HOW PHILOSOPHY
SHAPES THEOLOGY

HOW PHILOSOPHY SHAPES THEOLOGY

PROBLEMS IN THE PHILOSOPHY OF RELIGION

FREDERICK SONTAG

HARPER & ROW, PUBLISHERS
New York, Evanston, San Francisco, London

HOW PHILOSOPHY SHAPES THEOLOGY: PROBLEMS IN THE PHILOSOPHY OF
RELIGION

Copyright © 1971 by Frederick Sontag

Standard Book Number 06–046349–X

Library of Congress Catalog Card Number: 71–170618

for
Sistie

THERE ARE THREE THINGS THAT LAST:
FAITH, HOPE AND LOVE; AND THE
GREATEST OF THESE IS LOVE.

—*I Corinthians 13:13*

CONTENTS

PREFACE

When any student, young or old, approaches philosophy, he must expect to have more questions raised than answered. Such is surely—and intentionally—the case with this book. The reader who wants a scholarly rehearsal of historical material or a careful analysis of the recent literature will be disappointed. This work aims at something different because its author, who is primarily a metaphysician, feels that the issue before us today is to reappraise *how we are to approach* the central issues in philosophy of religion.

Thus, if anything profitable comes from a reading of this volume, it should be not a new set of precise definitions or conclusions, but a fruitful framework within which to deal with the philosophical problems raised by religion. I ask the reader to step back from recent discussions and seek a fresh approach to ancient problems. The revolutions threatened on every front offer some evidence that we need a new approach in theology too, and such widespread discontent should make us unwilling simply to take up where previous thinkers have left off. We must learn to loosen our thought before we can hope to tighten it up again profitably.

The reader might like at the start to have a clear understanding of the author's outlook on philosophy and religion, but for several reasons, that will not be given. First, the author believes that no one simply begins with a fully formed position. That must grow out of the material and the problems worked with; hopefully, the reader will understand the author's position at the end. Second, this treatment of the issues facing us in the philosophy of religion is not intended to be a systematic theology but only an introduction to the problems, one which may result in a fresh approach and possibly even in fresh answers.

It might seem that we would begin a basic work on the philosophy of religion with the traditional problem of faith *vs.* reason. But neither 'faith' nor 'reason' means one thing. Their meaning and definition can become clear only at the end of a long process of consideration. Since our search is for a new approach, we begin in Part I with 'philosophy,' 'theology,' and 'religion' (plus 'creation' and 'eschatology') in the belief that realigning these fundamental concepts might give us a new approach to both 'faith' and 'reason.' If we live in an age in which achieving faith is extremely difficult, we need to see whether a fresh approach to the philosophy of religion might open new possibilities for faith too.

To be fair, the author must warn the reader of the basic difficulties that will confront him. Detailed arguments are seldom given and little attempt is made to rehearse the history, past or present, of the traditional problems—for example, the 'proofs' for God's existence. That would be too much to undertake in one book. Further, our aim is to help the reader readjust his thinking about the traditional questions and arguments, rather than to continue the debate as if the premises were already agreed to.

However, perhaps the most crucial omission is the author's other writing. At many points an issue is not carried further because I have done that extensively in print elsewhere and could not duplicate that treatment here. I have avoided the questionable practice of constantly footnoting myself as an author, since that only distracts the reader and does not really supply him with the missing argument. Instead, I shall describe briefly at the outset how this volume fits into the overall scheme of my writing.

Our century has been unwilling to accept any transcendence

of the natural order, not even God's. In such a situation, we are not very likely either to accept the traditional reasons for ascribing perfection to God or to understand why classical concepts felt forced to attribute perfection to God in the first place. My first book[1] explored the various ideas behind the notion of divine perfection and discovered that there are several ideas of perfection and not one. Since how 'perfection' is conceived depends on a series of other concepts, it has some variability, although all of the divine attributes were intent upon preserving God's self-sufficiency. Thus, God can be conceived of in various ways and still be consistent with the traditional notion of perfection.

Although the beginnings of a (hopefully) new idea of God were contained in that first exploration, it was necessary to go back before we could go forward. Kant's restrictions against metaphysics and theology had to be explored to see whether a new basis for contemporary metaphysics could be found. The result was to propose a metaphysics without the modern characteristics of necessity and certainty, together with a God who preserves his self-existence but is much more capable of entering into the qualities of both natural and human existence.[2]

Theology, as is obvious, has been passing through some revolutionary days which hardly could have been predicted from the work of previous theological giants—for example, Tillich and Niebuhr. Theology's future course is very much an open question.[3] The kind of theology we need and the role philosophy can play, either to help or to hinder, needs to be reconsidered afresh. Locating a different philosophical approach might be the key to opening new theological possibilities. In doing this, the peculiarly American philosophical tradition might be more usable for theology today than we have

[1] *Divine Perfection: Possible Ideas of God* (New York: Harper & Row, 1962).

[2] *The Existentialist Prolegomena: To a Future Metaphysics* (Chicago: The University of Chicago Press, 1969).

[3] *The Future of Theology: A Philosophical Basis for Contemporary Protestant Theology* (Philadelphia: Westminster Press, 1969).

supposed.[4] If Christian preaching lacks force, and if its missionary work is apologetic and dispirited, oddly enough this may indicate a new need to examine theology's philosophical base.

If theology is in revolution, so is the religious life, and this is nowhere more evident than in Roman Catholic circles.[5] In any era, some situations are more illuminating than others, and Protestants as well as Catholics can be enlightened religiously if we become clear about the origins of crisis in our religious life. Authority is under attack among Roman Catholics, who almost alone preserved that notion religiously in the modern age. This challenge has the helpful effect of forcing everyone again to question and to locate the sources of authority he will accept in his religious life—surely always the central question of religion.

Metaphysics as a basic philosophical enterprise has probably always been under attack, but the effect of this on the philosophy of religion has been more noticeable since the time of Kant and the Logical Positivists. Our crisis may be based upon metaphysics as much as upon religion or theology. In an age of fundamental upheaval, when every first principle is challenged, we ignore metaphysical exploration at our own peril. We need to become clear about what metaphysics deals with[6] and what our options are in defining answers to these problems. In doing this, every traditional source and classical philosopher is equally available to us, and our only danger lies in restricting ourselves arbitrarily to contemporary sources.

As far as belief in God is concerned, it may be the problem of evil that more than anything else has blocked faith in a postmodern age. Traditional treatments of theodicy suddenly all seem inadequate, so that we are forced to question God directly again about his own involvement in evil—or else not

[4] *The American Religious Experience: The Roots, Trends, and the Future of American Theology*, with John Roth (New York: Harper & Row, 1972).

[5] *The Crisis of Faith: A Protestant Witness in Rome* (New York: Doubleday, 1969).

[6] *The Problems of Metaphysics* (San Francisco: Chandler, 1970).

I

PHILOSOPHY, RELIGION, AND THEOLOGY

Philosophy of religion came into full bloom in the nineteenth century, but the problems it deals with have always been important to man.[1] They still are.

Philosophy of religion originally involved treating its problems on the basis of certain philosophical assumptions. This, however, is no reason to shy away from this enterprise, for no question can be considered without some framework, and we can both criticize old frameworks and develop new ones. We are in danger only when we think the way a question is posed does not matter, for then we can fall into both error and blindness. We become the unknowing victim of an answer that is dictated merely by the assumptions forced on us from the way we have asked the question in the first place.

A sensitivity to the way a question is phrased, and an acquired skill in uncovering basic assumptions and developing new forms of the question, are the life of philosophy and the discipline it teaches. In some areas (for example, mechanical engineering) philosophy may not be too important. Where

[1] For a historical account of this process, see James Collins, *The Origins of Philosophy of Religion* (New Haven: Yale University Press, 1968).

religion is concerned, however, it becomes nearly all-important. It is not a substitute for belief, but a protection against undetected answers being concealed in the very questions we ask.

This book is not an inquiry into the historical origins of the concept of "philosophy of religion" or even into the assumptions built into it as a way of approach to religion. Instead, this book is an attempt to find a contemporary philosophical framework within which we can deal with the questions of religion. Such a new context cannot be developed without taking on assumptions of its own, of course. Still, it can be done in consciousness of them. First principles can be selected not blindly but with deliberate choice—that is, philosophically.

To attempt this seems especially necessary in our own century. It is an understatement to say that our world is in radical and rapid transition, and it is an oversimplification to say that we seem unable to accept religion without constant questioning. To paraphrase Kierkegaard, in our own day no one is content to stop with faith. Thus, we neither have an inherited framework for our questions nor does it seem easy for us to develop one—particularly where religion is concerned.

If we are to answer our questions about religion, we must first reconstruct the framework within which we shall consider them. The issues at stake may very well be the same as they have always been, but the form a previous generation gave the question is not our own. To be free to ask the question in our own way is a crucial matter if we are to secure answers we can adopt as ours too. We are condemned to become philosophers in order to find a new form for old questions. If we could merely accept inherited formulations, we might ignore philosophy, but that is not possible in an age of basic challenge.

There perhaps was a time when enlightened men expected soon to be able to dispense with religious questions, so that both this philosophic probing of assumptions and the reformulation of questions (for example, what Plato carries on in his dialogues) might come to an end. But now, in almost no area do we have an end in sight to the reformulation of theory. Instead, we can only predict that ahead of us lies a wave of newly formed theories without conclusion. Perhaps partly because we have discovered this lack of finality in every other intellectual area, and perhaps partly due to the unsettling questions existentialism has asked about man's nature—whatever the factors may be—to vast numbers of people religious questions do still seem meaningful if not urgent today.

If it is the form of the questions that is at issue, and if philosophy alone can provide the structure that would yield a satisfactory answer, then ours is a metaphysical age—that is, one of basic philosophical inquiry. This is precisely because it is a religious age, and metaphysics and religion cannot be disconnected. If we could accept religious doctrine without thinking inside some framework, this might not be so, but we must think in some specific fashion before we are able either to accept or to reject.

Unless we can rephrase our questions in an acceptable fashion, religious belief will not be satisfying. Even disbelief may seem a little artificial. In order to be either a professional theologian or a happy ordinary religious man, we must first master the philosophical art of reframing questions and then go on to the metaphysical skill of uncovering and reshaping first principles. Religion is no longer easy.

Of course some men do tackle philosophical questions without the benefit of philosophical training, but they must be content with an unsophisticated result. Religion is usually born in crude surroundings; its sophisticated forms result only when something else is added to it—a particular philosophical structure. For each of us to do this himself, or even accept the sophisticated answers developed by professionals, a certain level of philosophical acceptance is required. The end-product will not be pure religion but will contain a certain amount of philosophy, and we must either master it or be mastered by it.

It would be nice if life were less complicated, if theory could be simply one, or else philosophically neutral, or at least independent of any premises. But if it is not, then in spite of our wishes, the whole theory—and the life based upon it—are called into question.

If once we hoped to reach a final philosophy that would parallel the one final unified scientific theory we then anticipated, it was in the modern era and not in our postmodern age. Modern man thought he had to have necessity and certainty with any theory worthy of the name. Only the vast effort exerted to accomplish this could have proven its impossibility. We simply produced one formula for certainty after another, each differing in some basic way from the preceding one. "Modern man" failed.

John Dewey thought this quest for certainty was identical with all of classical philosophy, but it is, rather, a hallmark of the comparatively recent "modern age." In our acceptance of multiple forms of philosophical theory today, we are actually closer to philosophy's classical tolerance of nonfinality. This also suits the transcendental quality of religion more naturally. Transcending sense experiences as religion does, the presence of a variety of theories suits its precarious status more accurately.

Today we begin our attempt to solve religious problems with a more modest goal. And if we do, perhaps we actually have a greater chance to be successful in finding answers than did a previous and more demanding—and more arrogant— "modern age." Now we can employ philosophy to produce a theology that is aware of the fragile nature of its sources, sensitive to its variety of forms, and more on guard to keep the alertness it needs if we are to discover its hidden and its basic assumptions. Yet, in such a situation we also are better able to control philosophy, to employ it, and to modify it according to the doctrine required.

If the form we give to philosophy is neither necessary nor sacred, then we may vary it without seeming to abandon 'reason' itself in differing from some one form of philosophy and in deviating from those particular assumptions and consequences. In this "postmodern" era, we are at liberty to experiment with form and to alter the means to achieve the result desired. That is, we are free in this enterprise as long as all of this is an open and a conscious affair and if we are always prepared to justify our procedure. 'Reason' now returns to its classical form of 'rationalization.' This means to give the rationale behind any particular form or activity, to give an account of an assumption and of its aims, to explain to one who himself does not follow that route why you do.

Such a sensitivity to the flexibility and to the adaptability of the philosophic instrument not so long ago was connected primarily with an antimetaphysical attitude. However, this was due to an overly narrow interpretation of metaphysics and to its identification with a necessitarianism that demanded a procedure without alternatives. The existentialists have pioneered the way back to metaphysics, and the British analysts now seem to have drifted there too. This trend is fortunate where religion is concerned, since its theological elaboration must come from some prior metaphysical development.

Religion's nature is not very amenable to becoming a rigid and a completed science, as was demanded by the form of metaphysics against which our preceding generation rebelled. Now that we have found a mode in which to do metaphysics once again, and since it is one that allows us to develop a variety of alternatives and to select from among them, philosophy can be of more use in the religious quest. An age, such as ours, that is fundamentally in ferment requires a philosophy with a metaphysical bent. It is the first principles themselves that are in question in an era of revolutionary thought. Our task is not to complete an already agreed upon enterprise, which the "modern age" dreamed was its good fortune.

What we propose to undertake in the following chapters is both an analysis of the forms of philosophy open to us for religious use and a reinterpretation of the primary questions of religion in the light of this analysis. The two movements must be carried out together, since the philosophical framework will determine the form of the question. Then, the nature of the question at stake can guide us in selecting the form of philosophy more naturally suited to its solution.

If such an interplay becomes fruitful, if a form of philosophy emerges that is definite enough to hold its shape and to be used by other men too, and if religious questions are by this procedure given a clear structure, if they are arrested in their natural motion and then fitted into a structure that, when taken as a whole, seems to yield rational solutions—if philosophy can do all this, then a new theology is born. Our hope is to come to some fresh understanding of the spirit of philosophy, since this activity is implied in the very meaning of philosophy. If we are successful, we can try to phrase the questions of religion in such a way that men in our time will be able to make them hold still, and we can also examine how a theology begins to unfold in this process.

Whether this attempt can be successful, even the author of this essay cannot say until he tries it out. Such is the uncertainty and the challenge involved in the life of philosophy. Whether the understanding produced in this way can be grasped and employed by others as well, this the reader alone is left to judge for himself. The attempt must be made again in each new day; this is the only certainty involved in the whole enterprise.

To discern this situation is to place us in the position of having to make up for lost time and for opportunities an earlier generation wasted on false hopes of finality and certainty. More recently, our religious options have often been squandered in an ignorance that was bliss—that is, in a failure to see that this task must be done. At least today we seem to be a generation free from illusion. We are exhausted from having tried out unsuccessfully for the role of God, and now we are amazingly willing to listen, even when we are skeptical of the very possibility of an answer. Such a period of danger, one in which the crisis can move just as easily toward health as toward destruction—this is the gift of our age. Now the stage is clear for fresh creative effort—or else for failure. Ours is the challenge and the choice.

1

IN THE BEGINNING

A. IS A THEORY OF ULTIMATE ORIGIN POSSIBLE?

In the past century we have not been unmindful of the fruitfulness inherent in having philosophers develop theories of creation. It is just that we were naive enough to believe that this matter could be settled scientifically. Evidence of the evolutionary change of species, much of which had actually been known for some time, inspired new theories of evolution at the beginning of the modern era. Of course, such theories were not totally new then either, but enthusiasm over the possibility for finalism in a single scientific theory sometimes blurred the distinction between the simple evidence of change and the incontestable validity of some one theory about how evolution had occurred and did proceed.

Today we seem more sophisticated and better able to accept the fact that more than one theory can yield an explanation of the available evidence. Not that all theories are equally valid, but we now recognize that the door is never closed to a new theory. It may be one that uses the same evidence but offers an intriguing possibility for extension or perhaps a greater simplicity than an earlier theory could provide.

Lack of finality does not apply to all scientific explanation, but uniquely to theories of origin. A new theory concerning available material usually can be tested against current data. But, as Plato observed, all theories of origin are "likely tales." It is important to note that he did not call them "unlikely tales." That is, not every account is "likely," but all theories of origin are "unlikely" because even those that do have the power to explain cannot establish themselves beyond the possibility of replacement. To a lesser degree this may be true of all theory, but it is clearly true of accounts of origin. Our own era may be combed for present evidence of a direction. Yet the time span from the era in question to ours—that is, from one that had different forms of life in existence—is so much out of our reach that no theory about it can be established with finality. Where theories of origin are concerned, we are always at a distance from what we need to observe directly in order to be sure of our conclusion.

If we have cured ourselves of the arrogance involved in thinking that the details of this question can be settled once and for all, or even that one theory can be developed to exclude all others, then we can again enter into an era of basic reconstruction and begin to explore various theories of creation. If one scientific theory could be established authoritatively, philosophy might have been excluded from investigating this question of ultimate origin, as some thought that it should be. But if our situation involves a certain flexibility of theory and an impossibility of experimentation, due to the theoretical barriers of distance which cannot be overcome, then philosophy and theology may again play a role in offering theories of ultimate origin for our consideration. About the mechanisms for organic, geological, and astronomical development scientists may still vie with one another for the (temporary) prize of offering the most acceptable theory. In relation to this process, philosophers may at best be observers and commentators.

Scientific theory can never touch the "why" of the matter, and neither does it offer an account that pays specific attention to philosophical first principles: form, unity, and so forth. Nor does it raise theological questions: God, evil and the divine intent, and the like. Perhaps even more than scientific theories, in connection with which some experimentation may be performed, philosophical and theological hypotheses cannot by their nature ever be established with finality or placed beyond possible replacement. But at least the way is now open to test various philosophical theories of origin once again—that is, by attempting to construct them.

Philosophical and theological theories of origin can be given this minimal test: Can the theory be constructed so that at least it can be completed? And this is something we cannot know until we try. Other checks on the credibility of any new theory are possible, of course. We have a series of basic questions in philosophy to which we are able to give possible answers—that is, if we have a set of first principles as a basis upon which to proceed. A theory of origin is a pivotal point in any such set of first principles. Thus, if the theory can proceed forward in ethics, politics, and so forth, then this gives at least a partial testimony to its validity in the sense that, as Thomas Aquinas says, a little mistake in the beginning becomes a big mistake in the end. If it is wrongly conceived, a theory of origin will stop its author (for example, Sartre or Heidegger) as he tries to wield it—that is, when he uses it as a theoretical tool in his efforts to provide a solution to another philosophical question. Success in doing this does not establish any one theory of origin as beyond all doubt. It merely confirms the fact that at least it is a possible theory and perhaps useful for other philosophical questions too.

As should now be clear, it is on this issue that philosophy and theology come very close together as enterprises. Wherever else they may diverge, neither one can function properly without a theory of origin, whether overt or covert. Theology must justify God's ways to the world, and to do this requires a theory about why the world was created in this form. Philosophy lacks a completely visible subject matter and an experimental apparatus. It can only attack its problems with a set of first principles, one in terms of which it is able to structure answers. In order to do this, it must understand how the ingredients in the world came to be selected. This can be explained (so that it in turn may be used to explain) only by giving an account of how they first came to be that way when other forms were possible. All this can be accomplished with or without a specific theory of deity, and the ability to proceed to a theory of origin without a God distinguishes the pure philosopher from the theologian. A theologian cannot be without being at the same time a philosopher, but the philosopher need not also be a theologian.

Perhaps nowhere more than in a theory of creation do we have an example of how philosophy shapes theology. In the first place, only philosophy can defend the right of theology to form such a theory. For example, in an era of aggressive scientism such as we have just been through, when science claims exclusive right to such theories and theology is excluded, then only philosophy can challenge this situation and gain readmission to the theoretical playing field for both itself and theology. If theology tries to defend itself or to establish its rights alone, all it has at its command are particular theological premises which in the nature of the case are recognized by only a few.

Such universalism as theology can gain is given to it by the philosophy that provides its structure, and any scientific exclusions of theology from the area of theories of creation is bound to be based on philosophical assumptions. Only another philosophy is in a position to challenge, or can hope to gain recognition for, a new premise which either excludes or supports theology. No scientific theory is in itself either conclusive or able to claim finality for itself. It becomes so only when it is joined with certain philosophical premises, so that it requires a counter philosophy to uncover and to oppose these important assumptions.

By the aid of philosophy, theology is born from a particular religious tradition, and by philosophy alone can it perish. If a way has now been opened to form a theological account of origin, a theory of the divine nature must also first be constructed. To develop this requires a philosophical frame, since no religious tradition, if its previous philosophical extensions are excluded, is by itself that explicit or detailed about the exact nature of God or the reasons for his operations. As a theory of God develops, its major function and its most rigorous test is to see what proceeds from it by way of an account of ultimate origin.

Depending on the particular view of God adopted, his action in creation will then be explained in one way or in another. We learn what kind of God he is by how he acts and by how his actions are to be explained. It is philosophy's business to develop the detail of this explanation, since God himself has been notoriously silent about direct self-explanation and apology. He refused, for instance, to answer Job's challenge directly, and thus it falls to philosophy to develop his missing answers or else we may not have any.

Philosophy and theology are competitors, it is true, for the market on theories of origin. Although the theologian is basically dependent upon philosophy for his source of structural material, a theological explanation has advantages over simple philosophy in many ways. In theology, the theory of origin usually draws upon a certain sacred literature which contains stories of creation, and these add color and concrete detail to the theological explanation as it is developed. In addition, a theory of creation is often accompanied by the other features of religious practice, which both lend it credence and tend to create a context for its acceptance.

In theology, a theory of origin is merely one part of that theory, and it gains its meaning from its function in the wider context of religion. Philosophy has, or may have, a wider context too—for example, ethical action. However, this extension to action is not crucial in order for it to be philosophy—that is, unless its emphasis is upon metaphysics, which means that its implications extend to all fields. Even here, where the theory of origin may exist in the context of a story or a myth as it does with Plato, it may also be sheerly abstract. This may give it depth, but it does not provide a context of meaning easily grasped or one that has a very popular appeal.

If once again the market is open for theories of origin, this may prove to be the best meeting place and area of cooperation between philosophy and theology since their union in the Middle Ages. Philosophy split away from theology at the close of that period on the basis of a growing rationalism and in the hope that, by declaring independence, it might achieve the finality and the certainty it then saw in modern science. Since that time science has left philosophy behind and alone with these goals and has moved on to accept a view of the flexibility of theory.

If philosophy follows science into this new variability and

into a continued receptivity to novel theories produced without end, the interesting thing is that science could lead philosophy back to cooperation with theology just as it once led it away. Today scientific theory is in itself no bar to theological construction, since it contains no exclusions or inherent objections to the inconclusiveness that necessarily characterizes all theological theory. Theology, of course, must give up its own claims to finality, which it developed in reaction to the early years of modern science and as a defense against philosophy's rationalistic withdrawal. Yet, on the basis of these revised aims, theories of origin can again become central in theology— and in philosophy too.

B. WHAT RELATIONSHIPS NOW BECOME CLEAR?

A reader who has followed us to this point without complaint might be unable to keep his silence any longer and will ask impatiently: "How in the world does the question of theories of creation introduce us to the issue of how philosophy shapes theology? Why have you chosen to begin that topic by considering theories about ultimate origins?" Any reply to these questions should begin by noting, first negatively, that offering a theory of creation is not a matter of treading on the toes of modern science or even of considering the difficult issue of the relation of theology to scientific theory. The complicated question of how the rise of modern science first restricted theology but has now again opened up both theories of origin and theology in general—this will be treated briefly in Section D.

The main point to be made in this section is this: Our aim is to understand what 'philosophy', 'theology', and 'religion' are and how they are related, particularly with respect to how philosophy shapes theology. In trying to do this, we shall eventually have to take up all the major issues and develop answers to the questions involved. The interesting fact, however, is that the question of 'ultimate origin' has the special effect of throwing philosophy, theology, and religion into the strongest relief each vis-à-vis the other. In considering some issues, the lines dividing these enterprises would be much less sharp. Why does a theory of origin make the relationship between these fields stand out sharply to our view? Let us try to give a brief explanation.

In the first place, we are dealing with questions that are handled by more fields than one and whose solution may require us to work out at the same time how these fields (philosophy, theology, and religion) are related and how their approaches vary. All this must be done before we are able to deal with even one particular issue. This is not too unlike the growing complexity of the relationships between the various physical sciences—for example, biophysics and mathematics. Some simple issues can be dealt with almost entirely within one field—for example, plant classification. Where religion is concerned, we encounter an overlap of various disciplines, and the question of ultimate origin makes this situation unavoidably clear.

Ultimate origin cannot be exclusively a scientific question, since the sciences attempt to provide a theory of how the structure we have first came to be. This is a different question from how the mechanisms from which our present world developed were themselves selected. After all, there might have been nothing at all in existence, or other systems might have been selected which would have produced a quite different world as they unfolded. Yet the scientific presentation of various theories about how our world came to develop into its present form provides a needed backdrop for philosophical or theological theories. It also serves to exclude philosophy from attempting to describe either the process or the mechanisms for the development for the natural order. According to the modern division of labor, that is a scientific question. However, philosophy still can enter here (as we shall point out) by analyzing the role of theory and serving as a critic of any theory that would take itself as being without alternative.

The religious treatment of this question lies at the other end of the spectrum from natural science. A religious account is perhaps best understood in contrast to the scientific treatment, and scientific theory is kept in its proper bounds by being put in contrast to religion's approach to ultimate origin. Usually the religious treatment comes to us in the form of a story in some sacred literature. These stories are as many as the various religious traditions, but, for our purposes, the Hebrew account in the Book of Genesis and the Christian account in the Gospel of John will do as illustrations. Without either presenting or analyzing these stories in detail, the point is that each defines the relationship of God to his people, of his intentions toward them, and of what action he either has taken or might take in the future. Neither account needs to be accepted as literal truth in every particular. Instead, each attempts to establish its religious doctrine as true in intent if not in the detail of its statement.

The account given in Genesis does not specify when this 'beginning' was, but it does intend to establish that God is to be considered as the responsible agent in creation. The time involved could be either considerably longer or shorter than the story represents; the mechanisms for its accomplishment might also be quite different or more intricate and complicated than the written account indicates, and still the point of the story would remain. The reason behind, and the ultimate aim of, creation continues as an extrascientific question, and yet both treatments are important to our understanding. The description of the mechanisms by which the natural order unfolds, or the various theories that govern these processes, neither of these tell us anything about the intent or the aim of creation. They do not enlighten us about any radical changes that might be wrought in the mechanisms as presently constituted. Yet this does set a limiting condition on all religious theories: they cannot postulate an aim that is in conflict with the facts of the order presently before us.

Even this condition, which is imposed by various scientific accounts, still leaves open a wide variety of theories about the intent and aim of creation. In the case of the Gospel of John, the portrayal of the 'Word' as with God in creation and as now having become flesh to dwell among us in a particular person, this contradicts no known scientific theory of natural development. It is not even opposed to the Hebrew account in Genesis, but it does postulate a different relationship between the creator-God and men, one that culminates later in the literal presence among men of the creative agent in the form of a person. Nothing known in science excludes this as a possibility, although such a reentry is not itself predicted or accounted for by scientific theory. If in fact such an event goes against any given set of scientific principles, then a religious account simply does the service of reminding us that any scientific account involves the postulation of principles that are not ultimate. Thus, in themselves, they exclude no other conceivable assumption or possibility.

Scientific accounts of how natural processes unfold, and the religious accounts given in a sacred literature, which concern the intent of creation, each stands at opposite ends of the pole of possible explanations of origin. Science limits religion to a theory that is compatible with the present factual state of nature. Thus religious stories may concern the areas behind and beyond the mechanisms of nature, which scientific theories may tend toward but do not reach—that is, at least not on the basis of the present order of nature alone. The future is not yet, and thus in itself it excludes no possible development or radical reconstitution. Since the aim of creation is "behind time," a wide variety of theories can be compatible with the order of the world as we know it. How one accepts or rejects any one of these will depend on the philosophical principles the reader employs.

Does this issue also define the role of philosophy as sharply as it does that of religion vs. science? What part can theology play that is different from either of these? Philosophy, in its metaphysical sense of an investigation of first principles, has the task of examining scientific theory to uncover its basic assumptions. This is particularly true of any assumption that might establish one scientific theory to the exclusion of all others, or one that might extend scientific theory beyond an explanation of the data to become a philosophical or theological theory of origin or aim. Not that scientific theory may not be so extended, but, if it is, then it must be recognized as standing on philosophical ground and as being no longer a scientific theory which somehow is established by "the facts." Theology is similarly defined by this issue of ultimate origin. It usually takes part of its basic material from the stories in sacred literature. Then, like a scientific extension beyond the facts, theology uses a philosophical mode to elaborate a more systematic and technical doctrine on the basis of these stories. However, in order to do this it often uses certain terms or symbols provided by the religious literature.

Philosophy can, depending on its self-conception, refuse to extend itself to consider such an issue as ultimate origin. Whenever this is the case, we learn its basic assumptions quickly. When philosophy does consider a theory of ultimate origin, it must use a first principle or set of principles or concepts, and in this case its metaphysics is clearly visible. Since religion always begins by having its accounts given to it in a sacred literature, its answers will always have a symbolic and an indirect quality, one that can really be significant only to those who are familiar with the literature. Theology stands in between these two. It is committed to a philosophical analysis and yet also to one that is not out of harmony with its given religious tradition.

Now we come to the main point as to why this study of the relationship between philosophy and theology offered first a view about theories of origin: *Philosophy and theology simply are not such that either one can be defined in the abstract.* Ultimately there are just too many forms philosophy and theology can take to define them simply in themselves. First, where ultimate origin is concerned, you must raise a specific issue and then not only ask a question but also plunge in and suggest a theory that will answer it. Next, in the context of that question's structuring power, philosophy and theology are distinguished by the way they organize themselves to deal with it. Of course, not all questions have this power. Some may leave philosophy and theology apparently unrelated—for example, a theory of perception or set theory in mathematics. However, theories of ultimate origin have the classical quality of bringing philosophy, theology, and religion together and then holding them in a clear relationship.

First, you plunge into an issue as a concrete example. Then, you step back and see if you can recognize these three elements as they operate in this instance. You work out a theory of origin and you deal with the issue as presented. Then, in looking back over what has been worked out, what philosophy, religion, and theology are and do will become clear in this context in a way in which they could not in the abstract. In one sense, a theory of origin is admittedly an abstract issue. In another sense, a theory of origin, as it is developed, can only proceed by giving a precise relationship to philosophy, theology, and religion. Ultimate beginning is one of those mixed issues in which all three are mutually involved and where any solution depends partly on defining this triple relationship.

In this way, philosophy shapes theology, and this function can only be seen clearly and in detail in such an issue as a theory of ultimate origin—that is, whether one is possible and how it is to be elaborated in contrast to a scientific account of the mechanisms for the elaboration of life. Relaxing science's grip on theories of origin and abandoning the wishful notion that one theory can ever be established or that origins and ends can be known with finality—doing this allows philosophy, theology, and religion to come back into a new relationship in our day. Now they can define themselves and their mutual involvement as a particular theory of ultimate origin is elaborated and analyzed. Theology has the material and symbolism of religion to draw from; philosophy must define a first principle (for example, a God) drawn from, and in contrast to, previous philosophical first principles in order to make a theory of ultimate origin possible.

C. THE "HOW" VS. THE "WHY" AND THE "WHY THIS WAY"

With regard to the structures of nature, the natural sciences primarily answer the question "how." On their own grounds, they may rightly hold back from attempting to answer the question "why," but that does not mean that this question cannot be given an answer on other grounds. In fact, it is philosophy's job to see that science does not either assume one particular philosophical view as alone true or exclude approaches other than its own. This leads us to the question of "why," and it probably cannot be dealt with simply on the basis of a scientific account of the mechanisms involved in nature and a description of how these unfold. How can we establish asking "why" as a valid question against the possible objections to it? In the first place, it should be assumed to be a valid question until it is proven otherwise. Then, any principles that would exclude the question must be considered against various alternative philosophical hypotheses.

This is the way in which a theory of origin cannot escape being philosophical. Insofar as "why" is permitted to be a legitimate question, in addition to the scientific "how," no issue arises and philosophy is free to consider the question. To the extent that "why" is ruled out, then an issue of basic philosophy is raised, and philosophy must enter in to appraise the principles that would exclude it. In some other areas (for example, logic), philosophy is not made to account for its own nature this explicitly. Its presence as logic is taken for granted, and thus no self-reflection is forced upon philosophy. When the question of ultimate origin is raised, philosophy cannot avoid defining itself, its methods, and its approach. The interest philosophy has in this question of ultimate beginning is a self-interest. As it deals with a theory of origin, the assumptions of a particular philosophy stand out in bold relief.

Theology does not have the same interest in this question as philosophy does; it has an even greater one. Theology's very life depends upon the legitimacy of distinguishing between the mechanism (the way the process unfolds) and the question of why or for what purpose it unfolds in that manner. Philosophy can exist, and is still free to pay attention to, other issues (for example, ethics and politics) whenever its development of theories of origin is temporarily restricted. Theology, on the other hand, can only live by describing God. Yet, since no image of God is given in sense experience as a beginning point, God's nature can be seen only in relation to the natural order, just as his purposes are best described in contrast to the workings of nature. Thus, theology's interest here is a matter of life and death. It can only go about giving explanations by explaining God's purpose as a wider context within which alone the mechanisms of the natural order can be understood. All this, of course, depends on the special purpose which accounts for their selection over other possible mechanisms and patterns of development.

Not only this "why," but also: "Why do we not have a different set of basic mechanisms in nature when we well might have others?" That question defines theology's even greater task. Now the natural order cannot be taken for granted. Rather, it must be seen as only one from among an unlimited set of possible mechanisms, and then God's function becomes that of a deciding agent. How his choice is described is limited by the existing natural order—that is, we know this universe and its features to have been his actual choice. We must be able to describe God's decision and his choices so that we can see them as leading to the order we do have, although not with necessity. Philosophy can become interested in the flexibility that is possible in nature's basic order. Theology can only give its account by referring to the decisive power of a God. This makes the explanation of why we do not have a different basic set of natural relations crucial in theology's approach to the question of origins.

D. WHY THE QUESTION OF 'ORIGIN' OUGHT NOT TO BE NEGLECTED

In many other areas, philosophy, theology, and natural science each can get the idea that it is autonomous, and there are questions within each discipline that do have little relevance to the others. When these areas are concentrated on (for example, logic, the sacraments, molecular structure), then each field can become arrogant over the idea that it is independent. Theories of ultimate origin do not, in the strictest sense, make each enterprise somehow basically dependent on the other two. Rather, they highlight both how an important and basic issue is shared by more than one discipline and the fact that its solution can be approached in multiple ways. Any theory offered in one field ought not to contradict the basic data of another—for example, the evidence for the evolution of species vs. theories about how this took place. However, more than one theory can meet this criterion, and so dogmatism and isolation are prevented by the existence of a pluralism of acceptable theories.

In this case, the issue of the relation between philosophy, theology, science, and religion cannot be avoided, and a theory must be worked out that prevents the tyranny of any one over the others. The nature of God and a theory of 'last things' (eschatology) also have this same effect. They force each discipline to come to terms with the fact that other disciplines approach a common question with a different set of assumptions and techniques. Yet God and 'ultimate ends' do this each in a slightly different way, whereas 'ultimate origin' does this perhaps more clearly, and it involves the natural sciences most dramatically too.

The question of ultimate origin is a 'defining issue'—that is, one against which metaphysical assumptions come to the surface clearly. If this is not consciously defended, at least it is asserted. Our aim in this study is to see how philosophy shapes theology, to see what the problems of philosophy of religion are, and to do this by coming to some understanding of what differentiates philosophy, religion, and theology. Then, in terms of how we understand these three, we can see how they relate to one another and how we can and cannot approach the basic problems in philosophy of religion today. (See Part III.)

To illustrate this thesis, consider Plato's account of the origin of the world in the *Timaeus* vs. the Hebraic story of creation in Genesis. If we eliminate the details, Plato's theory is still quite acceptable in essence. What it asserts is that a plurality of basically independent elements come together to explain creation. God imposes forms on a place of chaos not ordered in itself. When you find any philosophy offering an account such as this, you learn how that philosophy conceives of its method and its task. In contrast, the biblical account presents a more powerful single deity who creates for a particular purpose, one who concentrates more on man. And you also see in Genesis, as you do in Plato's story, how this account enters into a religious tradition and shapes the attitude a follower of that belief will take toward his God. Theology must pick up this story as an element in its account. With Plato, on the other hand, unless extraneous issues are borrowed and added in, the question remains much more strictly a matter of the metaphysical principles adopted.

Neither theory can stand as it is without being given a redefinition in the present day, but then that is true of every theory in any field. Neither theory is of necessity incompatible with any of the available scientific data, although each does move along on different principles and goes further than the data by dealing with ulterior questions. These issues are perhaps raised by the data, but they are not answerable in those terms. The account in Genesis is not strictly philosophical in origin, but it may be used philosophically. Each theory has its own strength and' weaknesses. Plato has to deal with the difficulty that comes from having an ultimate plurality of first principles. The Genesis account is more graphic, but it lacks a technical precision which must be added to it if it is to have a theological use. By using these theories and others, however, it is possible to build the context within which we can learn the rules for handling a theory of origin.

Plato's 'demiurge' in the *Timaeus* creates because he is good. He is ungrudging; he communicates himself freely with as much order and purpose as the original chaos can accept. This is creation without a beginning in time. Although such a theory could be reworked to allow time to have a beginning, that would require quite a drastic change in Plato's God. The Hebrew creator begins a process which was not always in existence, and he does so with a definite dramatic plan in mind. Both accounts raise the issue of purpose, one that it is hard to answer on scientific terms and one that could only be ruled out on the basis of the assumptions of some particular philosophy. The question of purpose can be eliminated. However, this cannot be done simply impartially or on scientific grounds alone, but only by the adoption of some philosophical premises about the relations between philosophy, religion, theology, and science.

In this opening chapter, our intent has not been to examine or to present any one theory of ultimate origin. We simply wanted to raise the issue as one crucial way to bring to light how philosophy, religion, and theology are related. In Parts II and III we shall give an analysis of how philosophy operates to structure theological questions and their possible answers. Yet before this can be done, we must state more clearly just what philosophy, religion, and theology are (Chapters 2, 3, and 4). Then, from an understanding of what each is in itself, we may combine them in order to see how theologies are born and how problems in philosophy of religion can be answered (Part III).

E. PROGRAMMING AND TIMING

We have argued that the doctrine of creation is useful because it again allows theology into this area to give its answers. Yet, a reader might object that it is perfectly easy to account for the present form of the world through the process of natural selection. It is true that what we now know about the mechanisms of selection tells us a great deal about why some features of the world came to have their present form and function. What this reply overlooks is that, basically, such a scientific outlook simply accepts and assumes the basic features of the world as we know it. Theologically, our task is to ask whether the mechanisms that control our structure could themselves have been either different in kind or else "programmed" differently so that they would yield different results.

We can trace and retrace the routes by which our biological world came to have its present form, but all of this assumes that the "evolutionary machine" was fixed to this program in order to produce this result. Even if we include chance factors and allow some contingency into the process, the basic ingredients and procedures are assumed to be set to unfold in a certain way. In the twentieth century, we all realize that a variety of programs is possible. We recognize that, if the original processes were programmed to yield other results, we could have a world quite different from the one we presently know. Somehow the program on which evolution operates must itself be determined first of all, and it is this radical question that is properly theological. What theology tries to understand is how the processes as they operate came to be established in the first place vs. simply tracing out the plan by which they have developed in fact. In how many ways might our universe have been programmed to yield quite different results, even if we allow for the elements of chance already included?

Take the example of 'time'. According to Aristotle's definition, time is "the measure of motion" (see his discussion in the *Physics*). This would indicate that time is relative to the objects to which it applies. If time is relative to the framework it operates within and is not something in independence, it might yield a false impression if time were simply "run indefinitely backwards" in order to calculate our evolutionary development. That is, what time is is a result of the evolutionary mechanisms selected, and this particular time may not be applicable anterior to the selection of those procedures or even to the process of selection itself. There may be as many forms of time as there are ways in which the universe could have been programmed to yield various resulting structures. We do not quite know just how numerous these are, although we are sure that the world could have been produced by different means and avenues than have in fact brought it to its present form.

Of course, in order for each of these to be 'times', all would need to share some factors in common. The point is that we may not be able to establish what time is simply by looking at the structures of our own existence and our world alone, as Kant thought we could. To try to do that may be excessively provincial in a theoretically sophisticated age. Our prime question now becomes: What can 'time' be, such that it might govern any possible means elected to produce a universe of which ours is only one representative? What could time be, so that it might embrace forms of existence radically different from ours?

When we consider the question of the variety of ways in which the universe might have been programmed to yield results different from our present structure, we uncover the radical question of how time's nature might apply to all possible structures and not merely to those existing before us in visible form. In asking this, we have been returned to consider the point of radical origin, and here theology can begin its account.

2

THE MEANING OF PHILOSOPHY

A. THE ELEMENTS OF PHILOSOPHY

Although perhaps obvious, it is nonetheless crucial to emphasize that how philosophy will shape theology depends upon what philosophy is thought to be. To say this, of course, assumes that there is no one single form of philosophy. For if there were, our problem would be solved, or at least it would be vastly simplified. This does not necessarily exclude the possibility that we might all agree on certain aspects of philosophy. In fact, we shall attempt to point out some of these later. What is assumed here is that both the history of philosophy and the failure of modern proposed reformulations indicate unavoidably that we are condemned to deal with a variety of philosophies. Not all of these basic alternatives treat theology in the same way; hence we must first make some choices in philosophy before we can be sure how theology will be affected.

Since the basic philosophical question is "What is philosophy?" we know that philosophy will always shape theology at least in the sense that a definition of philosophy must be worked out in order for any theology to know clearly where it stands in relation to it. In forming the answer which it will give, any theology in that sense defines itself against philosophy, since philosophy can only be stabilized from among all of its possible forms by a philosophical definition.

We need not either accept one view of what philosophy is or catalog all the forms philosophy has taken or might take. There is a third alternative, which is suggested by the title of this section: we can define the elements of philosophy—that is, the basic materials out of which all of the varieties of philosophy must be fashioned. For our purposes, it is enough to state what the basic elements are and then to see if, from these, we can gain an understanding of the meaning of philosophy. This approach should yield a definition sufficiently detailed for us to be able to forecast how it might operate to shape theology.

Available theories and present experience may shape the words chosen for any new theory, but whatever its specific sources, a theory of philosophy can still best be understood in terms of the way its words and concepts affect the reader and direct his thinking. What objects philosophical words reflect and refer the reader to, that question is a matter of continuing debate. But if we at least agree that the basic "life" of philosophy is found in its written words and in their ability to guide a reader to discover what the author first "saw," then we have accepted an approach we can use to understand all of philosophy. From that we can go on to study how it shapes theology in general, without considering any one form philosophy may be given by any one philosopher.

What, then, does 'philosophy' mean? Its meaning is defined by its basic ingredients. First and foremost, this involves historical material, specifically, previous philosophical theories. To some men this might indicate that the study of philosophy is historically oriented, but this is not necessarily so. All that is involved basically is the assumption that we always begin "doing" philosophy by studying our predecessors. Then we use this data as part of the raw material for the construction of new theories. This means that every philosopher does not have to begin afresh and define philosophy for himself without receiving any help. That makes the job of doing philosophy easier. At least we do begin with a body of already existing material which can orient us.

From this source material the philosopher selects and uses what he finds most stimulating. If the process is successful, he and his reader have a tool with which each can detach himself from immediate involvement in, and thus gain a perspective on, the world. The theory, once formed, provides a stable and a fruitful framework for achieving a theoretical grasp of the structure of the world. Since more than one theory about the world is clearly possible, we can neither accept our world as self-explanatory nor assume some one theory to be adequate simply because it accounts for a certain amount of experience. In reaching beyond immediate involvement, philosophical theory detaches the mind by forcing it to move among various possible theories. And we can compare as many theories as we find in order to see if we can discover any superiority one might have over the others for the problems at hand.

B. EXPERIENCE, WORDS, AND READING

If we decide that a theory is "closer to" our actual world, and does not merely describe some possible world, we probably do this on the basis of some comparison with present experience. Yet, immediate experience of itself seems incapable of settling our philosophical perplexities, or else it would have put an end to our uncertainty long ago. Nevertheless, we use immediate experience as a concrete base of reference, even though this is not enough to help us decide once and for all in favor of some one philosophical theory, as some empiricists have rather idealistically hoped could be done. A number of factors form the material out of which philosophy arises, but this variety does not give us one specific and final theory of philosophy.

Although we learn what philosophy means only from some specific philosophical theory, yet we can define philosophy in general by indicating which materials make it up and by describing how it functions. 'Words' clearly are a part of this, and the effect of philosophical words on the reader is perhaps the other crucial question. In this sense philosophy means the ability to mold and to present words in such a way that they become stable and powerful enough to lead a reader to the discovery of abstract structure. Philosophy is this kind of verbal enterprise and the ability to exert power over it. Every philosopher must work out a theory of the nature and status of words and how they function. When he has done this, then at least we can learn what 'philosophy' means—according to that theory.

Words do impose a structure, and, as we discover this, our thought in turn is structured, although it was the philosopher's thought that first structured the words we now read and are guided by. However, our situation is more complicated than this, because the terms we use are never neutral; they themselves have a structure. Thus, the words we use to express thought alter the thought in its concrete expression. To understand philosophy means to understand how it employs words and how the terms employed help shape the thought. It is not possible to study philosophy or to be a philosopher without developing this sensitivity to the operation of a theory. Words do not only facilitate our expression; they also offer resistance to our thought, and the sensitivity generated in this process helps make an ordinary man into a philosopher.

A theory may be formed from this effort. Then, it may incite a later reader to discover again what the author of the words discovered first in the process of writing them. Reading, strangely enough, can cause a written theory to decompose into its elements; and, as the reader learns what went into the construction of that theory, he learns what philosophy means to that author. The fact that theories can decompose simply by reading them is what makes discovery possible. The reader is led to more than the theory's surface, and this activity may be sufficient to guide him to discover what he might not have had the energy to do unaided. We are induced to form concepts and to think in terms of them, and concepts are what give us the kind of focus we need in order to reduce the world's multiplicity to some simplicity.

The fact that philosophy leads us to discover certain sets of concepts is what makes philosophy useful to us. The world and experience are too much to understand, either all at once or unaided, and concepts offer a point of focus that enables us to get a hold on the world. Whenever this happens in the study of philosophy, then that philosophy can be useful. It becomes a tool for understanding, and through understanding certain problems can be dealt with which cannot be handled without a theoretical framework. When we come to understand the elements of which philosophy is made, how they combine to form a theory, and how the reader is affected by the theory, then we have learned how a theory can be said to "work" and to be "practical" and "useful."

Of course, not all philosophical theories either conceive of or use their elements in the same way. To understand any particular theory is to apprehend how the author conceives of its elements and how he treats them in his theoretical construction. However, if all philosophical theories use the same basic elements, in that sense all philosophy may be understood by learning what those elements are and how they may be combined, in spite of the fact that in each theory this may be done in some special way. The real way to understand philosophy is to read crucial passages in various theories and attempt to discern some common elements and the special way in which each of these directs thought.

As any adequate concept of philosophy is brought forth, it should enable us to gain a fresh grasp on theological questions and, in so doing, to structure "new" answers. In Part II, we shall attempt to illustrate how philosophy functions in theology according to the way in which philosophy has been conceived in certain historical instances, and in Part III, we shall set out the central problems in philosophy of religion. Hopefully, the conception of philosophy developed and employed here will help us solve these problems. How philosophy can function in this way will be discussed briefly in the last section of this chapter.

In order to make the definition of philosophy more clear, three illustrations will be analyzed in sections C, D, and E. These are not the only forms in which philosophy might appear; however, if what we want is not a series of special views but an understanding of the elements basic to all philosophy, we should be able to uncover them in a few comparative examples. We need to make some comparisons, for otherwise we might mistake what is peculiar to one theory for what is basic to all of philosophy. In this quest, which is so typical of the Plâtonic *Dialogues* (that is, the search for common elements in apparently opposing definitions), we shall use Spinoza, Hume, and Kant. After we learn what philosophy means for each one, perhaps we can see what philosophy always is and how a reformulation of these basic elements might make possible new solutions to the problems in philosophy of religion.

C. SPINOZA AND THE USE OF REASON

We can understand philosophy in the manner proposed in this chapter only if there are common elements in all of philosophy, whatever the particular doctrines. Thus, in understanding philosophy in a generic sense, we can also learn how some one particular doctrine might have been arrived at. In this and the next two sections, we shall proceed by reversing that process. We shall take a specific work of Spinoza's as the example of an end-product and try first to extract from it what he takes philosophy to be, without considering any of his doctrines. Then we shall compare Spinoza's understanding of philosophy with Hume's and Kant's. Thus, in considering how they differ, we may begin to form some idea of the variety possible within philosophy.

To do this should require the examination of only a few important and representative passages from a man's work. Our ultimate aim is to understand how philosophy shapes theology; but, in order to do this, we must first understand what philosophy is and what the possible forms of its elements are. Admittedly, the three men chosen here are all modern philosophers. Still, it should be as easy to understand philosophy in its essence through them as through any other set of men. Furthermore, it is modern thought that has shaped our present context and set our problems in philosophy of religion. Thus, it seems more relevant to us to understand philosophy first in this setting so that we can see how it might have worked to shape theology in our own era. In Part II, we shall use a little broader historical selection in an effort to see how philosophy actually has shaped theology in various historical eras.

At the moment, what we want to understand is philosophy in itself. Our first example is from an early work of Spinoza's, his *Thoughts on Metaphysics.** It might be interesting to compare it with the more fully developed doctrine in his *Ethics* or to discuss the intricate relationship between the definitions Spinoza sets up in this work, but such is not our main concern. In reading a very few passages, our first job is to understand how an author conceives of philosophy as he pursues it, for this conception always is behind the way he approaches any particular issue. Moving on from this, we should be able to come close to an understanding of what philosophy always is even when it is not done in Spinoza's style. The particular and unique way in which he conceives of philosophy will help him define his problems in a new light and suggest new solutions. However, in order to appraise this crucial framework, we need to understand his concept of philosophy against the background of philosophy in general.

Spinoza begins in a classical way with a definition of 'Being' (Part I, Chap. 1), and this marks his as a metaphysical approach to philosophy. More important than this, however, is his equation of 'Being' with 'necessary existence' and his proposal that this equation should be comprehended by clear and distinct perception. It quickly becomes evident that Spinoza believes that philosophy's job is the discovery of necessary existence and that this is also the goal of all thought. There are, to be sure, forms of thought, such as 'accident', that do not indicate necessary existence, but these modes do not represent real being, just as logical beings are not real and are not to be taken as an appropriate object for philosophy. 'God' is introduced as the cause of all things (Chap. 2), and this indicates Spinoza's view that philosophical thought aims to understand all things in relation to God. As a philosopher, man grasps Being just as God understands it—that is, he can do so if philosophy is successful.

For Spinoza, possibility and contingency represent only defects in our understanding. They reflect nothing real in Being but merely an imperfect mode of thought which philosophy

---

* In *Early Philosophical Writings* (New York and Indianapolis: Bobbs-Merrill, 1963). All references in this section are to that volume. The reader should keep in mind that, in this work, Spinoza is commenting on Dutch scholastic manuals.

seeks to overcome. Our thought of a thing as contingent comes only from a failure to consider its cause, which means ultimately to discover its dependence on God (Chap. 3). Since these are defects in our perception and represent nothing real, it follows that our task in philosophy is to correct the failures in our understanding and to bring our thought into correspondence with Being. This involves understanding as God does—that is, necessarily and without possibility and contingency. Time, then, does not really characterize things but instead indicates only an imperfect mode of thought (Chap. 4). A true idea will be clear and distinct, which means that it will remove all doubt by being certain.

What can we now say about this conception of philosophy, and how can it show us something about all of philosophy?—including modes that differ quite radically from Spinoza's? First, (1) it is clear that philosophy does not accept thought either as it is found or as representing things as they are. The task of philosophy is to improve our understanding and to train it to a more perfect mode of thought. How do we determine what this more perfect mode of thought is? From (2) an understanding of God's nature and of his relationship to all of Being. This can be grasped, and, when it is, we can see what it is about human thought that is defective. Here (3) clarity and distinctness are important criteria, and they indicate that Spinoza must feel that Being in general is put together in this way. Thus, what is clear and distinct is therefore its truest apprehension just because Being itself is like that.

Perhaps the most important characteristic of Spinoza's view of philosophy is that (4) philosophy seeks necessity and certainty and attempts to avoid possibility and contingency. If this is so, then metaphysics and theology are closely joined together. In fact, they become one enterprise, and the philosopher's chief concept is God. For this to be true, human thought must be very close to divine thought—that is, when properly corrected of course—and words must be such as to be capable of directly reflecting the nature of Being. Conversely, Being must also be such that it is commensurable with language in such a way that nothing about Being defies expression. This requires, of course, that nonbeing not be real and that it be defined in terms of inadequate perception. This whole process is the natural task of reason, and reason represents both philosophy's tool and its whole goal. All of this gives us a clear picture of Spinoza's view of the role of philosophy, but how can it also indicate what philosophy is like in general?

In the most general sense, we see that philosophy is (1) a verbal enterprise, one that is gone about by defining terms, and that often it begins with concepts that previously have been important to it—for example, 'necessity' and 'God'. By working with these traditional concepts and by changing some parts of their definitions, (2) new concepts are formed which relate to each other in slightly different ways. These concepts now form patterns through which the reader is oriented and enabled to look at the structures of Being in new ways. A change in one definition (for example, equating Being and 'necessary existence') requires changes in related concepts (for example, 'nonbeing' and 'contingency'), and all of this orders thought in new ways as these theories are studied by an attentive reader. Such new patterns, which are formed by reshaping the elements and materials of philosophy, (3) enable the reader to understand Being in new ways—that is, in ways it would be impossible to grasp without these new verbal and conceptual patterns.

What a glance at Spinoza teaches us is that one who reads philosophy must always attend to two things at once. He must first follow the words and the formation of the definitions and watch this pattern form as the connections are developed in print. Yet at the same time, he must watch his own response to the unfolding of this verbal pattern. As he reads, his thought is moved by the structure of the words set down by Spinoza; but, in order to understand both Spinoza in particular and philosophy in general, the reader must first become conscious of how that pattern of words affects his thinking. Philosophy is to be understood in its power to move the reader to observe new relations; and, as we watch this process with Spinoza's doctrine, we see how philosophy has the power to create a vision of things it would be impossible to attain without its verbal aid.

When we understand how Spinoza can unfold his vision for our inspection, we see how Spinoza saw the world and we can understand the power all effective philosophy can exercise by the controlled use of words. A way of viewing the world that has not quite been suggested before, or a perspective not available simply by looking at the world, these are open to us for inspection. Now we are able to consider the world from that perspective, in this case Spinoza's stress on the use of reason. When we see how it functions for him in philosophy, then we see the world as Spinoza would have us see it—and which we could not have done without first following his written structure.

D. HUME AND THE APPEAL TO EXPERIENCE

Just as Spinoza is content to move immediately to God and to form philosophy as an abstract connection between a set of definitions of terms, so it is equally clear that Hume does not trust philosophy in such an abstract mode. Instead, he stresses an appeal to common, immediate sense experience and to custom. On the surface it would seem that Hume and Spinoza disagree about what philosophy itself is, but let us consider a few of Hume's specific doctrines and see whether there is still some common meaning for philosophy which both share. Even if the details of the doctrine of each are and ought to be different, can the function of philosophy still be the same for both men? It might be that we can only discern the meaning of philosophy when we contrast opposing specific doctrines. If we take a difference over specific theory to be a disagreement over the function of philosophy itself, we may confuse all of philosophy with a particular doctrine. Whereas, if we can begin by distinguishing these, we can appraise various opposing doctrines and do all of this with a common reference to what philosophy is and how it functions.

Hume's views on what philosophy ought to be and do are clear and specific.* He shuns what he calls "abstruse" philosophy, since he thinks it has no effect on action or conduct (p. 16). Rather than embracing any opinion whether contradic-

* Cf. *An Inquiry Concerning Human Understanding* (New York: Liberal Arts Press, 1955), particularly sections I and II. Page references are to this volume.

tory to common sense or not, Hume prefers to view philosophy as proposing only to "represent the common sense of mankind" (p. 17). To do this serves as a corrective to philosophical speculation; it keeps philosophy on the right path and secure from illusion. Thus, clearly, Hume believes in the existence of a "common sense" shared by all mankind, that it can serve as a norm for philosophy, and that its elucidation defines the philosopher's task.

Obscurity, metaphysics, and abstruse questions—all these are to be avoided, and the only way to do this is through exact analysis of the nature of human understanding (p. 21). Thus we learn to confine ourselves to immediate questions and to shun remote and abstruse subjects, since we discover that our understanding is not suited to them. From this Hume passes to one of his most fundamental philosophical assumptions: "that what is really distinct to immediate perception may be distinguished by reflection" (p. 22). This establishes "immediate perception" as his basic norm; and, with this as the touchstone, it is already possible to see both how philosophy will be bound to proceed and the shape its resulting doctrines can take. Hume will reject all questions he feels lie beyond the compass of "human understanding." However, the crucial issue is to decide what these are; and, in this regard, it becomes clear that Hume proposes to give "immediate perception" a key role as a criterion.

Since this criterion is so important in Hume's view of philosophy, it is not hard to realize why, for him, philosophy takes the form of a study of the origin of ideas. Immediate "impressions" are of such things as the feeling of pleasure or pain. Given this as our base, Hume contrasts immediacy with the "ideas" of these impressions as they are recalled later. It is bound to be that, given this criterion, all ideas will be "inferior" to impressions. The problem, of course, lies in the starting point, for it is neither clear that immediate sensations are either the best or the only criteria of thought nor that all thought is somehow traceable to and derived from such a basis (pp. 26–27). However, approaching philosophy with these first principles (that is, with this metaphysics) is Hume's project, and accepting this starting point does have important consequences. Thought, for one thing, turns out to be confined to very narrow limits—that is, if we accept this account of its origins and this test for its validity.

According to Hume, thought derives none of its "material" from itself (a crucial point later disputed by Kant); rather, all its raw material comes either from some perception or from its copy in an idea (p. 28). No thought is originally complex; it is to be understood instead as composed of simple ideas each of which is derived from some impression. Given this account of thought, it is easy to see how philosophy will proceed, and this will not be by constructing theories about the nature of things but instead by analyzing all thought on the basis of this theory about its nature. Our attempt must always be to reduce thought to these simple components and to use this as the test of its validity. Since Hume begins by assuming that all ideas are derived from impressions, he can then demand that every idea be traced to some impression as a test of its validity—that is, if his assumption is granted. Only by either feeling or sensation, Hume is certain, can ideas be introduced into our thinking.

One of the implications of this theory is that all abstract ideas are necessarily faint and obscure (p. 30). This conclusion should make us pause, since it is not at all clear that this is so, and yet on Hume's theory it should be true. At this point considering Hume's aim is probably more important than questioning his basic assumptions, since he makes it clear that, by using these assumptions, he hopes to bring all ideas into a clear light and to remove all dispute regarding them. If our attempt is to understand the meaning of philosophy, this is a crucial issue. It is evident that Hume wants to end disagreement in philosophy, and his theory of ideas is not so much something independently discovered by him as it is a means employed to achieve this goal, which he takes to be philosophy's primary task.

If we could still allow for ultimate theoretical disagreement in philosophy, this account of the origin of ideas might not be so important. However, if we think philosophy must be free of dispute, Hume's scheme of ideas suggests itself as one of the few possible ways of providing a clear test for all ideas, and yet this does depend on whether we first accept his view of philosophy's goal. As is widely known, beginning with clear, simple, and independent impressions, Hume's next task is to account for the association between ideas. If Hume had begun with complexity as original, this might not be a problem, but he cannot do so, for that would not give him his clear and definite test for individual ideas in immediate sense experience. Hume develops "principles" according to which ideas are associated, and for some reason he seems sure that these are the only possible principles of association (p. 32). Of course, it is a well-known fact that Hume never really finds any connection between ideas he feels able to trust with assurance, not even his favorite, "custom."

The details of the way in which Hume goes on to develop the implications of these first principles, and the problems they generate, do not concern us, but the basic theory of philosophical investigation does. What is 'philosophy' for Hume, and how can his view share anything in common with one so apparently different as, say, Spinoza's?

As we noted with Spinoza (see p. 31), Hume would agree that (1) we neither accept thought as we find it nor agree that it represents the state of things accurately. What Hume and Spinoza disagree upon is how one goes about correcting thought. Spinoza seems to let reason correct itself—that is, when it is connected to a metaphysical account of the real nature of things. Hume, on the other hand, does not trust thought but prefers (2) an appeal to a certain kind of experience—that is, immediate sensations plus custom. We must refer thought to and test it by something external to itself if we are ever to eliminate the dispute between theories. Clearly, Hume's view of theory is that (3) it should ultimately be one and ought to reflect the basic simplicity he seems to find in experience—that is, in the immediate impressions of sense.

In a way, Hume seems to agree with Spinoza in seeking (4) necessity and certainty, although he cannot find it in the complex theories themselves, since the basis for certainty is located in individual impressions. It soon becomes clear that ideas can never be connected in groups with a degree of certainty equaling that of the individual impression. In this sense, philosophy can never achieve the unity and certainty Hume first hoped for, since nothing can be found to connect ideas into theories to give them the force of an individual impression, and that was what we accepted as our test for certainty. This leads Hume to a "mitigated scepticism," one he is willing to extend to apply even to his own theories. He realizes that it is inconsistent of him to hold on to any theory—including known doubt—as if it could achieve a certainty similar to that of an impression.

Like Spinoza, Hume does proceed by (1) defining his central and crucial terms (for example, 'experience' in terms of 'impressions' and 'ideas', and 'custom' in terms of 'regularity of experience'). Then, (2) because he has defined these previously used terms in a new pattern of relationships, as he proceeds to take up questions about the validity of an idea or the connection between ideas, new theories about these matters (for example, causation and miracle) result. A reader who views things in this way sees a pattern he could not have discerned simply by looking at Being unaided. The world has never been different than it is, but (3), with the aid of a new theory constructed by relating and defining crucial terms in different ways, the reader is enabled to understand it differently. A newly developed theoretical structure, such as Hume's, enables thought to grasp the world and our experience of it in a unique way.

If we follow the rhythm of our thinking as we read Hume's crucial opening passages, where the important terms are defined and the approach to philosophy is made clear, then we can see again how all philosophical theory operates and how philosophy has meaning as an enterprise. The same elements are present for Hume as for Spinoza, although differently related and organized. What has prominence in one theory (for example, reason or God for Spinoza) gives place to a different emphasis (for example, immediate customary experience and individual impressions for Hume). The reader first learns the form of any theory and the relation between its crucial concepts, and then he moves on to various problems. Some of these are traditional and some the particular theory itself gives rise to. This framework provides him with a context within which he can both understand the problem and begin to give an explanation of it.

E. KANT AND THE LIMITATIONS OF PHILOSOPHY

It is traditional to begin to understand Kant by using either his *Prolegomena* or his *Critique of Pure Reason*. As Kant's three critiques unfold, his thought naturally becomes more complicated. In order to understand Spinoza, we used an early piece of his writing, one prior to the famous *Ethics* and one in which the doctrines are not yet so rigid or fully developed. To understand Hume's view of the meaning of philosophy, we referred to a later presentation, one simpler in form than his basic *Treatise of Human Nature*. For Kant let us try a more difficult task and use the last part of his three critiques, the *Critique of Teleological Judgment*.* It might be foolish to attempt this if all we wanted to gain was an understanding of the detail of Kant's thought. Actually all we need to find is one clear point simply in order to understand what Kant took the meaning of philosophy to be. For this, any essential portion of a man's writing should do, and it is true that Kant himself thought that, in this part of the *Critique of Judgment,* his thought had attained a high degree of lucidity.

It soon becomes evident that he and Hume agree on at least one thing: our task is to be accomplished by limiting the scope of philosophy. Their difference comes in specifying how, and to what, philosophical thought is to be limited. For Hume, as we have seen, this limitation tends to be to custom and to the immediate and the individual impressions of sense. For Kant, on the other hand, philosophy begins with a critical appraisal of our faculty of understanding. As a result of this, we find that our understanding demands certain things as a condition for its very operation, and this provides a form of necessity to philosophy, one which cannot be found simply by examining the objects of nature. If we limit philosophy to what is necessary for our understanding, its goal may be accomplished.

In this light we can see why the concept of 'teleology' (a purposive direction to nature) would have perplexed Kant and also why this might be a good place to begin to under-

---

* *Critique of Teleological Judgment,* trans. James Meredith (Oxford: Clarendon Press, 1928). Page references are to this volume.

stand his view of philosophy. If we see a purpose to nature, this can appear to be a part of things themselves. Yet, to assert this is to overstep Kant's self-imposed limitation of philosophy —that is, to uncover only what is required as a necessary condition for our understanding. The idea of nature does not in itself give us the idea that the things of nature serve one another as to ends (p. 3). Thus, where does the idea of such teleology, such purposiveness in nature, come from? Experience cannot prove the existence of such ends, since only by limiting ourselves to the conditions for our understanding, and not by turning outward, can philosophy hope to prove anything—that is, according to Kant's sense of proof as a necessary deduction. Kant begins by saying that the knowing mind introduces the notion of finality into its representation, although it is such as to have the appearance of coming from an external source (p. 10).

Kant finds that a principle of finality is intrinsic to any organism. If so, this universality and necessity cannot rest on empirical grounds, since necessity, for Kant, comes only from the conditions of the understanding, and therefore it must have some underlying *a priori* principle (p. 25). In order to find an end for the existence of nature, it might seem that we would have to look beyond nature (p. 27). However, Kant cannot allow that as being legitimate, since he views philosophy as capable of succeeding only by accepting its limitation to the conditions required for understanding. Any necessity we may find (for example, when certain ends in nature are seen as the result of a cause) does not come from the constitution of things but rather depends wholly on the combination of our conceptions (p. 34). This being the case, we can see how Kant operates. No phenomenon is rejected, however difficult it may be to account for. Without transcending his self-imposed limits, which are to explore only the conditions for understanding (in this case, the difficult concept of teleology in nature), he still tries to account for all of this in terms of what our understanding requires as a condition for its operation.

Using only this brief sample, what is it possible to say about Kant's concept of the meaning of philosophy? It is clear that, almost even more than Spinoza or Hume, (1) Kant does not accept thought either as it is found or as if it represented things as they are. Kant differs in the method by which he proposes to correct thought. He does not follow Hume in accepting sense impressions as they present themselves. Rather, (2) Kant turns inward to investigate the very conditions for sensing or understanding, since he hopes to find in these a universality and a necessity Hume could not find in simple impressions. (3) Kant's criteria are what the understanding finds as necessary structures in order to explain what appears to come to it with necessity *in* experience but which, of course, could not come *from* that source. Philosophy does (4) seek certainty and necessity; however, these are to be found not by constructing Spinoza's complete metaphysics. Instead, we must restrict philosophy to deriving its rules only from what our understanding must assume as a condition to explain what, in fact, it experiences (for example, teleology in nature).

Almost more than with any other philosopher, in reading Kant we become aware of philosophy's necessity of proceeding by (1) a technical definition of important terms (for example, 'nature', '*a priori*'). Kant gives old terms new meanings (for example, 'nature' now means "a complex of objects of sense"). Limiting philosophy as he does and orienting it inward toward an examination of the conditions that make experience possible rather than outward to the experience itself, (2) Kant's new ideas begin to orient us differently. The patterns formed by these concepts and their relations (for example, *a priori* and *a posteriori*) order our thought in novel forms and direct it to apprehend structures it otherwise might not have known to exist.

It might seem hard to say, in Kant's case, that (3) Being and its structures are understood in new ways as a result of the reformulation of terms, and yet this is still true in a restricted sense. Not all of Being is brought to light; Kant's conceptual patterns themselves place some of it beyond our grasp. Yet a few genuine modes of Being are revealed as structures that are necessary for all human understanding. Being is neither ignored, as it might seem to be by Spinoza's standards, nor left shrouded in skepticism except for the certainty of single immediate impressions, as might seem to be the case for Hume. Instead, Being comes to have a new meaning; that is, it is the necessary structure of human understanding, which applies to everything that exists, just as Being formerly meant those structures of all existence themselves.

Kant's laboriously constructed and revised terminology enables us to see the world in this way, and it would not have been possible to do so without his careful redefinition and rerelating of certain key terms (for example, nature, form, experience). His doctrine is most certainly radically different from that of either Hume or Spinoza, but the basic function of philosophy seems to be much the same. It involves a careful reworking both of important terms and of their ultimate definition in order to form a pattern of relationships, and these reorient the reader's thinking. Thus he can grasp Being (whether all or part or with whatever degree of success) in ways that would be impossible without his having read these verbal patterns which represent a new way of conceptualization. Now, if philosophers disagree in doctrine but can be said to agree on the meaning and method of philosophy, what does this tell us about philosophy's theological use?

F. PHILOSOPHY FOR THEOLOGICAL USE

In a sense, this whole book is an exploration of the question just posed, so that at this point no detailed conclusions can or should be drawn. We considered first how the revitalization of a doctrine of creation might place philosophy and theology on a new footing, and in this chapter we are trying to locate a common meaning for all of philosophy. Our proposal has been, not to find for philosophy a single definition which seems to exclude other forms of philosophy whether past or present, but to try to see how philosophical doctrines might vary and yet still enable us to draw from all of them a general conception of the meaning of philosophy itself. In spite of the notoriously wide divergence of philosophy where specific doctrine is concerned (for example, what importance is placed on sense experience), are the elements of philosophical theory and their effect on the reader always the same? We have used Spinoza, Hume, and Kant as examples, and at this point we need to say something more about the meaning of philosophy in general and about how assigning such a function to philosophy might affect its theological use.

If all of philosophy seems to operate according to the same basic principles and to have the same effect, then whatever the specific doctrine, any philosophy can still play the same role in the construction of theology. If so, the theologian can select and use specific doctrines according to his knowledge of the individual effect each will have on the topic under consideration. In Part III, we shall attempt some theological answers to certain central issues both by using this meaning of philosophy in general and then by testing in each case how a certain specific philosophical doctrine makes possible an answer of perhaps a different kind to the problem at issue. Of course, we shall be assuming that philosophy actually is as we have described it here. In the classical spirit of philosophy, anyone is free to disagree with the view of philosophy we outline, and that is the first question for a theologian to consider.

We need to say a little more about this view of philosophy, so that we can more easily appraise the way it will affect the problems in philosophy of religion. To disagree over a certain view of philosophy and to establish an alternative is certainly possible, and that is a philosophical way of proceeding. To reject one philosophy or all of philosophy requires that you define your understanding of philosophy, and this inevitably involves you in philosophy yourself, since someone else is always free to challenge your view of philosophy. In which case, any antiphilosophical arguments made on behalf of theology always risk failure, since, if the view of philosophy upon which the rejection is based is not accepted (and philosophers have never been in agreement about its meaning), then the whole issue of philosophy is raised once again.

According to the understanding of philosophy offered here, there are many possible doctrines of philosophy. These are not indefinitely many so that handling them is impossible, but there are a variety of classical views and an unknown number of doctrines still to be developed. In spite of this irreducible multiplicity and an ultimate lack of unity among all theories, every philosophy seems to proceed in the same manner and by producing the same effects on its reader. Whether the work is

Spinoza's or Hume's or Kant's, the reader would never have looked at the world in quite that way (although portions of the doctrine may certainly have suggested themselves naturally) prior to reading that written doctrine. The successful philosopher first takes the classically important terms, and then perhaps he adds some which before had not been used technically. As these terms are redefined and as they define each other, the structure of that doctrine comes into the reader's view.

Because there are many philosophical doctrines, it is clear that our world is exactly like no one of them. And yet the structure of the philosopher's words, when taken in technical combination, can and do open to view aspects of Being and existence which otherwise a reader might not be able to grasp. The reader's job, then, becomes one of determining which doctrine presents a structure that, however possible in itself (the existence of it as a mere possibility often deceives us), might in fact be most like the theoretical structure God elected to use as a pattern in creation. It is, of course, clear that on this view of philosophy neither in God's operation in creation nor in man's construction of philosophical doctrine nor in solving theological problems are we bound to necessity and certainty. If we live in a genuinely contingent world, the theories we use about it are also contingent, and the solutions to our problems will also always be subject to some variation.

An outlook on philosophy of this type can help us in theology and in philosophy of religion, but the one thing it cannot do is to provide answers that are certain, final, and unalterable. Its use in theology is less prejudicial and less subject to suspicion than some more rigid versions of philosophy, since its variability and variety force theology necessarily neither in any single direction nor toward any specific solution to a problem. We may study the effects of various philosophical doctrines on questions of theology, and we can argue for the use of any one as an instrument according to its merits. We also see how the redefinition of terms leads to new theoretical doctrine, if it is successful, so that we can alter the definition and relation of key philosophical concepts consciously. In giving certain new terms priority and prominence (for example, anxiety, nonbeing, dread), we know that this will yield us a new instrument for theological construction and that it will be one that, if successful, makes new answers possible to old questions.

Reading Spinoza causes us to see the world through a certain view of God. Hume takes a particular definition of sense experience and applies it as a test to redefine a variety of problems. Kant withdraws from Being-itself and sketches for us a structure necessary to our understanding, one in terms of which we can now provide answers to various problems and rule out other questions as beyond our scope. None of these theories are like physical structures in the world; all are verbal patterns of crucially defined terms. Gradually, each of these will form a clear structure for its reader, so that through them the world may be grasped, but in a different way for each one.

Philosophical terms potentially have this power, and, when we understand this, we can employ them cautiously in approaching the problems that religion raises. What philosophy is and does is real, although not in any physical sense. Whenever any philosopher takes his special distinctions and then defines concepts as if they were the only way to speak about things, his philosophical soul is lost. On the other hand, if we can understand what is real about the life of religion, a philosophy, if it is sensitive to its own nature and limitations, can be brought into relationship with the life of religion. Now it can aid in the solution of the problems which arise without damaging religion's independent existence or simply turning it into a form of philosophy.

3

THE PRACTICE OF RELIGION

A. A NONVERBAL MODE OF LIFE

What always puzzles the philosopher—and what may also teach him something—is that it is possible to lead a religious life without discussing it or verbalizing very much about it. Since to question and to define are the philosopher's lifeblood, it is hard for him to understand that there is any good way of life that does not proceed in the same fashion, although this realization should create in him a certain modesty about the philosophical way. It is not that the religious man leads an unexamined life but that his examination is largely internal and often not visible to an observer.

In understanding this fact about the religious life, two things may confuse us: (1) Much verbalization goes on within the religious life and about it, and it has a certain connection to written documents and to preaching. Seeing this, it is possible to confuse such connected verbalization with the life itself. (2) Christianity as a religion has always been closely associated with theory, perhaps because its early success took place within lands under the influence of Greek philosophy. This close association with verbalization can blind us to the fact that the actual practice of religion often is very different.

The most important fact to note is that, if this is true, then religion as a way of life can be quite independent from philosophy. This does not mean that it cannot be related to philosophy, as will be worked out in the last section of this chapter. However, it does mean that, in order to understand either religion or philosophy, the independence of the religious life must be realized. 'To do' is different from 'to think', even when the thinking is about doing, and to this extent religion differs radically from philosophy. When this crucial aspect of the religious life is grasped, as it is from time to time by various individuals, many will impulsively reject all philosophizing in reaction against the confusion between thinking and doing. One who is interested in following it must recognize that the religious life is primarily a nonverbal mode involving action and life-style, but this need not demand the rejection of philosophy—that is, as long as the two forms of life can be kept clearly distinct. In any religious life, we must speak, but we must not take this as its essence.

Let us try to state now what kinds of action a religious life involves. (1) The religious life implies a seeking after God. Because God is not a simple object in the world, this quest involves philosophical structuring (in a way considered in more detail in the next chapter). Nevertheless, it is primarily an action—one that commands the individual's total activity as well as his thought. (2) The religious life often produces certain changes in the individual. Perhaps these are also reflected in his thought, but primarily they involve, or ought to, how he lives and acts. The report of personal change is always the central experience in the religious quest. The individual's ethical relationship to others is thus at the center of the religious life, not so much in what he says as in the way he acts toward those with whom he comes in contact. (3) To practice religion always involves a certain feeling of vocation, which takes over and tends to guide one's life and activity. It does not matter whether this is expressed as "following the will of God" or whether it is simply taken as the necessity to obey certain ethical injunctions and ritual practice: a sense of divine obligation is always present.

(4) Ritual practice is always involved. This is true whether it is simple or elaborate, whether it is considered to be near the

center of the religious life or simply a subsidiary part or means. Although words may be uttered in the process, it is the ritual aspect of the religious life that offers the clearest example of the way in which it is essentially an active way of life vs. a verbal form; all of its characteristics point to its central stress on a change in behavior and action vs. simply being thought. Because of this, someone who is unskilled in intellectual formulation may lead an exemplary religious life, whereas, somewhat ironically, "thinking too much" may interfere with successful religious practice. "To do" is what is required, and, unfortunately, thought may block action as well as make it possible. One may be fully religious without being a philosopher, even though it is true that God expressed himself via the 'Word' and so theology finds its verbal basis in God's own action.

Philosophers have a natural professional tendency to want to view every form of life as either philosophical or at least as involving philosophy in its conduct. Where religion is concerned, this outlook may actually be a hindrance. To say this is not at all to turn our backs on the famous philosophical maxim that "the unexamined life is not worth living." In the rest of this volume we shall be pointing out all the ways in which philosophy relates to and can aid religion, particularly theology. Certainly, many do rush blindly into activity when it would be better if they thought more about their action first. Unquestionably, many unreflective zealots do great damage with their physical power when a little philosophical reflection might soften and temper their actions in desirable ways and also alleviate the suffering which follows impulsiveness. All this being true does not detract from the fact that religion is essentially a form of practice. Since it is a nonverbal form of life, to confuse it with philosophical reflection is to damage it as a form of existence and often to prevent the very action necessary for the fulfillment of the practice of religion.

There is, of course, a simple sense in which philosophy must enter in before practice is possible. That is, the action enjoined by religion must first be understood before it can be enacted. Furthermore, we always encounter a problem regarding just what any religious doctrine requires of a man. Once an injunction (for example, "love your neighbor") has been understood, however, then the life of philosophy and religion split. We must first understand what "Love thy neighbor as thyself" means, but, once that has been done the issue is one of practice and not primarily of thought. Comparatively speaking, the injunctions of religion are clear and simple, so that, religiously, our fault is not so much that we have not understood properly as that we have not done what we understand the command to be.

It is also true that a religious injunction to engage in a form of practice (for example, "love your enemies") can and does often become encrusted with accumulated interpretation and specific rules. Then the religious life grows burdensome and its ways become unclear. In such a situation philosophy can become an aid to practice. It enters in as a tool to uncover the essential meaning once again and to clarify and to reduce complex interpretations to simple statement. Philosophy can be a preface to the religious life—that is, provided that it does not mislead us into thinking that the problem is one of definition alone. Clear definition is philosophy's task; but, whenever inattention or disuse or overelaborate interpretation make this procedure necessary again, the danger to the religious life is that the whole problem will appear to be an intellectual one. The vitality of religion is lost whenever it acts as if the issue is entirely a matter of systematic definition rather than primarily one of action.

This leads us to point out that religion is more a matter of personal discipline and an attitude of belief than of intellectual debate. Of course, philosophy also requires a certain mental discipline for its practice, but the philosopher's personal habits are immaterial to his professional life. Such is not the case where religion is concerned. The believer's mental equipment may be completely incapable of abstract construction while his moral and physical discipline may be near perfect. He may live out a life he cannot think about or express in words. This fact is central to the attitude of belief, since religion is never an obvious affair but requires the practitioner's prior acceptance in belief. Philosophy, on the other hand, may actually block our ability to commit ourselves in an attitude of belief and acceptance; and, whenever it does, religious issues are turned into a debate rather than into practice.

The precise kind of attitude philosophy takes toward religious belief depends, of course, on the type of philosophical doctrine involved. Some forms will work against belief (for example, Hume), while others render it unnecessary (for example, Spinoza's rationalism), and some philosophies make religion possible but do not support it philosophically by positive construction (for example, Kant). All philosophy, if we have interpreted it correctly, leads away from commitment in belief and practice in action, but some doctrines are more compatible to these goals than others. Before accepting any philosophical doctrine, the man interested in religion must first determine how its specific formulas affect the religious goal of practice and the cultivation of belief. Does a particular philosophical doctrine redirect attention exclusively to a problem of systematic definition, or can it allow the primary attention to remain on action? Does it tend to suspend practice due to an instilled scepticism, or does the philosophical doctrine leave the matter of practice open to the strength of the individual will?

In the sense in which any religion can enjoin a way of life, to that extent it is not primarily dependent on philosophy, whatever subsidiary role philosophy may come to play. The accomplishment of a program of action is a practical affair, and to have talent in this area may be unrelated to philosophical acumen. Philosophy almost of necessity involves an intense awareness of the thinking self, and religion often brings with it this heightened sense of self-awareness too. In philosophy, this may never disappear; but, the religious life is successful just to the degree that self-concentration relaxes and selfless practice is thus made possible without intellectual blocks. Too great an amount of self-concentration and self-awareness makes action difficult, particularly where others should be the aim of the activity. Philosophies differ in the degree to which they accentuate this tendency, but religion as a way of life requires that all self-concentration be reduced to a minimum so that action can proceed, discipline be accepted and individuals other than the self become the focus.

In order to illustrate religion as a nonverbal mode of life, take the matter of silence. While most Protestants tend to talk their way through their religion, Quakers and some Roman

Catholic monastic orders stress silence as a religious way of life. Some Eastern philosophies, which perhaps are more closely identified with religion, use silence as a philosophical tool, but on the whole most Western philosophy is a verbal affair. It aims at direct and explicit articulation. By way of contrast, silence as a religious discipline trains the believer to obedience and to waiting, and this disposition is quite central in all religious practice. It may very well be that God is not to be found in much talking and thought but is only discovered when one can discipline himself to listen in silence. Philosophy's tendency is to say everything as clearly and completely as it can; in that sense philosophy and religious practice may be at odds with one another.

Philosophical thought can lead to silence too. If it does not come at first, perhaps it does at the end of the analysis when thought has exhausted itself. Religiously, one may not be ready for silence, and he may need to be prepared for it. Philosophy can clear the air of ideas, depending, of course, on the kind of doctrine it is and on how open it is to see and to accept an ultimate limitation upon itself. Silence is not natural for any man; it is a matter of disciplined practice which can only be induced by an acceptance of belief. Philosophy is not action, even the activity of silence (since to maintain silence does require the controlled release of energy), but it can prepare the way for that. That is, it can if the particular doctrine is inspected and is found to be compatible with such a religious goal. In certain forms and in certain times and places, philosophy can either help religious action or block it. In order to control the potential help or harm present here, philosophy needs to be distinguished carefully from the primarily non-verbal form of life that is religion.

B. A MATTER OF ACTION

It is true, of course, that words can also be a form of action. In religion, we often speak about "words of healing," and in the secular life we know that harsh words can be severely damaging and even bring us to the edge of insanity. However, the "healing words" of religion may not come from the person who possesses a precise intellect but from the man who exercises a compassionate disposition. Nothing prevents the philosopher from cómbining both traits, but the point is that this form of the power of words—that is, when words become an action—comes not from philosophical skill alone but from the religious attitude. Nevertheless, when once-powerful words become dull and ineffective, they move few where formerly they moved thousands. Now the philosopher's art is desperately needed in order to revive meaning and to give fresh definition. He must use his skill to extricate important terms from the complications that have rendered them powerless.

Even when this philosophical discipline is needed to free the entrapped power of religious words, everything still depends on how the concepts are employed by an individual, and here it is right belief that the religious individual seeks. Of course, even the best intentioned religious man can do harm with wrongly employed good words. In fact, organized religion in any form is particularly prone to this sin precisely because of the arrogance that seems to grow up naturally within any religious institution. Words, then, can be a form of action for help or for harm, and here religious deed and philosophical theory come the closest to being one thing. Still, because their effect depends upon how the words are employed, the use of words as a form of healing action or of damage is more a matter of a religious vs. an antireligious way of life, even though the latter always seems to be mixed in with the former.

In light of this, it may seem too severe to say that the practice of religion is a matter of action and of what is done and not of what is spoken. Yet essentially this is still true. Words wrongly intended may be helpful, and the best intended words may be harmful to the individual to which they are spoken. Still, where religion is concerned, the action (whether verbal or overt) is to be judged by its intent. This is not a matter of what is spoken but of what is done—that is, the individual's practical attempts to shape his attitudes and his intentions. Religiously it is important that the action be attempted whenever the need is present, so that not to speak can at times be a religious defect. To attempt action religiously does not insure that it will be helpful; the best of intentions may produce harmful results. The judgment of help or harm is independent of the attempted action; but, religiously considered, primarily the concern is over a matter of action and not so much over what is spoken.

This leads to a somewhat subtle meaning of 'action', since it involves an interpretation that is not immediately apparent. This cannot be measured either by the overt action itself or by its results, although these factors are surely not irrelevant. To be a "witness in the world" is perhaps the concept we need here (see Chap. 12). That is, by one's mode of life and intentions as exhibited in attempted action, whether verbal or physical, the "presence" one has in a situation will be the measure of the "action." To say that he may act by simply being what he is puts this too passively, but the mode of presence he exhibits in the world does direct the course of action he will take. It is by this that the action is to be judged and is to be distinguished from mere talk. The concern is over whether the results of the action are harmful or healing.

Of course, most of the time one does not intend to harm; true religious action always aims to help, but its outcome is often not that pure. In considering the sense in which the practice of religion is a matter of action, what help or insight can we gain by taking the New Testament as an example? On a biblical basis, what does the practice of religion involve? Of course, we cannot sort out all the injunctions to action the biblical documents contain, but, on the basis of a few examples, can this help us to distinguish religion from philosophy as a matter of action? However, before proceeding here we must recognize that the New Testament contains a great deal of stress on God's action. In this sense, man does not accomplish his religious aim by himself alone. Furthermore, in the sense that belief in God's already accomplished action is required, action on the part of man is involved in only a special sense.

Still, in addition to these two important factors, the New Testament documents do contain, as most religious literature does, a great many injunctions to live and to act in a way that is not natural to all men. If this is true, the way in which religion is a matter of action involves a very strong sense of the meaning of 'action'. For if normal patterns are to be reversed or avoided, great strength is required to accomplish this. It is not done simply by living naturally. It is not, as some action is, a matter that can be accomplished without much concentration. Rather, the type of action the religious life requires would seem to involve both a 'conversion' of many normal dispositions and a reshaping of many natural human tendencies. The kind of remaking of an individual that is required gives action a special form which places it at a distance from all action that simply flows naturally without thought or effort.

Take for example the famous injunction of Jesus that we should "love our enemies." It does not even need to be pointed out that this is contrary to natural instincts of self-preservation and also to the drive to enhance one's position, not to mention its opposition to the nature of love itself. It is not sufficient simply to utter this injunction in words. If it were, surely those words would be meaningless. This must become a matter of radical action if it is to be accomplished at all. First, there is a natural tendency to strike back at one's enemies whether in public or in private. This has to be overcome, and then it must be replaced by an attitude that at best is rarely natural. Such conversion of one's dispositions cannot be accomplished except by intensive action. Words alone seem to have very little effect here no matter what we keep saying to ourselves, and the results must come in actions toward other persons and not simply in words. In fact, words often cover up a true disposition, in which case the word is kind while the thought is not.

Not considering for the moment how much of this change might be accomplished by God's effort, the point is that the issue concerns primarily a matter of action. The effort necessary to produce this change in disposition is the first problem, and then it must lead to the action (not the words alone) to give evidence of that changed attitude. A man may read a book by himself and have his thought changed by doing so. To alter human conduct on a basic level is not an easy affair, although it is still true that such change can come about. When it finally appears, often it arrives suddenly and with great speed. The point is that such results take a great deal of background preparation, and this is a matter to be taken up in the next section and in Chapter 5.

One example, which perhaps is even more difficult to account for, is the famous section of the Lord's Prayer, repeated by Jesus in his prayer in Gethsemane: "Thy will be done."

Men vary in the strength of their will, and yet it is still true that both the greatest evil and the greatest good in the world are produced by strong-willed men. Many deeply religious men have fantastically strong wills; this is the stuff from which religious zeal, devotion, and fanaticism all are made. Yet it is clear in this prayer that a proper religious attitude requires the surrender of the individual will to the divine will. If this can be done easily, if the human will is simply weak and if it seeks support by conforming to others anyway, then to follow this injunction is not much of a sacrifice. In this case, it is little likely to result in any very powerful positive action but more likely to end in weak submission.

An intense self-will, on the other hand, can be a powerful religious force if it is genuinely converted. Yet surely this is not a matter of words alone, however directive they may be, but of forceful action. It must be an action strong enough to take a will intently bent on its own aims and mold it instead to aims other than its own. Perhaps as with St. Paul this trans-formation will affect even those aims that originally were opposed to the individual's natural goals. This is a real sense in which the religious life is not a passive observance but a matter of action. Ritual performance may even mask this issue and make it more difficult to see the depth to which the will is selfish and is not at all God's. Particularly if it has become covered over by religious observance, it may take powerful action (whether from self, God, or others) to reveal the orientation of a will for what it is and then to convert it to a direction not originally its own. A philosophical analysis of the meaning of the phrase, "Thy will be done," may be of some initial help, but in the end this is primarily a matter of interior battle and of strong action.

Such a struggle with God is a life-and-death contest of forces and forms a classical definition of the heart of the reli-gious life. Yet in examining this biblical injunction, which is properly phrased in the form of a prayerful petition to God, an additional complicating factor is involved. Often God is not very real to the individual who is repeating the prayer, how-ever earnestly he may speak. In that case, it is little likely that he can be very clear about what "God's will" is, since it is difficult enough to be precise or to be sure about this, even when God's nature is clear in only very general terms. In order to carry out the change required by his injunction and then to act in accordance with such a new direction of the will, the individual must first discover God as real, or else be discovered by him. Even then the detail of the divine will may remain hidden.

When the precise goal is obscure, as it so often is where God is concerned, this leaves man his freedom as well as his indecision. Now the issue becomes even less a matter for philosophical definition and more a question of decisive action. That is, to discover the divine will one must venture and commit himself in action in order, hopefully, to find the direction of the divine will by being corrected in his error. One must be willing to be wrong, perhaps even dreadfully wrong (for example, Paul first slays the Christians). This means that we must accept the constant risk of action coupled with a sensitivity to the right and the wrong and to the good and evil that may be revealed in the process. There is no safe way in this matter. Action is always a risky affair, but it may be the only way to stumble across God and to uncover the divine will which we pray to conform to. When God is encountered in evil and in error, then the real struggle for a change in the direction of action can begin.

C. AN ORGANIZED WAY OF LIFE

Perhaps now it can become more clear why, in spite of all the defects to which institutions are subject, the religious life seems to require a structured organization into groups. Such community life is something philosophy does not need, and often it seems to be bad for the philosophical life when it happens—that is, it leads to a closed mind rather than to an open one. The action required in the religious life is so strenuous, and the needed changes of direction are so basic, that the individual can hardly be expected to accomplish this on his own. He needs the support of a community who share his goals and who can give him both support and direction, particularly in the crucial transition stages. Eventually, the individual may find his own mode of life and activity, but, at least at first, he is little likely to find it outside of some already organized way of life. So drastic are the religious requirements for action that no man seems able to convert himself to accomplish these alone.

There have been philosophical schools that bordered on being religious groups (for example, Stoicism), and in the East a blend of religion and philosophy is much more common. Yet, philosophy in the West on the whole does not form churches which support and propagate its theories. This fact tells us something both about the philosophical life and about the practice of religion. Philosophy is more a matter of reading the written theories of other philosophers, of reacting to these documents and then perhaps letting them structure one's view of things. It is for the most part a mental affair. It seeks to dispel confusion and to bring the individual to a clear conceptual grasp of the world as a whole or of some aspect of it. Philosophy may have many ethical and even political implications, but, at its core, it is a lonely affair of an individual seeking understanding through theory.

If one practices his religion within an organized group and not on a solitary basis, this circumstance makes demands upon him for certain types of action (for example, community prayer). Accommodating to these demands means an alteration in behavior in order to join in the group activity. These simple and overt changes are seldom the kind of basic moral changes that are either desired or needed, but they can serve as an opening wedge. Then, hopefully, this mild alteration makes other more fundamental changes possible once a previous pattern of behavior has been altered. Even solitary religious practice (for example, individual prayer and meditation) shapes the daily routine in different ways and imposes a certain type of organized life. Philosophy has no requirements for the behavior of the individual who reads it, although an absorbing philosophical theory may have profound effects on some. Religion at the very outset demands certain types of action, and this clear fact deters some people who resist all such demands. Even the demand for faith can be interpreted, if it is not superficial, as involving action and change and not simply as intellectual agreement.

This fact about religion is neither accidental nor arbitrary. These demands for action are based on the realization that

THE PRACTICE OF RELIGION 57

certain new structures are necessary to produce and to sustain a change in patterns of action. Just to alter one's way of thinking is not necessarily to change one's deed, and the New Testament at least is clear in rejecting a verbal confession that is not accompanied by overt deeds which represent it. Religion requires a deeper penetration into the personality than words sometimes are able to accomplish, although at times verbal forms can be powerful enough to effect change, or at least they can open us to that possibility. Yet even when words or thoughts have this effect, in order to support and sustain such altered behavior, a more elaborate structure than words and writing is needed—that is, some form of organization.

Religion at its very outset seeks to establish a more fundamental hold on and influence over an individual's action. Religion seldom accepts him as he is and seeks not so much intellectual enlightenment as moral reform or regeneration. As we shall discuss later, there are theoretical elements involved here, but that is not religion's initial or primary thrust. Those who study philosophy should seek a clarified understanding which is mediated by a theoretical structure that improves the mind's grasp. On the other hand, one is mistaken if he comes to religion and does not expect to be altered by his participation in it. If he does not desire such personal change, he is approaching religion for the wrong reasons, and he would be better off to join those who shun religion precisely because they are perfectly satisfied to continue just as they are.

This being the case, group life within religion becomes a necessity, or at least a logical expression of any genuine individual or inner religious life. If each person could change himself through his self-will in isolation (as some have thought possible), religion would be unnecessary. But basic change seems harder to achieve than that, and some group support, plus a favorable context, are required in most instances. Most people are not strong enough to go it alone, even with God. The religious person who speeds change consciously does so by exercising his free will. He does not will his own change directly, but he places himself in the context of the group where the desired change is more likely to be achieved. The religious community requires that each member share in certain common activities, so at least to that extent one cannot associate with religious groups and remain unchanged. Where religion is concerned, "free will" means to place yourself in the context where the desired change may be urged upon you.

Religion organizes a way of life in the hope of sustaining some new modes of activity in the individual. Thus, the person who deserts the religious life may be leaving the only circumstances in which he is strong enough to be successful. The new patterns of life demanded of the participants may open him to change. Any new action which he either initiates or desires may be sustained just because a religiously organized way of life keeps that person open to change and supports his new action with a sympathetic structure. Of course, in any given situation or for any given individual, this change may not be observable, or that may not even be the effect a religious group has upon him. Nevertheless, this is the rationale behind the fact that religion tends to organize its way of life; and this power to change is a potential in religious groups which always can be brought to the surface, even though it probably does require constant renewal if these purposes and powers are to be kept alive in any religious group.

Every organization tends to take itself and its structure for granted as soon as it has achieved a definite form, but there is still some significance in the fact that religion is organized into a structure, no matter how much we tend to rebel against formal structure today. There is a benefit to be found in this fact, if it can be made to assist the individual as it should. Our problem is not to take the particular way of life of any religious group for granted but instead to understand afresh each day why religion seems to require some form of organization in order to achieve its desired effects on individuals, whereas philosophy is a much less regimented affair. Why does my religion have the form it has and what is this intended to accomplish? These questions the healthy believer will ask every day.

In considering religion as a matter of practice and in trying to understand how this naturally leads to life within an organized group, it is clear that such a phenomenon cannot be identified either with only one group or any one pattern of organized life. If it could be, making a choice in religion would not be so difficult an affair. Granted that a religious group neither is nor ought to be organized simply for its own sake but rather that its form comes in response to some teaching or set of religious beliefs, still to share this common faith is only one part of religious life. It is a very different matter to agree on the form of organization that will most effectively preserve this or on the pattern of organized activity that most clearly gives it visible expression. This means that anyone interested in religion is constantly faced with a choice between alternative forms each of which may be genuinely engendered by the same belief.

This fact of the irreducible plurality to the overt expressions given to the religious life helps to explain why so many individuals are still restless even after they are inside an organized religious group. It might seem that making the decision to join that pattern of activity and form of organization would cure restlessness by giving it a stable form. Yet, as long as the form of religion is subject to alternate arrangements and its activity open to new modes, the organization of spiritual life will always create a restlessness at the same time that its function is to provide stability. The realization of the lack of necessity in any particular form of religious organization constantly re-excites the desire to give a new form to the very experience that perhaps caused the individual to adopt such a form of organized life in the first place.

Philosophy suffers from the opposite fault. You can seldom see its theory embodied in a concrete form of life. The fact that philosophy does not function as a religion makes it more difficult to see the faults of any given theory, and it also means that it is easier simply to stay within one philosophical theory. Whereas, in religion the tendency is to embody the belief in practice and to organize groups to accomplish and to sustain this. Thus, at least in going about this you do discover the problems inherent in the theory (see the chapter following) in a way in which they often cannot be seen as long as they are simply matters of belief which are assented to.

Once it is given concrete expression in an organization, you quickly become aware that any mode of life does not and cannot perfectly embody the belief and that other organized forms of life can give expression to the same ideal. In this sense, organized religious life both provides more stability for the individual (in the support of the group and its routine) and at the same time leads to a greater instability than adhering to a philosophy ever does. This natural tendency in religious life, either to keep modifying the organization or to move on to other forms of life which express the same ideal differently, may lead one to the erroneous conclusion that philosophy has a greater stability. The mind may be more content with a theory than the body ever can be with a community. The apparently greater stability of the life of theory offers a false contentment which often makes it difficult for men to see the need for effort at concrete embodiment.

In any case, it is clear that religion is a matter of practice in ways in which philosophy can never be. It is also clear, we hope, that this orientation toward practice and organized forms of life, particularly when it is inspired by a desire for change, in turn raises problems in the religious life which no activity or new organization in itself can ever quite solve. If either the organized religious life, or the forms of activity that express it, could ever be made both one and necessary, the religious impulse could pass smoothly into action, as is its tendency, and never even be connected to thought again. Since this is not possible, the discrepancies inherent in the concrete expression of all religious life of themselves give rise to theology—that is, to necessary verbal and theoretical forms accompanying belief and action.

D. BELIEF VS. PRACTICE

The content of any religious belief may in itself raise problems—for example, unclarities and apparent contradictions in the sacred documents, or those arising from symbolically expressed doctrines whose literal meaning is always subject to doubt. Yet, these could be dealt with by "church theology"— that is, by a dogmatic theology which worked out internally for the group some accepted definition and then established that as normative for their practice. Any organization can set up machinery for settling its points of difference, and, if these procedures are accepted as authoritative, philosophical questioning need never enter in.

Because religious belief flows so naturally into forms of

practice, this would at first seem to exclude philosophy all the more, but in fact the opposite is true. This natural urge to embody belief in practice is precisely both where philosophy gets its relevance to religion and where theology as a theoretical enterprise is born. An isolated belief can only meet the mild challenge of internal consistency and the need for clarity. The life of philosophy can be carried on as a debate in professional journals. Where the matter of the action and the way of life implied by that belief are concerned, anxiety is generated by the problem of how these thoughts are to be given concrete expression. Since philosophy seldom concerns direct action, its only solutions come on the intellectual plane and not by increased or altered action. In spite of the fact that anxiety has the defeating quality of causing us to think that activity in itself will solve the problem, when we do act our anxiety is only increased if the action miscarries. Thus, intelligence is called on to solve the problem of the discrepancy between thought and action, and this would not be the case if a given belief were of necessity tied to a certain form of action.

If we could always agree about the specific practice which a religious belief required of us, philosophical involvement would not occur where religious life is our concern. Philosophical reflection would be excluded and direct action would always solve our spiritual problems. Since we do not and cannot agree on either one form for organized religious life or on the specific action (or the lack of it) that religious life requires of us, we must turn to philosophy. If not, we will find our religious life blocked and our common belief degenerating into a quarrel over particular actions. Philosophical criticism is necessary to keep religious life from dissolving either into an idle routine or into deluding itself by thinking that a certain form of practice is the obvious way to translate belief into action.

Belief gives rise to voiced anxieties which can only be answered conceptually and not practically, since the problems generated by a particular practice are what give rise to most deep-seated anxieties in the first place. Sometimes we know what a certain belief requires of us ("Thou shalt love the Lord thy God"), and we are only disturbed because we do not do it, or at least this is so at times. More often, however, our greatest anxieties come because we simply do not know what we should do about our convictions, practically speaking. We would move to action if we knew what to do, but the required activity is not clear. In this case philosophical analysis must enter and work on a conceptual level first before action can be released or anxiety alleviated.

It is for these reasons, then, that both philosophy and a theology of a more speculative type cannot be avoided. We do not all agree in seeing one form of life as required, even if it follows from a common belief (for example, "love thy neighbor as thyself"), and often the commands themselves are not perfectly clear. Although we hear, we still do not always know what to do about it. Religious life is not simply one explicit action but is subject to many expressions. Yet this problem might remain submerged if it were not for the fact that the opposition of belief vs. practice makes avoiding the issue impossible. If religion were either simply all a set of beliefs to be assented to or else a prescribed pattern of activity simply to be followed out, it could escape its involvement with philosophy.

The constant discrepancy between belief and practice requires us to relate religion to philosophy again after it had first seemed to escape such intellectual affairs by being an activity. Certainly, not every believer in a religious group necessarily is led to philosophy by his religious practice. Those who do not question their mode of life or the action required of them may simply believe and live their religious convictions without reflection—a desirable state whenever possible or when it is not misguided or destructive. But, since practice itself presents problems, any vital religion must support some reflective activity which inquires into these problems and which attempts to bridge the gap between belief and practice by means of new intellectual concepts that allow clear expression.

According to the account given above, religion is, strangely enough, more closely tied to philosophy than other forms of practice are or even different forms of theoretical endeavor—for example, science or art. In other intellectual fields, a man may never turn to philosophy but simply carry out his theoretical inquiry as the state of the enterprise of the day inspires him. He may become interested in philosophical questions, or he may even introduce such basic reflection on first principles into his work, but he need not do so, and nothing in his theoretical field (for example, physics) in itself forces him to do this. On the practical level, he may be a carpenter or an engineer and simply make and build according to the rules of skill and the design employed. Such is the life of pure action.

In spite of their frequent antagonism, religious life and philosophical reflection stand more closely tied together and more necessarily associated than almost any other forms of human activity. Religion by its nature cannot concern what is wholly immediate or present, and this abstractness always raises problems of interpretation and understanding. More important, although religion naturally drives toward practice and action for its fulfillment, it is always partially frustrated when either the form of life or the specific action do not seem clearly required. We must act and change and not merely observe or else religion dies. Yet the forms these actions should take are constantly in question, and at least some men are continually driven toward intellectual inquiry. Their hope is to release blocked activity through clarified and reformulated theory.

Since theology has traditionally been thought to have God as its primary object, this drive toward philosophy which the religious disposition involves is perhaps most clearly in evidence where God is concerned. Religious documents seldom tell us much about God's nature in detail. Or, when they do, such information tends to be fragmentary and incomplete. Yet, for worship we need to have an object that increasingly becomes more real. Ritual practice and religious devotion are designed to lead in this direction. Yet, ultimately, to make God concrete must be the task, ironically enough, of an abstract speculative effort. The mind works simultaneously to analyze in greater detail that toward which a religious spirit feels driven to seek out in action and in its specific religious practice.

If either our action in the name of religious belief, or our ritual observance or our way of life, could ever become identical with God or even be clearly seen as necessarily required by him, then religion could free itself from theory and pursue action without reflection. However, in order to separate out what action God really does approve of for us vs. what human

motives have foisted off onto the divine, we need a detailed
theory of the divine nature and its operation, and this does not
come from religious documents or practice alone. And now the
problems only really begin, for more views of God's nature are
possible than one. We are driven to the most difficult of all
abstract questions: a comparative study of all the concepts of
God in order to justify one form of practice vs. another. Thus,
the most abstruse of all intellectual objects, God, is immediately involved in the difficult problems of concrete action and
the choice between a variety of forms of life.

Could the practice of religion be carried on without constant
reference to a theory of divine nature to support the practice,
philosophy would be less necessary to the religious life, and
the practice of religion would not be so subject to question,
even by those who engage in it. One not involved in any form
of religious life always seems to suppose that those who are
become the most certain of all people as to the rightness of
their activity and the necessity of some particular action. (Unfortunately, in its bigoted and intolerant form, religion is often
just this certain and then it can stoop to persecution.) Yet
anyone who comes to be familiar with a sensitive religious
spirit is perhaps startled at first to find, either in himself or in
others, that such a spirit tends to be the most uncertain about
itself of all human animals. Then we must call on the conceptual clarity of philosophy to provide assurance and
support.

Why is this so, and what insight does it give us into religion
as a matter of practice? On the practical side, we are led to
conjecture that one reason why religion may tend to reject
philosophy is because this relationship exposes its uncertain
roots. Thus, dogmatic behavior in that sense is an extreme
reaction against the uncertainties inherent in the religious life.
Religion must be a form of activity and not simply a theory,
and yet the unbridgeable gap between belief and practice
naturally causes constant theorizing to arise. This, in turn,
interferes with the simple translation of belief into action and
tends instead to bog religion down into a paralyzing set of
unending questions when it should lead to altered practice.

In reaction against this, religious belief often leads to the
demand for a rigid adherence to one ritual and form without

questioning its adequacy as an expression of belief. It is here that theology, as something different from religion, is born and cannot be dispensed with. The uncertainties inherent in the religious spirit inevitably tie religious action to philosophical speculation—that is, unless they are hidden by a rigid and unyielding attitude which ultimately kills the spirit. Philosophy has the sensitivity and tentativeness needed to keep religion from destroying itself by attempting to cover up its uncertainties, just as Adam hid from God when he discovered his nakedness in the Garden of Eden.

4

THE CONSTRUCTION OF
THEOLOGY

A. APPLIED PHILOSOPHY

Although religion is primarily a matter of practice, it is not an activity without its problems. The same thing, of course, could be said about any human conduct; and, in that sense, our political and economic life also lead to philosophy. However, very special and important factors about the practice of religion drive it toward philosophy and necessitate the formation of theologies. Most important of these reasons is the centrality of a concept of God, but we shall take that up as a separate matter in the next section. Beyond this, it is the involvement of religion with the inner or the spiritual life that necessitates philosophical assistance. Since these matters are neither obvious nor ever easy to handle, problems constantly arise and precise guidance is necessary if the religious life is not to go astray.

Religion also involves ethical directives for action, and often these are not clear in themselves or else they need clarification as times change and new circumstances arise. If the ethical advice happens to be of a very general nature or if it is phrased in parables or in a symbolic form, then it requires a constantly fresh interpretation, and great care must be exercised if it is not to·be misunderstood and misapplied. Leaving God aside for the moment, these practical problems might actually be taken care of without the direct involvement of philosophy. However, they still tend to take religion toward philosophy, even when they are dealt with as questions regarding the rules to be worked out by the religious community to guide its common life. For, when one step is taken beyond the basic formulation of the religious belief, then something else must be added to give additional structure to these clarified rules. Dealing with problems by the use of clarified definitions, of course, is precisely the meaning of philosophy.

In this chapter we shall consider what theology is as an enterprise and how it relates to what we understand both philosophy and religion to be. Theology occupies a strange position as a "mixed enterprise." It is, we shall argue, essentially "applied philosophy." Philosophy is an ancient enterprise, however we evaluate it, whose status and mode of procedure are rather clear. Of course, philosophy may have its practical sides, but essentially it is an intellectual enterprise involving the development of intricate technical doctrine.

Religion too is an ancient and traditional practice, but involvement in it does not necessarily include philosophy. Yet, without religion we would have no theology. It is true that many philosophers have developed doctrines of the nature of God, or at least some criticism of these. Such arguments for and against God come to us not so much connected with religious practice as simply a part of the development of that philosophy's technical view of the world. In this sense, philosophy has a theology of a certain kind within it, which is independent of the religious life. We shall consider this special connection between philosophy and theology in more detail in the next section. Except for its role in philosophy, however, theology would not arise from the practice of religion if it did not encounter certain problems.

As we have already mentioned, some of these religious problems arise over ethical commands and over how these are to be applied in each new era. The story of the Good Samaritan in the New Testament is simple enough; but a religious man runs into a number of questions in attempting to follow this example and determine exactly who his "neighbor" is.

Practical application is hindered by the lack of a clear understanding of exactly what is required in different circumstances, and it becomes a matter crucial to the vitality of the religious life that these issues be explained satisfactorily. To do so means to employ both philosophical reflection and philosophical terms and concepts in order to create an intellectual framework that makes a new understanding possible.

These are the internal problems of practice that lead to the use of philosophy to provide a theological answer. But there are also external problems that call for the application of philosophical methods and doctrines to religion even more clearly: we call this "apologetics." That is, religion can become ingrown, and, if it does, the members of the group will encounter no problems of understanding as they carry out their practice, only because they never challenge the context of meaning that unites them. However, the very meaning of religion involves the fact that not everyone else shares your beliefs and convictions. In such a situation, it often becomes both necessary and desirable to explain your beliefs to those outside your community who do not share them. Such continual attempted justification before an unsympathetic audience is the greatest possible corrective for religious blindness and self-preoccupation.

Often the success of the religious practice is at stake—that is, the practice may be hindered by hostility unless it can make itself understood outside its own circle. Furthermore, if the religious group seeks converts, such proselytizing may proceed by emotional appeal or by demonstrated acts of mercy which convince the other person of the great worth of that belief. Sometimes "works of love" of this kind are the most effective explanation of a religious belief that can be given to one who does not understand it. Yet, there are times when the belief needs to be explained in intellectual terms capable of being understood by someone who does not share that group's basic conviction, loyalty, and frame of mind.

In this sense, apologetics (that is, explaining clearly to another what the religious belief means in terms that do not require him to believe in order to understand) is a part of missionary activity, and this places philosophy in the odd position of aiding the spread of a religious belief. Philosophy, however, has been put to even stranger applications than this, and its use here is crucial if religious beliefs are to be explained to nonbelievers in clear terms. Philosophy, to be sure, is not hurt by this employment. As long as its original life is kept clear and free, it actually gains clarity by being used for such practical functions, since one theory begins to look like every other theory when all are simply left in the realm of ideas. The formulas that yield understanding in one era do not alway do so in the next, so that in this sense every religion must be constantly involved in the philosophy of its day. It need not use any one contemporary view uncritically, but theology at least must be made constantly philosophically aware.

The penalty theology pays if it does not keep philosophically active in each day is that it loses an ability to converse intellectually with those who are outside of its own particular tradition in that era. Theology is not and should not become simply another philosophical view of the time. Of course, its origin in the life of religious practice (if this is not lost) tends to prevent this by its involvement with immediate human concerns, and in the next chapter we shall consider the nonphilosophical elements with which theology must deal that also make it a mixed enterprise and not simply another intellectual discipline. Theology is philosophy applied to those nonphilosophic elements—for example, religious practice and its problems, sacred literature, and the traditions of the community. Just because that is its nature, theology is best understood as a mixed mode and as an impure intellectual discipline—but, nevertheless, it is an intellectual affair vs. simple religious practice.

If this account of the status of theology is at all correct, it is absolutely crucial that we understand the role philosophy plays in shaping it. Then we must develop a critical sensitivity to philosophical doctrines, together with some systematic ability to handle philosophy in independence from theology. To see philosophy always in relation to theology is to misunderstand it, and to do that is actually to render it ineffective for its theological use. Philosophy is the formative element which brings structured doctrines out of materials that, if left to themselves, would neither be systematic nor yield intellectual answers—that is, religious practice, sacred literature, and the like. In a strange sense, we actually set theology free to do its work consciously when we recognize and accept its philosophical dependence—that is, when we admit that the forms it borrows from philosophy will in turn give specific shape to its materials.

We might define theology in this way: *a philosophical view developed and applied in order to structure a problem raised in religious practice or belief, such that the difficulty is met and action can then issue from the religious belief on that basis.* Seen in this light, theology is primarily an intellectual affair, just as philosophy is, but it is the theoretical attempt to wrestle with a problem that involvement in religion always raises. Except as philosophy considers the problem of God on its own, this means that there are no theological problems for one who is neither interested in nor actively involved with the practice of religion. Even for the man who is committed to a religion, theological problems may not arise. Theology does not serve any useful practical purpose (although it can be played with as an intellectual game) unless difficulties arise in understanding the demands of religion or in attempting to carry out its specific practices.

This centrality of philosophy is less evident in the details of religious practice. Here theories may be formed and questions raised (for example, what degree of penetration is necessary in order to consider a marriage consummated?), but such theories seem to be a matter of legal detail and elaboration and are not very much concerned with philosophical principles. However much there may be of this kind of detail in "church theology" (that is, a theology that is internally oriented and of no relevance to the nonpractitioner but instead is centered on the details of practice), philosophy can enter in again in perhaps an even more crucial way.

That is, now philosophy is needed as a corrective to help protect both religion and that particular form of theology against its greatest danger: losing the important matters of religion in a mountain of detail. Now philosophy plays a vital role—that is, helping religion to keep a constant stress on its important issues and preventing the religious life from drifting into unconscious trivial routine. The application of philosophy helps religion to express clearly in each new day its most central concerns by its philosophical criticism of an overelaborate "church dogmatics" which make unimportant points appear more important than they ought to be.

This view of theology as "applied philosophy" does not necessarily depreciate theology as an enterprise provided that the specific philosophy to be used is not dictated to us, and provided that the theologian is not restricted to the use of only those philosophical views he happens to find current. In fact, in order not to fall victim either to any one philosophical view or to some particular trend of the day, the theologian must apply philosophy critically in his work in order to know that he need not of necessity use these special terms or employ that particular doctrine; he need not do this unless it seems to be conducive to his theological aims. The intellectual air of any day is full of philosophical doctrines, and this is a fact we recognize even in the formation of the Gospels. No theologian can be free of this, so that in self-defense he must himself become a philosopher in order to use philosophy critically. He does this so as not to be either determined in his conclusions by any hidden and unexamined assumptions or prejudiced by the connotation the terms he employs happen to have.

Such a view of theology is not prejudicial to the purity of the religious life—that is, provided that we distinguish it sharply from theology as an intellectual discipline. If we do this, the theological doctrine can be taken for what it is and incorporated into the community's religious life only when it is found to be helpful. In point of fact, this is what tends to happen between practice and theory anyhow. Furthermore, such a view of theology, and such a sharp separation of it from religion, mean that philosophy can actually be of service to the religious life—that is, it functions as a critic who helps to expose theological doctrines that rest on particular philosophical assumptions which have perhaps unknowingly worked their way into religious acceptance. All theological doctrines require constant scrutiny as to their origin, and it is particularly important constantly to reassess their suitability as a form in which to express the basic convictions of that religious community. In this case, to grant theology autonomy is to create a great danger for the religious life. Philosophy should hold theology back from destructive arrogance by keeping it subject to the demands of the religious life.

B. PHILOSOPHY AND THE SEARCH FOR GOD

This view of philosophy as an impartial evaluator of the impure forms of theology—that is, of those that have continued to establish themselves in the religious life long after their usefulness or long after the assumptions on which they rest have ceased to be accepted—this view can be made most obvious where God is concerned. If God's nature were clear from the beginning, religions probably would not exist with each one claiming as it does to embody some vision of God's nature, his actions, and his commands. If such a vision of God, one that sparks a religious movement, always stayed fresh and clear—even to the members of that group—then, obviously, we would not experience the phenomenon of the decline of vitality of once powerful religious movements. Even if once firmly grasped, it seems to require constant effort in order to keep a view of God alive, and in this process philosophy has a crucial role to play.

Why is it that the "search for God" cannot go on successfully without the aid of philosophy? To assert this seems to make things difficult both for the idea that philosophy is an independent discipline and for the view of religion as primarily a matter of practice. However, this need not trouble philosophy, particularly if we see that a majority of classical philosophers have in fact introduced a concept of God as part of their systematic thought. This does not commit all philosophers to share such a concern, but it does indicate that to develop a theory about God is not incompatible with the independence of the philosophical life. On the side of religion, the issue at stake concerns the clarity and the definitiveness of any particular religion's revelation of God. Without philosophy, religious belief may fail to define or to sustain its most valuable aspect.

Religions—even groups within Christianity—do differ on the view of God which they present. Therefore, no religion can afford to take its concept of God for granted. Each religious group is based on some revelation of God's nature, and yet the religious experience itself never makes it completely clear just how this is to be developed or worked out in detail. The religious presentation of God is always different from its technical elaboration, so that 'God' becomes a definite concept and a principle that offers guidance in the approach to the theological problems only when that idea is philosophically elaborated. Furthermore, no religion can avoid the necessity of giving technical formulation to its original vision, since problems and questions regarding its teaching arise that can only be dealt with by some technical (that is, philosophical) elaboration.

In addition, the initial presentation of God, which may have had great impact on those who received it or were converted to it, tends to lose its forcefulness unless it is continually renewed, and this involves primarily a technical elaboration. Of course, to the extent that this view of God and his action moves those who believe it to exemplary and model action, that vision of God is not lost and it can continue to communicate itself with the unmatchable forcefulness of action. Still, what words once conveyed can be forgotten, and then fresh formulation is always called for. Somewhat ironically, whatever the manner in which the first revelation of God was communicated (more likely via carpenters than via philosophers), it does seem to require philosophical reformulation after that in order to renew its vitality and to preserve its form by elaborating it more technically.

In a more systematic sense, philosophy is vital to a religious quest for God because God is not a simple object. He requires quite a complicated theoretical structure in order to make the concept of him concrete. However God is said to be revealed, this is never done in technical detail. Thus, if this is to be added, it must come from philosophy, and this is why the philosophy to be adopted is neither an inconsequential nor a neutral affair. It may almost be said, simply, that it is the theologians' task to speak "in the name of God." To propose this is not religious blasphemy, as long as we remember that this is done by the detailed philosophical structuring of what originally is a nonphilosophical experience. Then, in terms of this technical elaboration, the theologian is able to work out what God's motives in any action may be or his views on any situation might have been. To speak for God is not a danger but a necessity—that is, unless the theologian confuses his words with God's own existence, since God probably is less rigid in his nature than the definite structure of any particular speech.

To speak thus for God is not as risky an affair in a philosophical-theological mold as it is in a religious form. Theologically we realize that our "answers" are a product of, and thus dependent upon, the philosophical elaboration we have provided. These answers may be helpful, but they are to be given no more solidity or authority than what we know a philosophical theory is capable of providing. When it comes to theories about God's "opinions," every philosophical criteria and criticism of assumptions should be applied. Yet within this context, it is still importantly true that it is possible to work out the detail concerning the divine nature only when aided by philosophy.

If it were the case that every religious search for God were successful, this quest might not be a matter that involved philosophy so intimately. But the religious struggle for God is sometimes frustrating, often even destructive for the person so engaged, and when successful it seems to need technical expression in order to be communicated. More important, it also involves philosophical concepts of the nature of God as an aid to the success of the project. It may well be that some philosophical presentation of God's nature is necessary before the individual person has enough concrete structure in terms of which to continue his quest. Philosophy may have the task delegated to it of forming a concept of God that is sufficiently clear so that, in its terms, the religiously interested person can find enough definite material to react against and thus define his relation to God.

This brings us to perhaps the strangest, but certainly theologically the most crucial, aspect of religious doctrine. That is, for all the importance God has, the bulk of theological doctrine is always concerned with more immediate matters than a direct description of God, and its direct statements about God are at best incomplete and certainly in need of much elaboration before they can be very specific. Particularly concerning the divine nature, most religious literature is at best symbolic or suggestive about the details of God's attributes, and the history of theology would seem to testify that the filling in of this detail is at least as much a function of the philosophical view employed as it is of the original religious insight.

If this is so, then the philosophy selected to be employed is not an insignificant concern. In fact, it is almost determinative of the kind of view of the nature of God that is developed. This does not mean that the religious view presented is not important, but it does mean that our situation is such that it is not at all so simple as having a detailed view of God given to us by the religious tradition alone. For example, if we take all of the statements that concern God as represented in the four Gospels, we would find ourselves very far from having a doctrine of God of sufficient detail to allow us to use it for theological construction. On the other hand, if we look at the views of the nature of God that have been given theological use in the Christian tradition, it is also clear that these do not at all agree in basic elaboration. More than one technical description of God seems to be compatible with the statements made by the Gospel writers.

We can, of course, argue that one theological doctrine of God better represents the Christian presentation than another (for example, Thomas' fully actual God vs. one who is at least partially subject to time). Yet the important point is that the appraisal of such an argument is not a matter for religious solution but rather depends primarily on the technical evaluation of an elaborate set of philosophical assumptions. Regarding these technical matters, we have precious little guidance from the religious tradition itself, whereas, ironically, the kind of doctrine of God we develop systematically has many implications for the way in which troublesome religious matters are interpreted (for example, evil and human freedom).

That the construction of theology should depend to such an extent on the philosophical context supplied and be so little dictated by the religious tradition—this situation is not so much at odds with the interpretation of religion given here as it would appear. If you take religion to be primarily an intellectual affair, you might expect it to generate a theory of the divine nature from its own materials and that it would be able to structure this without outside assistance. However, we have taken religion to be primarily a matter of practice and activity (in the next section we shall take up the matter of religious literature and tradition). In this case, religion is not of itself a technical intellectual enterprise. As an affair that has other important interests, it cannot be expected to be intellectually sophisticated or precise in its own documents and practice. Its basic orientation is in a different direction.

If this is true, it has implications for our interpretation of 'revelation' in religion. In Christianity, for instance, if God is assumed to have revealed himself there, this must be primarily through his activity and not necessarily in any way that offers precise intellectual guidelines. It is possible for an action to be clear and definite and to constitute the revelation, but then the revelation did not take primarily an intellectual form. This does not mean that it is not subject to various intellectual formulations, but it does mean that we are left with some mental flexibility even after the revelation. We must make our own assessment of which philosophical forms give it clearest expression; and, most important, we discover the necessity to add philosophical materials to the religious data if we hope to produce anything like a theology. If God has determined some things definitely, at least the Christian revelation has been given a form (action) that is theoretically imprecise enough so that it preserves our intellectual freedom.

Precisely at its central core, then, theology needs the support of philosophy in its search for God. Action may be demanded of a believer; a particular technical form of thought is not. A concept of God becomes real only as it is structured, even if some of the materials used for it do come from the religious tradition and its documents. Theology solves the problems posed for it by the difficulties encountered in the religious life—that is, when for any reason its practice and activity are blocked—but to do this it builds around a central concept of God. Just as there is not one theology but many, so there is not one concept of God but many possible Gods. Were this not so it would be hard to explain the ferocity of the individual religious effort to find God and to discover his will. The rigidity of the theologian testifies to the fact that his concept of God is variable enough to need such protection and artificial defense. If one concept of God were either evident or one to which all men were eventually led, it would be hard to explain why the religious struggle begins in such basic uncertainty.

One must know the possible ways to conceive of God's nature in order to have a firm object to direct attention toward. In this case, philosophy becomes crucial, since its very business is the construction of concepts, the exploration of all possible ideas, and then the testing and the evaluation of the merits and demerits of various conceptual forms. This would seem to explain why, when philosophy grows sceptical about its ability to operate metaphysically with any success, then, despite all of the religious fervor or energy, the clear vision of God which religion ultimately needs seems to disappear and theology too turns its attention to apparently everything but God. Just because religion and theology are what they are as enterprises, if they are without philosophical support, at this point their constructive ability is lost—at least in the possibility of achieving any freshness or novelty where God is concerned.

C. THE THEOLOGICAL FAILURE OF PHILOSOPHY

If philosophy is as crucial and as central to the theological enterprise and to the religious life as has been made out here, why has philosophy been treated with such hostility in these circles so many times? Not that it always has been ostracized, but any account that claims philosophy to be basic to theological success must also account for its repeated rejection. Two obvious answers suggest themselves. (1) Not all philosophy is in fact sympathetic to religious interests, and (2) philosophy has a tendency to lead away from action and to turn religion from its practical concerns into an intellectual affair. Unless these tendencies are dealt with, an antiphilosophic reaction may set in whenever religion sees that its central life-interests are threatened.

In spite of the fact that many of the classical philosophers have had an interest in religion and have made technical use of a concept of God, not all philosophers are so disposed—particularly in modern times. Moreover, much of philosophy is concerned with other matters, and some of these are even antithetical to religion's concerns. Thus, all of philosophy cannot be accepted openly, and often it is a direct threat as religion's competitor, since many people find philosophical thought a sufficient guide to life and thus feel no need for religion.

Some philosophies not only prefer to develop other interests but also concentrate on views that systematically either eliminate religion (for example, humanism) or restrict it severely (for example, empiricism). In this light, philosophical dependence is not without its dangers for theology. Some philosophical attitudes can make it more difficult to achieve theological solutions, depending, of course, on the kind of philosophy employed. And worse than that, philosophy can turn would-be theologians away from their theological enterprise, either by converting them to a strictly philosophical approach or by restricting theology from accomplishing its goals for religion by the adoption of antithetical theoretical assumptions.

The difficulties in philosophy sketched above briefly do not encompass the most serious reason why philosophy sometimes receives a hostile reception in theological circles. A wide variety of philosophical views are available, so that, in order to overcome any possible theological restrictions, all that is necessary is an astute philosophical sensitivity. Given this, it is possible to forecast the theological consequences of any philosophical view. Of course, philosophy is not such a simple affair as to involve merely taking over one view and then applying it. No philosophical theory is ever completely worked out, so that to approach a philosophy is not to get a finished product but to find oneself absorbed into the intricacies of trying to extend the insights present there. To clarify these areas of uncertainty often merely raises problems instead of solving them once and for all.

To follow Kant is not to get a complete system but simply to continue the various lines of debate that always come along after a creative philosopher. Those who owe allegiance to Plato and Socrates are many; but, if you examine their doctrines in detail, each reaches quite different conclusions. Following one man may lead in many directions rather than in one only. This makes it necessary for someone who uses a particular philosophy to become a philosopher himself, in order to pick and choose and explore and develop and blend other views into the original one. It is not possible to accept one philosopher's approach and to be loyal to him without sharing in his own creativity. Simply to apply a philosophical view in theology is to be false to the spirit of philosophy and to make that philosophy dogmatic—which certainly is to abuse it.

If this is the case, it is not possible to take over philosophical views without getting drawn into the controversial and constructive life of philosophy itself—that is, unless you are willing to be false to the philosophy you adopt. And now it is easier to explain the second reason (number 2 above) that philosophy is feared in religion at the same time that it is used. Philosophy has this tendency, which sometimes is unfortunate for religion, in that it cannot provide a framework for solving certain difficulties without exacting its price. That is, at the same time that a given philosophical view is of assistance in theology (for example, Whitehead's 'God'), it also tends to draw the theologian into the difficulties, into the unsettled and uncertain aspects of the theory itself, and thus to divert his energy and attention into this area (for example, how to explain 'prehension').

In the strictest sense, this kind of involvement with the actual life of constructive philosophy is what must take place before the theologian either learns enough to know how to employ philosophy effectively or has a deep enough understanding of any view in order to control its use and to alter the defects it may possess for his particular purpose (for example, to give an account of the Trinity). Still, this often does have the effect of turning the theologian away from his concern with religion as an actual practice. Theology may now become, under the influence of philosophy, such an exclusively intellectual affair that even the theologian ignores its essentially mixed mode. He forgets that theology is dependent on philosophy for its technical form but that it still arises from the practical concerns of religion—that is, to explain itself to non-believers and to remove intellectual barriers that develop to hinder its practice.

In a slightly different way, philosophy may disrupt the religious life by introducing more quarrels than it settles, or at least by introducing questions of its own which divert religious interests to expend energy on questions little likely to be beneficial to it. In many ways, religious practice is a simple affair (for example, "except ye become as a little child"), whereas philosophy's very job is to add sophistication, to point out hidden and subtle problems, which the average man is likely to pass over as not worth worrying about. The practical man acts on the basis of a lack of concern over a technical understanding of the theoretical concepts he employs. Philosophers have always tried to bring to the surface hidden unclarities and basic disagreements over principle (cf. Socrates and the disagreement over the meaning of 'justice' in the opening sections of the *Republic*). Raising fine distinctions which others pass over lightly has a value, and it is this philosophers always stress.

Nevertheless, such concern can be detrimental to religion, so that what once seemed simple and a matter to implement in action now becomes so complicated that the whole world and every subtle problem must be solved before the religious life can proceed. Much in the religious life (for example, acceptance, humility) fights with the traditional goals of philosophy, since religion seeks first to change its life and action and that of others along certain lines.

Such a tension can be fruitful for both concerns; it can heighten the philosophical-intellectual life and the religious life of action. Yet it is clear also that philosophical interests do tend to make issues more complicated rather than less (at least at first). If action depends on the simplicity of an issue so that our choices become clear-cut, philosophy can defeat religion insofar as it turns theology into a very complicated intellectual affair. If this intellectual subtlety demands that it be mastered before any practical decision can be made, religion, whose life is action, dries up and theology loses its reason for existence.

D. CAN THEOLOGY BE DISPENSED WITH?

Given some of what has been said above, it would seem that religion would in some ways be better off without theology. Some religions have felt this way at times, a few have tried to avoid theology from the beginning, and still others have worked to keep theology as an enterprise while at the same time denying its philosophical dependence. The last alternative is perhaps the most dangerous one. Our history indicates that neither religious literature nor tradition is enough to give rise to a single consistent theology. Thus, something must be added to these rare materials to yield our various theologies. This, we have asserted, is either a particular philosophical structure or some combination of various ones. If we pretend that this is not the case, then a particular theological view simply arrogates a kind of importance to itself which it perhaps ought not to have. If its fallible roots in human philosophical doctrine can be acknowledged, it really is easier to deal with such philosophical involvement and to bring its assertions under criticism where they need to be. Our religious life is better off if theology can be kept subject to some external controls.

Whenever a theological view denies its partial dependence on philosophy, then it moves itself closer to being a religion in itself. This has the ironic effect of making it less possible to distinguish religious practice from theological theory. When the incorporation of philosophical views into theological construction is freely admitted, then theology stands out more clearly as something quite different, and as differently based, from the religious life and the practice of religion is not confused with a theoretical endeavor. The clarifying importance theology does have can now be recognized, while it does not somehow seem to require us to accept any certain theological formulation on pain of rejecting the whole of the life of religion.

Because of this subverting effect which theologies can have when they try to deny their human origins, some religious movements have been both antiphilosophical and antitheological. The evangelical Protestant groups in America are good examples of this. Judaism, on the other hand, by not developing a series of theologies about itself and by confining itself more closely to a people and a ritual practice, has been able to be philosophical in a wide variety of detached ways without feeling that philosophy must be held at a distance in order to preserve the life of religion. Yet the tendency to avoid both philosophy and theology can be effective only for a limited time. The success of such neutrality usually lasts while the religious movement is in the bloom of its initial vital attraction as a new way of life, or while it is dealing with people who are either not already intellectually sophisticated or who by birth are predisposed to membership.

When the religious way of life itself is challenged, or when it is changed enough to be different from its original conception, or when those to whom it speaks or attempts to reach are already trained in philosophical thought, then in any of these circumstances some theologizing must come first. This starts as an attempt to clarify the original purpose and to give that way of life the rational underpinnings it needs in order to continue to attract a group of people who must be met on the plane of intelligible explanation. Thus, every religious movement tends eventually toward theological purification and rethinking. Somewhat ironically, the power of a religious movement (for example, Methodism) is seldom intellectual and philosophical in its origin. There will come a time, however, when the continued expression of its influence depends on its success in working out philosophical foundations for its original non-philosophical message.

Without attempting either a brief history of Christianity or a comparative study of it as opposed to other forms of religion, it still seems clear that Christianity as a whole has been centrally theological in its form and has thus constantly been deeply involved with philosophical theories. Without considering the objections of those who feel that Christianity has been distorted in its philosophical involvement (for example, the argument over abstract Greek modes of thought vs. biblical imagery), it is still possible to point out the factors that have forced Christianity to be more theological than some other religious forms. For instance, Christianity began within Judaism; but, as it broke away, it needed to define clearly what made it another religion as opposed to Judaism and not just another sect within it.

Furthermore, as the decision was made to break away and not impose the requirements of contemporary Judaism, and as those of many races and previous creeds were admitted to membership, no regional or racial or historical bond was sufficient to unite such a disparate group. Thus, a common belief, one that united men of widely varied cultures and backgrounds as Christians, had to be worked out. From the moment of this dispersion, the union of Christians had to be first of all a theological union, however divisive theology may have become in later eras of Christianity. In order to define themselves as a group, any union had to be consummated on the basis of the acceptance of common beliefs. This meant that the beliefs needed to be clarified and systemized to the point that theology, not background or practice, could serve as the common bond.

Furthermore, and again without analyzing Christian assertions in detail, it is clear that Christianity stressed a life of the spirit and tended to look harshly on the prescription of religious ritual as the means to establishing community. Whatever the common practices may be that ingrained themselves in Christianity (for example, baptism and the Lord's Supper), still its emphasis tended to make it a matter of the spirit and of inner intent rather than of specific and prescribed forms of action or ritual practice. Set free from the Mosaic law, the observance of which could define the Jew, Christianity demanded a more abstract (that is, a more philosophical) definition of itself as a religion. Thus, there are good reasons why the early Church Fathers saw Platonic philosophy, not as a subverting force, but as kindred spirit and as an aid in giving expression to Christianity.

Platonism—and any other philosophical theory for that matter—may have certain difficult features for the development of Christian doctrine, and this is perhaps even more true in a later day than in an earlier era. The exact suitability of Platonism for molding Christian theology is not the issue here. The point is that Christian theology's affinity to Platonism and to philosophy in general is both quite natural and necessary, given the fact Christians (like philosophers) can never take either themselves or their lives for granted. Instead, they are condemned to the life of a constant definition of both their faith and their practice; it is the only way to keep outwardly divergent forms of life and diverse cultures united in theory and in belief. To accomplish this is essentially a philosophical enterprise and that is why Christianity cannot escape the life of philosophy, in spite of its frequent dangers.

Sometimes the result of expounding theology is to block the

activity of the religious life, and at other times it acts as a purifier to keep religious practice from being misled into irrelevant and even corrupt actions. Strange that religion's conscience as an activity should be found in the life of philosophy. Sometimes, theological construction can free power when it has become enfeebled by the loss of a clear vision of its purpose. Primarily, this leads back to the point elaborated in section B above—that is, that effort is required to maintain a view of God. Religious practice goes healthily on its way as long as its vision of God and his commands are clear. This vision probably did not come originally from a philosophical exploration nor is its power derived from that source. Yet, after a time, God fades unless a secondary defense is established in the development of a theology. This is designed to keep the vision clear and to distinguish it from its accumulated unessentials and to protect it from the natural tendency of man to adopt any view of God that will justify his own purposes.

Some men in religion may lead a purely practical life, and then they shun theological sophistication in order to preserve their noncomplicated source of a clear drive to action. Other philosophers may lead the life of pure philosophy, never compromising their goals with the unclarities and inconsistencies religion tends to gather about itself. To the religious man, the philosopher seems to produce endless complications as if in an endeavor to escape a direct confrontation with God and the practical demands of religion. In contrast to both, theologians are condemned to a life of mixture, whereas both the religious man and the philosopher can take a mixed life or leave it for either the purity of simple action or the life of theory alone. To construct theological theories means never to be free to turn wholly to a life of theory and its lack of outside responsibilities. Yet it also means never to be able to avoid absorption in a variety of philosophies as the only means by which theologies can be built.

5

THE USE OF
LITERATURE AND TRADITION

A. LITERATURE AND TRADITION AS PARTS OF PHILOSOPHY

Sometimes we may be tempted to think religion unique in that it has extraphilosophical sources. That is, religion is not merely a matter of defining carefully a set of beliefs. In addition to its practical side, religion draws from both an accumulated literature and an inherited practice in a way in which simple philosophical belief does not. It is true that, as we consider religion's effect on theological formation, the importance of its literature and its tradition cannot be overlooked; but it is also true that philosophy does not lack these elements. To understand exactly how philosophy has, and how it uses, a tradition and a literature and how religion differs from it—all this may help us to distinguish and yet to relate these enterprises.

Of course, it is true that philosophy differs both in its appraisal and its use of its own literature and tradition. In so doing, it defines its peculiar approach. Certain radical philosophical movements have wanted either to reject their inherited literature, to render it obsolete, or else to see it in some dialectical or evolutionary sense as leading to some later formulation. Without explaining these issues further, it is still true that previous literature is important to any philosophical movement as that against which it defines itself. In this sense, it is almost impossible to conceive of philosophy without a body of historical theory behind it. Then, either in opposition to or as a continuation of these trends, the new theory takes its form.

If it is clear that any new philosophy begins by either considering or reacting against a previous theory, its need for and preservation of tradition is not as obvious as it is in theology. Yet tradition is still there for every philosopher, no matter how differently he regards himself or his enterprise. Almost every philosopher, for instance, recognizes in the Platonic dialogues at least a kindred spirit of inquiry, however much he may disagree with Plato or with his specific doctrine. No matter how various the specific definitions of 'reason', still every philosopher feels some allegiance to a rational approach. He feels bound by an attempt to explain a problem as fully and as clearly as possible in spite of any inherent difficulty or how far any problem may ultimately transcend reason's grasp. The rational effort must still be made and pushed to its limits.

Even Hume's scepticism has a basis in reason, as he himself recognizes. That is, Hume is critical of reason's scope and ability, but still it is only by the use of reason that reason can be analyzed and evaluated. While Kierkegaard and Nietzsche are more extreme than Hume in their criticism of reason, Hegel is completely dependent upon it as an instrument. Yet, however different their approaches, at least each man's means of presentation is that of rational conveyance. This observation is not offered as an argument that all philosophies share some common notion of 'reason' or are part of a rational tradition. It is to point out that, according to its approach and its definition of reason, each philosophy defines itself. Furthermore, all philosophy seems to share this common orientation to the use of reason as its instrument no matter how qualified or redefined it may be.

Thus, it is clear that the teaching of philosophy is best done through its literature and its tradition, however specially restricted this may be in any individual case. Whatever natural tendencies he might have toward abstract thought, a philos-

opher is made and not born, so that it is in reading philosophical literature that the method is learned, even if this is by a
negative reaction to what is read. In sensing its tradition the
spirit of philosophical inquiry is caught and then perfected. Of
course, this accumulated literature is not an extraphilosophical
source. Rather, the material itself internally preserves the life
of philosophy, and it may be this fact that most sharply distinguishes philosophy's from religion's use of literature and tradition. That is, if religion is essentially a matter of practice and
philosophy one of thought, then whatever their role in religion,
literature and tradition always remain something separate and
independent from it.

One important distinction is needed here. Although philosophy may be taught through presenting its literature and its
tradition, once a new philosophical mode is formed, it may
then cut itself off from its antecedents and rightfully demand
to be evaluated only in its own terms, as it defines its novel
method and new doctrines. It no longer is judged in relation
either to its past literature or any previous concept of what the
philosophical tradition means. This novelty can also be somewhat characteristic of religion, but it is so always to a lesser
degree. In most cases, the religious practice involves a much
more obvious carrying forward—in whatever new forms may
be found—of its past. Its literature is always more central to
its present definition than is usually the case in philosophy.
Thus, religion depends more on, and also uses more specific
materials from, its refined and inherited literature.

This means that theology is never quite a free intellectual
discipline. Not only must it learn its trade from a theological
literature and tradition, but it must also interpret and incorporate its theories back into a religious literature and practice
which is philosophical neither in its origin nor in its primary
intent. This gives theology an added burden; it can never be
as free to work out doctrines on its own ground as some forms
of philosophy are. It is true that this is characteristic of
philosophy's approach to theology. To learn this kind of self-
dependence is good for the theologian, and it is philosophy's
contribution to his skill. However, in the end, the theologian
must come to grips with the literature and tradition to which
he speaks. Thus all new theological doctrines both receive

material content from and are partially shaped by something external to the theological method itself. The theologian is never completely the master of his own house as the philosopher can be in his.

This difference in the appropriation of literature and tradition has advantages and disadvantages for philosophy and theology. Philosophy is more free to be contemporary and is beholden to nothing outside of itself. This flexibility makes it easier for a new philosophy to break with its tradition, but it is also more difficult for philosophy either to be specifically relevant in any day or to wield practical influence. Theology, on the other hand, must constantly fight for some independence from religious practice in order to serve its function as a critic of institutional religion. Still, theology has a natural tie to immediate relevance and to material with a wide human appeal, and this should more easily assure its contemporary relevance.

Take as an illustration three issues: (1) the concept of God, which both philosophy and theology share, (2) logic, which is philosophy's special concern, and (3) the proper use and administration of the sacraments, which would never become a theological question were it not for the necessity of religious practice. Where God is concerned, philosophy has a literature and a tradition, but its relationship to them is rather loose— that is, the philosopher is free to ignore both. He need not use a concept of God or consider first principles. Or, if God is considered, the philosopher's approach may be dictated strictly by a combination of present materials and the context of the philosophical view being worked out. However, because God is not an ordinary object, philosophy may draw upon its own literature and tradition in order to orient itself. From the study of various concepts of God, a variety of intellectual approaches can be learned. From the detail of the theory and the terms used to describe God, the literature can provide materials to make the issue more concrete.

However, for theology, God is an inescapable subject: it forms the meaning of the enterprise and is the key concept around which other problems are arranged and dealt with. Of course, a theologian may play down or ignore dealing with the problem of God, but he does this at the risk of a failure in his theological structure. Because of his connection to the practice of religion, he is not free to ignore the past literature on God. If he does, it is at the risk of defining a religiously irrelevant God. While this necessity gives the theologian the advantage of a vast background and context for his consideration of God, it also may restrict the freedom of his thought to form fresh insights. Such a skill philosophy should and can teach him. Furthermore, his religious literature, because of its non- (or mixed) philosophical nature, also contains materials that make a systematic construction more difficult.

By way of contrast, (2) philosophy may at times share logic as a field with mathematics. However, on the whole, logic is an independent enterprise with its own literature and tradition. It can be studied historically, but logic usually is a contemporary enterprise which derives its methods and its problems from comparatively recent discussions. In the very general sense of the term, theology may employ logic, but this is not a part of philosophy that is very relevant to its concerns. This fact also indicates philosophy's greater detachment as a total enterprise from even its own literature and tradition. On the other hand, theology is bound to its past at this point, except perhaps where it is a matter of metaphysical exploration and a search for new and more expressive terminology. Because of its almost total inability to escape dealing with its accumulated literature and tradition, theology needs to guard and cultivate its small pure philosophical side in order to provide a needed area of detachment and to find a source for its new norms that will revise the tradition.

Philosophy has no interest as such in (3) the administration of the sacraments. These are so important in the religious tradition and community that theology cannot ignore giving them continually fresh treatment. Rather than simply distilling an accumulated tradition on the matter, you would think that here theology would first cultivate its more systematic and philosophical side—for example, the concept of God. Then, with this for leverage, it could turn to tackle the problem of checking its basis in tradition while still having as an aim the restoration of some given religious practice to contemporary meaning and relevance. In order to do this, theology must consider how to interpret and to preserve the traditional meaning of that ritual action. In this sense, it is not as free as philosophy simply to put forth new concepts. Theology's involvement with religious practice dictates that any new view of the sacraments needs a tie to past practice in order to insure its present meaning.

B. THE SPECIAL STATUS OF THEOLOGY

The issue of the use and administration of the sacraments is a problem that is important to theology because of its implications for religious practice. Yet, the problem would not arise philosophically were it not for the active nature of religion. This being so, we can see both theology's concrete advantage over philosophy and its potential pitfall. Since no philosophical issue *per se* is involved, the question of how to administer the sacraments can become a problem all too subject to endless detail and refinement. In this case, it appears to have great theoretical significance—for example, shall both wine and bread be administered to each communicant or only one? Actually, no intellectual problem is involved at all. Such being the case, it is important to insure that this issue arises only from the necessity of clarifying a matter of practice. Otherwise, the question becomes involved in a mass of intellectual detail which in point of fact had no original theoretical basis.

Because theology cannot avoid its inherited tradition and literature, it naturally has more relevance and connection to practice than does philosophy. Somewhere in the practical problem of the sacraments there may be a relation to a theoretical issue, but care must be taken to show what this importance is. If not, theology can simply lose itself and become the victim of the weight of its inherited literature and habits. When this happens, the connection to practice is lost and theological spinning continues to refine points by using intellectual apparatus. The word-building goes on without either a clear connection to some intellectual problem or any demonstrable importance to the religious life. Theology can isolate itself and lose itself in its own accumulated concerns, and then it is no longer able to free itself for a critique of its first principles. At this point, philosophy's greater detachment from its literature and tradition can help gain a release for theology from its self-made prison.

Of course, theology's special status in relation to literature and tradition does not come from itself but from its connection to religious practice. The theologian may treat the past theological theories and traditions in his field as theoretical documents, just as the philosopher deals with his past. The theologian may build views just as the philosopher does—that is, insofar as it has a relation to only past and present theologies and theologians. Yet, except for the purest philosophical speculation, in which theology is identical to a portion of speculative philosophy, all past theology has its connection to a religious literature and tradition. Present theology can stumble across this connection, either in discovering its own present tie to a religious practice or else by recognizing that the same attachment is present in a previous theological theory as the theologian studies it.

Unlike philosophy, then, theology really has two sets of literature and tradition of which it must take account, and these join to give it a unique intellectual status. As far as technical theology goes, it has its own past theories just as philosophy does. It may either orient itself by this material or else attempt to lead a more independent and contemporary life. This is the same choice the philosopher makes, and it has the same advantages (freedom) and the same disadvantages (possible irrelevance). Beyond this lies the literature (for example, the biblical documents and spiritual counsels) and the tradition (for example, the institutional church), and the necessity of accommodating to these realities complicates the life of theology severely. That is why it is perhaps easier to understand what philosophy is than theology, which includes so many various endeavors under one title, from church laws to ritual practice to speculative theories of the divine nature.

These complexities, and the wide divergence among the activities called theology, indicate that theology cannot understand itself clearly unless it first establishes a definite relationship to not one or two but to three sets of literature and tradition. (1) Whether positively or negatively, the past and present literature and tradition of philosophy must be given their place. (2) The literature formed by past theological

theories cannot be ignored, and it is important to understand
in what way a new theology proposes to go about its work in
relation to its theological tradition. (3) Religious literature and
church tradition are different from either of the other two sets
of material. Not that theology cannot be done in detachment
from these; but, again, as in its relation to philosophy, either
positively or negatively some actual religious practice must be
either excluded or incorporated.

One important point to note here is that religious practice is
much more dependent on the use of a body of literature and
tradition than either philosophy or theology. Theology may
tend more toward such involvement, but religious practice is
given its meaning and its concrete context only as it grows out
of its accumulated literature and practice. This does not mean
that this procedure is either simple or automatic for religion.
Far from it. In fact, the sheer weight of its involvement causes
it to tend toward a loss of meaning in its practice. Any religious life needs connection, refinement, and constant distilla-
tion in order to find power and vitality in its tradition. To do
this it needs both theological effort and the kind of independent critique that only philosophy is in a position to provide.

Although the question is too complicated to go into in detail
at this point, it is interesting to note how Protestantism and
Roman Catholicism are mutually defined here by the way in
which their theology and their religious practice relate to the
question of the use of literature and tradition. Of course,
Protestantism is not all one thing, and this makes it difficult to
define as opposed to Catholicism. Still, Roman Catholics must
give a very heavy weight to their inherited literature and tradition whereas Protestants can, but need not. As a religious
practice, Protestantism can sever all connection to its past
literature and its own inherited tradition, although if it does it
risks irrelevance. The Protestant may reject or set aside, either
bypass or eliminate tradition and attempt a fresh formulation
of its religious beginning point in a way in which no Catholic
is free to do.

The Roman Catholic task is much more cumbersome at this
point, and we must understand this if we are to understand
why its theology will take a special form. Believing as it does
in the inherited authority of its tradition as an independent

source, Roman theology is always forced to work through its entire tradition before it can shape any contemporary outlook. This makes it difficult ever to reach any really fresh formulation, but it also saves Catholic theology from the risk of the irrelevance that comes from breaking all ties with a meaningful set of previously accepted doctrine. Because its religious practice is also more detailed and specified, Roman theology has a more natural tendency toward involvement in the details of church structure and practice. This gives its theology a dangerous burden of detail, but it also assures it a concrete connection to religious practice, and this is not always true of Protestant theologizing. Although any given Protestant theology may carry with it all the weight and detail that Roman Catholic thought does, and although it can be equally involved with the life of the institutional church and its practice, the main point of difference is that Protestantism need not be.

Let us say that a given set of literature claims to be "the revelation of God's will and nature." What is the implication of this assertion for the theology? First, the literature is not itself the original revelation. That is, God either acted in certain ways (for example, the covenant with Israel, the Incarnation) or else certain individuals were moved in being confronted by the divine. In response to these events, statements were made and words were used to describe the action, perhaps first in oral tradition and then later as set down in written form. Now, if this description is anything like the origin and status of religious literature, that literature cannot itself be a theological norm in its literal written form. Rather, the theological norms we need are actually found in those now distant divine actions which these surviving forms of literature were first shaped to express.

If a theology wants to be sensitive, its accumulated religious literature actually does contain a norm for its theological formation. The difficulty is that the literal text is not this norm. If it were, it could serve as a much more definitive guide than in fact it does. There are also questions of impurity in the revelatory material, which can cause distortions (this problem will be considered in the last section of this chapter). The central point is that, if only God's revelation had been given first verbally, the status and use of religious literature would be much more clear and definitive. However, God acted instead of speaking, and it was nondivine men who responded to his action with words. Thus, these words always have a secondary and derivative status and, being words, are subject to a certain fluctuation. Any action, whether divine or human, simply is what it is. The issue is that an action cannot be made this clear and simple in the words that express it. It cannot be easily preserved as such, not even when the words used approximate the idea contained in the action.

'Tradition' is in the similar situation of lacking finality in itself. That is, any religious action or inherited formal procedure celebrates not itself but that to which it refers, and this is usually some divine action, just as is the case with religious literature. Since no tradition of ecclesiastical procedure or ritual receives its significance from itself but only from that which it seeks to preserve, commemorate, and renew, it is material that has theological relevance when taken as a body. Yet, whatever revelation of God's action and will it preserves, it does not do so in its original mode (action) but in a quite different mode (symbol, dress, or prescribed routine). Thus, if either religious literature or tradition is taken as a fixed entity in itself, it can easily distort theology rather than direct it. Recapturing that to which it refers is always theology's first interest—and that of the individual's religious life as well.

C. DO LITERATURE AND TRADITION PROVIDE THEIR OWN NORMS?

From what has just been concluded, the answer to this question should now be clear. Unfortunately for the simplicity of theology, the answer must be "No." In giving such a flat answer, it is true, we have not considered any specific issues— for example, the use of the story of Job or how the account of the Second Coming is to be treated by Christian theology. To consider such cases is a time-consuming and intricate job, and it is not the function of the treatment here of literature and tradition. That we do not take up particular illustrations itself indicates one important conclusion: No single set of rules can be laid down as to exactly how any piece of religious literature or particular religious tradition is to be used theologically. How this is done will depend on the particular historical connection, from Baptist to Roman Catholic, and it may even vary considerably within a given group.

Still, the additional and important point to note is that, for all theology, some accommodation to and appropriation of a literature and a tradition is inescapable, and yet the norms for their appropriation are not given. This necessarily involves any theology in the use of philosophically established criteria, so that the factors that differentiate theology from philosophy as a discipline at the same time establish a necessary use of philosophy in order to handle the inherited religious tradition. It might seem that we have been hasty in concluding that any such literature does not carry with it its own norms for its use. For, if it did, theology might be independent as an enterprise rather than so philosophically structured at this point. This question, of course, is based primarily on the issue of "revelation." We shall try to work out an answer in a little more detail in Part III; for the moment it is enough to note that even if one group does feel that it has an independent norm for the interpretation and the use of its literature (for example, a literal interpretation of scripture or an inerrant divine revelation in its composition), still it is true that not every one (in fact, probably very few outside the group formed around such a norm) will accept such a view. This does not mean that any group is forbidden to hold any view about either its literature or its claim to revelation or its use of its tradition—that is, if they are willing to work out carefully and defend their assumptions. It does mean that no group can either consider its norm universal or take it for granted.

What we must conclude, however, is that these norms are not such as to be evident to all, not even all who claim to follow that religion or to accept its revelation. If even those who accept it do not agree, this at least indicates that the norms are not self-evident to all sympathetic eyes. If literature and tradition are thought to contain revelation and are to be taken as a material basis for a theology, it does appear that God did not give his revelation in such terms so that it was perfectly clear and unavoidable and not in need of constant further interpretation. God could have been this definitive if he had wished to be, so that our only conclusion is that, if he was less clear in his revelation than men are capable of being, he must not have intended any literature or tradition to be independent of the need for continual interpretation.

This problem is not bypassed basically even by those who might claim that an authoritative guardian of true interpretation has been established—for example, in some church leadership or distilled tradition or series of church councils. It is not that this cannot be believed if one wishes to, but, even if it is, it places the norm for interpretation outside the literature itself and even actually outside the idea of the tradition too. That is, it is not the accumulated total historical tradition itself, with all of its variety, that interprets itself but rather some process or person who has been established and accepted to do so. This is a possible answer to the question of how any religious literature or tradition is to be used, but it still does not get around the fact that such norms are not self-contained but must be established by reference to something else. That is why not all people agree with any one way that has been worked out to deal with this problem. Such plurality of viewpoints indicates that the norms of interpretation are not self-contained; they must continually be added to the religious literature and tradition.

In any case, even for those who might argue for some single, central, and 'authoritative' norm of interpretation (for a further discussion of this important term, see Part III), it is still true that a constant process of purification of the material is necessary. Christianity inherited four gospel accounts and not one, and now we should understand the involvement of the literature in its origins in such a way that a single, definitive, and consistent interpretation of the documents is not ever likely to come about. If the literature is always under the demand for constant reinterpretation, tradition as a norm is even more so. No religion will accept all of its past as either normative or representative. Therefore, it must establish ways to define constantly what the "essential tradition" is. It must find ways to weed out needless accumulations and to revive important aspects that may have wrongly fallen into disuse.

It is, of course, probably true that it is religiously necessary to place this burden upon us and that without it the religious life itself would grow complacent and lose the vitality to accomplish its aim. And complacent is the one thing religion can never afford to become, since it is built on a condition of heightened sensitivity. Although it would be easier for us not to have to fight constantly for our norms, it would not be good for us religiously to have such a degree of certainty, since there is no evidence that this is what God intended to provide in any revelation. If he did, the means he used (for example, a religious literature that is not entirely consistent or a tradition that itself needs purification and defense) seem incapable of achieving that end, as twenty centuries of debate testify. It is a hard thing if we accuse God of intending to provide us with religious certainty but then of failing to use a medium that could accomplish this end.

Yet, we are not without all guidance religiously. This chapter has tried to consider why and how theology must incorporate a religious literature and tradition into its structure as a *partial* guide. However, it does seem better to decide that, in any revelation, God must not have intended it to be self-contained but instead wanted it to depend for its use on additional norms which must be humanly constructed. Thus, it is only by human and always debatable additions that revelation is able to serve as a clear guide. The material of the literature and tradition is given to us (whatever human elements partially account for its formation too), so that we do not fabricate the whole theological construction ourselves by any means. Yet this material, whatever its religious value, cannot give a single account of itself theologically without the introduction of philosophically clarifying terms and philosophically established norms.

How are the norms for interpretation to be derived if they are not provided? We have already indicated that there are as many answers here as there are various religious groups, since it could be argued that a religious group is formed by the common acceptance of a norm that is able to guide the group's practical life and define its belief. Even within one group, there may be differences over the norms to be used to make such judgments, and the religious community may even be based on a principle of allowing a greater or a lesser degree of individual decision on this matter. In any case, it is essential for the clarity and the vigor of any religious group for it to have a clear notion of both what its norms of interpretation are and what its conception is of their source.

Even if it is asserted, and believed, that these norms of interpretation are ultimately from God, this cannot simply be accepted but must be inquired into. Why? Because these very statements are not themselves divinely uttered but are our interpretations of God's intent. Such an interpretation may be believed; that is not the point. The issue is that the argument that asserts this is itself not divine; therefore, even if God did intend a more definitive norm than is apparent from the lack of simplicity of the material of the literature and tradition, the discovery and the formulation of this norm appear to have been left to human argument. Thus, it is always capable of being challenged by another human being. When any norm is accepted as divinely founded, then somewhat ironically it is human testimony and argument alone that lead to such acceptance. It is human reasoning that must first be believed, even if the end result for one individual is to believe that the norms of interpretation are of divine origin.

Again, our question: How are the norms derived for the interpretation and the use of religious literature and tradition? Not all that is contained in these two mediums, either separately or when taken together, can ever simply be accepted. And even if it could, not all of it is on a par as to value or importance. Surely it is obvious from its history that any religion has a tendency to forget its essentials and to drift toward trivia and detail unless it is carefully guarded. Thus, the value norms, which define both what the essentials of belief are and which items are important, must be added to the materials. Otherwise, we can never explain why we go astray if such corrective norms are simply built in.

Our answer: In every day and age we must derive the norms anew. Even if we are associated with a religious group that takes it as a corporate responsibility to do this for its members, it still is true that the exact use made of literature and tradition cannot be seen by an individual until he receives it for himself. No matter how clearly they are defined externally, any individual does not see this until he himself has gone through at least some process of intellectual purification. If this is not taken as a matter of corporate responsibility, the individual has an even greater burden placed upon him. Neither the norms to be applied nor the terms and concepts used to convey them remain exactly the same in any age. And if the interpretation is to be meaningful, it must be worked out carefully, since not every interpretation can contain meaning for every person in every age.

D. THE IMPURITY OF THE SOURCE

However, if the meaning and the interpretation of a tradition and a literature in a later age is such a source of trouble, it may be that the religious literature is itself best understood as first having faced this same problem at the time of its formation. In this case, its origin is not independent of such a process but actually is the result of it. To view an inherited tradition in this way is perhaps not to treat it falsely but actually to understand it in the way most likely to allow it to provide guidance for us. That is, if we treat the particular tradition or religious literature we use as if it were different in kind from our present situation (which always is one of a struggle to achieve clarity), we may both misunderstand its origins and misjudge its nature. When this happens, we are unable to draw the assistance from it we should, because we fail to discover how its situation is also ours.

We know that the canon of scripture was not self-made but was brought together by men. This does not necessarily mean that any mistakes were made in what was selected. Its essential form may be beyond reproach, perhaps precisely because those who formed it sensed the material that contained the greatest potential significance for all later religious struggle. However, the important factor is that scripture is never produced as a whole but comes to us as the result of a distilling process. If God had issued a detailed manual to Adam, instead of a brief and perhaps figurative injunction, it is possible that neither Adam (I cannot speak for women) nor anyone later might have gone astray, because the rules would have been so definitively laid down. Such is neither the clarity of the text which we have nor the way men hear God. The nature of the medium is not precise and orderly and definitive in contrast to our situation. Rather, the literature as it was established is able to speak to us precisely because it is the product of uncertainties and struggles such as our own.

Given this view of both literature and tradition, it does not mean that each cannot serve as a guide in a later day or that each cannot be normative in some degree for a construction of theology. We do conclude that revelation cannot take the form of a clear, precise, definitive, and singular norm originally formed as such. Instead, revelation's own origins are not pure but rather are in need of constant refining. We have always longed for a pure source, the contact with which would put an end to our uncertainties. Such could have been provided; but, since it was not, our only conclusion is that God did not intend to act in such an open and unquestionable manner. We seem to have been given an impure source, not a pure rule, from which a norm must continually be extracted and refined but never simply handed over whole.

Our conclusion, then, is that any literature and tradition is not a source for norms to govern our religious practice in complete independence from philosophy and theology. Instead, both need the application of clear philosophical rules and the development into theological principles before their guidance can be very helpful. Neither literature nor tradition is a formal theology or technical philosophy as it stands. Each in fact is an earlier blending of various elements, including both philosophical ideas and theological concepts. Thus neither is independent of all philosophy. Rather, philosophy must be applied to these sources both in order to understand them and so as not simply to fall victim to forms of philosophical interpretation present even in the earliest sources.

This impurity and mixture in the source makes the use of literature and tradition a difficult problem for any theology. It would be easy if they could simply be normative, but their nature does not allow them to serve in that clear function. In theology, we cannot reject them and then build pure theological systems on a selected systematic basis, because theology is not such a pure speculative discipline to begin with. We must relate to, and make use of, a body of religious literature and a distilled religious tradition. Yet, how we are to render either of them normative itself is a problem. This is why theology needs philosophy, and yet at the same time it can never afford the luxury of simply becoming that alone. Its source of meaning and significance, and also its ability to move men, come from its connection to religious practice as it is reflected in its two sources of literature and tradition; its power is not from the technical theological structure as such.

In order to release and guide such potential change, an abstract structure is needed, since we have agreed that the codified material itself does not have that much clear and singular power. We need philosophy to appraise critically the philosophy already present in our religious sources; we use fire to fight fire. Although philosophy has little practical power in itself, we need its clarifying structure in order to be able to release the potential influential force in religious documents and tradition. Power flows only when it is given a clear line of direction and a precise form. A religious tradition does not have this feature in its own mixed existence, but philosophical refining can draw it out.

At this point, of course, we come up against the question of the guidance of the Holy Spirit (this complex issue will be considered at least briefly in Part III). It is possible to assert, and some have done so, that guidance in the interpretation of scripture and in the application of tradition comes from the Holy Spirit and never from philosophy. It is not easy to say in what sense the Holy Spirit serves as a definitive guide; but, without denying that it is possible, at least this much is clear: The Holy Spirit is a norm that is not universally applicable. It has not moved men at all times and in all places in the same way. If this is the case, it may be judged an excellent individual guide, but even the Holy Spirit would still not answer the problem of providing a clear norm for theological construction.

It does not matter if the individual theologian claims the guidance of the Holy Spirit; its operations are hidden enough so that this cannot be offered as a norm to those who read the theology, no matter how helpful it may have been to the man constructing it. The judgment of the fruits of those who are under the guidance of the Holy Spirit must be made in terms of more general and less restricted norms. A spirit may guide the person, but it does not appear to evaluate the result. Similarly, the Holy Spirit may operate in the biblical documents or in the tradition of the church, but it is clear that it does not do so in such a way as to remove all doubt in those who read or interpret it. In whatever manner the Holy Spirit may decide to guide, its direction is mixed with other defects which are not automatically sorted out.

We are left with the conclusion that the movement of the Holy Spirit may be present in any given section of religious literature and tradition, but it is not uniformly and obviously present and it does not label itself as such. Whenever its guidance is present, it is we who must discover it and announce it as such. If its presence were certain, or if the authority of its guidance were inescapable, its work would not be said to be secret. Then, only the blind or the stubborn could ever overlook this clear source. As it is, many have sought such guidance and failed to find it, which means that it must be possible to mistake it. This is not to say that others have not found such guidance; but, if its regulation is not uniform or obvious or unavoidable, it is not sufficient as a norm upon which to erect a theology.

In fact, it would seem that, whatever guidance the Holy Spirit may give, it also needs other instrumentation. What this may be for the individual we shall not attempt to answer here. For theology, in its use and interpretation of literature and tradition, this would appear to come through the medium of a clear philosophical principle. Not that this norm should itself be allowed to become sacrosanct. For instance, a passage such as "He who hath seen me hath seen the Father" first needs to be understood before any "seeing of God" can take place, since it has not provided sight for everyone who has read these words. For the individual, further meditation on scripture may add enlightenment; but, as far as theology goes, such literature cannot serve as a norm until it has been understood at least to a certain degree. Such interpretation involves philosophical structuring of the meaning involved in order to open it more fully to our grasp.

Since religious literature and ecclesiastical tradition are data independent from philosophy, independent from the practice of religion and the technical construction of theology, they must not be reduced to any of the considerations of the previous three chapters (that is, religion, philosophy, or theology). Each must be held as a valuable source with an existence and a life of its own. Yet important as these two sources may be, what we have attempted to point out is that they are not self-sufficient either separately or when taken together. Religious life has sources and goals of its own, however much it may draw on other areas. This fact may be what first produced the literature and the tradition. If that is true, we must not kill the goose that lays the golden egg by confusing a body of literature or an inherited ritual form with the activity that gave birth to it but never is identical with it.

Surely, theology must have a life different from both literature and tradition, in spite of any elements of past theological theory that either enter into their original formation or are necessary for their contemporary interpretation. Yet theology already has a more philosophical base, a more systematic intent, a more elaborate method of statement than religious literature can ever afford for the sake of its clarity, and insight-producing qualities, and its availability to unsophisticated men. Theology is not intended for everyone's edification, but religious literature and the guidance of tradition are. When we learn precisely how to distinguish the areas and the life of the material taken up in this chapter and in the previous three, then we are better able to understand the religious life. This holds true both for the materials that go into it and those that come from it, and also for the precise way in which philosophy enters into the structuring of a theology.

6

THE FINAL RECONSTRUCTION

A. BEYOND PHILOSOPHY

It is important to understand why we end Part I by discussing the question of last things and why we opened it by considering a theory of creation. Our aim is to understand philosophy of religion by trying to comprehend what philosophy, religion, and theology each is. When we determine how they can be combined, we need next to explain how the issues both of this chapter and of Chapter 1 relate to that question. Why is it, then, that placing such considerations as these at the beginning and end of Part I helps to clarify our thinking on the meaning of "philosophy of religion"?

The questions of 'creation' and 'last things' tend to challenge philosophy's right to give an account of such matters. Thus, insofar as we decide whether philosophy can take up these two issues, we come to a clear understanding of what we understand philosophy to be and what its limits are, and such clarification is crucial in our understanding of what philosophy can and cannot do for the problems of philosophy of religion. In Chapter 1, we argued that theories of creation could once again become a subject for philosophical discussion. If this is true, philosophy will have a much wider application in religion.

However, when we come to consider last things, the situation is somewhat different, but it is no less crucial for defining the role philosophy can play in religion. The question of last things, sometimes called eschatology—that is, the consideration of whether there can or may be a final reconstruction in the future that will place the world and our lives on a different footing than presently exists—is an issue that in a genuine sense is "beyond philosophy's domain." Yet, just as we learn something important by discussing whether and how philosophy can take up theories of creation, so if we learn how and why the question of last things is extraphilosophical, we also learn something crucial about philosophy and the role it can play in religion. In the last chapter, we saw how religion and theology differ by necessarily drawing on a sacred literature and an ecclesiastical tradition. Now the question of this chapter can also help us understand more clearly what philosophy, religion, and theology each is, what each can and cannot do, and thus how they may be related.

In other words, the question of last things sets the limits for philosophy. Around the question of creation, a new view of philosophy could be developed; but, where eschatology is concerned, our only answer is that it is "beyond philosophy." Why is this so? In considering the possibility of a final reconstruction and an end to time, we mean by this neither the issue of what can come out of our present structure by evolutionary progression nor that of what alterations can be made by us because the potential is available within the natural order we have now. Rather, this question centers around the possibility of a more radical reconstruction which would alter the very framework we presently know and constitute it on quite different principles than we now experience.

Such a radical revision is not inconceivable. It may be thought about and discussed on a rational plane, but philosophy ordinarily orients itself by the structures we find before us. On that basis, it does not predict the coming of a radically different structure for the world. Philosophy is silent partly because the force necessary to accomplish such a reconstruction would have to come from outside the present structure. Due to this fact, such intervention cannot be predicted on the basis of what we now see and know. Kant based belief in a final judgment and in an afterlife on a necessity to balance the present ethical injustice, but that holds true only if one assumes a God of a certain type, a factor that lies outside the structure presently evident.

It is true that God is not an entity totally excluded from philosophy, and it is also true that philosophers construct theories about God on the basis of which they can predict certain things about his relationship to the world and how he might react toward it. In this sense, to consider a final reconstruction of the world is not nonphilosophical. It can be discussed rationally and various concepts can be formed. It is just that, considered philosophically, God is usually a principle viewed in relation to the presently known structure (for example, Aristotle's Unmoved Mover); he is not conceived of as a principle independent of it who might revise it radically. Philosophically speaking, how do we ever arrive at the concept of a God who might so drastically revise our structure?

This thought usually comes as a suggestion from religion. Thus, it seems that, if it were not for religion's assertion about a radical reconstruction, philosophy would be prone to accept our present structure as ultimate. It is true that, in the postmodern period, we have tended not to accept our given structure as being ultimate. This is true not only in the sense that its form may have been altered evolutionarily. Even the basic principles of the form itself are now taken as contingent; each mechanism for change might have been different. This makes us more amenable to religion's suggestion of a radical reconstruction, so that our present scientific age is better able to consider such a suggestion than early modern science could be. Nevertheless, actually to predict the coming of such a radical change—this is beyond philosophy's capabilities.

What the finale will be, how the last act will end and whether it will contain any surprises that are not predictable on the basis of the present scene alone—to write that ending or to talk about last things must transgress philosophy's limits. Depending on the philosophical view, you can be led up to that point, however, and we can consider such suggestions as rational even if they are not demonstrable. An examination of various theories of eschatology—that is, the explanation of how the end will occur if it is not simply a natural phenomenon but an interruption—all this can be gone about on a philosophical basis, but the 'proof' for any hypothesis is not forthcoming from philosophy itself. Thus, anyone who accepts philosophy as the sole approach to questions is not likely to see any possibility to consider the radical perspective on our present structure that eschatology involves.

On the theory we have been developing here, we can consider philosophy as being self-contained and yet admit that other problems arise out of other areas—for example, in this case, from the religious life and the shape of its literature. In this experience and in these recorded documents, we encounter the question of whether the form of the present world is ultimate or whether it will have an end and either be destroyed nonnaturally or else be reconstituted along different lines. Such a question is again "beyond philosophy" in the sense that, normally, it does not arise internally from philosophical considerations. On the whole, it arises in the life of religion and from suggestions coming out of its literature. Then, it must be given philosophical structure and consideration, but its basis is beyond philosophy's sphere.

Given the analysis of what philosophy means which we developed in Chapter 2, it is easy to see why this is not a question that naturally arises in philosophy. And yet it is equally easy to see why it is a question that automatically comes up in religion and also that it is one that religion cannot avoid. Precisely at this point we come to a clear delineation of philosophy, religion, and theology and their possible relations. According to how you approach a "final reconstruction," you learn how philosophy understands itself, what its relations to religion can be, and how a theology is to be constructed from this combination.

However, not all questions that are technically "beyond philosophy" because they do not arise from its normal considerations need to be beyond it in every sense. We are told in the literature of religion that God will eventually intervene and render a judgment on all men. At the same time, we are told that he will do away with our world's present framework and rebuild it along different lines—for example, making immortality possible where it is not presently. Philosophy cannot assert this to be either true or false, but it may attempt to understand what this might mean and then work out what it could involve. Since philosophy is independent of religion as an enterprise and has no interest of its own in this issue as it might about a theory of knowledge, it can be appealed to without prejudice in order to consider and to develop this question.

As a matter of fact, to maintain its health the life of religion actually needs philosophy most urgently just at this point. That is, many of religion's injunctions (for example, "Thou shalt not kill") are fairly simple to understand and to discuss. However, any assertion of a final and a radical reconstruction of the entire natural order is at once crucial to the life of religion and at the same time the most difficult assertion to understand, given the obviousness and the physical solidity of our present world's form. Such a possible reordering will have to be elaborated in more detail, and whether it can be incorporated into theological doctrine is largely a matter of the philosophical premises the theologian uses. Not all philosophies are neutral in this matter, and this is a crucial fact we shall have to discuss further. What philosophical attitude we adopt determines whether and how a doctrine of last things can be included theologically.

B. PHILOSOPHY FOR NONPHILOSOPHICAL USES

If eschatology is a question unique to religion and theology, and if it is omitted in philosophy's normal considerations, how can philosophy be put to such nonphilosophical uses? And how does the conception of philosophy involved determine the attitude taken? Whenever philosophy is brought to the consideration of something formally outside its domain, this highlights philosophy's own conception of itself, particularly of how widely or how narrowly it defines its own limits. Thus, interestingly enough, it is often the conception of philosophy that determines the attitude taken toward a religious declaration of an expected radical end ("Time must have a stop") or any projected reconstitution of the basic structure. Why is this? Simply because a religious doctrine or statement as present in the sacred literature raises the question or predicts the outcome, but this is not the same as to analyze, to defend, and to consider the implications of such a radical proposal.

To do this is philosophy's job, so that as soon as one opens up the question of last things the attitude taken will clearly reflect the assumptions of the philosophical premise involved. Spinoza, for instance, cannot allow this suggestion, because the present structure of the world, properly understood, already reflects God's ultimate aim. Hume would not reject it due to some conflicting metaphysical view, but his philosophical base in custom and in immediate sensory impressions cannot provide any ground for such assertions. They may be considered, but there is no way to establish such propositions or to lend any validity to the expectation. Hume's attitude stems from an epistemological restriction. Thus, eschatology does not provide the context for its own theological consideration, but philosophy does.

One reason why this nonphilosophical use of a philosophy puts it to the test is attributable to the problems raised by eschatology. That is, it is impossible to consider any ultimate reconstitution of things without becoming involved in the problem of evil and the questions of theodicy, that is, to explain why God created as he did. For if this world is the most perfect possible, as Leibnitz somehow seemed to think, it would both be wasted effort for God to rearrange things and it would also be impossible to arrive at a better combination. Any reconsideration would simply, logically, lead back to the same structure and situation we now experience. Furthermore, eschatology always depends on a doctrine of evil, since evil must be present in the world in a fairly serious amount (whatever its source) in order to require such drastic final action on the part of God to eliminate it. To mention these issues is not to solve them but merely to illustrate the network of other problems and assumptions a doctrine of last things rests upon.

This, then, is one reason why philosophy comes so heavily into play on this issue, even in spite of the fact that the origin of the assertion is nonphilosophical. The nature of God and his intentions in creation are, of course, involved here, too. Only a God of a certain type would or could create so that a final reconstruction would seem both necessary and possible. His intentions toward the world in its present form must be taken quite differently if we expect him to end its present form someday. The issue involved is whether we are to accept our world and its basic structure as ultimate or whether they can be seen as provisional, no matter how firmly locked into place the principles that govern them may be for the present. It follows that we cannot reach God by an examination of the natural order alone, since it represents only his provisional disposition and neither his ultimate nature nor his final intent.

We may postulate God's nature on the basis of what we know of the world and do so in connection with the religion's assertion of a coming new order, but at this point in time his nature and intentions can only be considered as partially revealed. A final moment alone can supply the missing portions of our thought about God. Religiously speaking, these may be revealed in advance of that end, but philosophically we can only consider these postulates as tentative. To develop what God's nature may be if there is to be a final reconstruction by divine interruption and not by natural occurrence (although we might use the latter as an instrument for our understanding, just as God might use some form of evolutionary theory as a basis for his creation)—to do this requires philosophical extension. Partly this is because, of all doctrines, eschatology is the least explicit in scripture and the most difficult to understand even on the basis of the assertions made in sacred literature.

Ironically, then, the least philosophical aspect of religion stands most in need of philosophical support and extension, precisely because it is the most difficult of religious doctrines to understand on its own. This is why, in an age in which philosophy does not seem to support theology, we are driven back to view religion as a set of ethical pronouncements. The other doctrines of the religious life are more metaphysical in nature—for example, they involve assumptions about first principles, and so they actually require philosophical development for their understanding, whereas in a sceptical age ethical injunctions are easier to understand simply on their own. Those religious doctrines that are the most nonphilosophical in origin are more in need of philosophical support for that reason, both to be understood and to prevent their religious rejection on implicit philosophical grounds.

Whenever a doctrine of last things is rejected or given a minor place, it is not religion's fault, since Christian documents assert its eventuality clearly enough. Instead, we must ask why the philosophical assumptions operating work to exclude this doctrine as either unacceptable or as not central because they cannot be explained clearly. In the most obvious matters, religion is independent of philosophy and involves simply following a way of life, and as such it generates no theology of necessity. When in our own day eschatology lacks centrality in theology, this is because it does not have a philosophical base for its expansion. The more esoteric the doctrine, the less it can be self-sustaining. It is not clear what practice is implied in such a belief, whereas the Sermon on the Mount is more easily connected with an immediate way of life. What are we to do and how are we to live, if the world will ultimately be transformed radically? Eschatology may lead to a way of life too, but not unless it is supported and elaborated into a doctrine, and we have already indicated how many abstract problems are involved in such a project.

Although theology may gain a certain independence from philosophy in some areas (for example, regulations concerning the sacraments), precisely in the more puzzling areas it seems impossible to have a theology concerning a final reconstruction without an elaborate philosophical base. Yet such a question is unique to religion and is omitted in philosophy as such. It becomes a theological issue only as a religious life struggles to understand it and is driven to employ a philosophical context in order to do so. The question of eschatology is unique to religion because its spirit is always connected to some dissatisfaction with the present framework. This discontent reaches such proportions that it takes the form of a projection of the present order's eventual destruction.

Should these predictions be taken as true, it is not inconsequential to the religious life, for it means that the present life is a provisional state and not a final form. In this case, it cannot be lived as an end in itself but rather as a preparation and an expectation. This need not imply either a rejection of the present world or a withdrawal. On the contrary, it can involve unending work to try to prepare the world for that eventuality, together with seeking a way in which to make the fact of an eschatological end a reality to those who hear it proclaimed.

In this changed mode of religious life, if it is based on the acceptance of a doctrine of last things, philosophy is all important. Without a working out of related concepts (God, creation, evil), any such assertion remains unreal, and therefore it cannot effect the conduct of a religious person very seriously. Philosophy is not immediately directed toward influencing conduct, and yet in this case the extraphilosophical use of philosophy is necessary in order to give force to this concept for any actual practice. This is not a strange role for philosophy to play at all, since Plato wanted philosophical insight and the support of a philosophical theory to be influential in the governing of a people. This is simply a parallel to Plato's central notion in the *Republic* of the combined role of philosopher-king. Where eschatology is concerned, you must form the concept of the philosopher-prophet.

In order to understand how the philosopher might possibly be tied to the role of the prophet, we perhaps need to call on Kierkegaard's analysis of the philosopher's relation to history, as outlined in the "Interlude" of the *Philosophical Fragments*. According to Kierkegaard, the philosopher will misunderstand the world as long as he looks at it historically. It will appear as a necessary process. Because of this, the future will seem indistinguishable in kind from the past. Kierkegaard feels that the philosopher must learn to look at history as a "prophet in retrospect." That is, he must recover a sense of wonder and uncertainty; he must view the past as if it were future and as if he were a prophet trying to predict its uncertain outcome. This indicates that an outlook that is strictly historically oriented cannot accommodate eschatology. Or at least it must change it so that the final reconstruction appears as a logical outcome of a present (if somewhat hidden) line of development. History cannot accommodate radical interruption that will make its course discontinuous, and this usually is precisely what eschatology involves.

In a philosophical climate such as existentialism, for example, it becomes possible to be radically future oriented once again, whereas a historical orientation usually implies understanding of the future on the basis of the past. Eschatology reverses this; both the past and the present are to be interpreted and understood in the light of what is yet expected. To do this is not a simple matter but rather requires a whole set of philosophical assumptions and contexts in which to make such a view meaningful. It is not surprising, then, that the dominance of philosophical modes of thought by historical forms of understanding has recently made eschatology not understandable and also seemingly not important. Nor is it any less strange that its revival as a central religious concept depends primarily on finding the right philosophical context for it.

C. THE END VS. THE BEGINNING

As a prelude to the next two parts of this text, let us pause and consider the first and last chapters of Part I taken together. Both set the stage for the central problem of this book, and yet each does so in a different way. First things (creation) and last things (eschatology) contrast with each other, but, between them, they perhaps define the context for a clear understanding of philosophy, religion, and theology. When we consider some questions, the roles of philosophy, religion, and theology might seem to merge and to be confused, or else to appear so different as to be essentially unrelated. With the questions of radical end and of first beginning, however, this is not the case. Each is different and operates on its own principles, and yet these issues make clear the way in which they work together so that each is essential to understanding the other.

Philosophy has formed and can form theories of creation (for example, Plato's *Timaeus* and Leibnitz's *Monodology*). Its ability to do so, or the denial of this ability in Hume's *Dialogues on Natural Religion,* clearly defines the basic principles of that philosophy—that is, its metaphyics is brought to the surface. When last things are considered, on the other hand, philosophy can make no suggestions from itself, although it may take up and treat, or provide a context for, the consideration of suggestions coming from religious literature. The essential difference is easy enough to see. Theories of creation may be formed by "running the present world backwards"—that is, by trying to see what first principles operate in what way to produce the world's structure as we know it. A theory of final reconstruction is, on the contrary, not an extension of known structure forward but the postulate of its radical reconstruction away from its present form.

In each of these, we see a different role for philosophy and for its relation to religion. Religion need not—although it may—suggest a doctrine of creation; philosophy can do that for itself. In fact, religion as such is less oriented back toward origins and is more directed to the future. In this sense, religious practice is a good corrective to an excessive philosophical absorption in historical research. Of course, it is true that, in its doctrine of God, any religion becomes interested in origins, and in tracing its traditions it is concerned with the religious community's past. Yet, considered as practice, religious activity is located in the present and is oriented to future change, and this indicates why religious life tends to lose its vitality and to dissolve into theological theories whenever it forgets its eschatological concern. Theology, as it derives its interest in ultimate origins from religious life, undertakes to develop a doctrine of God and of his intentions. Yet, religiously speaking, this can be distorted if it is done solely on a historical basis and by an acceptance of the present fundamental structure as ultimate.

Where eschatology is concerned, the forecast of a final reconstruction casts philosophy in a different role. While it is true that philosophy occasionally takes up such questions, even in the case of Plato's casual interest the problem seems to derive from religious origins and always has an unreconciled status in philosophical doctrine (see his *Republic* and its ending). Religion suggests that such questions are central to its concern, but they are less substantial than simple ethical rules. They stand in need of theological development in order to keep the centrality of eschatology clear, and this cannot be done without making use of philosophy. Here the nonphilosophical development of a philosophy seems vital if the religious life is not to lose its future orientation and to degenerate into accepting present practice as religion's sole preoccupation.

How does this chapter's consideration of last things summarize the essentials of Part I and forecast the theme of this whole study? We have just pointed out how the present issue sharply defines the differences—and yet the possible relationships—among philosophy, religion, and theology. This would

seem to fit in with the idea of meaning vs. practice vs. theoretical construction as outlined in Chapters 2, 3, and 4. Furthermore, particularly where eschatology is concerned, the
suggestion of a radical future change often comes primarily
from the religious literature and tradition. Yet, it can be lost
in the practice of the religious life itself unless that life is
constantly brought into contact with its accumulated literature
and its continuous tradition. Thus, eschatology stems from
sources not quite identical with either religious practice or
theological theory.

As far as the question of creation is concerned, it has been
argued that to consider eschatology is necessarily to form a
theory of creation at the same time. Since this involves a view
of the nature of God and an explanation of evil in addition to
creation, it naturally requires that a theology be developed
around it. Doctrines of creation seem related to similar possible interests on the part of philosophy, whereas eschatology
is a nonphilosophical interest, and yet it requires a philosophical context for its elaboration and explanation. Following
this problem, we see how philosophy lives in independence
from the practice of religion and yet how in eschatology it is
necessarily brought in to shape a theology. Either philosophy
or theology may reject this association, but, when it does, the
vividness of an eschatological sense fades from religion.

As doctrines, eschatology and creation are related, and yet
they exist on different planes. Where creation is concerned, we
see before us a clear picture of what resulted from this effort,
and thus we can project backward to first principles and
intent, although never with certainty. We postulate a principle
(for example, Plato's 'Good' as not grudging but as diffusive of
itself), and then we can check to see whether all the goodness
a created structure can reveal has in fact been communicated
to our particular world. (Leibnitz answers "Yes," but I say
"No.") Where eschatology is concerned, we cannot simply do
the opposite of this procedure—that is, postulate a final transformation and then see if our present situation seems to anticipate that. It is true, of course, that we may judge the
present scene to be in need of radical reconstitution. In that
sense, present observation can support a theory of final reconstruction, but actually to postulate its eventual happening

cannot be done simply on the basis of what is before us. However, with creation we are at least certain that the event did happen, because we find a world before us, even if we remain uncertain about its causes.

We do not see the coming change, even if it is true that Christians have been given a sign of its future (that is, second) coming. We can listen to such an announcement; but, if we insist on seeing its truth visibly forecast in the present, probably we shall either cease to believe in it or tend to treat it as an evolutionary outgrowth of tendencies presently to be discerned. Contrary to this, eschatology in its radical form means a breaking of the laws governing our present structure and the substitution of a new order rather than its evolutionary development. Eschatology is incompatible with an evolutionary metaphysics.

As Kant long ago pointed out, in order to think about a limit you must in some sense already stand outside of it. The beginning and the final end are both limits, or at least they are attempts to think about what sets a limit to our world's order. In this sense, the only standpoint from which to consider either limit is God's, and this means that a fully developed doctrine of God must first be achieved in order to provide a context for the mind to undertake such considerations. This is why, in any era in which theology is either lax or weak in its development of a forceful doctrine of God, we become disoriented and do not know how to handle either a doctrine of creation or eschatology. Our conclusion is: No clear God, no understanding of creation or final reconstruction.

Philosophy plays just such a strong role in either the development of a detailed description of the divine nature or in the rejection of the task. When philosophy does not support theology, these two religious doctrines tend to lose their centrality in the religious life, since we have lost the context within which to deal with them. They require interpretation to make them graphic enough to produce change either in religious practice or in the religious individual. We must learn to think as God did think, does think, and will act, or else we cannot deal with first and last things. Since these problems are religiously suggested to philosophy, all would be simple if we had (as Descartes seemed to think) one fixed and accepted concept of God. If, on the other hand, what we have are many possible concepts of God, plus many grounds on which to deny him, only as this crucial issue is settled and a specific description of God emerges can any stability be introduced into a consideration of our ultimate beginning and our last end.

It is interesting to note a similarity between scientific theory and philosophy in their relation to eschatology. If the same force that first constituted the present order intervened to reorder this structure along different lines and did so by using different sets of first principles, certainly there is nothing to prevent either philosophy or science from considering such a possibility. It is just that, normally, this is not the main consideration of either one, nor is it the starting point for either theoretical enterprise. Both philosophy and science start from a given structure, but it is true that, on certain theories of the function of each, it is possible for them to be amenable to such considerations rather than to eliminate any given suggestion as not possible. That is, philosophy in its metaphysical stage does not accept first principles; it challenges them. In constructing a theory of creation, it attempts to account for the present order in terms of the principles that first combined to form it.

If it moves in this direction, philosophy can encounter a theory of 'possibles'. When it does, then it considers this world as only one from among an infinite variety which were possible, although one (that is, our present order) was in fact chosen. Still, in this light, a theory of final reconstruction simply involves a shift by the originating first principle from one selected form, on the basis of which our world has been running, to another. It is not philosophy's business to suggest this, but at least, within such a framework, it is possible to consider such a change. Time does not stop itself, but there is no reason why it cannot be stopped by that which first constituted it. In "science fiction," modern science can and does consider orders of nature other than our own. Its relation to these theories is not as strong or as central as philosophy's consideration of possibilities; but, although science more than philosophy accepts our present order as given, nothing prevents its consideration of a vast range of possibles. We can think of our order's radical end due to other than natural causes—that is, by intervention in a manner similar to the way our present principles were first brought together to form a particular world (ours) from all that was and remains in itself possible.

D. THE TIME IN BETWEEN

One of the most interesting things to note is that, given a theory of eschatology, the time in between creation and that anticipated end takes on a different character. It does not matter whether one accepts a form of evolutionary theory involving even millions of years for its accomplishment. Some original beginning point had to be first, and this was the moment when the particular rules governing our order and evolution were brought together. It is true that some have pointed out a negative aspect to this new view of time, which comes with a theory of eschatology. That is, it can lead to an abandonment of all effort within the present order, to a depreciation of it, and to turning our present life into nothing but a waiting period. A theory of a final reconstruction can do that, but it does not have to. This depends on what the theory specifies, for it need not depreciate the present order. In fact, it may place this present life under even greater injunctions to accomplish something in its span in anticipation of a final judgment, and it can do this much more so than if our present order is accepted as ultimate.

At its best, a theory of eschatology throws the present time span into a bold relief, and this can only happen when there is a stopping point and a projected transformation against which our present time can be considered and understood. What we often need is some detachment from our involvement in this order, so that we do not take for granted what can be changed and so that we may understand our life by criticizing it against other possible forms it might have taken. To anticipate a change in the present order is to feel that it is under judgment, since what is perfectly adequate does not need basic reconstruction. Any metaphysics that takes this world as the most adequate structure obtainable is at odds with eschatology then. However, to feel that you live in an imperfect interval certainly does change your perspective on the present age.

Not all religions have theories of such radical reconstruction, and many will vary in degree as to how serious they think the reconstitution must be. If we take Christianity as an example, let us not focus on the Book of Revelations, as difficult and as important as it may be, but rather on the traditional concept of the Second Coming of Christ. Our aim in doing this is neither to explain this as a biblical doctrine nor to consider its treatment in various theologies. We simply want to examine how this doctrine changes the individual Christian's attitude toward the time in which he lives. If Christian doctrine simply presented a theory of divine incarnation in the birth of Christ, or if it could settle for his life work and teaching as a model, or even if it stopped in so important a point as Jesus' suffering, death, and resurrection—it would be so much easier to comprehend.

However, primitive Christianity did not stop there. It promised a return of Christ, even if the exact time of the Second Coming is subject to much misunderstanding. How does the addition of such a promise and prediction change the Christian's attitude toward the time in between? As recorded in the Acts of the Apostles, some early Christians expected this additional event very soon, and they abandoned their concern for the world in favor of an immediate expected transformation. Clearly, this particular expectation was based on a misunderstanding, but if this time still lies at an unknown distance, how does this fact affect our present attitude? The first thing to note is that actions that Christians attribute to God as present in the life of Christ are not complete. Christianity in its contemporary state does not possess a full revelation but rather only a partial revelation plus a future promise.

Our attitude toward an incomplete doctrine, then, is quite different than if it could be accepted as complete. Had God given a full revelation of all he intended at one time, then those who accept this as a divine revealing point (that is, Christians) could have a fixed doctrine. As it is, Christian theology must always remain incomplete. The matter is not closed with the assumption of divine incarnation and then return. Rather, we live in a state of expectancy; we are left intentionally unsure of the time or exact form of the predicted divine reappearance. In fact, one could treat the whole series of events that Jesus represents as merely the announcement of a proposed eventual change in the basic structure of things.

We are doomed to a period of basic uncertainty of undetermined length, and no intellectual reconstruction can be expected to close the gap. The needed material to complete the account is not yet at hand; it is only expected, promised, and anticipated.

Christians not only believe in one divine interference in the normal operation of things (for example, either the birth or the resurrection of Jesus)—after God's original constitution of our order along certain possible lines. They also take this one intervention after creation as simply an announcement of a further and more drastic interference such that the present order will neither evolve indefinitely nor exhaust itself by natural means. Those who possess a final revelation can be more secure in their religion. Christians, because of the forecast of a Second Coming, are constantly more uncertain in their religious convictions and more tentative in their attitude toward the end of the present order together with all philosophies which explain it. Each faithful Christian may enjoy it, work for its improvement, draw from it all that he can; but, if he held a final revelation rather than a provisional revelation, his intellectual situation would be quite different.

Of course, the complication here lies in the doctrine that the presence of the future kingdom is already in the midst of us. The question of in what sense we already now participate in the promised radically altered future kingdom is a complicated matter, and one we shall not attempt to solve at this point. The issue is that, even if there already is some present inauguration of a new age, it was never made out to be a complete and an open coming of a new form of life in unavoidable and visible garb. However, although such an anticipated new age may be presently experienced or shared in since the day of the appearance of Jesus, its full realization will still lie at some future point in time. At the moment, the present world's structure must be broken in order to make life in a new form possible. To be given a promise and to live in that future promise now is in some sense possible, but to do this is always different from the actual fulfillment of that promise and the overt constitution of a new order.

Such a situation of "being always in between" must give a strange and an unsettled quality to the religious life. Therefore, those who come to it expecting to find the full peace of a perfectly constituted new order are bound to be disappointed when they discover that, instead, their condition is such that they must wait unendingly in time in hope and expectation. They do not live in the midst of an assured reality but simply exist on the basis of a promise as yet unredeemed. Were it not for the doctrine of the Second Coming, Christians might be able to achieve their anticipated new life now. As it is, they exist with an incomplete revelation, and so their religious life itself remains necessarily unfulfilled. To discover this is bound to disappoint many who come seeking greater security than is possible on the basis of a promise.

The result of this will, or should, make quite a difference in action and attitude if we must live constantly in the midst of an uncertain expectation. Some actions we know are necessary to this life, or perhaps they are required of us by ethical or religious codes. Regardless of this, we cannot view them as final, since the very structure in which we incorporate them will itself be destroyed. According to the doctrine, in a final reconstruction not all will be destroyed but rather our basic elements will be reconstituted along different lines. This attention will omit some things now possible (for example, evil) while allowing other things not presently permitted (for example, a fully expressed and received love). Our present, past, and future actions may be reincorporated, but not if we act as if they depend only on the present makeup of our structure. Some actions may not rest on any particular structure (for example, compassion) whereas others do, and therefore they will pass away when that structure passes (for example, physical monuments).

When viewed in this light, our attitude is bound to affect our action, or at least it should. We do not accept the confines of our present world as ultimate, even as altered to the maximum of our ability and its capacity. This means that we constantly eye our own actions and those of others as to how they might survive a radical reconstitution and as to how they might or might not fit into an order of a different quality. Not all—and in fact very few—will ever be able to live for long in such an attitude. Many will prefer to accept our present structure as ultimate, for after all its presence makes it rather obvious. However, those who do see Christianity's forecast for the future ought to have their outlook and action altered by accepting this forecast.

The state of the Christian is one of constant anxiety and waiting. He expects something, but it is not here. And even if he finds it as in some sense already present ("The kingdom is within you"), still it is not present exactly as promised or as predicted or in a way that allows its full realization. A promise as yet unfulfilled, particularly if it is accepted in the knowledge that it probably will not be fulfilled in your lifetime, is always bound to cause a certain basic anxiety and to prevent that person from relapsing into security. This need not mean that he neglects the present world. If he does, his action rests on a misunderstanding, since he has plenty of injunctions which tell him about his work in the world and his present obligations toward others. It is just that the Christian's work of charity to his neighbor is done in an attitude of nonfinality. He is enjoined to preach his gospel and to minister unto the needy, but he knows that these acts, good as they may be, are not done simply for their own sake but in anticipation of a still future transformation.

Part I closes with this consideration of a more difficult—but perhaps also more important—feature of the practice of religion as it is affected by the doctrines contained in its literature. Our aim is to understand what philosophy, religion, and theology are, and therefore how they can relate to or even participate in the life of each other in spite of the essential uniqueness of each mode. We end with eschatology precisely because it is not one of the easy doctrines where the three enterprises seem to be close (for example, simple ethical injunctions). Rather, it is when caught in extreme issues that each enterprise can be understood and clearly distinguished from the others, and after that each can then be related back to the others in certain ways. Philosophy, religion, and theology stand out most clearly at the radical points of each—for example, logic for philosophy, eschatology for religious practice, and regulations concerning the sacraments in theology. Highlighted by these extremes, we may then see what they can and cannot share in common and also how they may or may not work together in any given instance.

II

THE ROLE OF PHILOSOPHY IN THE SHAPING OF THEOLOGY

In Part I we tried to work out a relationship between philosophy, religion, and theology from which we could then work forward. In Part III we shall try to proceed systematically by examining the role philosophy plays in defining and clarifying a series of important issues. In this section, we want to examine six specific cases. There is nothing crucial or particularly significant about the six authors and works selected as the bases of Part II. A sensitive reader may recognize that these are, for the most part, theological theories where we would expect to find the influence of philosophy most strongly. Such a selection was made deliberately because where philosophy is the most consciously present, one can perhaps most readily see how its doctrines influenced the development of a theological position.

It is hoped that the presence of philosophy in lesser amounts may be more easily detected in other situations once we have become sensitive to its presence and its general modes of operation in theology. Our aim is not specifically to meet directly the challenge of those who deny philosophy's presence in theology. The majority of theologians admit the presence of philosophical theory in the formation of theology. The question is not whether philosophy has had this effect on theology but whether it is possible to do without it. We shall attack that question indirectly, by trying to understand both how philosophy has actually shaped theology (Part II) and how it might do so in the future (Part III).

Most of those who either object to or reject philosophy's role in theology do so not out of any basic antipathy to philosophy itself, but from a strong desire to protect theology's independence (for example, Barth). They want to prevent any particular philosophical view from either distorting a theological doctrine, if it is incompatible, or from deflecting theology from its aim by turning it into simply another philosophical view. Certainly, according to the analysis given in Part I, theology does have both a different aim and a different status from pure philosophy. However, such a rejection of philosophy may rest on a false understanding of what philosophy either is or needs to be. If philosophy is more flexible than is sometimes imagined, and if in fact theology cannot be structured without it, perhaps we can protect theology's special interests and even promote them more successfully by the careful application of a philosophy open to a variety of forms.

What we propose is to examine six important works by six now-classical authors to see if we can learn in each case (1) what view of philosophy each man held, and (2) in the light of this, what influence this idea of philosophy had on the doctrines that man formed. We cannot examine each man's thought as a whole; that would be too complicated. We need to talk of philosophy and theology in the abstract, in order to be free to form new theories of each, but we also need to examine how the two disciplines actually have operated together in the concrete work of an individual author. It is the task of this part to analyze that question.

As we begin to consider Origen in Chapter 7—and the same will apply to the five authors after Origen—no attempt will be made to understand each man against the background of his time. Each author undoubtedly borrowed or constructed much that was based on the philosophical ideas of his age. Researches into this area are important and are the province of historical scholars. Rather, what we want to do is to take one concept, or a set of concepts, and see if we can trace their influence in shaping certain theological doctrines. Then, hopefully, we can gain greater control over the use of philosophy in our contemporary theological construction.

If in the following six important instances we can gain any insight on this matter, we might move on to build a set of philosophical principles more consciously—that is, we can proceed with an eye to the kind of effects these may have in their theological employment. Too often, it seems, we discover the consequences of certain views only after we have found ourselves struggling against the form a theological doctrine seems to be taking (for example, Bultmann fighting to recover a meaning for traditional Christian affirmations after he had adopted modern philosophy and existentialism). Our basic need is to develop greater ability to forecast theological implications before the philosophical premises are ever set.

7

ORIGEN AND FIRST PRINCIPLES

A. CREATION AND A FINITE GOD

As we have already pointed out (Part I, Chapter 5), it might be easier for us if the philosophical sources used in scripture were unified and if they all agreed in outlook and terminology, but such is not the case. Even when a man uses biblical sources and references, as Origen does, it is interesting to observe that this does not guarantee that he will come out with any one position on the major religious questions. Nowhere is this flexibility more clear than where Origen develops his concern with God and creation. And his use of philosophy provides an interesting example, since he is one of the earliest Church Fathers to turn to philosophical sources.

In choosing between a finite God and an infinite God, it would seem that scripture might lead more toward a concept of infinity, although this is not absolutely clear. Origen, in defining his first principles, argues for a finite God. If we can understand why he moves in this direction, it might be quite instructive for our interests. Given our philosophical aim, we probably shall not find a more enlightening passage than the following:

In the beginning, as we contemplate it, God created by an act of his will as large a number of intelligent beings as he could control. For we must maintain that even the power of God is finite, and we must not, under the pretext of praising him, lose sight of his limitations. For if the divine power were infinite, of necessity it could not even understand itself, since the infinite is by nature incomprehensible. He made therefore just as many as he could grasp and keep in hand and subject to his providence. In much the same way he prepared just as much matter as he could reduce to order.*

What is important for us to notice here is first the way in which Origen's view of God is shaped by philosophical considerations, and next, how this, in turn, influences his other theological conclusions. *The most crucial route by which philosophy shapes theology is via the doctrine of God.* That most central of all religious concepts and biblical considerations is the least well-formed without philosophy, and ultimately it is the most influential in theology. A theology without God, it would seem, might dispense with philosophical assistance, but one that treats God as central cannot. We might have thought that, where God is concerned, theology would be the most independent. Instead, it appears that theology cannot even be sure of a concept of God without philosophical assistance.

If we want to understand where Origen got the idea that God must be finite, we must turn, not to scripture, but to certain philosophical principles. What is the basis of Origen's reasoning here? He argues: if the divine power were infinite, it could not understand itself. Why? Because Origen thinks that the infinite is by nature incomprehensible. This is not the place to go into detail on the history of the inclusion and exclusion of the attribute of infinity in the concept of the divine nature, but Origen accepts unquestioningly the philosophical association of limitation and finiteness with rationality. It is clear that some philosophers have argued this way (for example, Aristotle), but the point is that others have admitted infinity to be

* Origen, *On the First Principles,* trans. G. W. Butherworth (New York: Harper & Row, 1966). All page references in this chapter are to this edition.

quite rational, although of course not without changing their concept of 'reason.' The point to note is that how one sees infinity is a function of a basic metaphysics and theory of knowledge, and this is not dictated by religion.

Even if this is so, what difference does it make to theology if various metaphysical assumptions lead to different attitudes on issues such as finiteness? Our quoted passage gives us an insight on this point too. Origen is considering the question of how many intelligent creatures God created. He argues that God could not have created an infinity, since this would have exceeded his grasp. And if we reason this way, we set up a very different context in which to consider God's relation to his creatures. The effects of this conclusion appear in many places in Origen's thought. For, if God is so limited, clearly his decisive power to intervene is restricted and his effectiveness with man will also tend to depend more on human achievement. If Origen could establish God as infinite on philosophical grounds, God's power relationship to man could certainly be placed on a different basis.

We are not helped much by sacred scripture at this point. Even if we view the biblical documents as recording God's actions toward man, these actions are simply reported but not explained or analyzed. It is theology's task to try to construct a context within which it becomes possible to account for God's actions, and this account can only be given by reference to a concept of his nature. After defining God's attributes, it becomes possible—in that context—to explain why his recorded actions proceeded as they did. And, in order to understand God's reported actions so that we can draw further implications from them, they must be set into a theory that explains them and thus allows an elaboration of the biblical reports. Since more than one interpretation of the meaning of God's actions has been given, it is important that this explanatory attempt go on constantly in order not to confuse God's reasons with one particular theory about them.

In Chapter 1, we considered theories of creation and how these play a crucial role in defining what philosophy, religion, and theology are and thus how they can be related to one another. Now with Origen we see how his philosophical stand on infinity and its irrationality almost controls his attitude concerning God and creation: If God's power is finite, he must conserve his strength, and it may very well be that what we see in creation is not a reflection of his unhindered choice but instead is a compromise forced on God by the circumstances related to his restricted power. In this case, God could still be conceived of as supreme, but his position in the universe, at least as regards its constitution and its creatures, takes on a quite different perspective.

Origen does not argue to his particular philosophical position as opposed to its alternatives, and what results from his position on creation is a much closer blend between philosophy, theology, and religion—one that leaves little distinction between them as enterprises. Thus, it is hard to see which principles from which source actually shape the outcome of any issue. Whereas, if the philosophical principles were argued out in greater independence, the consequences of their use would be easier to trace and to appraise as the theology is developed. Otherwise, it may appear either that the biblical documents suggest this outcome or that theological investigation demands it on its own. God, certainly, may have "limitations," but the issue is whether these stem from his finite power or from other sources. "What God cannot do" is a very important question. Some of its answers may have biblical foundations—that is, the argument that he will not reject his creation. Yet, on the whole, the answer given to this issue depends upon a series of philosophical questions and principles.

B. A FRAMEWORK FOR SCRIPTURE

Origen, of course, is famous for the development of a framework within which scripture can be interpreted, but that fact only raises this question: From whence does the framework for the interpretation of scripture arise? Origen proposes a threefold way for presenting the meaning of sacred writing —that is, according to its flesh, according to its soul, and according to the spiritual law (p. 276). We shall not discuss the exact meaning of these distinctions, or how each relates to the biblical material, or how each affects our thinking. We are concerned with a more basic question: Does the framework within which scripture is to be interpreted come from scripture itself or from some other source? If we accept what seems to be the easiest answer, we actually wind up in the greatest difficulty. That is, if we say that the framework for interpreting scripture comes from itself, we then have to account for the great variety of interpretations which have, in fact, been offered. And we must also explain our present disagreements and the difficulties we have in understanding. This is particularly true if we give up the romantic notion that some day we shall arrive at one final understanding.

Faced with these past and present difficulties, any simple explanation is apparently so little effective just because it leaves our difficulties not only unexplained but impossible to account for. If we agree, however, that the framework for interpretation is external to the actual documents themselves, perhaps the most attractive theory would be the one that has absorbed so much attention in the past century—namely, that the proper context for their understanding is to place these documents in their original background in order to devise from this a norm to determine "the original meaning." There is no question but that this technique of historical inquiry has had a certain clear success. It can eliminate assertions about meaning that are simply false, and it can help a reader to uncover a richer context for his understanding. But can this approach in itself provide a single, definitive framework?

The answer, of course, itself depends on the view one holds on the status of language, the definitive theological intent of the scripture and, most important, about whether the original thought context from which the writing came had, in fact, a single clear meaning for each term. If so, we can be sure if our author used it at that period that he used the meaning universal to the time. Many have based their enthusiasm for such historical inquiry into the background of the scriptures on a positive answer to these crucial questions. However, this does not lessen the fact that, if we take a different position on any one of these important philosophical assumptions, the whole import of our inquiry into the background and into "the original meaning" assumes a different tone. In spite of its helpful and even enlightening assistance in understanding scripture, historical scholarship cannot provide a definitive context for interpreting scripture that is extraphilosophical, since its ability to do this itself rests upon the acceptance of a nest of answers to philosophical questions.

Unless we can securely establish that scripture is only to be understood in the historical context of its original meaning and that this can be done in a definitive manner, then our question becomes one of asking (1) what can provide a context for understanding, and (2) where does this come from and of what is it made? It is true that Origen seems to think that scripture itself argues to and supports certain crucial questions—for example, free will. "Indeed there are in the scriptures ten thousand passages which with the utmost clearness prove the existence of free will" (p. 166). Even in order to comment further on what seems to Origen to be such decisive evidence, we first have to understand more clearly the status of a philosophical term and the doctrines that grow around it. Few philosophers explicitly deny freedom of the will, but, in any case, everything depends on how this issue is worked out explicitly. A supposed common concept can be developed in many ways, and the results we get depend on how this is done. This is particularly true if we consider how widely theologians have differed in interpreting 'free will'.

Spinoza, for example, affirms his belief in freedom of the will, but, when the meaning of this is examined, it turns out that nothing can be other than it either is or is ordained to be. Everything depends on the way in which a particular meaning is developed in technical fashion, and certainly scriptural documents do not pretend to have this kind of detailed development as their aim or as their mode of approach. A biblical statement does not draw implications from itself. That is a philosophical way of proceeding, as far as such close analysis of terms is concerned. Thus, if this is to be taken from scripture, it would appear to come by means of something being applied to that body of writing. The biblical documents simply use any available term or concept to express a meaning, rather than to inquire backwards into either its root meaning or its possible systematic extensions. That is done only later.

The biblical records may, in fact, contain statements about free will, but these cannot be fully understood without some intellectual framework, and the application of this changes the situation. Even if this theoretical context is said to be its "original meaning," that may or may not be acceptable when its full implications are elaborated. To carry out this kind of inquiry did not seem to interest the scriptural writers, but it is absolutely necessary to enter into this philosophical discussion before any fixed theological implications can be drawn. Our problem seems to be that biblical authors, having other motives in mind than the purely philosophical, tend to use a term to express a meaning in their particular context and neither to inquire into the meaning of crucial terms nor to examine the possible variety of meanings. Yet, when questions and challenges arise, the theological task begins to specify particular meanings and clarify concepts.

'Free will' is an important concept for Origen, for he goes on to assert that external things do not lie within our power (p. 163), which is essentially a Stoic doctrine, although he admits that we may use them in certain ways. Origen draws implications from this for a doctrine of salvation [it comes from ". . . the will of him who has mercy when he pleases" (p. 106)]. Thus, it is perfectly clear that 'free will' is an important concept where the intent is to define a doctrine of salvation. While it is true, as Origen points out, that scripture may mention 'free will', we know that that concept is subject to a variety of interpretations and that much, if not everything, depends on how we give a specific definition to the concept. To bring in philosophy at this point in order to adopt a specific meaning is not false to scripture but actually is true to it, as long as we realize that any specific interpretation is the result of our philosophic addition. This stricture prevents us from attributing to scripture a more specific doctrine than its author perhaps intended, and it removes the issue from the cloak of sacred scripture and puts it where it belongs—that is, on a philosophical level. To the extent that we succeed, a theology is born.

Origen, for instance, himself observes that "The term 'incorporeal' is unknown not only to the majority of Christians but also to the scriptures" (p. 5). If we are not to freeze biblical terminology, and if we can admit that it is not itself sacred but simply consists of available concepts used to express a sacred intent, it may be very important to theology to develop later a meaning for "incorporeal." To do so, then, requires the application to scripture of another interpretive framework which, as long as the two are kept distinct, need not confuse either. There may still be better and worse frameworks in which to interpret crucial passages of scripture. Some will alter its original meaning more and some less, but this does mean that some framework must be applied and that the arguments over the merits and demerits of each are essentially philosophical.

C. HIERARCHY VS. DEMOCRACY

One of the most striking examples of the application of a philosophical framework to scriptural interpretation is Origen's clear use of a very elaborate scheme of hierarchies. It is not our place to argue how much of biblical (or specifically New Testament) thinking is ordered by hierarchies; the question concerns Origen's specific use of 'hierarchy' and the theological implications he draws from it. In examining this, we are interested neither in the issue of Origen's orthodoxy or heresy, nor even in the fact that his doctrines are obviously heavily dependent on philosophy. These facts others have pointed out and commented on. What we do want to show is how the philosophical doctrines he used worked to shape his theological conclusions. If we can become conscious of this, perhaps we can be more sensitive to the theological consequences of the interpretive schemes we employ and then use them with greater discrimination.

"The Son, being less than the Father, is superior to rational creatures alone (for he is second to the Father); the Holy Spirit is still less, and dwells within the Saints alone" (p. 34). As indicated above, our interest is not to debate the orthodoxy of this particular view of the Trinity (it is not orthodox, clearly, at least as the doctrine came to be defined). We want to know what could have led Origen to interpret the Trinity in this way. In the first place, of course, the Trinity as a technical doctrine is not developed within the scriptures as such, whatever suggestions regarding it may be found there and however important the Trinity has become as a doctrine. Consulting scripture alone, one might just as well declare the members of the Trinity to be coequal as not. It seems clear that what was in Origen's mind, and which led him in the direction it did, was a neo-Platonic love of hierarchies. Even more important, he is moved by the Plotinian preference for absolute unity and the accompanying tendency to place all multiplicity on a secondary level.

Thus, it seems perfectly clear that how the Trinity is approached is heavily dependent on the classical metaphysical problem of the One and the Many. If you follow the neo-Platonic love for unity in its pure state as supreme, it will be very difficult to form any notion of Trinity in which any ultimate plurality remains. But if you follow Plato's way in the *Parmenides,* which involves a compromise with plurality, some multiplicity can be introduced into God's nature without logical scandal. Scripture cannot provide the detail of this outcome, but metaphysics can. And the importance of the outcome should already be clear from seeing Origen's solution. We do not want to deny that scripture does provide much material for theology and that a great deal of it is clear in its intent; but, in refining the unclear concepts and in building a theology, the pivot of an argument often swings on a philosophical assumption, especially where the original material leaves us with an area of choice.

This is particularly true for the kinds of questions we have been picking out in Origen—for example, creation, God's infinity, scriptural interpretation, and the use of hierarchies. The last section of this chapter will take up the issue at the point where his philosophical refining seems most prominent— that is, the doctrine of the soul. Yet the point to emphasize is that, in every case, our situation is one in which we are dealing with entities whose nature is such that they are incapable of definitive verbal formulation. If this is so, and if these concepts are also important to religion, perhaps the situation we are in is one that leaves us no choice except, in each age, to develop a definition of these concepts that is workable for contemporary theology. If the meaning of each of these terms is such that it cannot be made to hold still but tends to fade, it is the classical task of philosophy to introduce stability into an essentially fluid theoretical situation.

For a moment, let us not pursue any further the implications of Origen's preference for hierarchies where the Trinity is concerned. The quotation above makes that obvious enough. If Origen does have a preference both for hierarchies and for unity as a guiding principle, what kind of effect does this have on his general interpretation of Christianity? First, it is clear that, as we shall see with the soul, Origen will tend to view all things as moving up a ladder, but there will be no equal downward movement toward participation in multiplicity, except perhaps that soliciting power that draws men upward. The Christian doctrine, however, seems to be one in which there is a movement of God downward, a subjection and a suffering and an entering into multiplicity. It seems that a more democratic theory is required in order to interpret this biblical picture, one with perhaps less stress on unity and with more ability to accept a divine identification with multiplicity.

Church doctrine as defined has corrected Origen and has perhaps achieved a more democratic basis on which to understand God's nature and intent. But any later interpretation is not free from its own philosophical context, so that perhaps no final formulation is possible—that is, one that does not bring along with it its own special difficulties. Probably our most important concept is the God we see as operating behind this whole process, and yet technically that is perhaps the idea over which we differ most. If he is a God who structures hierarchies and then identifies with them, we shall interpret Christianity in one way and build church structures along those lines. On the other hand, if he is a more democratic God, one capable of receiving multiplicity and of acting in independence from any structured hierarchies, our view of Christianity may be quite different and our church structure certainly can be less bound to hierarchies too.

D. HOW CAN THE SOUL BE UNDERSTOOD?

If the soul were a simple matter, it would not have been subjected to centuries of debate. In considering this crucial concept, let us set down a series of revealing comments by Origen —that is, revealing of his philosophical assumptions. Then, we shall comment on them, and next see what conclusions they lead us to concerning the role of philosophy.

1 And that the soul of the sun is older than the covering which serves it for a body can, I think, be logically shown from a comparison of the sun with man and after that from the scriptures. (p. 63)

2 There is resurrection of the dead, and there is punishment, but not everlasting. For when the body is punished the soul is gradually purified, and so is restored to its ancient rank. (p. 146)

3 . . . the soul when saved remains a soul no longer. . . . There was a time when the soul was not a soul and there will be a time when it will not be a soul. (p. 123)

4 But there remained some souls who had not sinned so greatly as to become daemons, nor on the other hand so very lightly as to become angels. God therefore made the present world and bound the soul to the body as a punishment. (p. 67)

5 Whole nations of souls are stored away somewhere in a realm of their own, with an existence comparable to our bodily life. . . . But by some inclination toward evil these souls lose their wings and come into bodies, first as men. (p. 73)

6 What else can we assign as the cause of its [the world's] existence except the diversity in the fall of those who decline from unity in dissimilar ways? (p. 77)

7 Now passion in the human soul is a likening to the irrational. (p. 73)

One conclusion, after reading these seven short quotations, might be that the soul is quite important to theology. Yet, in its biblical setting 'soul' tends more simply to be mentioned, rather than explicitly defined, and usually it is employed as connected to certain current usages then. Thus, if it is to be explicitly defined so that it can become a principle for systematic theological construction, 'soul' cannot be understood unless it is structured further, and this requires philosophical development. Of course, another reaction to these excerpts could be that of theological condescension. That is, we might acknowledge that Origen was philosophically guided and perhaps wrongly so, but what is to be concluded from this is that we ought to prefer a theology less obviously philosophical. Here the key word is "obviously," for it might be that in other doctrines, perhaps ones more orthodox or currently acceptable, the philosophical structuring is no less present even if it is perhaps less obvious.

It may be that it takes temporal distance, when certain terms and concepts are no longer obviously accepted, to be able to discern the effect the adoption of any implicit framework has for theology. Whether we are able in any age to get outside of such an acceptance in order to appraise it critically, this is an involved question, yet, at least it can be answered simply by saying that the attempt to adopt one's first principles knowingly and critically is the traditional first business of philosophy often called metaphysics. Granted that we may adopt a theology that is less heavily slanted than Origen's, does that mean that it will really be any less philosophical? Or is it simply that the philosophy has been picked with greater scriptural sensitivity and with an eye to how doctrine has, in fact, developed? What is true of Origen may be true of every theologian, except that Origen does us the favor of showing his use of philosophy clearly.

If we consider quotation no. 1, our first reaction should be to ask "How did Origen ever become interested in such a question?" Reflecting on this brings to light one other interesting fact about the theological use of philosophy—that is, it tends to highlight certain problems and to cause others to appear as important, according to the philosophical views involved. Thus, the first question to ask any theological work when it is initially approached is "Would these same problems be as prominent or be structured in this way if it were not for a certain philosophical view?" After this, the philosophical questions can be isolated and recognized as such. For instance, Origen is able to pose his question in this way only if he already has in mind a doctrine of soul such that bodies like the sun possess souls. Neo-Platonic doctrine does lead to such a view of soul, but so can other doctrines such as Plato's. However, it takes a view that treats soul as prior, and with physical body generated secondarily, even to raise the question in this way. The manner in which we conceive of the soul in theology is not only important but almost all important, and it cannot be gone about without the aid of critical philosophy, or else it will be decided for us.

When Origen considers the effects of punishment (quotation no. 2), it is probable that he can find strong biblical support for a doctrine of eternal punishment. Why does he reject it? Clearly it is because he has a concept of the purification of the soul through punishment. If one accepts this, it is easy to see why Origen might decide that a soul would be restored by punishment. Such a doctrine of the effect of punishment is not obvious, unfortunately; it needs a philosophical defense. And all of this is coupled with the underlying assumption of quotation no. 3, that 'soul' is not an ultimate entity. Soul is an important being, but, for Origen, it is still descended from something higher to which its aim is to return and thus to cease its identity as soul. This doctrine is connected to an idea of hierarchy and of unity as absolute. If these neo-Platonic metaphysical sets of principles are accepted, it becomes easy to follow Origen's theological reasoning.

As quotation no. 3 indicates, it makes a great deal of difference whether the soul is considered as an inferior and a descended being or whether it is taken as an ultimate principle. Its nature and its relation to the body are no less important, and the details of this must be worked out philosophically. Perhaps we can discern enough of Origen's view of the soul's status to see why in quotation no. 4 he considers the soul's presence in a body to be a punishment. For, if the soul is descended from something higher (as in the neo-Platonic account), and if it seeks both further purification and to transcend itself as soul into a higher principle, then attachment to the body is a movement downward and away, and it is always a punishment. God's own entrance into a body in the doctrine of the incarnation becomes more difficult to explain on this theory too, since it is a movement against the natural divine direction. Using a different theory of the relation of body to soul and with another concept of the status of soul, much of this difficulty could be eliminated.

The reference to Plato, specifically his *Phaedrus*, is most evident in quotation no. 5. For there Plato gives us an account of the soul's presence in the world as having come about through a loss of wings. We also get the notion from Plato of a whole realm of preexisting souls. Thus, when Origen talks about his view of "the fall" in quotation no. 6, it is clear that his metaphysical notions on the primacy of Unity are operative again. That is, the fall is here interpreted as a tendency away from unity. This, of course, can be used as an account of the fall; but, when the whole world's existence is attributed to the tendency away from unity, it is clear that this will also be the context within which to understand God and his actions in relation to the world. To treat God without such a framework is impossible, but how much choice of metaphysical contexts do we have?

In many ways, quotation no. 7 may be the most typically Platonic, and it is also the most important in considering what kind of doctrine of the soul we ought to adopt and in what directions various doctrines will lead us. For it is well known that Plato was at least suspicious of passion; or, even if Plato saw some good in it, he still had a tendency to connect it with the irrational. Must passion be considered as akin to the irrational? Certainly not necessarily, and Plato himself defends the possibility of a "divine madness" in the *Phaedrus*. However, later Platonists often take over the side that links emotion with the irrational; and, if this is done, Christian doctrine will be quite radically altered. It is hard, for instance, to see how God could 'love' men, since passion in his nature (on this theory) becomes an imperfection. Furthermore, it is particularly hard to make any sense out of God's 'suffering' for man, because such action would be inappropriate for divinity.

Where theology is concerned, the answer to these questionable interpretations ought not to be to reject philosophy whenever one context, as in Origen's case, can so easily be seen to alter theological problems and to make the solution to some questions more difficult rather than less. Spinoza later returns to this classical view on the inferiority of passion, and he demands the exclusion of emotion from divine existence. Studying Spinoza, we can see the consequences of these assumptions regarding the soul very clearly. Our response should be to observe this shaping of theology by various philosophical first principles and then to learn how to accept and to reject basic assumptions in philosophy, according to our knowledge of their theological tendencies. With Origen it is quite evident how this process works, and we also discover a brief list of the first principles we must watch carefully: creation, God, infinity, the framework given to scripture, free will, unity, hierarchy, and the soul. To become sensitized to the crucial importance of how these concepts are defined and related, this is to derive a great deal of theological help from philosophy.

8

AUGUSTINE AND THE TRINITY

A. A PROPER GOD

We did not attempt to treat Origen's doctrine in detail but intended, rather, simply to uncover the first principles operative in his views in the hope of understanding better how philosophical first principles function in theology. Now it is easy to see that, with Augustine, almost nothing could be either more indicative or more important than the Trinity.* Implicitly, our aim is to uncover how Augustine thought about philosophy, since philosophy in doctrine is many things and not one. If philosophy were simply one thing, its relation to and its function in theology could be fixed once and for all and then either established or dismissed. As a major part in our understanding of any theologian, then, we must isolate his view of philosophy and understand its role in his thought.

The criticism of any theological doctrine often begins with a

---

* Augustine, *The Trinity*, trans. Stephen McKenna (Washington, D.C.: The Catholic University of America Press, 1963). All page references in this chapter are to this volume. Note: This single work is used for the sake of simplicity, but the reader interested specifically in Augustine will want to consult the specific writings devoted to time and free will, as well as those chapters in *The Confessions* that treat the Trinity in a personal religious manner.

careful appraisal of the philosophy operative in the doctrine and then the formation of an alternative philosophy. If we differ philosophically, and if we next work out the consequences of this, we often gain the leverage needed to break up a rigid theological doctrine. At the same time we are provided with a basis upon which to begin to reform it. This being true, our first task is to determine the exact extent to which a philosophical difference affects the theological conclusions reached. Having done this, we may discover where we can begin if we would like to obtain different theological results.

In spite of the fact that Augustine reportedly uses something like 42,816 biblical quotations in his writing, and although it is certain that he intends to draw heavily on scripture in his theology, Augustine himself is perfectly clear about the crucial areas in which sacred scripture is either silent or else indecisive. "But the divine scripture rarely mentions the things that are properly ascribed to God and which are not found in any creature" (p. 5). Here again we note the most crucial deficiency in any use of the biblical documents as a basis for theology: They talk about God, they describe his actions and even attribute words to him, but there is little or no technical description of his nature.

You might say that, in this case, theology should shape a doctrine of the divine nature so that it will fit the religious accounts. The problem with this idea is that the history of theology teaches us that more than one technical account of the divine attributes will meet this requirement. If one and only one doctrine of God were compatible with either scripture or the tradition of a church, theology would be an easy and obvious affair rather than the crucial and debatable enterprise it is.

Augustine surely thinks that his view of God fits the biblical account, and yet, given such a central doctrine for Christianity as the Trinity, what we hope to show is that the crucial and debatable aspects of his doctrine are really philosophically determined. When he says

Some things in the Scriptures concerning the Father and Son are, therefore, put in such a way as to indicate the unity and equality of the substance of the Father and the Son. . . .

. . . but some are so put as to show that the Son is less on
account of the form of a slave. . . . (p. 53)

It is clear that the *problem* of the relation between the Father
and the Son is set by the biblical account, since only those
interested in Christianity will see the importance of this question. But the *solution,* that is what scripture does not provide
from itself.

In thinking about the Trinity, then, what assumptions can
we see at work shaping Augustine's views? What can we trace
to this basis rather than to scripture? In the quotation just
given, Augustine is working with the problem arising from the
fact that the biblical documents do not give one account of
God but say a variety of things about both God and Jesus.
Therefore, our problem becomes to find a concept capable of
reconciling this multiplicity into a coherent view of God—that
is, one capable of serving as a theological center. In this case,
Augustine is worrying about the traditional assertion that
Jesus appeared in the form of a servant, as a slave. If a doctrine of the Trinity is to be worked out to allow Jesus to be
fully divine, these assertions and others must also be reconciled with a concept of God.

In discussing this, Augustine follows a traditional route and
decides that not every description about Jesus applies fully
and convertibly to God. This decision eases the tension, but
where does Augustine get the distinctions he employs to solve
this problem? Surely they do not come from the biblical account itself, or else there would have been no issue over how
to describe the relation of Father and Son in the first place.
However, behind even this question of the source of the philosophical distinctions lies an even more basic question: Where
does Augustine's concept of God come from? It is this concept
that determines what must be separated out and which actions
and qualities of Jesus are not to be attributed directly to the
Father. Only when you first see what is inappropriate to God
does a need arise to develop a distinction in order to clarify
and to protect this relationship.

In this case, it is easy to see that Augustine balks and does
not want to attribute "the form of the slave" directly to the

Father. He tells us that some things in scripture apply to all persons of the Trinity equally and that others do not—for example, the slave. Yet scripture itself does not distinguish these attributes into such groups. In fact, this becomes necessary only after you have formed a concept of God clearly enough to see that some attributes cannot be accepted—that is, if you are to hold that concept of God consistently. How do we determine what is "proper" to God and what is not? Surely that is theology's first and central task, and yet nothing given to us in religious experience is sufficient to determine this for us with finality. Our arguments over God center not so much on what is presented in the New Testament as around what God's nature must be like in order for the assertions made about him to be true.

We are not left guideless here, of course. The philosophical and metaphysical tradition is full of clear sets of criteria on the matter. Although these do fall into patterns, we are not dictated to but rather are free to make certain basic choices in the definition of concepts—for example, unity, infinity, nonbeing. How we do this determines what becomes 'proper' and 'improper' as attributed to that concept of God. In Augustine's case, it is easy to make out what shapes his thinking on this question. Not that Augustine feels that he has any alternatives in this matter, but what one theologian takes as a bedrock assumption may later turn around and yield a new theology as it becomes evident that other assumptions are also possible. The first principles of any man mean that which he assumes and builds upon, so that to learn what Augustine takes as self-evident is to learn what shapes his thought on God and where the first attack for any desired change must be directed.

B. UNCHANGEABLENESS AND SOUL

In order to understand Augustine's views on the Trinity, perhaps the most important concept to examine is 'unchangeableness'. What does this mean for Augustine? If it involves a variety of meanings, are all of them equally necessary or could some be changed while others are still preserved? In its most basic sense, and perhaps this is the meaning most clearly derived from the biblical accounts, 'unchangeableness' means God's own self-existence and lack of coming into being or passing away as the universe and its creatures do.

It stands to reason that He Himself was not made through whom all things were made.

For the moment, let us not challenge this assumption of unchangeableness as an attribute of God and as limiting what can and cannot properly be attributed to him. It does pose certain problems for the doctrine of the Trinity, since, at least in form, the Son does come into existence and pass away. However, it is not so much this basic aspect of divine perfection that shapes Augustine's thoughts on the Trinity at certain crucial points as it is his further assumptions about what unchangeableness means.

Here are some other things Augustine has to say about this central concept:

1 . . . true immortality is unchangeableness, which no creature can have, because it is proper to the Creator alone. (p. 5)

2 For this reason it is difficult to contemplate and to comprehend fully the substance of God, which makes changeable things without any change in itself, and creates temporal things without any temporal movement. (p. 5)

3 . . . the life of the Son as that of the Father is unchangeable. . . . (p. 54)

4 . . . the form of the slave was so assumed that the form of God remained unchangeable.

Regarding no. 1, we can say that, if Augustine means only self-existence and not passing away, it is true that this quality does belong uniquely to God. But in no. 2, a different notion of 'unchangeable' is brought in, one that is more debatable and perhaps one not so necessarily connected with the basic divine attribute. For here Augustine asserts that there is to be no internal change in God, but this is not obviously true, and it rests upon a whole set of assumptions.

For all his Platonic background, Augustine appears to be Aristotelian at this point, since Plato, interestingly enough, does not exclude all change and motion from the divine and eternal. Aristotle linked change with both lack and incompletion, and thus he associated it exclusively with creatures and excluded it from the divine. Following this metaphysical course, it is easy to see why Augustine is forced in quotation no. 3 to move on to attribute unchangeableness to the Son too. This quality is not biblically derived; in fact, no simple reading of scripture alone is likely to lead to this assertion. Rather, it is Augustine's special view of God that dictates that, if the Son is to be divine (which Christianity does require), then he is going to have to share this particular set of divine attributes. Actually, as we shall go on to point out, this special view of God is going to prove difficult for Augustine in the end, and it will force compromises on him. But he is right: No solution to any basic theological questions are possible unless we begin by forming a concept of God and then use that to structure and to solve the problems given to us in theology.

It is, of course, the biblical use of "the form of the slave" that worries Augustine the most, and it is interesting to see how certain metaphysical assumptions about God tend to modify the significance of this manner of describing Jesus' divinity and his relation to God. In no. 4, we note that Augustine cannot allow God to change in his assumption of the "form of the slave." Yet, to conceive of a creator God who manifests himself in this way does seem to involve change, since the last thing slaves do is to create universes and dictate the unfolding of evolutionary patterns. Augustine might mean (in no. 4) only that God can achieve this condescension without passing out of existence, but clearly Augustine really wants to exclude *all* change from God for reasons that depend on the view of the divine nature he has adopted.

Our central question is "How do Augustine's metaphysical views on 'change' affect his analysis of the Trinity?" Consider these quotations next:

1 Neither God the Father, nor His Word, nor His Spirit, which is the one God, is in any way changeable with regard to that which He is. . . .

. . . the Father, the Son, and the Holy Spirit can in no way
be visible in itself, since it is in no way changeable. (p. 119)

2 . . . it was not the Word of God Himself in His own substance, by which He is equal to and coeternal with the Father,
nor the Holy Spirit in His own substance, by which He is also
equal to both, but assuredly a creature, which could be made
into and could exist in these forms, which would appear to
corporal and bodily sense. (p. 127)

3 . . . why may not He be understood as having appeared
often to Abraham, to Moses . . . through a changeable and
visible creature subject to Himself, while He remains in Himself and in His own substance, by which He is unchangeable
and invisible. (p. 71)

In no. 1, it is clear that Augustine goes beyond asserting the
simple eternality and self-existence of God. He wants to exclude all change as being incompatible with his theory of the
divine nature. Since this is one important way to think about
God, it does not seem strange at first—that is, until it becomes
clear that this forbids God to become visible, since clearly this
would involve some connection with change. The assertion of
the divinity of Jesus runs into a problem at this point because
of his obvious visibility as a man.

Augustine's solution appears in no. 2. The Word of God
itself did not 'appear' (since that would subject it to change),
but rather it is a creature that appears as subject to God's will.
This is, of course, one way to deal with the perplexities of the
Trinity, but what is it that gives Augustine this particular
problem? Assuredly it is not scripture, which simply asserts
the 'appearance' of God. Rather, it is philosophy—that is,
Augustine's decision to reject any form of change in the divine
nature. Such an interpretation of 'change' does introduce a
difficulty into the Trinity: God himself cannot 'appear' since
that would involve him in change, which Augustine does not
want. Should we then eliminate all philosophy in order to save
theology from being pressured in this way? No, because then
the crucial assertion of the divinity stands unresolved. However, what we can do is question whether Augustine's particular philosophical assumptions have any alternatives.

In quotation no. 3 Augustine worries about the earlier assertions of God's 'appearance', since these were not via the special
mediation of the physical Jesus. As a solution, he is forced to a
"robot theory," one in which God can remain eternally without
change and yet "control" visible creatures subject to himself
via someone who represents him. This has certain advantages
as a solution to the problem of change in God, but only if we
wish to stick to Augustine's absolute restriction against all
forms of change in divinity. However, this clearly has the disadvantage of not representing God fully, since in the "changes"
observed in Jesus, nothing of God's essence is revealed except
his eternal decision to cause change. As a result, Jesus has
important difficulties as a revealer of God's true nature, not
because of any scriptural assertions but because of the relationship dictated between God and the Son by Augustine's
metaphysics of change.

Where the nature of 'soul' and the 'divine will' are concerned, this becomes even more clear:

1 . . . although it [soul] is changeable still it is not visible.
[The Wisdom of God] . . . is not only invisible, as the soul is,
but is likewise unchangeable as the soul is not. (p. 68)

2 Thus, the will of God is the first and highest cause of all the
forms and movements of the corporeal being. (p. 104)

In no. 1, Augustine sees clearly that, of necessity, soul is associated with motion, but he follows Aristotle (or perhaps more,
Plotinus) in considering this to be inferior. The wisdom of
God is thus superior in the divine hierarchy, and we know that
soul must be beneath it, not as the consequence of any biblical
command but by virtue of Augustine's views on change.
Granted that the scripture may attribute 'unchangeability' to
God and that we might wish to keep this divine attribute, it
can be interpreted to mean 'without origin' and 'never helpless
to control change', but it need not exclude all meanings of
change unless our metaphysics dictates this. Where God's 'will'
is concerned, it must be made the cause of all movements in
corporeal being only if one is determined to exclude every

form of change from the divine nature. Otherwise its perfection might be so interpreted as to allow us to attribute some independence of decision to corporeal beings.

C. GOD AND MAN

How does Augustine's rigid interpretation of 'unchangeableness' affect the way in which it is possible for him to relate God and man, which is the central question at issue in developing a doctrine of the Trinity too? Consider the following:

1 The divinity, however, cannot be seen in any way with human sight. (p. 15)

2 Although He appears in visible and sensible forms, still He does so through His own creature, not in His own substance. (p. 126)

3 . . . the Son of God is understood to be equal to the Father according to the form of God in which He is, and less than the Father according to the form of a slave that He has received. (p. 52)

With no. 1, as we have seen before, divinity is excluded from sight because of the resulting connection with change, as Augustine has interpreted the senses. The difficulty this gets him into becomes more clear in quotation no. 2, for Christianity has asserted the 'appearance' of God, and it is actually this central assertion that gives rise to the doctrine of the Trinity and makes its interpretation so crucial.

Soul, according to other theories, can be considered as divine (for example, Plato's) although not necessarily in every form but only in its perfect exercise. Similarly, in the *Phaedrus* Plato can allow a certain form of 'madness'—that is, being possessed—to be divine. Augustine cannot accept this position attributed to soul because of his view on change. Thus, God's asserted 'appearance' in Christianity cannot be considered as an appearance of his 'substance'. Instead, he appears through a creature that does not act on its own but is subject fully to God's will as fixed from eternity. God's existence from eternity may be assumed in the New Testament, but it does not necessarily involve the complete determination of his will from eternity. It is Augustine's philosophy that requires this. If not, the creature could not represent him but would be independent, or else God's substance would appear directly in a creature, all of which Augustine's doctrine of God cannot allow.

It is, however, perhaps quotation no. 3 that is the most important for the interpretation of Christian doctrine. The Son can be equal to the Father in certain respects; but, when it comes to the traditional assertion that God has appeared "in the form of a servant," Augustine is forced (as are also thousands of men in the church's history since his time) to make the Son not equal to the Father where the concept 'slave' is involved. Why not? God's acceptance of this form is clearly asserted in the scripture. Why is Augustine pushed to introduce a distinction into his doctrine of the Trinity and to assert that the Son, insofar as he has the form of a slave, is not equal to the Father? 'Slavery' and 'servanthood' indicate, as the outcome of the gospel story evidences so clearly, the availability of God to accept suffering, abuse, the imposition of human will, and even death. We in America understand all too well the difficulties arising from slavery. Yet, why is it impossible for Augustine to conceive that this aspect might actually be crucial in order to reveal God's full nature?

If Jesus is to be taken as a full appearance of God in this form, he needs to be capable of some mode of change. However, this need not involve either a loss of self-existence or a lack of original or ultimate control through unlimited power (although perhaps it could be voluntarily limited for a time). This is a fully possible concept of God's nature, even with perhaps some advantages for Christianity, but it clearly does not fit Augustine's concept of God. Thus, he is forced to place God's appearance in the form of the 'slave' as that part of the Son's nature that is not shared fully with God. God 'appears' in this form only in the sense that his unchanging will has been fixed on this manifestation from eternity, but, according to Augustine, to seek God's essence in the form of the servant (as some Christians have) is never to see God fully.

What kind of relationship between God and man results from this kind of view? With this question we uncover perhaps the crucial consequence of the way in which Augustine shapes his doctrine of the Trinity. If God is so different in nature from man, either we must reinterpret human nature in order to find a possible core of similarity with God's complete unchange-ableness (which is Augustine's tendency), or else any close relation of God and man, *qua* sensible creature, will be very difficult. It is well known that Augustine goes on to uncover trinities in man's nature, particularly in his mind, which gives us a natural basis for understanding how three persons can be one in the divine nature. Yet, in reading Augustine it is clear that his tendency is to look for aspects of unchangeableness in man, imitations of eternity, rather than to question his view of God in order to relate God to man more closely.

To get a little ahead of ourselves, it will be interesting in the next section to see how closely Bonaventure brings God to the natural order. A different concept of both God and man will appear there, but we have seen Augustine restrict God's manifestation to the Son and not allow God's full presence in other corporeal things. Augustine's ability to have God mani-fest in the Son is only accomplished by excluding, as not fully applicable, certain sides of creaturely life because his God is not like them in kind. Bonaventure finds God to be much more fully present to natural beings, because he has a God whose nature does not exclude the basic principles of creaturely existence. Augustine, however, will not allow the incarnation of the Holy Spirit because the presence of God in one incom-patible creaturely form (Jesus) offers problems enough. Thus, it is clear that, if revelation cannot be full and complete through this means, further incarnations would not help solve this difficulty and so are to be avoided unless necessary.

Augustine's view of God makes his association with cor-poreal entities a very difficult matter. Traditionally, these prob-lems are brought to a focus in the doctrine of the Trinity, because this is where the concept of incarnation must be dealt with. In our own day, we face many who deny the divinity of Jesus and the existence of God for reasons precisely opposite from those that gave Augustine his difficulties with God. Today, any transcendence of natural modes of existence is denied by some, whereas it was Augustine's conception of a God so different in kind from changeable men that gave him his problems in relating God and man. Augustine was ready to compromise the full humanity of God's appearance as not manifesting his substance, but today we seem more ready to abandon God's transcendence in order to make natural processes ultimately revelatory.

Perhaps truth lies in neither extreme, in spite of the fact that this concept of God seemed natural to Augustine and to others for centuries. What would a God be like who could manifest his substance in the form of a slave, and make this a full revelation, and yet be God and not simply another slave? Wouldn't this God be closer in his own nature to the natural qualities of the world? Yet clearly he need not of any necessity be subject to their limitations, unless he voluntarily submitted to this for a shorter or a longer period of time. This is not the place to develop such a suggestion further, but clearly it requires a God who could accept change in his nature without surrendering his self-existence or his ultimate control. And equally clearly, it is Augustine's views of both divine and human nature and the attributes of each that govern the way in which the persons of the Trinity can be related.

D. TIME AND FREE WILL

If it was ever in doubt that Augustine's views on 'time' and 'free will' are central to his theological interpretation, a glance at the following quotations should indicate their philosophical importance in shaping his doctrine of the Trinity.

1 . . . it was certainly decided before time, at which time that Wisdom of God should appear in the flesh. (p. 61)

2 . . . for the order of times is certainly without time in the eternal Wisdom of God. (p. 61)

3 For the essence of God, whereby He is, has nothing changeable, neither in eternity, nor in truth, nor in will; because there the truth is eternal, love is eternal; there the love is true, eternally true; and there eternity is loved, truth is loved. (p. 130)

4 Hence, because there is One Word of God, through which all things were made, which is the unchangeable truth, all

things in it are originally and unchangeably simultaneous, not only the things which are now in this whole creation, but also those which have been and are to be. (p. 132)

Where quotation no. 1 is concerned, why is it so clear that before all time it has been decided at what exact time God would appear in the flesh? It could be that such a revelation was always intended in principle but that its exact form, time, and place were left to later determination. Such a view would account equally for the biblical assertions. However, it runs into trouble, not because of Bible but because of Augustine's inability to admit change in any form into God. The Trinity is concerned with the way in which God appears, but how this takes place in turn is dependent on the conception of the divine attributes.

For instance, in no. 2 why must the knowledge of the order of times be itself without time as it exists in the divine wisdom? Augustine excludes time from God's nature because time involves change, so that a particular interpretation of 'unchangeable' seems to shape his whole notion of God as well as his doctrine of the Trinity. There is no logical impossibility about forming a view of God in which his own nature reflects the qualities of time itself, although this need not be exactly as it happens in man's nature. And already it becomes clear here that 'free will' must be denied, since it is incompatible with a divine Wisdom that is fixed, incapable of being affected by change, and exclusive of time. Augustine must eliminate free will in man, not because it is somehow impossible for man to have this power, but in order to allow God to use changeable creatures for his own purpose without involving himself in change.

As we pointed out in sections B and C, the doctrine of the incarnation forces Augustine to give some account of God's presence in creaturely form. This raises problems for him that do not face Aristotle's 'Unmoved Mover', since it was not asserted to have appeared in such unlikely forms. Augustine can accomplish this difficult reconciliation only if God may use creatures for his own purposes, as fully determined and as instruments, without reflecting change back on their source. If

as creatures we·had any freedom of will, God's entrance into
one of us might subject him to change (a consequence Augustine perhaps fears more than God does). This necessitates
Augustine's elimination of time in the divine nature, and
human action must be fixed from eternity in order that God's
relationship to man will not involve him in attributes Augustine thinks are unfavorable.

In no. 3, we meet the famed qualities of Augustine's conception of God, and it has a certain majestic peacefulness
about it that lends it to liturgical and religious development.
However, our issue concerns the Trinity, and that problem is
raised for us because of the assertion of God's incarnation.
Therefore, our question becomes "Granted the peacefulness of
this view of God, does it really fit and best express the Christian doctrine of the incarnation? Or does the view of unchangeability actually force undesirable consequences on any
explanation of the Trinity?" Augustine is very strong on seeing
truth as eternal (that is, as without change). In such a situation, love does seem secure and the contemplation of it has a
quieting effect. The majesty of such a view of God is un-
deniable, and yet it is clear that its effect upon man is neo-
Platonic. That is, it draws him up and away from his nature as
man and transports him to a realm very unlike his daily
existence, and therein lies its attractiveness as an escape from
the unpleasantness of our world's difficult features.

Yet, if this is really the condition of God's nature, does it
seem likely that it would ever manifest itself by incarnation in
a lowly form in the first place, as Christians have asserted?
Augustine, it is true, does hold to a doctrine of incarnation,
but we have already noted that God's substance cannot be
fully expressed in a creature. It still might be true that
Augustine's view of God actually works against placing real
emphasis on incarnation as a way to understand God. For, if
his existence is as it is described above, his natural intention
would not be toward incarnation and his essence would not
best be revealed or understood in this event. Instead, the incarnation becomes a problem that Augustine's view of the
nature of God makes more difficult than necessary to solve. He
cannot interpret God's nature in the light of his appearance in
the form of a slave, but rather we must interpret this difficult

assertion in the light of an already established doctrine of God.

In interpreting the Word of God (no. 4), Augustine is forced to see it as containing all things "unchangeably simultaneous." Now, granted that God might view all things in a simultaneous manner rather than partially and sequentially as we do, still this alone does not demand that all change be excluded, unless Augustine's other assumptions require this. If the future must be contained in God's understanding in the same manner as the past, this eliminates all possibility of freedom of human choice, since contingent choice requires that past and future be different by nature from each other. The future would have to contain an indeterminate quality that has been eliminated in the past. Starting strictly from the assertion of God's incarnation, there is no reason why the future should not contain some unresolved uncertainties, since even the mode that God's revelation took (the suffering servant) is asserted to be surprising. It was not generally expected, and it still is not widely accepted, precisely because of its incongruity with some classical notions of God.

In all of these matters, it is apparent that Augustine's metaphysics has shaped his doctrine of the Trinity, not entirely, of course, but in its crucial and undecided features. If so, one response to this discovery might be to demand the expulsion of philosophy from theological construction. In the case of Luther, we shall examine whether such a proposal can succeed, but for now it is enough to note that Augustine did form a doctrine of the Trinity which is both highly influential and acceptable. This technical formulation was called for, not by philosophy, but by problems in religious doctrine and in the biblical account, which would have gone unsolved without it. If religion's problems remain unsolved without such an addition of philosophical principles, the answer would seem to be not to withdraw philosophy from the religious life but to differentiate between the two—carefully. Then, when the resulting theological doctrine seems to run into difficulties, we can ask what other philosophical options are available for our use and examine the product that results when it is compared with our original religious problems and aims.

9

BONAVENTURE AND REDUCTION

A. THE INNER LIGHT

In discovering what it is that makes Augustine reach a certain crucial distinction regarding the Trinity (that is, an implied philosophical principle), perhaps we have also uncovered why it is not possible to build a theology without philosophy—for example, directly on simple biblical interpretation. Beyond the fact that such a source is not itself pure and simple (see Chapter 5), the point at issue revolves around an understanding of how crucial concepts function. Unlike simple terms, concepts such as 'incarnation' are not precise in their use but become so only when a philosophical context draws and shapes them in one implicit direction. Augustine does this by using a special interpretation of 'unchangeable', and he gets a specific theology as a result.

Without such specific definition, religious meaning remains vague and subject to misunderstanding. All it is important to remember in this process is (1) how religion differs from philosophy, (2) how theology arises as a combination of the two, (3) that one philosophical context must never be assumed, and (4) that this is avoided by carrying out the critical development of one framework always with an eye to its possible replacement by another explicit philosophical extension. A knowledge of how crucial concepts function will tell us why simply to use scriptural terms (for example, 'unchangeable') is not enough, not even when they are legitimately biblically derived. The most important terms are, somewhat unfortunately, subject to the widest interpretations. Thus, it is imperative not to leave them undefined, for otherwise they cause misunderstanding. Only a philosophical analysis can specify a flexible term for one definite use so that it can function systematically.

When we turn to consider Bonaventure, we seem to face a doctrine that asserts almost the opposite of the thesis of this whole investigation. His famous little work, *Retracing the Arts to Theology,*[*] appears to place philosophy in a secondary position and in its place to make theology basic. However, the crucial point to notice is that the presentation of his theory is itself based on an elaborate philosophical scheme. That is, the argument depends on many philosophical premises which, *if accepted,* lead to a certain ordering of the other disciplines in relation to theology. As we shall see, both an intricate theory of knowledge and a metaphysics of the world's structure are crucial if we are to agree to the whole argument, and these are both philosophical in origin and subject to philosophical reappraisal. *If* that perspective is adopted, *then* all arts are seen to stand in a certain relation to theology, but it is a certain philosophical argument that outlines this position for theology —certainly it is not scripture.

Bonaventure's 'reduction' or 'retracing' of the arts is an explanation and a classification of the various arts, each of which is independent and sufficient in itself. This is not so much a 'reduction' in the usual sense as it is a definition of God's relation to all things through a theory of knowledge that is able to discern God's immediate presence. Not all men have found God so available. Those who have not will not discover

---

[*] Bonaventure, *Retracing the Arts to Theology,* trans. Sister E. T. Healy (St. Bonaventure, N.Y.: The Franciscan Institute, 1955). All footnotes in this chapter are to this edition. Readers interested in the development of Bonaventure's own thought will, of course, want to compare this work with his other writings to note the concrete shifts in his thinking about theology as he considers it in other contexts.

actually evident on all levels and if their essential similarity were only discerned when theology is reached (defined).

1 . . . all speech signifies a *mental concept.*

2 Practically the same procedure is seen in the beginning of the Eternal World. . . . (p. 35)

3 Now the fourth light, which illumines the mind for the understanding of *saving truth,* is the light of Sacred Scripture. This light is called *higher* because it leads to things above by manifestations of truths which are beyond reason and also because it is not acquired by human research, but comes down by inspiration. (p. 27)

4 Wherefore, all our knowledge should end in the knowledge of Sacred Scripture. . . . (p. 29)

It is important to note that the first quotation indicates a certain philosophical view which, if rejected, spoils the whole structure, since no. 2 asserts that the same procedure is present in God's begetting of his Word. The crucial point in no. 3 hinges on the particular theory of knowledge outlined for the function of scripture. Is this really what scripture does, and, if so, in exactly what sense does it accomplish this? An interesting view of the function of scripture is involved, but, if rejected or modified, it spoils the parallelism as much as a change in the concept of philosophy would. Most important, since it rests on a theory of knowledge concerning the function of scripture, the basis of the theory is itself philosophical, and it becomes theological only after the theory of knowledge is accepted.

This basic role assigned to philosophy can perhaps be seen even more clearly in the concept of 'reason' as it appears in no. 3. For instance, whether something is 'beyond reason' is not a fixed matter but depends entirely on the way in which reason is defined. Thus, even to know that the truths of scripture are 'beyond reason' requires, first, a detailed analysis of reason's powers, and this itself is a philosophical matter to be accepted or redefined on those grounds. It would have been easier for us all if 'reason' had been given a fixed meaning and an agreed sphere, but the center of philosophical debate has focused on this point since philosophy began. Reason may be either relatively restricted or greatly expanded, depending on the way in which philosophical first principles are developed (for example, Hume vs. Plato).

Whether our knowledge should end in sacred scripture, as quotation no. 4 suggests, is now seen to rest on a set of assumptions, primarily the scope assigned to 'reason' and the interpretation given to the function of the biblical documents. We have mentioned the breadth of interpretation possible for 'reason', but, when it comes to 'scripture', it is clear that we have no agreed principle for its interpretation either. To say this is not to argue against either the clarity of the doctrine or its possible religious value. Both of these may remain intact, and still it is true that the issue of how scripture is to be treated as a norm in theological questions is one for which there is no fixed internal doctrine. It must be worked out again and again as the material is taken up. Not that the documents do not contain elements of both theology and philosophy, but they do not contain them in a single, developed, systematic form, so that first this must be provided.

We are now in a better position to understand the famous definition of philosophy as the "handmaiden" of theology:

> It is evident too how all divisions of knowledge are handmaids of theology, and it is for this reason that theology makes use of illustrations and terms penetrating to every branch of knowledge. (p. 41)

In the first place, the status of handmaiden applies to all divisions of knowledge, although it is true that this defines philosophy (according to an older understanding of that discipline) as including all of the arts. Bonaventure's simple meaning here is that theology uses or borrows from all other arts, and in that sense they serve her. This is a relatively harmless view of what it means to be a handmaiden, and it is true that theologians are more likely to borrow from art or scientific theory than artists or scientists are to use theological doctrines.

However, from what we have considered before, it is clear that Bonaventure also has in mind another way in which philosophy and the arts serve theology as a handmaiden. If the procedures in theology turn out to have such strict parallels in philosophical operations and goals, it is true that, once theology is reached, it will become clear just how theologically dependent and directed other quests for knowledge have been, even if they have gone on without realizing this fully. If the theory outlined by Bonaventure is true, every enterprise points to (that is, serves) theological purposes and understands itself better as this similarity to theology is more fully understood. However, as we have already said, this whole scheme is itself a philosophical construct, and so the "dependence" of philosophy on theology itself depends on accepting that philosophical interpretation.

C. THE IMMEDIACY OF GOD

Perhaps the most pressing question behind Bonaventure's whole theory concerns the immediacy of God. The overwhelming impression the reader gains is that Bonaventure senses God's presence everywhere. If this is not quite so evident at first, it becomes so as one advances to the "Higher Light."

1 It is likewise evident how wide is the illuminative way and how in everything which is perceived or known God himself lies hidden within. (p. 41)

2 Furthermore, if we consider the delight of sense perception, we shall see therein the union of God and the soul. Behold how the Divine Wisdom lies hidden in sense perception. . . . (p. 31)

In considering no. 2, the first thing we have to note is that not everyone (in fact, very few) actually sees God as that closely connected to sense perception. This does not mean that it cannot be true, but it does mean that the burden of proof lies with the asserter of that philosophical proposition.

Bonaventure clearly finds it advantageous to discover God to be so close to natural experience. As far as knowing God is concerned, it certainly helps if knowledge of him lies that close at hand, whether or not this is easily recognized. But there are problems with this theory too, since it is in such things as the experience of the beautiful and joy in the harmonious that Bonaventure finds God hidden within his sense perception. First, whether we accept this depends upon the kind of view one takes of the divine nature, so that, if you view God differently, these experiences might not seem so close. Furthermore, many sense experiences (for example, pain and anguish) do not fit this pattern. Thus, either only certain areas of sense experience lead to a certain concept of God, or, if all sense experience is to be accepted as a base, a very different kind of God will have to be constructed to correspond to our confused mixture of actual sense experience.

Perhaps an even more pressing problem than what kind of God will fit what kind of sense experience, however, is the question of the theory of knowledge that locates the apprehension of God so close to us. For, if this immediacy of the divine is true, how can so many men fail to see it? This failure includes not merely those who do not care enough to seek. Many who earnestly search for God fail in this attempt. Bonaventure's theory works best for those who do find God close to ordinary experience, but the close parallels he sets up do not account for those who yearn to, yet cannot, see this. The number who cannot find God in close proximity would seem to argue for a much more separate relationship between God and the world, such that it is possible to study the one without being led to the other. And does this seem to be the case more often than not?

All men do not discover God's immediacy, not even all religious men, and every aspect of the natural world does not seem to fit into ultimate beauty and joy in harmony. If this is true, it does affect Bonaventure's view of theology and its immediate presence in all of the arts—that is, their "retracing" to theology to show their involvement. For if God's relationship to the world is a more distant one, the arts cannot so easily lead to him, and then theology will become something a little more specially placed and not simply a kind of model for all the natural arts. This is not to prejudge the rightness or wrongness of Bonaventure's theory of God and his proximity to simple experience. However, it does suggest that the key to the whole theory is not only a specific theory of knowledge but also a special view of the divine nature, which must be appraised first. And, if that is rejected or modified, the whole view of theology is altered.

Bonaventure finds God mirrored in everything, but if those who do not are right, theology cannot have .the function Bonaventure gives to it. This possibility brings us back to his argument that God is, in fact, to be seen mirrored in the various natural arts. Of course, his argument could be correct, even if a majority refused to accept it. The argument, then, is not obvious but a philosophical theory. If one accepts it, theology comes to have the position ascribed to it. If God's nature and position were obvious, theology could have a clearly recognized position and not simply one established by a special philosophical argument. If God is not evident, we are dependent on a philosophical construction to make him clear.

The problem is God. His nearness to created processes would enable all the arts to trace their relationship to theology clearly. But, if he is not conceived of in this way, theology must function in a different manner. The point is that theology cannot simply be defined and its functions worked out. What it is depends on what God is like. That is not something we can assume. Instead it is our first unknown. A different philosophical assumption regarding God's nature would shape theology along other lines. For instance, if we dwell on evil or on the negative side of life, a markedly different God is required to account for these forces than Bonaventure's God of beauty and harmony.

D. NATURAL INCARNATION

We saw how much trouble Augustine had when it came to interpreting the Christian doctrine of incarnation; his particular views on God's 'unchangeability' made it difficult (if not impossible) for God to be represented by a form of flesh and particularly by the concept of a slave. As we might suspect, Bonaventure has the opposite problem: His vision that God is so easily visible within the natural order that God is led to 'incarnation' as the most natural tendency (cf. the account of

Hegel following). Augustine's God has certain incompatibili-
ties with the time and change always involved in the natural
order, but Bonaventure's God is so closely associated with the
natural order that incarnation is a matter of little difficulty.

Our question at this point is, How evident is this close relationship which Bonaventure sees so clearly?

> And so it is evident how the *manifold Wisdom of God,* which
> is clearly revealed in Sacred Scripture, lies hidden in all knowl-
> edge and in all nature. (p. 41)

If what is revealed in scripture does lie hidden in all knowledge, once this is discovered, it is easy to see how one might
then turn back and find all forms of knowledge as prefiguring
this, even if it cannot be seen in advance but only from the
perspective of theology. However, is this so "evident"? For if
not, God might not be found present elsewhere in the same
way as he is in scripture. And if God is not evident, can he
really be shown to anyone who does not see or who is uncertain? This is where the argument must begin—not with a fixed
view of theology but with establishing that God really has the
nature he is asserted to have.

Even if we accept Bonaventure's 'close God', there is still a
question as to whether this makes 'incarnation' too natural an
event and no longer one that is extraordinary or unexpected.

> . . . all natural philosophy, by reason of the relation of pro-
> portion, predicates the word of God begotten and become in-
> carnate. . . . (p. 39)

According to this theory, philosophy in its natural function
repeats and parallels the divine incarnation. Considering the
difficulty Augustine had with this concept, there is something
attractive about finding incarnation so similar to other ordinary philosophical procedures. Yet there are also dangers.
That is, clearly there are millions who do not believe the
Christian story of incarnation, and yet, according to Bon-

aventure's account, this should be a very natural idea—one that is readily accepted once suggested.

Whenever a theory makes something appear easy and all the while we know in fact that people do not act as if it were easy and natural, we ought to suspect that we are dealing with a theory that is attractive in itself but possibly just not in fact the design on which our actual world was built. That is, the world could be constructed along the lines of such close theological parallels; God could be so readily available, and incarnation could appear as an event that is constantly paralleled naturally, but in point of fact millions of intelligent people do not see it this way. This suggests that God actually is more distant than Bonaventure pictures him; perhaps he is also less beautiful and harmonious than described. In this case, theology has a much more ambiguous position than simply being a clear example of the knowledge all arts covertly seek.

If God really is everywhere, admittedly beneath the surface and yet close to its surface, any beginning anywhere should lead to God and get us to Bonaventure's 'reduction' as a natural outcome. That is, once God is discovered, his position as parallel to all pursuits ought to become clear. Then theology stands supreme both as having made this clear and as possessing the knowledge that all, knowingly or unknowingly, seek. Such a view certainly changes philosophy from the position we have assigned to it previously. Interestingly enough, it also raises scripture more toward being a finished theological doctrine than we have been willing to allow. Scripture for Bonaventure contains a special source of wisdom. It is not just an account of events that are basic to a certain religious way of life. It is much more a systematic and single universal insight such as philosophers have sometimes sought in metaphysics.

Thus, when scripture itself becomes more like a philosophical source, then philosophy also changes its position in relation to theology. However, like the view of God's closeness to nature which does not seem to fit the way men in fact act about God, such a view of scripture (as containing a higher wisdom) does not really fit either with the origin of those books or the history of their use. To be sure, some have treated scripture as if it were the source of a single and complete wisdom, but it seems clear both that its original intention had a more modest religious purpose and that many have not found in it this route to all wisdom. In any case, whether unrealistic or not, this view of the role of scripture is subject to all the virtues and defects of a philosophical theory. That is, it shapes a particular theology if it is accepted. If not, then it raises once more the issue "What basic philosophical approach shall we follow?"

10

LUTHER AND THE BOOK OF ROMANS

A. THE OPPOSITE OF KNOWLEDGE?

Moving from Bonaventure to Luther will provide a good contrast. Many readers, as they consider the thesis of this volume, will remember that Luther protested against a too philosophical rendering of theology, and in some sense Protestantism can be seen as maintaining a constant alert against any unfriendly philosophical intrusion. (Strange, that in our day so much of Protestant theology is dominated by unsympathetic forms of philosophy.) Thus, to test our thesis, we shall examine in Part II three pre-Reformation figures and three post-Reformation writers, one a biblical theologian, one a speculative philosopher, and one a philosopher of religion. It has never been our assertion that philosophy has only one role to play in theology; we propose that philosophy shapes theology according to the kind of philosophic theory employed. Furthermore, this choice should be made consciously from a consideration of the full range of our philosophical alternatives and not by a quiescent surrender to one form whose basic assumptions have never been challenged.

Luther's *Lectures on Romans** may seem an odd choice for

* Martin Luther, *Lectures on Romans,* trans. W. Pauck (London: S.C.M. Press, 1961). All page references in this chapter are to this edition.

our purpose, but, upon examination, it should prove to be an enlightening one. If Luther wished to free theology from a philosophical overlay which did not allow the gospel to come through clearly, the best place to test his philosophical freedom should be in his biblical commentary, and this volume is perhaps the one in which Luther himself formed his revolutionary understanding of the Christian message. As we see Luther's new biblical understanding emerge in his *Romans,* is he still in any way involved with philosophical assumptions? If so, does this affect his own biblical understanding?

Luther was all too aware of some of the philosophical shaping of theology we have discussed in the preceding three chapters, and against this he rebelled. However, did he really escape philosophical influence? Or is it the case that our only choice really is to use various philosophical instruments or to have no theology at all? If Bonaventure had a highly philosophic theory, even if the outcome was to turn all arts into imitations of theology, Luther's aim is to do the opposite. Starting from the New Testament, he sought to release a fresh understanding of Christianity. Consequently, Protestantism has from that day on had a slight antiphilosophical tendency and has been famed for its use of scripture as its "only basis." Luther's writing, then, is a good place to examine the possibility of doing theology in a nonphilosophical—that is, scriptural —form. Or rather, this is a good place to ask whether this really is a possibility.

Both Bonaventure and Luther actually give scripture a central place. And as we pointed out, Augustine too uses scripture constantly, so that the issue cannot be a simple question of either the use or the absence of scriptural reference. All the men we have considered think their view is fair to scriptural doctrine, so that the difference must be found more in *the way* in which scripture is used. And yet, if all use scripture and use it in varying ways to produce different theologies, scripture itself alone cannot dictate its own theological norm. Or, if any sacred scripture is asserted to have this norm contained within it, it surely cannot be an obvious affair but rather one that requires explication in order to be seen. In this case, the principle of interpretation in use is itself open to possible philosophical appraisal and rejection, since something other than

scripture must enter in to produce the various norms of interpretation.

Luther says of Paul's epistle to the Romans:

1 The sum and substance of this letter is: to pull down, to
pluck up, and to destroy all wisdom and righteousness of the
flesh.

2 There have always been some among the Jews and Gentiles
who believed it to be sufficient if they possessed virtues and
knowledge, not of the kind that is outwardly put on but that
which is inward and comes from the heart. This was also the
opinion of many philosophers. (p. 3)

3 But here just the opposite shall be taught. (p. 3)

In approaching Luther on this issue, it is important to note
that he is commenting primarily on the writings of Saint Paul
and not directly on the Gospels. Whatever philosophical elements the Gospels contain, Paul's writings are certainly already one step removed from such simplicity and directness as
can be found there. His writings are the evidence of a theological view shaped by certain principles. They are the work of
one man who is not giving a report simply as a witness of
events. He is one man who is developing and structuring a
theological view to meet problems which already are arising in
a religion and require intellectual and systematic development. If no scripture is completely free of philosophical ideas,
still the Gospel should always have a primary place. Doctrines
that develop out of any other part of scripture should be distinguished and considered as already representing overt interpretations. Yet, even with this in mind, it is clear that Luther
wants to oppose his message to all philosophy (no. 3). But
can this really be the opposite of knowledge, or is a heavy
dependence on scripture only a way to correct certain questionable forms?

Luther begins (no. 1) by asserting that it is Paul's intention
to oppose all wisdom of the flesh in order to defend the
Gospel. This would seem to put philosophy and religion ir-

reconcilably at odds with each other, but later (no. 2) it is clear that only if this wisdom is considered sufficient in itself is it a hindrance to Christianity and must therefore be opposed. Something more is needed beyond even inner righteousness (that is, the action of God); but, as long as any form of learning is not irreconcilable with this, no basic incompatibility appears. Only a natural reason that seeks self-sufficiency is a philosophical danger.

Is this necessarily either an antiphilosophical teaching, or is it even a nonphilosophical doctrine? It might be, but only if a commentary on, or interpretation of, scripture could be either philosophically free or in need of nothing other than itself to be understood. However, we shall see that at two crucial points Luther's own interpretation (sections C and D) is dependent philosophically.

It is clear that Luther thinks the interpretation of scripture is not subject to variation at its central core:

> It makes no difference whether Matthew or Thomas wrote it down and taught it and in what words and in what language: the gospel of God is the same. (p. 15)

If this is true, it would appear to do away with philosophy, and yet the interesting fact is that this apparent exclusion of a variety of philosophical interpretations itself rests on a certain philosophical premise (essentially Platonic) about the use and the function of words and language. Those who will differ most with Luther on this point are not the philosophers who somehow reject scripture but those who cannot accept this Platonic notion of the singularity of knowledge, which is such that it remains one in spite of a multiplicity of words and variety of concepts. Surely, most current biblical interpretation is based on a different epistemology than Luther assumes. Thus, biblical interpretations will differ fundamentally, not over scripture but over the philosophical basis for its interpretation. Luther seems to forget that not all men accept Platonism as the Gospel or agree with its account of fixed objects of knowledge.

B. FROM BEYOND OURSELVES

Perhaps what Luther means to say, even more than his apparent opposition to secular knowledge, is that what is important to us religiously does not originate from us, whereas our accomplishments in the arts seem to. Thus, it is only when we use our knowledge as a basis to refuse to see that anything comes from beyond ourselves that we restrict God's asserted action and distort the Gospel by treating it as another human product. (Is Barth's message in our own day essentially anything different from this?)

1 For God does not want to save us by our own but by an external righteousness which does not originate in ourselves but comes to us from beyond ourselves, which does not arise on our earth but comes from heaven. Therefore, we must come to know this righteousness which is utterly external and foreign to us. That is why our personal righteousness must be uprooted. . . . (p. 4)

2 . . . a true Christian must be so stripped of all that he calls his own that neither honor nor dishonor can affect him, because he knows that whatever honor is done to him is done to Christ. . . . (p. 5)

3 . . . there are few who for the sake of obtaining Christ's righteousness regard as nothing the goods at their right hand, namely, spiritual goods and righteous works. (p. 5)

4 Human teachings reveal the righteousness of men. . . . But only the gospel reveals the righteousness of God . . . by that faith alone by which one believes the word of God. (pp. 17–18)

It is worth pausing to observe that, amazingly enough, Luther and Bonaventure actually share one important attitude, although it is not related to philosophic theory. Bonaventure sees God's action as tied to nature everywhere, and he allows him very little actual independence from the natural order or from human arts. Luther similarly reduces everything to God's action, although he differs from Bonaventure about God's nature and, thus, about his relation to the natural order. What we must ask, again, is whether this difference over the conception of God is ultimately to be traced to a different philosophical framework? Luther does not place God and the natural world in parallel in the way that Bonaventure does. Luther's God is more opposed to the natural world, more to be seen in contrast to it, and yet it is true that both men discover God beneath everything—in spite of the different ways in which they describe him and his relation to natural knowledge and art.

Luther's stress on that which comes to us from beyond ourselves (no. 1), then, turns our attention to the central question of the nature of God, since everything now will depend on this. That question is the topic of the next Section (C); the issue at hand is "Why must our natural knowledge be uprooted in order for this goal of purity to be realized?" Clearly, this must be true if knowledge of this kind considered itself both sufficient by itself and also self-sufficient. However, the necessity for this attack depends upon the view of knowledge held, and Christianity might not need to be so radical in its opposition if it faced a more amenable theory of human knowledge. Perhaps the Gospel does reveal "the righteousness of God." Still, in order to present this discovery about God, perhaps his nature must be made clear through a systematic development that cannot be solely biblical in origin. It is not self-evident that what God revealed was a technical doctrine about his nature.

Our question is, What forms of knowledge is the Gospel opposed to?

1 . . . God makes us appear foolish and weak before men— and this is our outer being. But the wisdom and power of God are the life according to the gospel and the very role of the Christian life, by which he makes and reputes us wise and strong before himself—and this according to our inner being. (p. 20)

2 The apostle turns chiefly upon those who in this world have power and knowledge. . . .

. . . it is they who most strongly opposed the gospel and the word and life of the cross and incited others to opposition against it. (p. 20)

3 For to no one the preaching of the cross appears so foolish as to the philosophers and the men of power, because it goes contrary to all they are and feel. (p. 20)

In quotation no. 1, of course, the most crucial distinction, and one on which the whole argument depends, is that between 'inner' and 'outer' being. Granted, these terms appear in scripture. If our analysis of the function and the difficulty of important terms is correct, these concepts are subject to at least several interpretations and cannot be left unspecified for fear of failing to see that some of our difficulties arise in a disagreement over interpretation. Where nos. 2 and 3 are concerned, the issue is whether in all cases power and knowledge actually oppose the Gospel, or whether this is so only in certain cases and probably in the ones Paul speaks about to the Romans. 'Knowledge' is many things, and power may be used in many ways, so that it is unphilosophical to generalize from one form of knowledge to all forms. We cannot know the relation of the Gospel to power and knowledge until we first work out a theory of knowledge, since that is not given to us. It must be built and defended by us anew in each day. What is true of one theory of knowledge in one day does not hold true for all accounts in all times.

Of course when the 'Godhead' is appealed to, our question is whether this concept is so clear in itself that it can simply be used without further philosophical development.

1 . . . [before Christ] they were endowed with a knowledge or notion of the divine nature.

Their error was that in their worship they did not take the Godhead for what it is in itself, but changed it by fitting it to their own needs and desires. (pp. 23–24)

2 God elects and favors only a soul that despises itself and considers itself worthy only to be rejected in the house of God. . . . (p. 48)

3 Inner righteousness is praised by God and reproved and persecuted by men.

This, then, is the lesson: one who has not yet evaded the condemnation of men, or suffered calumny, reproof, and persecution for his action, has not yet attained to perfect righteousness. (p. 57)

Luther admits that there are pre-Christian notions of the divine nature, but, even granting that scripture reports certain special new facts that if taken into account would shape a new understanding of the divine nature, is this all developed automatically? Or rather, is it not the case that the crux of the argument comes over precisely how the 'Godhead' is conceived and that the detail of this view must never be taken as fixed but should be subject to constant philosophical reappraisal and critique? For instance, where quotation no. 2 is concerned, is it self-evident that scripture makes this assertion *uniformly* (not that certain passages cannot be found) as strongly as Luther does? Or is it not the case that this categorical rejection of self-value arises only from the particular way in which Luther comes to structure his understanding of God?

What is so striking is that sometimes Luther rejects all of our pretensions to possess a knowledge of the criteria upon which God operates, and at other times he seems himself to know *precisely* how God operates, for instance as in no. 2. It can be said that an assertion of precise knowledge of God's nature and operation is acceptable as long as it comes from scriptural sources, but what we must examine is whether any doctrine of God could come entirely from scripture alone (answer: probably not). Does Luther's own understanding of God itself have clear sources which are external to the Gospels, however interesting or valuable his insight may be? It is just that, when human exposition of God's nature is taken as if it were somehow divinely revealed and the only way to interpret scripture, the situation is made more difficult. A philosophically based interpretation has been provided with a kind of divine sanction that actually is antireligious. It gives a protected status to an interpretation of God that should stand on its own and be subject to constant critique.

In order to understand Luther's views on human righteousness and condemnation (quotations nos. 2 and 3), the important question to consider is this: "Is the human will exactly as Luther describes it, or are different interpretations of human nature possible?" Of course, we must grant that scripture does not give us one complete doctrine here that if adopted would change the situation. If human nature (and God's nature) are different in any significant way from Luther's description, perhaps his view of the necessity of persecution (quotation no. 3) is a little too strong, just as Kierkegaard's is often too violent on this issue. That is, the strong opposition and rejection of the world, and the world's persecution in return, may be as much a result of Luther's theory of knowledge and his view of the divine nature as it is an absolute requirement of scripture, even granted that it has a certain basis there.

C. GOD AS HE IS

When we turn to this issue, our first question must be "Is it that clear what God is like, even for a Christianity that claims some revelation of him?" Luther, of course, would be the first to answer "No," but then the question becomes "If Luther's views assume a knowledge of God and if all of God's nature is not claimed to have been revealed in technical detail (rather more his actions than his nature), then from what does Luther's knowledge of God arise? And how can we be sure which parts of God's nature are derived from revelation and which lean upon a philosophical context for their elaboration? If Luther assumes a knowledge of God as he is, can we assume this to be the content of revelation?" It may be, but then again it may not at all have been God's intention in revelation to describe himself in detail. In this case, our knowledge of his nature must draw upon other sources as well as scripture.

Luther has some very definite ideas about how God ought to be thought about:

1 . . . even today a great many people think of God in a way unworthy of him.

For no one can think rightly about God unless the spirit of God is in him. (p. 33)

2 . . . people even today come to commit spiritual idolatry of a more subtle kind, and it is quite frequent: they worship God not as he is but as they imagine and desire him to be. (p. 26)

Yet, our first reaction to this might be that even granting that Luther's problem developed because of wrong ways of thinking about God, times do change. Our present difficulty seems to be that we have no satisfactory concepts of God at all and have even lost the power to think about him. When philosophy offers many ideas of God, some at variance with Christianity, that is one situation. When we have no adequate ideas of God to begin with, our plight is even more extreme than Luther's, and it may not be remediable by scripture alone.

Nevertheless, even granting that it is theology's task to argue against false gods when they are presented, is this not possible only on the basis of proposing some view of God and then criticizing other concepts in relation to the asserted virtues of one? Scripture, whatever its normative function may be, does not seem intended to provide us with one, fixed concept of God which can serve as a single basis for elaboration. Consider even such a scripturally normative concept as 'love', which probably can be considered to be part of the Christian revelation of God's nature. We know from our own experience with this phenomenon that its assertion or even its appearance does not settle the matter. Love's meaning is in doubt and in need of specification even when its presence is assured. And if this intellectual task is not accomplished, we seem to be in danger of losing its presence because, if love's nature cannot be clearly understood, it becomes subject to misunderstanding. Theological elaboration is actually crucial to the continuance of a religious spirit—even if that spirit is not conceptual in its origin.

However, we need to consider Luther's assertion that the presence of the spirit of God is necessary for right thinking about him (quotation no. 1). Let us not argue about this for the moment but assume its truth. What then? The issue becomes "How can we distinguish the presence of the spirit of God from its absence?" Many have asserted its presence and, at least in intellectual conceptualization, they certainly do not all agree. It is too easy to dismiss disagreement as stemming from a lack of the Holy Spirit, and it is too easy to support one's own view by asserting its presence (which actually is a very un-Lutheran thing to claim). The spirit of God does not seem to have left us with definite norms for discerning its presence, or at least not with norms beyond question or interpretation. However God can be thought about, he seems to have placed the burden upon us for establishing norms to test this. 'God as he is' may be our goal, but we are not able to receive God except on our variable terms.

In distinguishing so sharply 'God as he is' from our conceptions of him, Luther runs into a major difficulty in addition to the need to establish the norms to determine "right thought." This is that the Christian assertion is one of the incarnation of God, so that what we must ask is whether Luther's view of the radical distinction of God's nature from the world actually has anti-incarnational tendencies, just as Bonaventure's close association of God with the secular order made incarnation almost a natural necessity.

It seems clear that the help we might draw from scripture in thinking about God is like this: (1) his revelation took the mode of self-incarnation in the form of a servant; (2) this event was not normally expected (the 'scandal' of the Gospel); however, (3) God should be such that this event fits (that is, reveals) his nature. We must live and think in the middle ground, one between making incarnation too natural an event (or else it will lose its status as revelation) and making God so disparate from us that it is hard to see how human incarnation can, in fact, reveal God's essential nature.

There are, then, norms for thinking about God that may be drawn from scripture, but they are not explicitly stated. They are in need of further elaboration and are such as not to yield one doctrine only or to exclude all flexibility of interpretation. 'God as he is' is in some sense always a theological goal, but ironically, it is the detailed specification and elaboration of this aspect of theology that is most dependent on a philosophical context. Luther has developed a strong sense of what God's nature is and how this stands opposed to certain other human conceptions. To do this is perhaps always theology's first task, but, when we examine some of the results of Luther's conception, it becomes clear that Luther himself was able to do this only by adding metaphysical notions that today require careful philosophical scrutiny. To remove theology from this possible critique is to protect artificially its most vulnerable elements, and reevaluation alone perhaps can keep new ideas from becoming dangerous to basic scriptural forms.

D. SIN AND THE DIVINE WILL

When we turn to these topics, we face some of Luther's most crucial theological doctrines. Unfortunately for him (although fortunate for us in our understanding of how philosophy functions in theology), it is also here that we encounter most clearly a mass of philosophical presuppositions.

> 1 For it is not correct to say that God orders men to do evil—no, one must rather say that he deserts him so that he cannot resist the devil, who now goes into action by the command and will of God. We may twist and turn the matter as much as we want, we must assert that it is God's will that a man be overwhelmed by sin; moreover, he wills this by his good pleasure insofar as he lets him be overcome by that which he [God] hates most. . . . (p. 27)

> 2 It does not follow from this that God wills sin . . . even though it is done by his will. (p. 28)

It is hard to remember that this interesting, if perhaps horrifying, picture of God appears in Luther's commentary on Paul's Romans. Even if we discount certain of Paul's philosophical interpretations as being added to the Gospels, it is still difficult to imagine that all of the detail of Luther's view is biblically derived. This concept of 'the desertion of God', for instance, is an interesting one, as is God's command to the devil. Yet, beneath this lies a certain analysis of the human will and also of the relation of good and evil in God's own nature. It may be that it is God's will that man be overwhelmed by sin, but exactly how and why this is done is subject to a variety of interpretations. And most important, where does Luther derive his knowledge of the inner metaphysics of the structure of the divine nature? This background, which is necessary for our understanding, is left vague—perhaps intentionally so—in a simple scriptural account.

When Luther talks about sin and punishment, what kind of concept of God is involved and where does it come from?

1 For he lets it [sin] be done by his will in order that a man be subjected to what he hates most so that this man may know what a terrible judgment hangs over him. (p. 28)

2 . . . God lets sin be done, not for sin's sake, but for the sake of penalty and punishment. (p. 28)

3 For he is not bound not to will that there be sin, although by his nature he necessarily can neither will nor love it, but he can will and love it, not insofar as it is sin, but insofar as it is punishment. (p. 28)

4 God . . . despises sin, to be sure, yet because he cannot bring about shame except in connection with sin, he wills that man commit sin in order that this shame should overwhelm him. If it were at all possible that such ignominy could become a fact without sin, God would bring this about and he would prohibit sin. But this cannot be. (p. 29)

We shall not analyze this position in detail, but pose several questions to highlight our point: How does Luther know that shame can be produced in no other way? But most important, how does he know that God has this view on the necessity of penalty and punishment? From the New Testament alone the picture seems to be more of a forgiving and loving God, although it is also possible that such a God might use Luther's rather extreme means. Yet, in addition to the questionable concept of God involved, what if man also is different in nature? What if man feels no sense of shame over sin, which seems more often to be the case today? What if he does not recognize his actions as sinful just because he does not share Luther's particular view of God? Our beginning point and our basic agreement in these matters seems much less fixed than Luther assumes.

Luther's view of human nature is quite explicit, but is it correct? And is it in any way a divinely revealed doctrine so that no religious man can oppose it, or is it only something obtainable by human construct?

> 1 For every law occasions sin unless, under the influence of Grace, feeling, mind, and will are bent toward the law. For the will always tends to go in the direction opposite to that in which it should go and it would rather do something else if it could, even though it does outwardly what the law commands. (p. 49)

> 2 . . . human nature is inclined toward evil and without strength toward the good.

> And so, unless helped from above, it continues to be held in evil longing contrary to the law, and it is filled with selfish lusts. . . . (p. 57)

Without questioning what sources are Paul's own as Luther discovers them in his study of *Romans,* and without questioning Luther's assumptions, it is clear that this picture of human nature is less charitable than what we might think of as the more tolerant and accepting attitude of Jesus in the Gospels. This severe picture of the human will seems a little far from the facts of human nature, and our natural attraction to the good may be much stronger than Luther allows. Was the intent of revelation to furnish us with an analysis of human nature, whether Luther's or someone else's? Or is it not the case that the range of views open to us is somewhat flexible and that Luther's is not the only one that will fit the Christian revelations of God's action? In fact, again as with his too drastic separation of God from the natural order, Luther's view of human nature actually makes it more difficult to understand why God is represented as having great compassion for man. Man's struggle toward goodness must be stronger and more natural to him than Luther allows.

It is not that scripture cannot be reconciled somehow with Luther's drastic views on human nature. But it is possible that God might have greater sympathy for man's struggle with good and evil. If true, this would fit more naturally with God's self-incarnation. Determinism of a rigid kind is not a very fitting idea for God, since it would seem that his whole intention could be prearranged without the difficulties involved in incarnation. Only a God with greater sympathy for our human attempts to combat evil and our desire for the good would go so far as to share man's lot. In Luther's account, there is nothing much to attract God to human nature and little to be gained by participating in it that could not be gained more easily in another and less complicated way.

However, when we ask Luther questions about why God acts in this way rather than another (which should be theology's theme), we often find an evasion of the theological argument.

> If you ask why this is so, we answer: God wants it so according to his hidden judgment. . . .

> Nobody has the right to define the rule by which God punishes sin and rewards the good. (p. 34)

The problem here is that Luther restricts others from inquiring into God's reasons, and yet he himself seems to have a rather privileged access to God's motives. Or, at least where this is not so, Luther knows precisely the point where questions must be stopped; and to know this in itself takes quite a bit of understanding of God. To prohibit questions and to demand belief and acceptance at a predetermined point is clearly an easy avenue for Luther, and it saves him an embarrassing analysis of the basis for the definiteness of his knowledge of God's reasons. But has God himself established what questions can and cannot be asked of him? What is it that leads us to think that he is not open to human interrogation? Is it the case that God is more receptive to questioning about the basic principles for his actions and beliefs than Luther is in allowing us to test his view of God? Job questioned God and obtained considerable religious understanding; why should Luther refuse to hear our questions, if God does not object but instead created a world that demands our inquiry?

Perhaps our crucial issue is this: "How do you know where to stop reason in a theological argument?" Granted, there should be some limit set to our reasoning about God. Is this fixed by God himself in some final way, or is it discovered more as a result of the particular theory a man holds regarding God?

1 For how could they possibly be evil and do evil if he did not permit it?

2 And he wills it in order that the good may shine all the more brightly in contrast to evil. (p. 30)

3 For how these two statements can be reconciled and by what criterion they are correct, namely that God wants to bind me and all other men to himself and yet gives his grace only to whom he wills to give it, and moreover, that he does not will to give it to all but reserves it for himself to elect some among them—this, I say, we shall see only in the future. Now we can only believe that this is just, because faith is the conviction of things unseen. (pp. 29–30)

It is undoubtedly easier for Luther to stop reason at this point, and it permits him to avoid troublesome questions. But is it not true that the difficulty in reconciling these aspects of God (for example, God loves good; God wills evil) stems more from the particular view of God and man that Luther has adopted than from some necessity in God's nature as revealed in scripture? Both the details of the problems that develop, and the limits set upon reason in order to provide their solution, come from the way in which the argument is structured philosophically (for example, Luther's view on free will). Very little stems from some clear, announced, fixed limit set by God himself and outlined clearly by him. A different view of God, another concept of human nature, good and evil and free will defined in new ways—all these might be reconcilable with the Gospels, and yet they would set different limits on the extent to which reason is permitted to go in seeking solutions. Perhaps today we must go further than Luther's assumptions would allow him to move in questioning God directly about his nature and his actions.

11

HEGEL AND SPIRIT

A. SPIRIT AND RELIGION

A shift from Luther to Hegel will provide us with another radical contrast. Luther wants to restrict all reasoning about God; Hegel is the ultimate rationalist in God's name. Luther tries to exclude philosophical interpretation in the hope of recovering a pure biblical theological doctrine. Hegel transforms all of theology, and even all of the religious life, into a form of philosophy. Luther has a God who by nature is not congenial to human form; Hegel becomes the supreme incarnationalist. God himself would be incomplete, in Hegel's account, without this appearance in nature. Luther makes interpretations of doctrine unknowingly that borrow from philosophical concepts; Hegel rewrites all of philosophy past and present on the basis of his understanding of Christian theological principles that assert God's involvement with and presence in the world.

Even if we shift to consider a theory the opposite from Luther's, as far as the role of philosophy in theology is concerned, our problem is still the same: How do Hegel's philosophical views, as reflected in *The Phenomenology of Mind,** change his solution to religious and theological questions?

1 . . . Religion . . . [is] the consciousness of Absolute Being in general. (p. 685)

2 Spirit knowing its self is in religion primarily and is immediately its own pure self-consciousness. (p. 687)

3 For it is only the whole which properly has reality . . . But the moments of the whole, consciousness, self-consciousness, reason, and spirit, have, because they are moments, no existence separate from one another. (p. 689)

4 . . . religion is the completion of the life of spirit. . . . (p. 690)

5 In the process of these universal moments is contained the development of religion generally. (p. 690)

6 It is actual only as Absolute Spirit. . . . (p. 693)

In a short account, we cannot stop to offer a detailed exposition of Hegel's concepts, which by their nature cannot be treated simply; nonetheless, it is clear how different his approach to religion is from that outlined in Part I of this account. The life of religion is neither independent from philosophy nor built on a different basis; rather, Hegel's theory makes religion a form of the philosophical life. This being the case, philosophy cannot be itself and not have a religious phase, and it would also be impossible to understand religion except through philosophical development. Religion becomes, not the practice of a way of life, but a general consciousness of 'Absolute Being' (no. 1). The self cannot know itself fully except as it develops in religion (no. 2), and both are involved in a process of development that cannot separate one · part from the others (no. 3).

If we make religion into a natural completion to the life of

* G. W. F. Hegel, *The Phenomenology of Mind,* trans. J. B. Bailey (London: George Allen & Unwin, 1949). All page references in this chapter are to this edition.

the spirit (no. 4), this interpretation would seem to have advantages for religion. This is true unless, in fact, this is not the case and unless religion becomes purely a matter of the development of consciousness rather than of practical action. According to Hegel, religion is not a phenomenon of man (not even his response to God), but it is the manifestation of the process of 'Absolute Spirit' (nos. 5 and 6). Again, this view might appear to have advantages, except that, on closer inspection, it tends to identify God himself with the religious actions of men. It neither leaves men free nor treats religious practice as a matter of human responsibility and decision. God's identification with the unfolding of religion would not be so difficult if the total history of religion could give us a less disgraceful reading of God's conduct.

It is easier for theology if God is clearly seen in the processes of natural development. That is, it is unless such processes actually yield an unacceptable view of God. When we cannot accept the historical pattern as a direct expression of the divine, then it is a hindrance to our discovery of God when philosophical processes and religion and God's self-expression all are so closely connected. Art too becomes simply a stage of religion, and language is likewise another way in which God manifests himself.

> 1 The work of art hence requires another element for its existence; God requires another way of going forth than this, in which out of the depths of his creative night, he drops into the opposite, into externality, to the character of a "thing" with no self-consciousness. This higher element is that of language. (p. 716)

> 2 Through the religion of Art spirit has passed from the form of substance into that of Subject; for art brings out its shape and form, and imbues it with the nature of action, or establishes in it the self-consciousness. . . . (p. 750)

Everywhere in nature and in every human construction, God is now to be seen. (Actually, this conclusion is not too unlike Bonaventure, but it is based on a different philosophical theory.) Hegel even speaks of God "requiring" a way, so that it becomes impossible to conceive of God except as these phenomena give him some opportunity for expression. This theory has the virtue of giving to God a certain concreteness, since all of nature, man, and spirit are now taken as his forms. But problems arise too in treating the natural order as so closely divine. In order to do this, one should be quite happy with what he finds in the world—or at least with what he takes to be its ultimate direction.

B. CONSCIOUSNESS AND INCARNATION

Divine incarnation now becomes, not an extraordinary miracle, but a natural direction of consciousness:

> This incarnation in human form of the Divine Being begins with the statue. . . . (p. 750)

Even in art the tendency toward incarnation is uncovered. Christian doctrine is seen everywhere. This is not because Hegel thinks it is this obvious to the unreflective mind, but because he believes philosophical theory will bring to light the essential religious nature which perhaps before was not grasped as being the rule of the secular world too. If we want to see God, our logical avenue is to move through a deeper understanding of the processes of human consciousness. Luther did not see this at all, but Hegel thinks that here God is both found and lost.

> 1 The "unhappy consciousness," the soul of despair, is just the knowledge of this loss. (p. 753)
>
> 2 It is consciousness of the loss of everything of significance in the certainty of itself, and of the loss of even this knowledge or certainty of self—the loss of substance as well as of self, it is the bitter pain which finds expression in the cruel words, "God is dead" [from a hymn of Luther's]. (pp. 752–753)
>
> 3 For actual reality, or self-consciousness, and implied being in the sense of substance are its [consciousness'] two moments; and by the reciprocity of their kenosis, each relinquishing or

"employing" itself of itself and becoming the other, spirit thus comes into existence as their unity. (p. 756)

4 Consciousness . . . does not set out from its own inner life, does not start from thought . . . , rather it sets out from immediate present existence, and recognizes God in it. (p. 758)

We come across God in following and in attempting to understand the necessary processes of consciousness. This is particularly true of the first moment in any loss of significance, for this experience reveals the self not to be a fixed substance but a process. Once this is discovered, the same will be found to be true of God. This "emptying," by which God's incarnation descended, appears now, not as so unusual, but rather as a necessary process. Here is Hegel's message for a godless time: God must be lost first as part of the necessary process of finding him, since this very process of loss reveals his nature. Spirit never simply is. It comes into being as a process of opposites which, followed far enough, become a unity. God is thus found in our immediate present existence, but, in order for this to be true, God's own nature must have a structure not essentially different from the processes discovered to be operative naturally.

Our problem with Hegel is to grasp how 'incarnation' is to be understood. In a sense, Hegel's concept makes divine incarnation easier to understand, since its law is also universal. However, once incarnation becomes a process of nature, this makes it not possible for divine incarnation to be an ultimate source of revelation, since actually it is not the birth of Christ alone that provides revelation. Instead, it is the philosophical grasp of this as a general process of spirit that makes philosophy the source of the basic revelation of which Jesus is only one instance.

This incarnation of the Divine Being, its having essentially and directly the shape of self-consciousness, is the simple context of Absolute Religion. Here the Divine Being is known as Spirit.

> For Spirit is knowledge of self in a state of alienation of self;
> spirit is the Being which is the process of retaining identity
> with itself in its otherness. (p. 758)

When we understand the nature of spirit, Hegel is saying,
then at the same time we discover the general pattern of incarnation. There must be separation and union, going out,
emptying, and the reunification. This now is asserted to be the
law of all things, not just God's special or unique action at one
time and in one place, contrary to all normal expectations. In
Luther we discovered a theologian who slurs over philosophical problems and invokes God to cut off debate at embarrassing points. With Hegel we encounter a philosopher who turns
everything into a general philosophical view to such an extent
that understanding God, as well as the special Christian interpretation of his actions, is only one approach to a metaphysical
power that permeates everything. No wonder we shall find
Kierkegaard rejecting metaphysics in order to preserve some
independence for religion from philosophical control.

When we consider Hegel's view of the person of Jesus, it
quickly becomes clear that a single event cannot have more
significance than the whole process, so that any incarnation for
Hegel is bound to become merely a single illustration rather
than a special locus of significance.

> . . . there arises, therefore, not the notion, but bare externality
> and particularity, merely the historical manner in which spirit
> once upon a time appeared, the soulless recollection of a pre-
> sumably individual historical figure and its past [the life and
> work of the historical Jesus]. (p. 765)

When all theological revelation becomes an example of general
philosophical procedure, then no isolated event can be any
more important than the incarnational principle in general. It
is easier to grasp revelation in the consciousness of a person,
but Jesus does not fully express God any more than any other
individual does, since only the movement of the whole process
could do this.

This leads us to such essentially Hegelian notions as "salvation history"—that is, that God's revealing action is not found in a single event but rather in the whole history of his relation to man. In this case, religion clearly cannot be understood or grasped on its own, nor can scripture itself be a revealing source, since the only true insight is found in a philosophical grasp of a process of which every individual event is a particular illustration. Lest that seem too much like the thesis of this whole essay, let me point out one significant difference: Hegel does not conceive of the possibility of an alternate philosophical view, and it is this insidious fact that makes him so difficult to deal with. When Hegel merges religion and theology into a general philosophical theory, we are left with the result that the philosophical account itself takes on all the sacrosanct qualities of a religion and all the revealed finality of a theology dogmatically proclaimed.

What we proposed in Part I is to give a greater measure of independence to philosophy, religion, and theology without reducing all to a single process, as Hegel advocates. Along with this, we also suggested a greater variety and flexibility for types of philosophical treatment, so that neither theology nor religion is coerced by the apparent necessity to adopt one philosophical perspective or else appear to be wrong. When philosophy is made singular in its process, as Hegel proposes by claiming to have discovered the ultimate truth (revealed in his philosophical dialectic rather than in the particular person of Jesus), then no theology and no part of the religious life can be free from its domination. Hegel apparently has done religion the service of making the whole natural process divine. But, when men cannot see God operating there (as it is difficult to do today), then their reaction is to reject God, because the process of the world is no longer found to be in itself revelatory of divinity.

C. DIVINE VS. HUMAN NATURE

The interpretation Hegel gives to the crucial term 'spirit' has the effect of merging religion as a part of philosophy (which has both good and bad effects), and it makes theology an inevitable consequence of a necessary philosophical dialectic.

One other result of centering thought around the concept of 'spirit' is that divine and human nature are brought very close together.

> 1 Spirit is known as self-consciousness, and to this self-consciousness it is directly revealed, for it is this self-consciousness itself. The divine nature is the same as the human, and it is this unity which is intuitively apprehended. (p. 760)
>
> 2 Here, then, we find as a fact consciousness, or the general form in which Being is aware of Being—the shape which Being adopts—to be identical with its self-consciousness.
>
> . . . and this existence possesses equally directly the significance of pure thought, of Absolute Being. (p. 760)
>
> 3 That the Supreme Being is seen, heard, etc., as an existent self-consciousness—this is, in the very truth, the culmination and consummation of its notion. And through this consummation, the Divine Being is given and exists immediately in its character as Divine Being. (p. 760)

The virtues and the defects of this view are that, if its philosophical premises are accepted, God is necessarily reached. Yet, since God and human nature are so much alike in basic structure, if the interpretation of human nature is ever seriously questioned, God's existence comes under doubt too. Human nature must be agreed to be a preliminary stage to the divine in order for the divine to be reached or to exist.

'Self-consciousness,' of course, becomes the key feature that characterizes both God and man, and it is this that must be analyzed when we want to understand the substance of all things (see quotation no. 1). Because of the immediacy of self-consciousness, the starting point is firm and clear, but whether out of this God and the whole world can be unfolded—this is a matter that can come under question. Whenever it does, religion, God, and theology are all crippled because of their intimate connection as parts of one form of philosophy. If one is aware of his own consciousness but fails to find God united with it intuitively, there is nowhere else to turn to find God, and he is lost. All of 'Being' is now understood on the basis of consciousness (no. 2). Thus, if we take a nonidealistic view of consciousness, the world takes on, not a divine cast as it does for Hegel, but a discouraging cast—if that is our attitude toward consciousness.

If consciousness is accepted as possessing divine qualities, then God becomes a part of philosophy very easily. Yet, because of their close association, when consciousness loses its divine interpretation we do not seem able to look elsewhere for God, and he dies in the sudden death of a romantic view of the self. It seems clear that, for Hegel, either God exists as "self-consciousness" (no. 3) or else not at all. If we are able, in contrast to Hegel, to attribute to God an existence different from that of human consciousness, we would not need to turn this aspect of man into something divine in order to find God. If we follow Hegel, of course, God is as close and as evident as consciousness itself. This offers a handy kind of certainty to theology, but such an advantage is entirely dependent on accepting his particular starting point for philosophy (that is, the self). However, if philosophy changes, all of religion and theology seem disoriented.

If religion and theology were more distinct either from one philosophical view or from all of philosophy as an enterprise, they might not appear as a necessary culmination to philosophy. Furthermore, their very existence as human enterprises would not be so closely bound up with the acceptance or rejection of one philosophical position—a rather precarious situation for so valuable a human activity as religion. Hegel, of course, finds his God and his religious experience in a philosophical culmination.

1 God, then, is here revealed as He is; He actually exists as He is in Himself; He is real as Spirit, God is attainable in pure speculative knowledge alone, and only is in that knowledge, and is merely that knowledge itself, for He is spirit, and this speculative knowledge is the knowledge furnished by revealed religion. That knowledge knows God to be thought, or pure Essence. (p. 761)

2 This joy, the joy of seeing itself in Absolute Being, becomes realized in self-consciousness, and seizes the whole world. (p. 761)

Such a picture has many advantages, and it guarantees religion a positive outcome simply due to the nature of philosophy. However, it is clear that Hegel thinks of this view as the very essence of all philosophy. He can foresee the unification of all strains of philosophy, but he cannot consider a possible rejection of this whole philosophical position and approach. In point of fact, that is what has happened, although this does not deny the vast influence Hegelian dialectic had for a time or even its present enlightening aspects. Nevertheless, its failure to bring all of philosophy onto this basis does place religion in an uncertain position. That is, it does if religion's very life depends on its inclusion in a particular philosophical view.

However, Hegel's theory does more than lead us from the human self to the divine, from philosophy to religion, as a necessary culmination. There is a return motion of the divine, as we have noted before, so that the tendency toward incarnation is natural and not unexpected, once this philosophical dialectic has been grasped.

> But its [that is, Absolute Spirit] truth consists not merely in being the substance or the inherent reality of the religious communion . . . but in becoming concrete actual self, reflecting itself into self, and being *subject*. (p. 764)

Just as we discover God's substance by understanding the human spirit, this view has advantages for religion and theology—as long as that philosophical perspective is accepted. However, just as religion is endangered when the human self is pictured in less exalted ways, so, if we do not find the divine tending naturally toward incarnation in the world, the religious life seems to have no other base for its existence. That is, if one finds the world process going on about him to be a kind of representation or incarnation of divine process, then as every historical event unfolds God becomes very real and near. But, if one decides to see history's events as completely secular and as not reflecting the divine as such at all, this God and his incarnation are then rejected too, since their acceptance depended on a philosophical view that made them a logical and expected consequence.

D. REVELATION AND DIALECTICAL NECESSITY

There certainly is divine revelation for Hegel, but it takes place as a process of dialectical necessity, and our becoming aware of this revelation depends upon understanding that the whole framework of the world is based on this pattern. Almost every religious concept of Christianity thus becomes a philosophical law. Take death and resurrection, for example:

> 1 . . . that element which has for its essence, not independent self-existence, but simple being, is what empties and abandons itself, gives itself unto death, and so reconciles Absolute Being with its own self. (p. 774)

> 2 This death [of immediacy] is therefore its rising anew as spirit. (p. 775)

Recalling our analysis of Luther's thought, simply reading these excerpts ought to be enough to make us smile, since Luther was so sure that the heart of the Christian gospel was "offensive" to philosophers and unreconcilable with their mode of thought. Now we find death to be a divine necessity, and 'emptying' is a process without which God cannot be God. His condescension and emptying into human form is not at all unexpected; it is the philosophical fulfillment of an inner divine (and natural) necessity.

> 1 . . . the divine Being "takes on" human nature. . . . it is not asserted but implied that *per se* this evil existence is *not* something alien to the Divine Nature. Absolute Being would be merely an empty name if in very truth there were any other being external to it. . . . (p. 775)

> 2 The essential Being is then Spirit only when it is reflected into itself. (p. 776)

Here what once was completely unexpected and unpredicted in God's action now becomes a metaphysical law. Theology has shaped all philosophy in one image (its own).

As long as such a metaphysics is accepted, Christianity becomes the most natural and rational culmination of the world's process, and it will appear so to all rational men. But when that metaphysics is questioned, Christianity has become so identified with one particular way of thought that it cannot separate itself from it. 'Resurrection' is not a miracle but a necessity of divine fulfillment (see no. 2). God must become flesh and enter into all the world's processes in order to fulfill himself (see no. 1). Yet, the man who cannot see that God is being revealed in the course of the world's history is left with no ground to see God at all.

This process, the Divine Being emptying itself, dying, and rising anew—all this is what makes God God. Thus, unless this same process is uncovered in the world and taken as nature's metaphysical law, there is no way for God to be realized either for himself or for man.

1 . . . the Divine Being is reconciled with its existence through an event,—the event of God's emptying Himself of His Divine Being through His factual Incarnation and His Death. (p. 780)

2 The process of carrying forward this form of knowledge of itself is the task which spirit accomplishes as actual History. (p. 801)

3 . . . History is the process of becoming in terms of knowledge, a conscious self-mediating process—Spirit externalized and emptied into Time. (p. 801)

The interesting fact about such a view, one that makes incarnation a dialectical necessity, is that now it all comes about, not so much for man's sake as originally proclaimed, but for God's own needs. God requires an incarnation in order to fulfill himself. Such an interpretation of incarnation is fine as long as this underlying metaphysics is also accepted. When it is not, then there appears to be no ground at all upon which to assert a divine incarnation.

The process is, of course, more important than the individual, so that Jesus becomes not ultimately significant as an individual person but merely an illustration and a necessary moment in the divine process. Death, for example, is not a free choice on Jesus' part but rather is forced on him in order to exemplify a dialectical necessity. No individual thing can be 'true' but only the whole process, so that the last place truth could be discovered for Hegel would be in a single, isolated event or person. Jesus as an individual is unimportant; the metaphysical principle is all-important.

> 1 Neither the one nor the other has truth; their truth is just their movement. . . . (p. 77)

> 2 This self-consciousness does not therefore really die, as the particular person [Christ] is pictorially imagined to have really died; its particularity expires in its universality, i.e., in its knowledge which is essentially Being reconciling itself with itself. (p. 781)

> 3 This particular self-consciousness [Christ] has become universal self-consciousness. What dies is merely the outer encasement . . . but also the abstraction of the Divine Being. For the mediator, as long as his death has not yet accomplished the reconciliation, is something one-sided. (p. 781)

What happens in this case is that any earlier revelation cannot be accepted as ultimate, since a single moment cannot be revelatory; only its place in the whole process is. Jesus as a self will not lead to himself but, quite naturally, beyond himself. When Christianity becomes a philosophy, as it has here, religion is nothing different from a philosophical system. Revelation is not surprising but is expected as necessity in order for God to become himself. Such a natural transformation of religion into a set of metaphysical truths gives great security to religion. That is, it does so until that whole philosophical view comes into question, and then religion tumbles and falls with it.

Hegel's account of evil is illustrative of one result of his account of Spirit:

> 1 . . . evil is itself the state of self-concentration. (p. 779)

> 2 . . . the Eternal Being manifests itself as the process of being self-identical in its otherness. (p. 770)

. . . but thought which contains otherness, and is, thus, the self-opposed thought of good and evil. Evil appears as the first actual expression of the self-concentrated consciousness. (p. 771)

3 But these universal powers of good and evil belong all the same to the self, or the self is their actuality. The alienation of the Divine Nature is thus set up on its double-sided form. (p. 773)

Given a doctrine such as outlined above, it is much easier to account for evil, because it becomes a dialectical necessity within the process rather than a result of free decisions and acts. Just as God requires incarnation and death in order to fulfill himself, so evil also reflects a necessity in the divine life. That we have no freedom in this matter is not a particular concern. That is, it is not if you are uninterested in the individual as such but value him only insofar as he is a part of the total process. Neither Jesus nor we have any ultimate choice in the matter. His death and our evil are needed to fulfill the divine process of self-fulfillment. God's needs drive us all.

Evil comes to be interpreted essentially as a separation, and in itself this certainly has a biblical ring about it. Yet, the process of alienation is ultimately a divine process, so that man's separation is not an independent or a free act of his. Instead, it is the reflection of a development within the divine nature. This naturally tends, first, to the opposition of good and evil and, then, toward their reconciliation. The "revelation" that God has overcome evil in Christ, therefore, is now not at all startling. Instead, it is a dialectical necessity, and over this process neither God nor man can exercise any free choice. The philosopher has spoken with necessity, since it seems to be he alone who has real insight into the nature of the divine.

12

KIERKEGAARD AND TRUTH

A. THE SUBJECTIVE PROBLEM

For Hegel, religion became the essence of philosophy, and in that sense Hegel gave philosophy of religion its origin and its meaning. However, in turning to Kierkegaard we discover philosophy of religion in a more simple and contemporary sense. That is, he cuts it loose from its heavy metaphysical moorings and makes it simply a kind of free reflection on matters of religion. As such, he develops, in the process, a mode of philosophy peculiar to this notion of religion's independence. For Soren Kierkegaard, of course, this new way of relating philosophy to religion appears in his contrast between the 'objective problem' and the 'subjective problem.'*

1 The objective problem consists of an inquiry into the truth of Christianity. The subjective problem concerns the relationship of the individual to Christianity. (p. 20)

2 Faith does not result from scientific inquiry; it does not come directly at all. On the contrary, in this objectivity one

* Soren Kierkegaard, *Concluding Unscientific Postscript*, trans. D. F. Swenson and W. Lowrie (Princeton, N.J.: Princeton University Press, 1944). All page references in this chapter are to this edition.

tends to lose that infinite personal interestedness in passion which is the condition of faith. . . .

For if passion is eliminated, faith no longer exists, and certainty and passion do not go together. (p. 30)

3 . . . all decisiveness . . . inheres in Subjectivity. . . . (p. 115)

4 Now if Christianity is essentially something objective, it is necessary for the observer to be objective. But if Christianity is essentially subjective, it is a mistake for the observer to be objective. (p. 51)

5 It is subjectivity that Christianity is concerned with, and it is only in subjectivity that its truth exists, if it exists at all; objectively, Christianity has absolutely no existence. (p. 116)

It is a difficult matter to appraise accurately Kierkegaard's philosophical relationship to Hegel, and it is a task we shall not even try to take up briefly here. At certain points (for example, the concentration on the self), one can recognize a heavy borrowing and dependence on Hegel. Yet it is clear that, beneath this, Kierkegaard is struggling for a new view for the relationship of philosophy to religion and for the function of theology. On this point, it is easy to see that he has established a radically different doctrine. Just as Hegel's philosophical view completely determined his treatment of theological issues (even if the metaphysics was originally religiously inspired, all of which merges religion into philosophy), Kierkegaard's radical view of the relation of philosophy to religion will likewise shape his treatment of theology. Or rather, it indicates why, unlike Hegel, who turned philosophy into a necessary theology, he did not and could not build a theology on this base.

Christianity instead becomes, not a metaphysically necessary scheme, but the opposite of philosophy and thus something that philosophy by its nature thwarts. It is hard to find a more direct opposition than this to Hegel's view of philosophy's natural culmination in religion, and perhaps much of this can be traced to Kierkegaard's rejection of metaphysics. 'Subjectivity' becomes an individual problem and not an exemplification of a universal process (see quotations nos. 1 and 2). Rather than leading to the truth of Christianity, scientific and systematic inquiry will block it precisely because Christianity is a radically different kind of thing. It requires personal, free decisiveness, and this is impossible in any universal consideration. Instead, Christianity comes to mean individual acceptance through passion. It does not exist as an objective metaphysical scheme but only inwardly and subjectively. It is not a universal norm but a personal mode of existence.

Philosophy no longer leads us to Christianity; it prevents it. Of course, it is easy to see that Hegel and Kierkegaard mean quite opposed things by both philosophy and religion. Because they disagree, they relate philosophy and religion in two very different ways.

1 . . . speculative philosophy does not permit the problem to arise at all. (p. 55)

2 But the difference is, that philosophy teaches that the way is to become objective, while Christianity teaches that the way is to become subjective. . . .

. . . the guidance of philosophy in this matter is a misguidance. (p. 117)

3 Faith is the highest passion in the sphere of human subjectivity. (p. 118)

When philosophy is thought to lead to the truth of Christianity as a set of metaphysical principles governing the world, then, since this is religion's problem too, the two enterprises converge. Now, if religion is conceived to be quite different (and here Kierkegaard seems to accept 'philosophy' as defined in its Hegelian form), then it is clear that philosophy is at odds with the needs of religion. Faith refers to nothing in an objective sense; it means only the passion generated between the subjective individual and his appropriation of Christianity.

Of course, whenever Christian assertions are taken as the highest and profoundest example of rational insight into the very structure of 'being,' then Christianity can be assimilated rationally. In fact, it becomes reason's supreme insight. However, as we shall see, Kierkegaard reverses Hegel at this point and thinks of Christian doctrine, not as the rational substructure of the world's day-to-day process, but as something reason cannot assimilate. The results of these changes are dramatic for the way in which philosophy relates to theology.

B. INDIRECT COMMUNICATION

Hegel may speak in complicated ways which must be grasped in their total connection or not at all, but certainly he speaks directly and sets no barrier to any reader's rational assimilation of the truth as he presents it. This is so because what is expounded metaphysically is taken to be the highest example of rational insight. Thus for its assimilation, it simply requires raising the hearer to its own mode of apprehension. In opposition to this, Kierkegaard stresses indirect communication, and this is only necessary if one holds a quite different view of the nature of what is to be communicated. Partly this goes back to Hegel's stress on necessity; Kierkegaard, however, is the champion of individual freedom.

Whatever is necessary can surely be communicated directly, since all that is required is to bring the other person to recognize its necessity as truth. If the preservation of freedom is your aim, however, you must use every means available to guard against a coercion that can only be distorting.

1 . . . the secret of all communication consists precisely in emancipating the recipient and for that reason he must not communicate himself directly. (p. 64)

2 . . . a direct mode of communication is an attempt to defraud God. (p. 69)

3 The inwardness of the understanding would consist precisely in each individual coming to understand it by himself. (p. 71)

4 . . . the entire essential content of subjective thought is essentially secret, because it cannot be directly communicated. (p. 73)

These changes in basic philosophical perspective are certainly all important to theology. Both theology and religion will receive quite different roles if we agree to Kierkegaard's philosophical stress on freedom and individuality.

Leaving the consequences for the religious life aside for the moment (and he sparked quite a revival here), what is particularly interesting to note are the negative consequences this view has for theology. That is, if Kierkegaard's stress on the necessity of indirect communication is accepted, not only is theology changed as an enterprise, but also it actually can be misleading. Quite consistently, Kierkegaard develops no theology. To construct theology is to stress an attempt at rational, objectively appropriate answers to religious questions, and, given the way in which Kierkegaard has set up religion, this would be to distort it.

1 . . . Christianity is the very opposite of speculation. (p. 243)

2 . . . it would first be necessary to give my exposition an *indirect* form. (p. 216)

3 The immediate relationship to God is paganism. (p. 218)

4 A direct mode of communication would not have permitted it [faith], since such a method is relevant only to a recipient of knowledge, not essentially to an existing individual. Existence in what has been understood cannot be directly communicated to any existing spirit, not even by God, much less to a human being. (p. 244)

Certainly, theology requires a degree of speculation, and, on Kierkegaard's terms, this makes it opposed to religion. Hegel found God immediately in consciousness, but Kierkegaard calls this paganism. In order to make religious faith possible, the freedom of the individual must be preserved, since religious experience depends not on a rational necessity of 'being' but on a free individual act. How Kierkegaard knows that God cannot communicate directly (no. 4), however, raises the question of just how far he really has gotten away from theology and from speculation. God is important to him, but how are we to form a concept of his nature?

C. HOW PHILOSOPHY BLOCKS THEOLOGY

While Hegel's view of philosophy turned all of religion and theology into a form of philosophy, Kierkegaard's analysis actually makes theology impossible. Philosophy and theology become opposed as enterprises. In fact, just because philosophy blocks theology, it tends to become philosophy of religion in the nonmetaphysical sense. That is, philosophy is a commentary on the individual's problems with religion, and no basis is left on which to build any kind of systematic theology. However, if between philosophy and religion there is a "third thing" (as has been suggested in Part I, that is, technical theology), the actual result is that the opposition need not be so sharp between what philosophy is and what religion attempts to do. Kierkegaard raises dramatically the problem of what philosophy of religion is. Is it the form philosophy should take in relation to religious questions, or is a more systematic approach toward the development of philosophical theology also possible?

At first, philosophy seemed to be antithetical to the interests of religion, but that was only in its old speculative form. Now Kierkegaard reinterprets philosophy to fit more into his analysis of the religious situation, just as Hegel reshaped religion along the lines of his metaphysics:

> Only by closely attending to myself, can I arrive at an understanding of how an historical personality must have conducted himself while he lived. But I cannot, by apprehending him as dead, learn from him what it means to live, that I must experience for myself. (p. 131)

What is particularly interesting to note is that Kierkegaard refers all understanding to the self just as Hegel does, except that he has a different notion of the self, which thus yields a different idea of the function of Jesus. Hegel stressed process, but he also stressed its final realization. Kierkegaard is not totally devoid of metaphysical assumptions, particularly when

he insists on the priority of 'becoming' and its use as an interpretive device.

> 1 . . . everything must be understood in terms of becoming;
> for the empirical object is unfinished and the existing cognitive
> spirit is itself in process of becoming. Thus the truth becomes
> an approximation whose beginning cannot be posited ab-
> solutely, precisely because the conclusion is lacking. . . . (p.
> 169)

> 2 If an existing individual were really able to transcend him-
> self, the truth would be for him something final and complete.

> It is only momentarily that the particular individual is able to
> realize existentially a unity of the infinite and the finite which
> transcends existence. This unity is realized in the moment of
> passion. (p. 176)

Because the individual is as Kierkegaard sees him—that is,
unable to transcend his subjectivity—truth becomes what it is.
Thus, if a different analysis of the individual were given, it
might turn out either that truth is not so momentary or that
religion is not necessarily built on paradox.

> 1 But the eternal essential truth is by no means itself a
> paradox; but it becomes paradoxical by virtue of its relation-
> ship to an existing individual. (p. 183)

> 2 Subjectivity culminates in passion, Christianity is the par-
> adox, paradox and passion are mutually fit, and the paradox
> is altogether suited to one whose situation is, to be in the ex-
> tremity of existence. (p. 206)

To watch Kierkegaard base religion on paradox, and then relate
it to truth and passion in this way, is particularly instructive
when we realize that he takes the prime example of paradox in
Christianity to be the doctrine of the incarnation of God in
human form. This is exactly what Hegel's metaphysics made
him see as the culmination of all rational necessity and natural
tendencies. With a change in metaphysics, the whole character

of religion changes. What once was a natural event according to one theory now becomes impossible for another to accept.

If we want to understand how a change in philosophy shapes theology differently, little could be more illuminating than the contrast between Kierkegaard's 'absurd' and Hegel's view of divine incarnation as a rational necessity. For if we accept Kierkegaard, not only is the construction of systematic theology no longer possible but to do this is actually to work against religion.

> An explanation of the paradox makes it clear what the paradox is, by removing any obscurity remaining.

> . . . does the explanation also take existence away from the existing individual?

> To explain the paradox would then mean to understand more and more profoundly what paradox is, and that the paradox is a paradox. (p. 196)

For Kierkegaard the incarnation of God is the source of paradox; for Hegel it is the culmination of logical necessity and the very completion of reason.

Considering such a dramatic opposition, it becomes quite clear that a very different set of meanings assigned to central terms is operating in the two cases. Without attempting to deny either one, or to reconcile them or to form some third view, it is clear that these key concepts are subject to a variety of analyses and that neither extreme position is in any way a necessity. Variations and modifications will tend to produce different doctrines, and each will alter the interpretation of religion in the process.

> The fact that the truth becomes a paradox is rooted precisely in its having a relationship to an existing subject. (p. 177)

It is clear that, were it not for the particular interpretation Kierkegaard gives to the existing individual, the resulting paradox would not be so extreme. Change the view of existence and then paradox changes—since paradox is not in truth itself but in a relationship.

Nevertheless, at this point it begins to become clear that Kierkegaard has more of a theology than his stress on individual existence would seem to allow him to admit. We have to ask what theology he appears to accept and what kind of metaphysics we detect as operating, even if we grant his view that these block religion rather than support it.

1 If I am capable of grasping God subjectively, I do not believe, but precisely because I cannot do this I must believe. (p. 182)

2 This conformity [of thought with Being] is actually realized for God, but it is not realized for any existing spirit, who is himself existentially in the process of becoming.

For an existing spirit *qua* existing spirit, the question of truth will again exist. (p. 170)

3 Existence here separates thought from being, and breaks up their ideal unity.

Existence is always something particular, the abstract does not exist. (p. 294)

4 . . . there is something which cannot be thought, namely existence. (p. 274)

5 All knowledge about reality is possibility. (p. 280)

What we must ask is this: in spite of all of his objections in the name of religion, what metaphysics does Kierkegaard hold and use, even if we still grant that it is different enough from Hegel's to make each come out at a different place? Although —and perhaps rightly—he has not argued to it directly, it becomes clear, as evidenced in the last quotations, that Kierkegaard has been developing a view of the world and its structure which is his own and against which his views on religion are formed.

From quotation no. 1 it is easy to see that he takes God to be such that he cannot be grasped subjectively. Why? This situation, of course, results from the way in which Kierkegaard has defined subjective existence and also from how he conceives of God. Interestingly enough, on the one hand he has been rather explicit in working out his definition of subjective existence, but on the other, we are left to infer that God has a status as an object, and thus is incompatible with existence. Certainly, if God's mode of existence were conceived differently, this sharp opposition could disappear. 'Becoming,' it is clear in quotation no. 2, prevents thought from achieving a conformity with 'being.' Of course, if 'being' were differently conceived (for example, using 'becoming' as a basis), a greater conformity might be possible.

Kierkegaard's strong oppositions stem from a fresh interpretation of certain concepts (for example, 'existence'). At the same time, he does not alter his interpretation of others (for example, 'God' and 'being'). Of course, his antisystematic and antimetaphysical tendencies prevent him from carrying out this complete revision, but it does seem sure that he has metaphysical and theological views nevertheless and that they play an important part in shaping his radical interpretation of religion.

Judging from no. 3, we understand what 'existence' involves, but why is it that this cannot be thought (no. 4)? In a certain sense, of course, it obviously can be. Namely, it has been "thought" by Kierkegaard in writing down this sentence and by his reader in reading it. Yet behind his assertion stands a conception of 'thought' that puts it at odds with 'existence.' Could 'thought' be reshaped to make it fit our understanding of 'existence' more easily? At this point, Kierkegaard's stress on 'possibility' (no. 5) becomes important; for, if thought demands necessity and if existence is built on possibility, they are incompatible. But what prevents us from reshaping our concept of thought in order to ground it more on possibility and thus to bring it more into accord with existence?

D. THE IRRATIONALITY OF SUFFERING

Even a brief exploration of Kierkegaard's metaphysics makes clear what changes could be made in it that might lessen its perhaps unnecessary tensions. Although these alterations cannot be completed here, in order to give an example, we might focus on the important concept of 'suffering.' For Hegel, such a condition is a logical necessity in God's process of fulfillment. For Kierkegaard, it becomes the epitome of ir-rationality. Why such a radical change in viewpoint? The answer is that Kierkegaard does not have Hegel's metaphysics to support his understanding; therefore, suffering becomes un-understandable.

> . . . suffering is posited as something decisive for a religious existence, and precisely as the characteristic of the religious inwardness: the more the suffering, the more the religious ex-istence—and the suffering persists. (p. 256)

What we sense in this quotation is a reaction against Hegel, because he made God's suffering too natural, rational, and necessary. Nevertheless, it also seems clear that Kierkegaard is operating with an implicit concept of God and that his God is just as important and just as much subject to question as Hegel's.

> The paradox consists principally in the fact that God, the Eternal, came into existence in time as a particular man.
>
> The paradox is that Christ came into the world *in order* to suffer. (p. 529)

The picture of Kierkegaard's God begins to emerge here, par-ticularly in his use of the attribute the 'eternal.' If God were conceived differently in relation to this attribute, the principal reason paradox results might be lessened. In order to have any idea of the consequences of suffering, we must understand the beings involved. We need, then, to understand Kierkegaard's doctrine of God and his Christology before we can appraise the way in which suffering affects religious faith.

On the matter of faith, Kierkegaard is quite explicit:

> Faith is the objective uncertainty due to the repulsion of the absurd held fast in the passion of inwardness. . . .
>
> Faith *must not rest content* with intelligibility. (p. 540)

It is easy to see that "repulsion" depends upon the way in which the factors involved are related. Suffering may or may not repel reason, and unintelligibility may or may not be ultimate. This depends on the way in which the principal concepts are defined. In some real sense, then, the basic paradox in Kierkegaard's thought can be said to be that he accepts one picture of what God's nature is like without arguing for it, and much of the radical conclusion of his thought rests on this unexamined assumption of God's classically fixed nature.

> God does not think, He creates, God does not exist, He is eternal. Man thinks and exists, and existence separates thought and being, holding them apart from one another in succession. (p. 296)

From this, it is perfectly clear that Kierkegaard has an explicit concept of God's nature. The issue: Is it correct? Kierkegaard makes God 'unthinking' and, thus, he is not amenable to thought. However, thought can mean many things, and is it so clear that we must remove all thought from God? That assumption requires our most careful examination. Next, Kierkegaard removes existence from God and attributes 'eternity' to him. Granted that God might not come into and go out of existence as men do, is it possible that he might also 'exist' even on his own terms? If he did, thought and being would not need to be so separate, as Kierkegaard makes them out to be, and in this case man and God might not be held to be so far apart either.

Whether suffering is 'irrational' depends entirely on how reason is conceived. Kierkegaard does not want to follow Hegel in making suffering a natural necessity, but, if reason were differently conceived, at least suffering need not be taken as irrational. Whether it is a paradox that God should suffer depends upon what God is thought to be like, even if he is not required to suffer as Hegel's God is. Kierkegaard's views on philosophy and religion have prevented him from moving to construct a theology directly. Unfortunately, that is not the same thing as to say either that he does not have a clear conception of the divine nature or that this does not shape his thinking decisively.

In Part II, we have considered six individuals in relation to six important concepts. Our aim has been to observe how each author's view of philosophy has shaped his thinking about theological doctrine. Little could be more important than Kierkegaard's definition of truth. Its subjective and paradoxical quality has the effect of shutting off the construction of formal theology, just as Hegel's philosophy of the Spirit made technical theology an unavoidable necessity. Still, it is clear that Kierkegaard has important theological views without which many of the oppositions that he sets up as crucial would not exist.

Thus, in order to question his theology, we must begin with his understanding of 'truth.' Although this is not his procedure, by moving in this direction we still might reshape theology in a new mold to conform to this philosophical suggestion, instead of leaving them, as Kierkegaard does, in an irreconcilable opposition. A new concept of theology and a new hold on God derived from a new philosophical understanding— that should be our aim. Proceeding in this way, we might even develop a theology from Kierkegaard's understanding of human existence and religious suffering. As 'experience' and our metaphysical interpretation of it change, God's nature shifts and moves either nearer or farther away from man.

III

SOME PROBLEMS FACING US

We have come to the hardest part of our examination of how philosophy shapes theology. For in these chapters, we must take up the major problems facing us in philosophy of religion and attempt to offer a solution—or at least provide some clarity about the issues involved. To do this, however, is not quite as difficult a task as it might seem. For, if philosophy does shape theology according to the theory used, and if the way in which we worked out the relationship between philosophy, religion, and theology in Part I was satisfactory, we now should have a clear context for the application of philosophy to the religious questions considered in Part III. One unchangeable answer to each topic will not automatically result from the application of the view of philosophy we have developed, but it will give us a context within which to structure each question. According to our account, that is more than half of the battle.

The analysis undertaken in Part II forms a prelude to this systematic construction. In order to be conscious of the effects of philosophy on theology, it is necessary first to work comparatively and to understand how classical theologians reached a variety of conclusions in structuring their doctrines.

Otherwise, we could remain insensitive to the philosophical principles already in operation even before the theological question is first posed. This type of analysis of Origen or Kierkegaard is comparatively easy, since we can now look back to their systematic struggles with a detached attitude. Of course, to engage in only a comparative historical analysis is to cheat in a very serious game. The problems in philosophy of religion cannot be solved easily by reading theories in books. However, to plunge into the midst of a constructive effort surrounded by the confusions of the day is to risk losing perspective.

The twelve issues taken up in Part III do not exhaust religion's important philosophical questions, but they do represent a cluster of concepts continually considered to be central to, if not determinative of, theological construction. In each case I shall state first what the issue is and why it is "a problem." Then I shall apply, not every possible philosophical view, but at least one theory which, I suggest, will shed contemporary light on the question. Sometimes the contrast with another philosophical view will provide the direction needed to construct a solution. The aim is not to provide a tight and neatly integrated set of answers, but to suggest fruitful ways in which to form an answer to these questions in the light of the philosophical aids available to us.

Easier and more contemporary examples could have been used in place of the classical theories analyzed in Part II. In other words, the present day also provides a full range of theologies which are shaped by philosophy. On the whole, contemporary theologians offer less subtle use of philosophy than do the classical authors treated in Part II. This is some of the reason why they are called "classical." That is, their theological conclusions are not blindly derived from some philosophical principle assumed unreflectively. Instead, each of the six authors examined is himself a critical philosopher, and thus he seems to proceed in full consciousness of the implications and the results that follow from the use of certain philosophical concepts and principles. The less subtle the use of philosophy, the greater the danger of distorting the critical and constructive power of philosophy and blinding us to its usefulness in theology.

Philosophy can, then, be an ally in creating solutions to religious questions and not just a blind tyrant that transforms religion to mirror its own views. Each of the authors considered in Part II needed philosophy to formulate his doctrine and to deal with problems that otherwise might have proven insoluble. An example of a challengeable use of philosophy is provided by a contemporary theologian whose analysis rests on the dogmatic application of a philosophical principle—a simple empiricism.[1] The author's position is not argued to or defended, but simply imposed as if it had no alternatives, and with predictable results: no God, no area for the sacred, and a stress on the secular. Who can—or dare—insist that one form of empiricism is the only possible philosophical view or that its truth is obvious?[2]

In order to protect ourselves from this sort of uncritical use of one philosophy, we must become philosophers before we allow ourselves the luxury of attempting to be theologians. Not to do so is dangerous. This section will treat a series of important concepts and attempt to determine how various philosophical assumptions either open as possible—or else shut off—certain possible interpretations. At least one philosophical interpretation will be suggested for each concept. To do this is to provide a core for more detailed theological construction, and this is philosophy's task.

What we want to show is how the philosophical context shapes the theological answer, but perhaps this can be understood most clearly by realizing that bits of philosophy are constantly incorporated into the pages of sacred literature. The reference material used in this section will frequently be from the New Testament, but a reading of either Old or New Testament will quickly reveal how their authors continually used philosophical theories then current. To say this is not to assert

[1] Paul Van Buren, *The Secular Meaning of the Gospel* (New York: Macmillan, 1963).

[2] Van Buren himself evidences the lack of necessity in the principles used in his early critique. Note the shift in position in his later work, *Theological Explorations* (New York: Macmillan, 1968). He does not seem to be the master of the philosophical principles he employs, but their obedient servant.

that the biblical documents are actually nothing but various philosophies pieced together. As a matter of fact, it is our intention to point out almost the opposite. Biblical writers vary in the extent of their use of philosophical doctrine, but in every case they employ these concepts to point up, in contemporary idiom, the ideas they want to convey.

The New Testament writers often refer to Jesus' 'ascension' into heaven. Some may label this a use of mythology, but that is a wrong way to phrase the issue, since it is clear that the author does not intend to assert something untrue. Rather, it is a symbolic way of stating very clearly a fact the author believes to be true; he wants the reader to share not a mythical outlook, but this factual belief. What the biblical writers accept as the true bases of their religion is, basically, clear enough. The philosophical concepts they use from time to time do not shape the message in any essential way. The biblical writer's intent is clearly nonphilosophical; he employs philosophy in pieces and usually in an illustrative manner.

How and exactly where authority is to be established in matters of religion is perhaps the crucial question, and in this respect it is important to understand what certain philosophical theories will and will not allow.

Our primary question, then, is whether there is a philosophical framework that allows Jesus' words and actions to be taken as evidence for his right to speak with divine authority—for example, to forgive sins as only God has the right to do. This, of course, raises the more basic problem of what philosophical theories allow all authority to reside in God (see Chapter 1, Section B), and then the even more difficult question of whether there is a philosophical framework that allows any man to represent or exercise that authority in God's name. This analysis requires the development of a theory of Jesus' relationship to God—that is, a Christology. However it is accomplished, the prior issue still concerns the philosophical framework that might allow such a claim to be accepted, whatever the specific detail of the formula.

The answer given to the question of 'authority' will be shaped at least partially by the kind of philosophical context used. Our situation in this regard might be different if God's authority could clearly be seen by all, or if those who claimed to represent him could ever be identified with him fully. If religion were completely self-evident, a particular philosophical doctrine might not be so important. But the evaluation of any claim to divine authority is itself at the very heart of the religious issue; it is this division that defines both the believer and the nonbeliever.

How does the admission of this different role for philosophy, as subservient to a religious gospel, affect our thesis of the way in which philosophy shapes theology? The answer hinges on the distinction between preaching or proclaiming a gospel and developing a theology. When proclamation and conversion are the goal, then philosophical terms are simply used; they are bent and molded as subservient to the message. Of course, this cannot always be done without either introducing distortion or decreasing effectiveness, but this is a concern best left to missionaries, preachers, and the writers of devotional literature. Where theology is at issue, the role of philosophy is different, and we have tried to point out the essential distinction between promoting the religious life and developing a theology. Such a narrow dividing line, of course, is not a hard and fast one, and in the biblical documents it is clear that a difficulty encountered often forces the development of a more technical theology. Then, as in some of Paul's letters or in the Fourth Gospel, we see philosophy taking on another role. It is no longer occasionally used to convey a message; its concepts begin to be important in working out a particular theological solution to religious issues.

To examine the various kinds and degree of the uses of philosophy in biblical literature is the opposite of our task in Part III. The construction of those documents is over and done, although we are still trying to understand their origins and intent in better ways. Our present needs are quite different. In this day we often do not seem to have any religious message worth such a strong proclamation. If this is the case, theology is our need. Then, in its defining light, one might be able to discern what he does and does not believe about Christianity's assertion. In providing a resolution to some of the difficulties facing us, philosophy perhaps has the key role to play in making a religious solution possible once again.

13

AUTHORITY

A. THE DEMOCRATIC REBELLION

Since the advent of the modern age, many have asked whether it is possible to accept authority in religion in any form. Thus, for contemporary man, 'authority' is perhaps the central question that he must answer before he can find a new religious solution. It may be true that the problems of reaching religious belief are perennial. Even so, it is also true that the context for their consideration is set by the prevailing social and intellectual climate. And it is also true that from age to age certain issues become more pressing while others seem less difficult. This is particularly true of the issue of religious 'authority'. Although it has always been a problem, it probably was not the pressing and primary issue it is today.

Whatever else has not changed, it is clear that the concept of authority has been drastically altered since New Testament times. Of course, religious problems are distinct from political ones. But—obviously—our continuing social revolution shapes (and is shaped by) the meaning of 'authority', which defines the context in which the religious issue is to be considered. Religion always requires the willingness to submit to an authority higher than the individual (though what form this should take is itself an item of debate). When submission to a king or the obedience of a slave to his master were accepted political forms, accepting religious authority did not seem to be so difficult by comparison. After an almost universal "democratic rebellion," the definition of religious authority has become a major obstacle in almost every religious life.

Although there are many theories concerning the locus of authority in a democratic structure, ultimately the individual member of the democratic group is the source of all political authority. The form may be that of a constitutional monarchy or a representative government or a committee of the whole. In any case, the authority rises from the people and is vested in the governing body. Authority flows from the individual upward, not from some authoritative figure at the top downward. Whatever theological difficulties this may involve, Christianity is compatible with such a political theory. In fact, the notion of 'freedom' is one central Christian concept that supports democratic forms (Chapter 2). However, God's relationship to man is not democratic. He does not stand as one among equals, and the issue of divine authority is a matter that induces a crisis for modern democratic man. It poses a more serious problem today for religious belief than it ever could have in nondemocratic times.

Large numbers of men actually think that continued belief in God works against the establishment of democratic principles, and this is why many leaders of democratic revolutions have been ardent humanists, or even have tended to become militant atheists. Not that democratic revolutions have always been coordinated with religious revolts, even though some have argued that they should be. Yet often, after the achievement of political democracy, the acceptance of divine authority either becomes much more difficult or is rejected as incompatible with individual freedom. Saint Paul accepted the Roman emperor's authority and so, at least politically, it seemed natural for him to recognize Christ's authority. Now, when political authority resides in the individual, can the believer still accept religious authority as being from God alone, and how can he bring himself to submit to it?

If we live in an era of violent self-assertion and of intense concentration on the individual, how does this define the problem of religious authority today? The first thing to note here is that self-assertiveness has always been a problem—personally, socially, politically, and religiously. Every person, and particularly the young, tests his power against the persons and institutions around him. He learns about himself and defines his individuality when their reaction to his self-assertion either expands his personal powers or limits and defines them. When it comes to the ancient struggle of man against God, the problem is compounded because God is not a concrete and well-known object and he does not always respond directly to man's assertiveness. If God is silent or is not clearly defined today, it is hard to have a stable background against which to test and define man's religious self-assertion.

In a monarchical and aristocratic society, it was much easier to discover and understand one's place. Today, we are often mired with confusion and self-doubt precisely because our extreme democratic tendencies preclude our recognizing or establishing a higher source of authority to which we willingly submit and thus find our place in a definite order. At its extremes, political democracy makes us unwilling to recognize any divine authority at all. Or, if we can accept the concept of submission to a higher authority in the religious sphere while rejecting it politically and socially, we still face a God who is less concrete than a ruler or a society, and we no longer have a parallel situation in our social experience to teach us how to act in the face of religious authority. Submission now goes against every social instinct and this compounds the religious problem.

In modern times, it would seem, the problem of authority cannot be treated separately from the problem of freedom. We will take up that problem next, but, for the moment, let us at least set out the background of the problem. If this can be done for 'authority', perhaps the solution to the question of 'freedom' will be easier. In political and social theory, freedom is perhaps the fundamental concept, but it is indicative of the unique nature of religious questions that the issue of authority is prior. Thus, freedom, as Christianity understands it, can only be defined as 'authority' is accepted or rejected. If this is religiously the proper order of procedure, it will be so by virtue of God's peculiar status, but that is an issue to be considered only after we know how we shall deal with 'freedom' and 'authority'. At the moment, what we must ask is "If we deny that ultimate authority resides in anyone but the individual, has one of the prime questions of religion been decided for us at the outset?"

Religiously, the question is something like this: "If politically we place the ultimate locus of authority in the individual, can we still grant God ultimate authority in all things religious?" It does not require much insight to see that part of the answer to this question will rest upon how God's nature is conceived, and it ought to be easy to recognize that the specific form the answer will take depends upon the mutual relation of several key concepts. However, every concept cannot be considered and defined at once, and some take on more central importance than others. Let us, therefore, try a provisional solution to the central question of authority, and see how this may affect the treatment of other concepts later.

In order to answer these questions, something emerges that is very much like the concept of the separation of church and state. If these two realms are not divided sharply, the assertion of unrestrained individual political and social autonomy will simply be carried over to challenge all authority in religion, accept what each individual approves for himself. As long as kings were accepted as possessing divine right, religion could link itself to secular government and not feel its own authority challenged. When authoritarian government disappears in the face of an almost universal desire for self-determination and democratic rights, then religious authority must either dissociate itself from all support of temporal power or face a challenge to its own locus of authority. Today, if God is still linked to kingship, we are likely to lose both.

What kind of theory might still allow men to acknowledge the authority of God—even if we no longer grant such superiority to kings? With this question we encounter one of the clearest instances of how the philosophical context we accept will shape our theological answer, or at least limit our alternatives. That is, the political and social theory we adopt, as well as our theory of human personality, must be such that it does not necessarily reduce *all* authority to a common base. Our political basis must not demand a common source for all authority; if it does, we can predict the religious outcome in advance. In order to make sense of the concept of divine authority in the religious sphere, we need a philosophical view that will admit an ultimate plurality to all theory and not dictate the unified reduction of all authority to one basis.

On closer inspection, it becomes clear that the general philosophical theory adopted will also have important consequences for authority. A royal family, its wealth and its power, are easily displayed, but it is hard to make God's authority evident. A strict empiricism, then, has difficulty in accepting the force of any unseen power. A philosophical basis is required that can grant reality and being to objects other than those physically evident. Otherwise, religious authority will be denied a solid base simply because of the metaphysical criterion for determining the modes of being and their degrees of reality. In the face of widespread democratic rebellion, God need not fall along with dictators and kings. That is, he need not be deposed if reality and power can be granted to unseen objects. A failure in metaphysics challenges divine authority today almost more than any political or social revolution.

Our problem in making this distinction between political and religious authority is to enable us to go through this transition without the loss of God. That is, in its origins religion usually was either connected with or dependent upon the authority of a ruling power which did not stem from the people. As we shall attempt to explain below, somewhat uniquely, this may not be the case with Christianity, at least in its origin. If the concept of God that comes to be real (in the way that it did for the tribes of Israel) is connected to military power and kingly authority, then either God is lost or the concept must be radically revised when this civil connection is broken. However, if God is no longer connected with either the right of political governments or with the superior social status of any group (including the priestly class) or with military power, then the concepts both of 'authority' and of 'God' will need to be radically reconceived in this new light.

B. GOD AS THE SOLE SOURCE

Whether the basis for authority we establish is plural or singular, one thing is clear in both the Old and the New Testament: God himself is *the* authority and the only source for all other claims to religious authority. Although God appears less directly in the New Testament, still throughout the biblical literature there is a constant claim to have received divine authority, either by election or calling or consecration. This is not the place for a full analysis of all of the roles which claim to manifest divine authority (for example, prophet, priest, or disciple), but the basic fact is clear that either that person is accepted as sent by God or he lacks authority. The debate rages around trying to establish the legitimacy of any claim to a delegated divine power, but the point is that all recognize God as the only ultimate seat of religious authority.

The connection of authority with another concept, revelation (see Chapter 16), now becomes clear. All revelation is either a disclosure of divine authority or a recognition of the granting of authority to another (for example, to Jesus). It is no wonder that if modern man has trouble finding a basis for accepting religious authority the concept of revelation loses all meaning. It is perfectly clear that still another crucial concept is involved here—'sin' (see Chapter 20). No action receives the strong label "sin" unless it is first recognized that divine authority requires certain actions and attitudes. If a great deal of the structure of religion can be seen to revolve around the ability to vest authority in God, it is no wonder that when the locus of authority becomes unclear, the whole structure of religion is also in doubt.

May God elect a man for a certain service? He may, if we grant God ultimate authority; he may not, if we think that all authority is human in its origin. May God send someone in his name—for example, a prophet? He may, if we can look behind the person and see that his injunctions stem from a divine authority conferred on him. May God reveal himself and his purposes? He may, if the revelatory act is taken as a sign of his authority—for example, a miracle. But he cannot do this if no act is acceptable as representing divine authority—for example, if miracles are ruled out. May God place the burden of a mission upon men—for example, preaching the Gospel? He may, if he has authority that he can transfer to men, and if the designation for such a mission is also accepted as a promise of support by divine authority. But if man believes that he, man, has full power and capacity to perform any mission, authority is denied to God. According to the original biblical view, man could not hope for success without first receiving a delegation of authority.

We encounter still another important Christian concept that depends on the status of authority: the function of Christ as mediator (see Chapter 17). It is perfectly clear that the issue of accepting or rejecting Jesus rests on his claim to possess divine power. It is also clear that the reason for his crucifixion was the blasphemy, to Jewish ears, of his claim of possessing full divine authority, which previously was reserved for God alone. It is also equally clear that the formation of Christianity rests on the acceptance of Christ's full divine authority (however it is expressed in formula) such that he has the power to set aside any previous divine command—for example, Mosaic law. These codes had been given to the Jews by God himself to be kept faithfully as a sign of acceptance of his sole authority. Removing them is either an action by God himself or a rejection of God by man.

It ought to be evident at this point that the acceptance of the account of the resurrection of Jesus also depends upon our decision regarding the issue of divine authority. The notion of 'resurrection' is bound to be misunderstood if placed in any other context or if the issue of the locus of authority is decided in certain negative ways without an open debate. The reported resurrection of one man is not sufficiently important to found a new religion on just that. And yet, as has always been claimed, it is central to the Christian faith and necessary to its continuance. Why? Because, in the issue over Jesus' power to represent God and to break the Mosaic law which had been instituted by God himself, his crucifixion is taken as the conclusive evidence that he lacked this ultimate authority and thus must fail in his challenge. Placed over against Jesus' death, his resurrection is the reversal of this negative judgment. It is the sign of Jesus' possession of divine authority and, therefore, of his ability to triumph over his enemies and to reveal God to the people by his life and work and teaching.

Those who carry Christianity forward from that point on do so because they accept this sign. Thus, they acknowledge his right to transmit authority to them in his great commission to minister to the needs of less fortunate people, just as he did this in God's name. They thence spread the Good News of God's new promise (or new covenant) revealed authoritatively in Jesus of Nazareth. *To be a Christian means to share in and to carry on this authoritative mission.* Thus, if no ground can be found for granting authority to God—that is, at least religiously if no longer politically—there really is no such thing as Christianity to carry forward. That particular religion came to be defined as the acceptance of a call to a certain life and work as authoritative. Unless the concept of religious authority can first be reestablished, there is little hope that anyone today can feel the force of Christianity as its first adherents did.

Often, this question degenerates into the issue of the specific powers of certain elected officials within the church—for example, pope, bishop, priest. Here again it is evident that the interpretation of another important concept (community or church; see Chapter 15) depends upon how authority is conceived and established. That is, no body or its officials can act authoritatively until it is agreed that God both possesses and can disburse ultimate authority. Yet, it is this locus of all power in God that seems to have the least contemporary reality and that modern man is most likely to challenge in the name of a democratic rebellion and individuality. Nevertheless, the concern evident in the New Testament over the authority of certain elders, apostles, deacons, and others must not be confused with God's primary interest. In the Gospels, men are already trying to establish favored positions for themselves (for example, to sit on Jesus' right hand), but this is a simple human striving for authority. Such struggles misplace the question, since the chief issue is, not how men will fight to divide the power, but whether, in the first place, God possesses such authority that he is able to delegate it at a time and place of his choosing.

The issue of God's authority is really where the major challenge comes in the contemporary world—that is, whether there is any authority to delegate. If this issue is faced up to first, at least it helps to keep human arguments over power in a better perspective—that is, as a secondary concern. If modern man's democratic clean sweep has removed God's authority from every realm except the religious, authority in religion may actually be better understood in its new isolation. Since external controls can no longer be thought to be God's aim, any religious power will have to take on a purely nonsecular quality. A claim to religious authority can no longer carry with it political or social privileges—or at least, if it does, such self-arrogation is not religious in its origin.

In considering any organized religion, every member or potential member must reach a decision about the status of the clergy and all church officials. This will be an impossible task if all authority has been removed from God, or if either the status of authority in the divine nature is uncertain or the method of its communication in doubt. Early Christians met and solved these problems for themselves, and once they did, they had no trouble in accepting certain authorities in the life of the church. If we approach this issue from the other side today—that is, having already abandoned all divine locus for authority—we are likely to be baffled as we face the hierarchy of any church and try to clarify its function. This does not mean that if we grant God authority and an ability to dispense it, there is one and only one status for clergy, or only one organization for the church. History seems to indicate that these distributions can take a plurality of forms. However, this does mean that the question of the status of clergy and church officials can be dealt with clearly only after God's position is determined.

'Prophets' have enjoyed little popularity of late, whereas in an earlier day their religious function seemed quite central. Without necessarily trying to revive this office for the twentieth century, it is easy to see that the prophets' words were not accepted as in themselves valuable but only as they were taken to be a representation of God's authority over man. When man will not recognize any authority above him, then neither can anyone feel impelled to speak in God's name nor can anyone be accepted in such a role. The question of the presence of a "divine spokesman" in religion is crucial, but it cannot be dealt with intelligently until the locus of religious power is established. Whether prophet or apostle, the issue is not the man but whether any authority can be found behind him.

Perhaps we can now understand why the biblical record

(and this book) opens with an account of creation. God's biblical claim to fame is constantly traced back to his role as creator. Thus, any satisfactory answer to our problems in philosophy of religion also depends upon the restoration of theories of creation to some central place of intellectual importance. If that radical role as the originating source is denied to God, it is clear that his claim to authority is also drastically weakened. If this is true, we are little likely to understand the account given of God's reply to Job. When Job challenges God over his ill-treatment, God asks if Job was present when he, God, laid the foundations of the world. If we do not accept God in this role and the authority that results from it, this will seem at best a weak reply to Job's attempt to understand his suffering and at worst a bullying tactic and an evasion of the issue.

Theodicy—that is, the problem of evil and the justification of God's ways to man—cannot be dealt with outside the question of God's role in creation. If he had that crucial decisive power—that is, to create from nothing external to himself—then he still holds it today, and it is the fundamental source of his authority. Thus, he has the power to elect a course of action as he wills it. Although this does not remove all of our complaints against God, it does set the context within which the discussion between God and man ought to take place. To deal with a creator God, and the power that represents, casts a new light on the problem of evil. This discussion may end, of course, by forcing more responsibility for the ills of the world onto God. If God were less powerful, his responsibility would be less, but so also would his authority. The possession of authority equips him to accept a greater responsibility for evil.

Every religion faces the question of evaluating, and then either accepting or rejecting, those who claim to be sent by God. We have not tended to treat such claims very seriously in recent times, and it is true that, when religious authority is removed from the political and social realm, it is more difficult to appraise the claims of any proposed divine delegate. This evaluation is easier when one occupies a position of tribal leadership as Moses did, and that is why it was so hard to assess Jesus' claims when he refused political leadership and did not identify himself with current social movements. The question of whether any man's claim to be sent by God can be validated is difficult enough to determine in itself, but it becomes an impossible and fantastic assertion unless there actually is a divine source of authority to be represented.

If, religiously, God is to be seen as the sole source of authority, our question in this connection becomes "What philosophical theories force us to deny authority to God?" To answer this, of course, is not to declare all such theories to be either true or false. It does enable us to see how much is changed or rendered impossible if the philosophical theory adopted prevents the attribution of any authority to God. Or, what is perhaps more likely, it may restrict authority in such a way that it will affect all the subsequent issues that involve the question of the locus of power. Thomas Aquinas falls into this trap in denying that the creation of the world can be established on rational grounds, and this should lead us first to examine his metaphysical basis in order to determine how it shapes his theology in that precarious direction.

C. LITERATURE AND TRADITION AS NORMATIVE

The question of authority is perhaps the key issue for philosophy of religion, but this cannot be decided in isolation from the question of the specific locus of authority. If at least general agreement can be reached to allow us to seek an authoritative source in religion, then it becomes a matter of trying to fix a proper locus of authority which even a free individual might accept. The issue of God as the sole source (Section B), and also of how God's nature is to be conceived, is undoubtedly the first question. For this answer, we must turn to religion's sacred literature and its accumulated tradition. The question becomes one of where God can be discovered, where he might have revealed himself, and how his nature and his desires can be discerned. Can the literature and the religious tradition be accepted as containing this desired authoritative norm?

Let us begin by asking about the function of 'creeds.' This question involves both religious literature and tradition, for it is now clear that many sacred documents originally had the function of a creed. That is, parts of these writings were designed and preserved for their value in proclaiming the fundamental tenets of belief—for example, Yahweh brought us out of Egypt; God was in Christ. From the earliest times, the followers—and the leaders—of religion felt the need to put their belief into formulas so that an individual could know clearly what was being asserted and then take a definite stand in the light of such statements. Much of any church tradition hinges around the continual process of a redefinition of the faith and the attempt to find new and more effective ways in which to express this new formulation. Certainly one source where we might expect to encounter authority would be in the sacred literature as it is preserved and in the particular church tradition as transmitted.

This is not to say that somehow literature and tradition serve as an authoritative source, either in any simple matter or independently from the individual's recognition of that authority and his willingness to accept it. Although he might have, God does not seem to have made the force of religious authority overpowering or even always very clearly evident. If authority is present in the literature and tradition, it is there in such a form that it can easily be overlooked and ignored. It depends for its effect on recognition and acceptance, and yet the interested person can discover authority there. Creeds—as the literature expresses belief and as the tradition continually works to define them formally—represent a distilled normative statement of the kind of authority that can be uncovered and acknowledged.

In considering how authority can be found in creeds, literature, or tradition, one of the crucial questions is "What gives these a continued authority for a person who did not himself form them originally?" That is, it is clear that a creed represents a person or a group's best effort to formulate at the time what it can accept as normative. Much of the biblical literature was written to express what had become an overwhelming conviction of its author. The problem is that one who comes along later cannot, in most cases, be expected to look upon these statements just as their authors did.

It is one thing to form carefully into words one's own religious convictions and quite another for a nonbeliever to read such statements. Reading expressions of the acceptance of an authority in religious life can only produce in the reader acceptance of those expressions as normative if they induce him to share in the same experiences that originally led their authors to make those formulations and to accept them.

Regarding these sources, the question is "What authority was discovered then and how can it be recovered now?" The first and simplest answer is the fact that what someone else came to accept, and his expression of it, became authoritative through its *use* by others. In that minimal sense, these materials are always authoritative. Beyond that, it is always possible for a later individual to come to agree with all or part of these expressions, in which case they become normative for him too. Thus, it is clear that the exploration of religious literature, plus the attempt to understand a creed or to come to terms with a particular religious tradition, is the first order of business. Since these were once expressions of the discovery of religious authority, they may exert that power again at any time, but this recovered power depends on finding an effective contemporary idiom.

We have to balance these assertions by admitting that literature and tradition very often are interpreted so that they distort the expression of a source of religious authority and thus prevent its later recognition. This can happen because sacred literature always must be interpreted if original meaning is to be recaptured. Interpretations vary, and sometimes they even change the original meanings by placing the ideas in new forms of expression. This is a not necessarily bad and probably unavoidable process, but it does tend to make both the recognition and the acceptance of the literature as normative a difficult or at best a complicated matter. Once the canon of scripture is established, at least the basic text does not change. Yet, where religious tradition is concerned, a group or a community always moves forward into new circumstances and so sees the old documents in new lights.

More important, however, is the fact that human beings make mistakes, and thus, whether knowingly or unknowingly, they can be false to their tradition. When a man first approaches any particular tradition, he is most likely to be struck by the deviation from its ideals and by its times of false witness to its claims. Thus, to find authority in the true witness of a religious tradition as expressed in a community life and in its deeds is complicated by the process of purification which must occur before any acceptance is possible. Just as the reader of literature must try to uncover a valid interpretation before he can accept any scripture as normative, so one who tries to join or to understand any religious tradition must begin by being able to discover its true core and to distill out this ideal from its past and present distortions. No simple reading or involvement in a community of itself reveals a source of religious authority, except perhaps by accidental encounter.

In this attempt to consider the normative power that might be found in literature, traditions, and creeds, what role does philosophical theory have to play? If one holds intellectual reservations against the profession of all creeds, he is little likely to attempt to confess them in order to try to locate any power in residence there. One's view of the past and its relation to the present and to the future will provide the context within which the question of the authority a tradition can exercise will be decided. This fact does not necessarily demand that we adopt a certain historical view; however, it does indicate that tradition is not self-validating, but depends for its approach and function on certain prior theories.

Particularly in the light of the recent vast effort in biblical research, it is clear that, where sacred literature is concerned, biblical documents can be quite radically changed in their import depending on the context within which they are treated. This is not so much a question of their meaning, interpretation, and translation as it is of the theory that determines what present reality and power an ancient expression can be said to have. Nor is this at all to say that religious documents have no clear meaning independent of philosophical theories. The words are what they are, even if certain philosophical expressions are contained internally. Their acceptance as authoritative will be twisted by some theories (for example, an empiricism of the present moment) and aided by others—those which at least allow for a continual discovery of authority there.

D. THE TEACHING AUTHORITY OF THE CHURCH

Biblical documents themselves testify to the church's constant function as a teaching authority. Not everyone automatically holds the same beliefs or even accepts them once an authoritative pronouncement is made. Thus, any church is involved in a constant attempt to explain its beliefs to its members, and this responsibility is clearly evident in the Gospels and the letters of the New Testament. It is not difficult to recognize any church's responsibility to instruct its members in their faith, but it is much more difficult and crucial to decide what authority over the individual this teaching function has and how each member can be brought to accept it. Our primary question is not so much the legal one of how such teaching authority can be located in, or exercised by, any given church. That is a very practical matter. However, if such instructional authority exists, how can it be recognized and how does it function?

We will not undertake an examination of the basis upon which any particular church claims to possess such authority. That is a complicated matter involving individual assessment. However, the central consideration for philosophy of religion is, what kind of philosophical basis will or will not allow us to grant such authority? Our interest is to discover the theory that can permit such teaching to be authoritative and in what ways. At least at first glance, religion seems to demand different treatment in this regard. If in other areas man functions as his own authority, why does the same situation not hold in religion? The first answer to this question should take the form of pointing out that in no area is education dispensed with. If in any area education is required before the individual can assume authority, there is good reason why in religion one should have to be trained by a qualified teacher before he can hope to practice his belief correctly.

If we recognize this necessity to submit to instruction before responsible decision-making can be expected, one portion of the problem is solved. Those who will not undergo religious training cannot be any more entitled to an opinion than a would-be engineer who will not study engineering. However, some churches assert that they possess a continued normative control and an authority to correct their adherents, and this involves an additional difficulty which is largely without parallel in other areas, at least in a free society.

Does religion require a more constant teaching authority—that is, one continued beyond an original apprenticeship? If this requirement does not rest strictly on the need for prior education, what can the source of the religion's claim be to a continued authority? Part of our answer lies in the fact that any religion harks back to an original event considered revelatory of God. Most other human enterprises have contemporary reference, but, with religion, recapturing a primitive spirit is always fundamental, and usually it is also prior. A church functions as the guardian of that origin, and its teaching authority rests on the necessity never to lose contact with that original source on pain of losing all vitality in the religious life based on it.

Do churches have the same status, then, that judges and courts do in our legal system? In law, we are involved with a primary constitution and accumulated legislation, and current problems require a constant process of interpretation so that the original constitutional aims will be understood, preserved, and promoted. It is easy to see that religious authority does function in somewhat the same manner as long as an individual remains a member of that group. However, one fundamental difference is clear: Since God is the source of the original religious "constitution," his existence and actions cannot have either the common meaning or the immediate reference that the words of any political document have.

Partly because of this greater difficulty in being certain of the definite reference of their basic norm, many churches vest a partially qualified teaching authority in their hierarchy, while others refuse to grant anyone such powers out of fear that they will be misapplied. The exact degree and form of teaching authority vested in any church is not a problem that can be decided here. What is crucial is whether, for religion, the question of authority at least can never be done away with even in adulthood. In many areas, it is easy to recognize provisional authority during an apprenticeship. Is it the case that in religion one never completely graduates? Why should this be true? If there is a constant need for teaching in religious matters, life in that sphere would involve a continued search for and subjection to authority. Now the only question becomes "What kind of authority and where is it to be found?"

Perhaps the situation would be different if the assertions of any religion could ever be known to be true. Of course, certain root assumptions in any political constitution (for example, that certain rights are "inalienable") may not be capable of demonstration beyond doubt either. Yet, on the whole, the assertions of religion are much more uniformly incapable of current demonstration—for example, we cannot perform another escape from Egypt or a second resurrection.

Belief in the founding events confirms the individual as a member of that religious community, but a continued exercise of authority may be necessary in order to guard the belief. In relation to this need, any individual remains constantly a student and a novice. This fact points to the derivation of the meaning of religious faith from the concepts of authority and trust. In the sense of immediate observance, the individual can never validate his faith. (However, for one basic qualification, see Section E.) This is defined by his trust in the accounts he receives and by his recognition of some authority for their interpretation.

The issue, however, goes deeper than discovering that the basis for faith resides in trust and in the recognition of authority. It might be true that authority itself makes faith possible. If religious faith cannot be given except on this condition, the issue of recognizing a teaching authority becomes crucial. That is, unless one can find a locus for this power, faith is not possible. It might seem that it is because of faith that one can accept a teaching authority in religion. What we want to suggest is that the opposite may be true: *Until a teaching authority can be found and accepted, the discovery of religious faith is not really possible.* As this chapter indicates, there are many available definitions and sources for authority, so that we are not arguing for any particular form but simply for the location of an acceptable authority as a prerequisite to faith.

Because of the constant uncertainties of religion, faith must be located "in something." Hence, everything depends on finding that in which one can place trust as authoritative. We do not seem to trust anyone who does not have authority in these matters, since that is the meaning of trust. To those who refuse to recognize any authority in matters of religion, all possible faith may be cut off. This is not to suggest that the recognition of authority is at all an easy matter. However, since religion derives its authority from its decisive originating events, the best source for authority would always seem to be connected with an original witness to those events. To the extent that any church's hierarchy is recognized as serving in this capacity, it becomes possible to vest it with authority and thus to make faith in those events again a possibility.

What philosophical interpretation of authority do we need so that, on these terms, a church might possess this power in its teaching function? What views on authority are such that they make it impossible for any church to exercise this function? It may be that one who tries to learn from his church's teaching will fail in this attempt primarily because he implicitly accepts a concept of authority such that he cannot grant this function to the institution from which he attempts to learn. In this case, the teaching office is frustrated, not so much because of what is communicated to him, but because he is not prepared to receive it on the only basis upon which it could be effective—that is, moving him.

Even in education in general today, it is hard to get a student to recognize authority in any teaching office. Information may be transmitted, and the student may even happen to educate himself unknowingly. Yet, where religion is concerned, such anarchy means in itself the disappearance of religious faith without even a fair trial.

Today we tend toward pure democracy and absolute equality in political and social matters; it appears that religion cannot exist on this base alone. In certain religious procedures and theories, pure democracy can still prevail—for example, perhaps in its service to those who suffer. However, when you seek instruction in religion, the prior recognition of a source of authority and the determination of its guardian—these are the crucial matters. If we have a theory of knowledge that is not built on obvious fact and one that allows the existence of entities not subject to the five senses, the granting of authority to a teacher is a condition for learning. A knowing submission is not folly but a religious necessity.

E. THE BEDROCK OF PERSONAL EXPERIENCE

The questions raised in the preceding three sections may seem to indicate a movement away from individual experience as the locus of authority in religion. The factors outlined, if accepted, certainly do not allow private experience to be a sole criterion. However, they do not prevent the inclusion of immediate experience as one of the factors that determines where authority is to be located. To relate a personal experience is not out of line where religious knowledge is concerned. For example, when I tried to persuade a student to break off from a revivalistic and evangelical Christian group, he admitted that my arguments proving the preferability of a more intellectually respectable group were all good, but still he refused to change his affiliation. When in exasperation I asked why, he replied: "Because, before I was different; since I have known them my life has been changed."

This kind of report is the absolute bedrock of all religious claims, and without it any religion will soon be rejected for simpler and more effective forms of belief. Perhaps only a felt need for change can ever bring a person to consider adopting a religious faith, and surely the personal experience of a changed mode of existence is all that can sustain it in the long run. To say this may seem to deny all sources of authority except those that are immediate and individual. The situation can be so interpreted, but it need not be. The issue depends on what makes possible such an experience of personal transformation or even rebirth. Perhaps this change cannot take place until the source of the religious belief is individually discovered. Perhaps, as we have indicated, the discovery of this is not at all a simple matter, but depends on the location of, and willingness to submit to, authority.

The experience of personal transformation may be the ultimate testimony for religious authority, but the point is that it can be reached only after the locus of authority has been uncovered. Follow Luther through his *Commentary on Romans*. It is an examination of scripture that Luther accepts as his authoritative guide, although he might not have recognized it quite that clearly at first. Because he discovered in Paul's letter to the Romans a new understanding of faith, Luther experienced a wide-reaching transformation. This experience testified to the letter's normative quality, and henceforth anyone who wanted to challenge Luther's faith would have to meet him on that ground.

The point is that Luther did not experience personal change

first and then accept a certain norm of authority. Rather, he first submitted to the testimony of scripture, and thus made himself capable of receiving new instruction. What he learned in this process induced his personal reorientation, which confirmed his discovery of the source of authority, but all this would not have been possible without the prior acceptance of the sacred literature as normative. Of course, God must be found in order for authority to be accepted, and then the question becomes "When will God appear and in what context and material can he be seen?"

The issue of a religious norm is not so simple, however, as to make an experience of changed personality the test of the accurate placement of authority. Such alterations are not always for the better, and, more important, they are often temporary, not enduring and fundamental. Many a person has been disappointed by experiencing a change under religious influence that proved to be a momentary emotion not capable of sustaining itself. Perhaps we should say that it is more the sustained action that flows from the change than it is some rare experience itself that counts.

An encounter with the Devil can also be a moving experience and induce extensive change, except that the Devil can be detected by his disruptive consequences rather than by his healing ability. On the other hand, goodness tends to communicate itself ungrudgingly to others without a jealous regard for self.

The Gospels indicate that such was the experience of those who met Jesus. But it is crucial to note that the change that results in evident good works was not experienced by everyone who crossed his path, but only by those who accepted his authority as being one with God's. In this sense, faith is not simply a forced and self-induced attitude. It is, rather, the discovery of divine authority and the acceptance of its teaching powers, coupled with the experience of fundamental personal renewal as clearly manifest in actions demonstrating the fruitful results. Such personal experience and clear action are acceptable evidence of the presence of authority.

If religion seems to agree that all authority is ultimately divine, does the acceptance of personal experience, changed personality, and a flow of charitable action contradict this

authority the disciples discovered and in the name of which they went out to preach. This involves all of the factors in the four sections above, since scripture, of necessity, becomes a locus for re-creating this transformation. The personal change experienced by the apostle becomes (for each individual) the primary evidence for the authenticity of all contemporary preaching. Whenever preaching is sensitive and self-reflective about its intent and how it can accomplish its aim, it can once again have the converting effect it originally had. Then, when a later listener shares in the apostles' original experience, preaching for him becomes a medium for the discovery of religious authority. However, in addition to the preaching role as an imitation of the apostles' original experience, no new experience is authoritative without proper listening.

Since he who speaks with words powerful enough to reveal authority will still have some listeners who do not accept these as authoritative, it must be that, if the listener is not properly receptive, no effect will result. Then, of course, neither preaching nor listening can be taken as evidence. Here, perhaps, philosophy enters in most decisively; for, if the listener holds a theory that rules out words as capable of being authoritative, he becomes incapable of hearing them in that way. If the listener demands that all words be verified before he can allow them to affect him, he blocks all possible verification which results from the discovery of the change induced. It would seem that how one approaches preaching makes all the difference. The words that are to be preached must be formed by learning both their origin and the intent of preaching. The listener, for his part, must be capable of allowing the words to reach him in this form with their original intention still intact.

It may be particularly instructive to consider Paul's claim to apostleship. Although he was never present during Jesus' ministry and did not participate in the events of the crucifixion and resurrection which gave authority to the apostles' words through their experience of these actions, Paul was always very strong in his claim to an original and equal apostleship, and he mentions this often. Omitting for the moment the special circumstances of his conversion experience, Paul's claim is that he received a direct commission to preach, and he is certain that he also had a direct experience of the events that establish Jesus' authority. This also gave Paul authority, just as well as those who were present at the actual time whose experience was first hand. Since he had no immediate participation in the events surrounding Jesus' own life and service, Paul stands as a model of how all later Christianity can be communicated by preaching and accepted by a prepared listener.

What this seems to require is a philosophical framework that will allow the claims made for Jesus to serve in a later time as evidence for his authority. The teller must be capable of portraying Jesus' authority, and the listeners must be able to comprehend the import of the claims. With Paul we have an apostle who understands his preaching role in this way. It is interesting to note that he gains more authority as an accurate preacher of that message than does Peter who was a direct witness, even to denying his Lord three times. Paul is our norm of how Christianity must be presented to all those after the close of Jesus' own ministry.

To return to Paul's conversion experience, however, the vividness of the events resulting in his personal transformation both opened him to hear and enabled him to preach. Thus, all preaching and listening is confirmed in the production of such lasting and fruitful transformation. However, the situation must be one which is conducive, first, to both preaching and hearing. Then the resulting personal transformation which establishes this situation is capable of providing the evidence. The conviction does not come before the listening but only after its recognized good results. Nevertheless, all this depends on establishing a situation open to attributing this function to preaching and listening before religious authority can be discovered.

G. CAN ANY MAN EXERCISE DIVINE AUTHORITY?

This question represents the basic problem of all religion. God, as such, never fully appears to exercise his own authority directly. Whatever their status, it is always others who exercise this authority for him and either act as his intermediaries or report God's command. It is never fully possible for such a person, or event, or recorded word, to have all of divine authority spread out on its surface. Yet, it is of the essence of religion that the individual believer must be willing to accept it in this way. Such is the meaning of faith: one trusts these reports as accurate—as representing God's authority and as the basis upon which one is willing to place his trust and his action. This, of course, does not mean that a great deal of evidence cannot be examined regarding any claim to represent divine authority, but it is clear from the beginning that no evidence can ever fully verify such a claim.

It is the believer's responsibility to accept or reject the claim after testing the evidence, and in this regard the individual always faces a constant paradox. The answer to the question "Can any man exercise divine authority?" is "He can't." You are always left with a man, or with written assertions, but never with a man who at the same time is clearly seen to be God. You hear reports of God's speaking, not God's speech itself. This may in faith be accepted as such, or the sacred literature may be taken as representative of God's word, but the equation can never be perfect.

In the case of Jesus, the Jews experienced not only paradox but even blasphemy in his claims. Not that others had not been anointed to represent God to his chosen people. Prophets had come and been accepted, but Jesus' claims were even stronger. They bordered on a claim to identity with God; in any case, he claimed authority to set aside previous religious injunctions. It takes the full authority of God to remove religious laws previously established by God's own authority, and Jesus claimed this power both in his words and by his deeds. Nor can Jesus' claim be taken lightly, since every religion must protect the purity of its tradition if it does not want to degenerate. The Jews have a bad record when it comes to the desertion of their God in order to worship false gods, and so they were rightly very sensitive to any challenge that might again lead them away from God and also away from his favor.

Since more claims to represent God than one have been put forward, evaluating these is not a trivial matter but the crucial issue. The believer must decide who possesses God's authority, and the religious tradition must guard itself against challenges that would remove its claim to represent God's desires. The Jews are not the only ones to experience this difficulty with Jesus' claims; the situation is essentially the same for all the apostles and for every believer in any time. The apostles claimed continued authority to represent God's revelation and, in that sense of proclaiming with authority, the paradox of a man exercising divine power remains. Every believer presents the same problem, since he too must determine from the claims where he will agree to locate divine authority. Whatever frees him—whether pope, priest, Bible, preacher, or creed—in itself always appears to be less than it claims to be—that is, as the eye sees it.

In the case of Jesus, this is precisely the reason behind the development of the doctrine of the Trinity. Whether such a technical formula can be found in Jesus' own words, or even in the first statements of the early Christian church, is unimportant. The issue is that Jesus' claim to speak with divine authority is so extreme that, in the end, he must be God in order to back up these assertions properly. He could easily be another prophet in a long tradition, but his assertion that he represents God demand that he have a closer relationship to divinity than that. It does not matter whether some particular technical formulation is accepted for a trinitarian doctrine. The issue is "What status must Jesus have in order to be able to support his assertions and the claims implied in his actions?" Any doctrine of the Trinity must be understood as one way to give adequate support to the status necessary to support Jesus' claims.

We ought to ask what proof Jesus himself offers for his assertion of divine authority. This question clearly comes up in his own life by the miracles he performs and again after his death in God's act to prove Jesus's authority to speak—that is, by reversing his death, and his condemnation for blasphemy, through his resurrection. These complex assertions cannot be considered in detail here; but, as far as philosophy is concerned, it is clear that any doctrine that in itself forces the rejection of miracles radically alters the conception of Jesus' mission and in itself amounts to the rejection of his claims. Some metaphysics allow miracles and other do not. It is not necessary that a philosophical basis in itself somehow authenticate miracles, but it is important that the possibility for a believer to accept them not be ruled out in advance simply by the theory of knowledge which is in operation.

14

COMMUNITY

A. AUTHORITY IN COMMUNITY

Any consideration of the question of religious authority and how it is established must take into account the possibility that authority is discoverable, not in an individual, but only in a community. This problem is distinct from the question of whether one special individual (for example, Jesus) represents religious authority. For even after the appearance of such a unique individual, it is still possible that authority can only be located in a community. If this is true, it is not a trivial matter. Rather, it becomes all important for any person other than those who knew that original authoritative individual. It may be, of course, that the basic issue is still the claims of the founding individual—for example, those of Jesus or Joseph Smith. The point is that perhaps the context for authority now is centered in a group.

As much as it may seem to, this possibility does not prejudice the question of what the group should be like or how it is to be organized or administered. If some assert that only one form of community can carry forward the claim to authority, this question should be faced first. The history of Christianity seems to indicate that a plurality of forms of community are acceptable. If this is the case, the issue is no longer whether only one form is viable. Rather, it concerns how many forms there might be and whether certain of these have advantages over others and in what respects.

It is interesting to consider how authority might come to reside in some forms of community to a greater degree than in others and how in some sense the test for authenticity lies in the effectiveness of that community—that is, in its work and its ability to carry itself forward and to adapt to new circumstances. The history of Christianity is one of a constant suggestion of new groupings as more effective ways to express the authority Christians accept in Jesus.

Societies always seem to be more efficient at carrying out the work placed upon Christians. Both a pragmatic test and the doctrine of the survival of the fittest operate here, for some groups evidence strength while others cannot sustain themselves after perhaps a momentary surge of vigor. Such a pragmatic test is, of course, not a complete guarantee of the adequacy of any theory of community, but it is at least a first screening device which can be used to eliminate the unsuccessful candidates.

Relevant to this discussion is Kierkegaard's use of 'the individual' as his fundamental category. In stressing the individual's absolute solitude and loneliness in the religious quest, does Kierkegaard automatically doom the venture to failure? Or, at least, does he make it more difficult than necessary? That is, is some form of community a requirement as the context for the success of any religious quest?

If this is so, he who refuses to consider working from within any community may, in his original choice, doom his efforts to failure. The discovery of a proper group context becomes even more difficult if only one form of community is deemed acceptable, for the religious quest is shaped in certain fundamental ways at the outset. A person then, must both consider carefully and be willing to accept the basic features of the life of that community, since its form is important to him. If he joins it physically but still refuses to accept its basic principles spiritually, his efforts are headed, if not to failure, at least to considerable frustration. He simply diverts his energies to fighting within the community when these energies are urgently needed for other spiritual issues.

Even if one accepts a plurality of forms of community, not every problem is solved. Much effort must be invested, at least initially, in deciding among the possible community forms. Of course, few will start this quest without some prior attachment, and, since much of the help of a community stems from the individual's emotional ties with it, a certain natural direction is provided. That is, he knows he should give an initial priority to the form of community he has inherited and in which his basic emotional commitment has been given before. If this direction is accepted, the next questions are "Can that inherited form of community profit from revitalization and an alteration in its structure?" And "Might other forms of community be even more fruitful for that individual, specifically, forms as yet only potential and not yet made concrete?"

Even if we reject Kierkegaard's radical doctrine of the absolute primacy of the individual, the importance of the isolated self in the religious situation is, nonetheless, apparent. Granted that he must work within a community, it is still up to the individual's free choice what community he chooses to work within. "Free choice" is present in the religious quest in the sense that one can decide to work to free himself from whatever nature and heredity have given him as a starting point. In establishing his basic context, the individual is very much alone if he does not simply accept blindly what he has inherited. If he takes this path of less resistance, it might kill the effectiveness of his community context anyway. The 'individual' is still the center of all religion; the problem comes over determining where individuality is primary and where the concept of community should be dominant.

In the issue of the individual vs. the community, the question of authority may be decisive. For, if the individual demands in advance that a given community's authority to represent God be demonstrated to him, and if such authority can only be manifest to a member of the community, then that man's efforts to solve his religious problems are headed for frustration. This is not to say that this demand is not right, but it is to suggest that the issue must be worked out in advance in order to avoid making an impossible request. What is actually more likely to be the situation is probably something such as this: The individual is prior in the sense that he must agree to enter a (or to stay within an inherited) community. In deciding to do this, he must first see in its life and work at least a potential locus for the discovery of divine authority. This initial commitment having been made, then, once within that group an exploration must be undertaken for the confirming presence of divine authority.

Although authority may be fully discoverable in religion only within a community, still the individual taken alone does have a central role to carry out if the total religious life is to be successful. If God is said to address a group, it is usually through the medium of some person (see the paradox of the voice of divine authority as being inherent in any single man). For the Christian, revelation is accepted as present in Jesus; he is a single individual who accomplishes this when there is no absolute reason why it could not have been done by a team. Most philosophy and theology and most religious authorship are primarily the product of single individuals, in spite of the fact that their work may be gathered together. Still, it may be that 'community' either naturally results from such unique thought and action, or that the development of these important insights could not have come if the individuals had existed entirely alone and outside of all community support.

It may be that God is disclosed only in the situation of individual-to-individual encounter. Yet, at the same time perhaps God is discoverable only in a community context (see Section E). If this is true, to seek God in isolation is to seek the impossible—and court insanity. Despite the prominence of amazing individuals as the medium for the expression of divine authority, it is still true that the results of these unique discoveries inevitably seem to call forth a community response. Perhaps in his creative insights the individual still can gain the strength of independence from 'community'. Nevertheless, no individual is strong enough to ignore the importance of community context.

B. THE CHURCH AS COMMUNITY

Until this point we have deliberately avoided the use of the term 'church'. Defining the idea of community is prior to the question of church, and many individuals, we suggest, are frustrated in their attempt to reconcile themselves to some institutional church precisely because they have never settled the prior issue of the meaning and function of community in their religious life. 'Church' refers more to some ecclesiastical body, with its title to properties, its governing structure and particular tradition, its accepted practices and procedures. Just as the question of the relation of individual to community must be settled, so must the question be resolved of the relation of 'community' to official and public structure—that is, to a 'church'. It seems clear that the two are never identical, but it is also equally clear that, like individual and community, they are never totally independent.

We all know what churches are, because they exist as public and legal and at least partially visible entities. We all know what a community is too, but its definition is more difficult and its existence is harder to discern. A church may continue to exist when all sense of community has been lost, but a strong sense of religious community, whenever it is discovered, tends to result in the formation of a visible body (a 'church') in order to give it an overt and a more concrete expression. A church is also needed to act as the physical means for the continued expression of that sense of community and particularly for its extension and manifestation in some good work. It is probable that neither community nor church can exist without the other, but it is also equally likely that a strong sense of religious community is prior to the formation of any church.

A community can be formed to express many things—for example, political views or a cultural phenomenon such as music. But a community cannot be religious unless it is "called by God." This important qualification returns us to the primary question of authority, for when a group or an individual discovers a locus or an expression of divine authority, then they feel called by this discovery to form a community to witness to it (see Chapter 24) and to carry out its required work. As such, it is the community that feels called by this disclosure, and any church or actual organization is only either an outer expression or an instrument for this new community spirit. Of course, most individuals enter this process backwards; they come into contact first with the outer organization.

Then, perhaps only later, they themselves experience the discovery that first called together that community.

Since all cannot be lucky enough to be explorers and founding fathers, every one who comes later must try to recover the original impetus behind the formation of the group. And once it has been constituted, the community's primary responsibility is to try to bring others to that original impetus. In doing this, the community is hampered by the fact that, of necessity, what most latecomers first confront is the group's institutional side. Then, somehow, that must be set aside and a way sought to reach the original spiritual experience once again. This is true of the relation of the individual Christian to Jesus. The problem always is to go behind the various institutional churches now representing him and to face that experience the reaction to which first called forth so many churches as a witness to it.

'Church', then, is a derived category and not a primary concept where religion is concerned. Unless the members of a church can be made to sense this, the existence of formal structures may actually become an impediment to the expression of the community convictions. Unless a sense of community becomes primary, every function of the church may be misunderstood. The hierarchy may seem to have authority in itself, when instead what it is intended to represent is the fact that all authority is God's. Its claim is merely to have this fact discovered in some particular context and by some divine action; its own right to authority is simply as a witness to this fact.

Any man in any church may come to take every function as significant in itself and to be enjoyed esthetically, or else he may see the church's function as an end in itself without further need for justification. If so, the stage is set for the disgraceful quarrels and even persecutions that continually mar the record of all religions. When a sense of the derived quality of all religious functions and church procedures can be maintained, then the individual can maintain a proper understanding and appraisal of the church and its institutional functions. Now the sense of community is primary and the original discovery of divine authority in some event or person is recalled once more. In this case, the significance of every ecclesiastical function can be judged according to its continued ability to express that originating experience.

Whenever the issue of church is raised first, then questions of ritual and administration become primary. When this happens, some progress can perhaps be made in reconciling differences over procedure and form, but, on the whole, these are issues that always divide us because by nature they are subject to extension in an infinite variety of forms. The subtlety of ritual practices and the possible intricacies of administrative forms cannot naturally yield uniform agreement if approached simply on their own terms. If left to that, they tend at best toward a loose multiplicity and at worst toward a rigid insistence on one form to the exclusion of all others. Fortunately or unfortunately, our world seems to have been provided with a variety of forms to express one thing. Unless the original community spirit can be captured, no criteria are available to distinguish between the multitude of variable forms, and an arbitrary rigidity is all too often resorted to.

The religious situation is hopeless if it is left to depend on our ability to find any one way to fix ritual or administration. Only an outside criterion can do that task and save us from eternal bickering over insoluble details. This needed criterion is the original sense of the community, but, unfortunately, this is neither precise nor concrete in intellectual formulation and so cannot perform this function infallibly. A common spirit may be expressed in a variety of forms, although only a few are probably really suited to preserving its power. Still, at least the starting point is agreed upon and the line is established by which we can trace the suitability of any particular expression. Although this task of testing institutional forms can never be done once and for all or reduced to one form, at least priorities and procedures can be agreed upon.

What is the function of any church and what might philosophy have to do with clarifying this function and implementing it? If the common spirit of 'community' stems from the discovery and acceptance of some source of divine authority, the church is the means by which this is presented and implemented in a vital way. Still, since those who first felt the full force of the divine discovery do not last and cannot automatically transfer their experience to others (not even to their children), the church springs up as a needed teaching instrument. It must try, through instruction, to perpetuate the reality of the original discovery by constructing the means to reproduce it perpetually.

Discovering the relation of church to community is dependent on philosophy, because it is not a relationship that remains clear without a constant defining effort. In fact, if left uncriticized, the two tend to merge. The community spirit seems to become identical with the practical structures which came after the experience to give it a durable expression. In order to maintain this distinction between community and church, we need a philosophical spirit that is sensitive to the priority of nonvisual entities. Otherwise, the functional church will always appear as primary. Furthermore, the original form given to the sense of community is not itself free from a variety of philosophical definitions and terms each of which has elaborate connotations, whereas the original religious experience may have been comparatively simple. In this case, philosophical skill is constantly necessary, from the second generation onward, in order to be able to keep the variety of later philosophical interpretations distinct from the primary experience.

C. THE NECESSITY FOR OUTER DIRECTION

If it is the case that a community is formed around the discovery of a source it is willing to acknowledge as possessing divine authority, still it should occur to us to ask why this inevitably tends to express itself in the formation of a church? Is it conceivable that such a community spirit might exist as it is simply within each of its individual members? Why, then, does it so often seek institutional form, especially if that is not the mode of its original appearance? Let us begin to answer this important question by admitting that much about the religious spirit involves a turning inward. In fact, it seems that, if there is no ability to turn inward silently without outward activity, there is no basis upon which the religious spirit can build. The fault present in this necessary tendency is that it can turn into morbid introspection. The individual can be lost in self-preoccupation, and then he becomes unable to break out of his exclusive concern.

Although the authenticity of religion appears to have no infallible tests, one valid standard seems to be that all genuine religious discovery breaks the bonds of exclusive inner direction and causes in the individual both a revolution in loss of personal concern together with a need to express his conviction in outer form. An unhealthy inner preoccupation can also burst forth as a result of religious conversion, but this usually comes only from the explosion of confined energy that is left without a constructive outlet. Its lack of authenticity can be seen in its destructive tendencies which are often directed toward those who do not conform to some standard, or, in extreme cases, fanaticism is turned toward the self in abusive fashion. As opposed to this, it is easy to tell the genuine spirit by its healing and reconciling qualities, by its gentle acceptance and lack of self-concern, and by its natural tendency to flow outward in service to others on their terms and not on his. The converted soul no longer whips itself, although it may volunteer to suffer for others.

The religious spirit can be fierce and terrifying and violent and intolerant. Whenever it is, it does not create institutions and ritual forms but destroys them in its self-righteous rage. Compassion and love, on the other hand, require an outer direction as a means of expression so that they may be made manifest and communicated effectively and not wasted by finding no suitable outlet. Love may take the form of a craving desire for exclusive possession, as Plato pointed out, but it may also become the selfless spirit of a desire to communicate itself to others without demand of repayment. In this case, love requires externalization in word or deed—or perhaps even in efficacious ritual. Not to give it this form, to keep it merely in the form of spirit, is to deny it and to distort it. Love and compassion require demonstrative and physical expression, nonobligatory communication to others, but this usually cannot be accomplished without the medium of institutional form.

Thus, the necessity for outer direction to this religious spirit requires church formation, and that also demands group support and existence within a community. When love ceases to be a desire with a tendency to exclusive possession, then there is a movement toward community formation as a natural basis upon which to share what is no longer hoarded within the self. Furthermore, it is not easy to implement the aims of a generous spirit and a compassionate nature. If not properly controlled, such good qualities not only are wasted but also may even become harmful if their application is uncontrolled, or if it goes without plan or rule. The business of finding an effective mode of expression for even such a good spirit is so difficult that the individual requires the support of mutually concerned comrades who embrace each other in their explorations for effective expression—as well as in their failures.

Without a chance for formal expression, a person might drown in a sea of his own unformed good intentions, and many suffer this sad fate. It is bad enough to see evil or selfish motives prevail; it is sadder still to see good intentions spoil through a failure to find a structured means for effective expression. The spirit of any community is unformed in itself, so that it needs the agency of some church structure if it is to be born into the world physically. Here the pragmatic test applies. Many forms have been tried and some clearly allow the spirit its free expression. Others, once able to do this, now seem hardened, while still other forms involve us in more handicaps than advantages. Perhaps what is most difficult of all to detect are those unrealized forms of expression that remain latent only because the religious spirit has not been directed to explore them.

Every spirit seem fated not to be able to give expression to itself easily and naturally. Probably this is because the forms available to it are more than one and are never neatly arranged in a hierarchy. When the selfless religious spirit is born, its natural desire is to communicate itself to others in nondemanding service. To do this it must have both a form and some guidance, and churches are to be understood as community expressions of this critical need. When approached in this way, churches are measured in New Testament fashion by their fruits, by their healing power, and by their devotion to, not themselves and their structural needs, but the needs of those outside their restricted membership. This necessity for love to find a concrete form for its outer direction both explains the existence of church forms and gives us a norm for the evaluation of their success.

D. WHAT BINDS THE GROUP TOGETHER?

In order to understand any church form, we must understand both the community spirit and the need that first called it forth. In order to grasp the spirit of the community, we must learn what it is that continues to bind the group together. When a church is old, it is sad but true that sometimes all that holds it together is a ritual practice, if the animating spirit is no longer fresh. And even when it is, it is true that sometimes this spirit is discernible only by the professionally trained. If so, then it is not communicated, as it first was, to the uninitiated too. Since no ritual practice as such was ever primary, its test must lie in its ability to manifest, both to the layman and to the pagan, the spirit that first made a particular community ceremony into a religious ritual. Otherwise, we may not be able to discover what binds the community together in any but a superficial sense. This exploration may, if the surface is ever broken, potentially be very divisive just because no common spirit exists any longer behind the ritual.

Usually, some common affirmation holds the community together. Not that the formulation of a creed or statement comes first and then the community assents to it. Rather, in some experience of divine presence and authority, a common experience is first shared, and it is then put in the form of an affirmation in order to communicate and preserve and perpetuate it. When it comes to the problem of settling the details of such statements, trying to reach agreement can split the community rather than bind it. This is particularly true if the technical form of the statement itself becomes the focal point instead of consideration of the words in the light of the original experience they try to express.

However, although rooted in a powerful experience of divine presence, such creeds and affirmations, even if properly understood as to their origin, are too intellectual a matter to be a very strong source of unity, particularly in light of the potential divisive power of fine verbal distinctions. Quite often the most powerful congealing bond derives from shared suffering, and this is why it is so hard to mold a strong sense of community (whether religious or political) in the face of victory and success. The church triumphant may very soon be a church without a strong cohesive spirit, and then it is reduced to celebrating its past glories. That is, of course, a strong theme in the New Testament—that it must be deemed a privilege to suffer. A too successful church or organization soon turns to disillusion and to arguing over the control of its wealth. It is no accident that so much powerful religious literature is the result of persecution and is written in prison cells.

A church may, of course, celebrate a victory, but usually this is not a temporal victory. Sometimes precisely because the victory cannot be shown clearly in the present, the community must suffer in its celebration of events that are not commonly visible—for example, the triumph over death in the resurrection. Suffering follows because one has come to accept these events as divinely authoritative, and yet this cannot be seen as the way of all things now at this point in time. Instead, all natural expectations are opposed to these assertions. To affirm such beliefs (for example, human brotherhood) is to suffer, at least internally, over the difficulties evident in the contrast between religious belief and obvious current practice. To try to implement this belief is also to suffer, because it is so hard to express it adequately or to gain wide acceptance for it. Physically, this is the most difficult situation, but, intellectually, it is easiest when persecution is the strong hand that binds the community together.

No common endurance of suffering, no strong community— this seems to be the rule. That is, this is true unless the community is successful in inducing its latecomers to participate vicariously in the suffering of its founders. Then, as these early hard days are recalled (for example, the amazing effort of the Mormon pioneers), the present community is bound together again just to the extent that they reenact and relive those original events. The danger with this method is that the glamor and distance of time may surround and rob the events of their primitive power by transforming them into beautiful literary stories rather than hard experiences. Ritual representation involves the almost greater danger of making original suffering pleasant in the beauty of its presentation (for example, the Mass). When all roughness is lost in gold and velvet, it is difficult if not impossible for these once stark events to exercise the same binding effect upon the community. The tendency is to become a theatergoer instead of a disciple.

When we understand how shared suffering binds, then no man or wife or religious seeker could wish to be rid of all hard and rough events. Of course, if one is destroyed or emasculated by them, then suffering binds us only in weakness and through the creation of a need for support. We can, however, also see this as a source of power—that is, if in the events the individual experiences an overcoming of them by divine power after his own power is gone. In this case, strength flows from the unpleasant event, and it gains healing power and a need to communicate itself. Now we are one step further in uncovering outward directed love as the real reason to build church structure. *Love is formed not in easy circumstances but in suffering that is overcome.* Then love is strong, and it moves out to communicate the same power of endurance against the suffering it has experienced. This is the origin of community, of all church structure, and of every personal strength capable of sharing its power with others.

In the religious sense, such transformation is never experienced in the abstract but only with God as its source and focus. This is the meaning behind saying that the common acceptance of authority is the source of community. In the social sense, of course, this is always true. Unless a common authority (rule, code, person, or group) is accepted, no real community can be established. In the religious sense, this must center around God and the recognition of the presence of his authority (in the Jewish covenant; in Jesus' actions). As we have just concluded, this is seldom a kind of accidental or detached discovery. Usually, it is born of suffering and need. When that need is great and nevertheless the suffering is healed, then the operative power is attested to be divine. This does not always happen, of course, but only when that outcome is not naturally expected or when it is not the result of human effort. A release from bondage must involve an overcoming of natural processes if it is to be accepted as divinely authoritative (for example, the New Testament miracles).

Still, whenever a community pledges common allegiance in response to this and accepts those acts as the locus of divine authority (for example, the exodus from Egypt), then a community bond is formed. Probably next it will receive structural form in church institutions and in ritual celebrations which can preserve that originating event (for example, the resurrection in the case of Christians). In accepting this experience as authoritative, the group submits to it as normative. Now the existence of their community hinges on this, however difficult in practice it may be to give it a precise formulation. Still, it is the acceptance of the authoritative event that forms the community, not the creed or ritual that results from it, whatever the importance of their future role may be.

In order to preserve any community thus formed, rules of procedure must be established, but these are never on a par with the authoritative event itself. Yet, most of all, it is the kind of common work the community engages in that preserves and strengthens its original bonds. In the case of Christians, they are enjoined to the love of neighbor and to serving the needs of others, no matter how small, if the need is vital. When self-searching and refining definitions cease and practical service to man begins, then a common spirit can be built and fostered. This is not to depreciate self-searching or creedal formation, but only to indicate that it becomes sterile if isolated.

The community, then, finds its strongest bond in externally oriented service, primarily to the nonmember but also to the member, as this is required in order to render him capable of effective service. No one labor or particular affirmation can bind all groups, so that there will be as many communities as there are forms of human suffering to be ministered to. And there will be as many ways to formulate this as there are means to express a common affirmation—that is, this desire to serve comes from the healing experience of the discovery of divine presence and activity. It is the result of the command that is at the heart of that experience, and it is acknowledged by the acceptance of the authority of that command—that is, "Feed my sheep."

E. SEEKING GOD IN COMMUNITY

We sometimes think that asking about God's nature and existence is primarily an individual matter. It may start there, but if we do not want to make a mistake, we ought first to ask if God can be discovered more easily in a community. It·might be that such a context is necessary and that to ignore it is to fail to discover God concretely. Why would it be that a community setting or a common endeavor might be necessary for this divine quest? One of the most obvious answers is that the task of God-seeking is admittedly such a difficult one that, personally, one simply needs the support of a community in undertaking such a burden. Furthermore, in starting to consider God, one of the primary problems is to find a fruitful approach, and a community can provide at least an initial background.

This need to seek God in common might be stultifying if there could be only one legitimate religious group. Then we would have to worry about being provincial in our outlook without being able to check on this by making comparisons. Interestingly enough, more than one religious group has grown up. Thus, the problem of community is not a simple one, for first a person must decide which community. A natural answer is one that has meaning for the individual by his historical attachments to it. But, in our day, many do not have such a natural starting point, and we must always ask whether another group might have an advantage over our own. Like marriage, however, you cannot move about indefinitely; sooner or later you must choose one context or one community as workable and agree to pursue the question of God within that framework.

Once accepted, a religious community can provide both support and orientation in the difficult search for God, although this is not absolute support, since the question of "which community" always lurks in the back of our minds. Still, the problem of finding stability within a community is a personal one and involves the history, procedures, and personnel of that group. On the more systematic side, we have to ask why it is that God is any more likely to be found within a community than by a strictly individual search. Most philosophical treatments of the question of God's existence approach the matter as if it were, in the extreme sense, an individual problem of each man thinking out an issue on his own. Behind this, however, what we have to ask is whether such independent questions about God actually presuppose some context of religious community within which alone the argument and the kind of God argued to make sense.

One key here is to realize that most reported "appearances" of God have been to a community. Or, perhaps more accurately, they have at least come to an individual as a part of an already existing religious group and have led immediately either to the formation of a new subgroup or else to a completely new community. To say all this or to accept it is neither to finish the quest nor to guarantee its success. The individual search still depends upon the individual effort; it cannot be done by anyone for anyone else.

At this point, we must make the issue of seeking God in community more difficult by asking this question: "Is God found when it is discovered that he is not in a certain designated place?" It is a very common and yet highly disappointing experience of those in some religious groups who read or hear reports of the ways in which that community has found or searched for God that he is not automatically always in that same place. Then, when the novice follows the proscribed procedures or looks in previously successful directions, he is often bitterly disappointed to find nothing, or at least nothing but the very human actions of his comrades. What we must ask is whether this disillusion is a necessary prelude to any actual discovery of God. If it is, this would support the argument for the necessity of a community context, since only by following some already established directions and procedures will you have the experience of God's absence at the very place where he has previously been reported (for example, in the Eucharist). Loss must precede finding, and 'loss' means to discover absence where presence has often before been reported.

If one simply seeks God on his own, he cannot know such disappointment, since he follows no existing directions but simply looks about by himself. Thus, he cannot be discouraged about not finding God in any particular place. An existing community usually disappoints at first because God is not found to be as real in that context as he had been reported to be. Why is this disillusioning experience a necessary one, and why does it argue for conducting the search within community rather than for abandoning a context that necessarily seems to induce misdirection on first encounter? The answer involves the classical *via negativa*—that is, God is found by discovering first that he is not where you might have expected him. Were he automatically present at some prescribed place, the quest would be too easy.

In this sense, the search for God in community is more rather than less difficult, so the question of community context is not one of initial ease but of eventual success. After the first disappointment of finding God not to be as real as others have reported, what the searcher learns is that God neither is controlled by simple formula nor does he appear on command. Then, in the disappointment of emptiness over the failure of a first encounter, a new sense of direction may develop. However, this is true only if the person does not let disappointment turn into a rejection of the whole experience but into new and matured determination. If encountered simply alone, this experience may make going ahead impossible. When you do what you are told and it is not successful, then the situation is both more precarious and more hopeful. If left alone, you are tempted to think that one failure is the final conclusion. Within a community, you may learn that it is a matter of continual and renewed attempt, always searching out new directions and returning to places of previously reported presence.

If the first attempt—and who knows how many more—to find God is doomed to failure and rightly so, then the community must provide sustenance when the individual has no other support. He learns about God by learning to depend on his fellow men. Left alone, the individual might turn back after one or two unsuccessful efforts, but given the support of a community, he may persist until one day he stumbles on the key. This situation is not really so different from training for any other difficult enterprise. Team support is needed in order to produce maximum effort continually and to provide expert coaching so that various styles are tried until one is found that fits that individual and opens success to him. If the divine quest is a team sport, it is not best played alone. In fact, it may even be dangerous and foolish not to admit the need for group effort.

Why should this be and, if it is true, what does this in itself tell us about God—a kind of first fruits of the willingness to surrender individualism? Alone, a man has no need to bend his will or to subject himself to anything other than his own desires. He may achieve self-discipline, but if left completely to himself, this is not a very likely outcome. A community context forces the individual to accommodate to certain common standards. This requires him to compromise his simple independence, and that is why so many break with their former communities out of annoyance. A God of rugged individualism unmindful of anyone but himself and his desires— such a God cannot be found in community because the very context does not lead to such a concept. In teaching the necessity for submission, the community may, if it is properly done, teach something about God that it is almost impossible to learn alone.

A God of community will have certain qualities an individual God cannot have. He must be of a certain kind or else he would not have associated with a group. If he does, he is a God of some concern for beings other than himself (*vs.* Aristotle's Unmoved Mover who is not a God to be discovered in community). If God relates and is present to a group, his qualities of personality are made clear in this way as they are not by any individual consideration of, say, the first principle of motion. A different kind of God will be found in a community context, there is no question about that. To refuse to accept the inevitable personal irritations of community life is either to risk failure in the quest or else to find a very different God.

What does the question of whether to accept a community context for God have to do with the philosophical basis each man decides to accept? First, it is clear that a God found in community will have the essential qualities of personality, however different from man he may still be. A philosophy that excludes the direct attribution of personal qualities to its deity (for example, Plotinus or Tillich) will work against the acceptance of a religious community as the locus of the search for God and will stress instead the solitary religious life. It is true that the question of the eventual loss of individual personality is at issue here, and it can be a community goal to prevent this. Without prejudging this question, at least we know that the goals of the community must be inspected carefully first, since they will shape the limits as to what kind of God can be found in that context. To join a group and then to seek a God incompatible with that community ideal—this is a common experience and a very sad and frustrating affair.

Second, any philosophy that insists on an absolutely individual approach to every question, together with the independence of the individual in working out every answer for himself, such a philosophical view cannot be conducive to the necessity for a community context in asking about God. A certain status must be granted to communities as opposed to individuals, and this is an issue to be discussed more fully in the next section. If God is found only after initial disappointment, he cannot be a simple God who is easily available. For this to be a correct approach, a philosophy of simple empiricism cannot be true, since our idea involves a God who does not always perform according to past experience and who is capable of refusing to subject himself to any simple form of verification. A God who can be found in community is possible only on the basis of certain philosophical assumptions.

F. WHAT STATUS CAN 'COMMUNITY' HAVE?

Where 'community' is concerned, it becomes perfectly clear that, unless this concept is granted a certain ontological status, the search for God is either seriously hampered or else redirected. If, on the one hand, all communities are dissolved, perhaps there is no context for God. On the other hand, if communities are treated as natural and necessary formations, all of them need not be religious communities—but at least such groupings would be justified. If communities not only are possible but also are considered central in importance, it does not seem so strange either that God might be most evident only within a community or that communities might be formed as the result of his appearance.

What philosophy perspective does or can grant equal reality to entities other than the individual? From this question alone it is clear why strict nominalism does not allow a community to have the status it needs in order to be a preferred context for God. Nor can nominalism explain the other phenomena associated with religious formation into communities—for example, their necessity both as an expression of inner change and in providing a means to communicate compassion. What we learn from all this is not that one philosophical position is somehow true merely because it is needed, but that, if 'community' loses its philosophical basis as a real and primary entity, God perhaps becomes unreal too because we have lost the context we need in order to approach him.

For instance, a philosophy that limits itself to the study of human nature can perhaps not be extended to God. Or, in the case of Anselm's ontological argument, the important point may not be the logical detail of the formal argument but the kind of philosophical view within which the very question and his procedures make sense. This is not to imply that a given philosophical context must never be changed, but it does mean that the most important point is to observe the effects of the shift from one philosophical context to another.

What kind of philosophic basis of community can we offer here? If authority is important to community, certainly we cannot operate on a basis of pure democracy. If we are able to grant ultimate authority to God, community can have a suitable importance. Those today who cannot understand religious communities and their function probably are also those who see no locus for authority other than the results of group decision. The governing structure of a community can still be democratic; it does not follow that if God is a king, men must be too. In fact, allowing God to be the locus of authority actually argues more that no one other than God possesses powers not voluntarily given to men by other men for practical reasons.

A philosophy of complete hedonism or self-seeking cannot support the idea of community, for we have argued (Section C) that communities and churches grow up from the need to express an outer directed compassion and love. If the accepted ethical basis is only that of the improvement of the individual's powers and potentials (for example, the self-fulfillment which is so prominent today), then this will work against the formation of a community as a necessary religious instrument. If individual self-fulfillment is the accepted criterion, communities will have no natural basis but one of expediency. Only a theory that naturally sends the person out of himself can support community. If his own salvation or improvement is the first concern, a community may actually present a barrier and seem unnatural to him. In any case, its existence will be for him a matter of personal convenience.

The ties that bind a group together must have philosophical support. Otherwise, if confidence in that theory is lost, the bonds of the community may dissolve too, or else they will be turned into one more business enterprise or power structure. In addition to the acceptance of a locus for authority, common affirmation, suffering in the pursuit of a goal, ritual practice, and common work are all factors that produce community. In theory, each of these must be accepted as having importance, or else the foundations of the community may be threatened. In addition to the individual search for meaning, is it necessary to provide for common affirmation? To do this is quite a different task from seeking individually an acceptable answer. In order to join together in a pledge, the individual must compromise his private intentions and be willing to submit to group consensus. Does he accept a theory that recognizes or rejects this as a goal? That is the fundamental religious issue.

15

FREEDOM

A. THE PRISONER OF CHRIST

Perhaps no problem has absorbed man so much as his quest for freedom. It is not unusual that this should appear as an issue in our religious life too, but what makes it difficult is that, in this context, freedom is strangely connected to the idea of bondage and of being made a prisoner. By way of contrast, the secular and political meanings of 'freedom' are not usually associated with such personal subjection. In fact, they tend to stress the opposite.

However, it may very well be that no kind of freedom involves a total absence of restraints. Yet, even if absolute liberty is simply a romantic secular notion, it is still true that, at least theologically, the understanding of freedom has been complicated by its somewhat paradoxical relationship to bondage. Thus, religiously speaking, freedom may simply mean to pass from one master to another. Understanding freedom in its religious form is bound up with this question: "What kinds of masters is man capable of being a slave to, and how does each one affect the personality of the captive individual?"

Freedom, as opposed to bondage, is a common theme throughout the Bible. In the Old Testament, a great deal of concern is focused on securing the release of slaves. Without question, a Jew feels loyal to his religion if he can affirm this traditional statement: "We were slaves in Egypt, and Yahweh delivered us from captivity." The Christian affirmation of freedom as a result of God's action is quite similar. However, somewhat ironically, it is now expressed as freedom from the very Mosaic law that originally was established to protect the Jew's sense of obligation to God for having given him his freedom. Still, even if the Christian feels himself free from the obligation of the ritual law, he keeps the idea of having exchanged one bondage for another. Understanding how such a situation can be called 'freedom' is at the heart of our problem.

It is Paul, of course, who speaks of being a "prisoner of Christ." Since he writes from jail and yet feels that he is free, it is fairly clear that, whatever the result of his religious experience, it did not depend on a freedom from all confinement. In what sense does Christianity 'liberate,' then, if it does not do so physically? As has been mentioned, Paul and other early Christians speak of freedom primarily as release from the observance of the elaborate Mosaic ritual law, but in our times that can be the source of Christian freedom for very few. And even this original release from the law must have been at least partially symbolic for Paul. Since the experience of liberation is often associated with a conversion upon hearing and accepting the Christian gospel, freedom must have something to do with a reorientation of attitude and a redirection of the self. To be a "slave" usually involves our inability to turn away from some practice (which either dope addiction or the slavish adherence to Jewish ritual law will illustrate) in order to realize our possibility to act in other ways.

Any release of the self from compulsion and involuntary action is an experience of freedom. In the religious sense, and in the specific case of the Christian, freedom also seems to be associated with turning away from outer demands and turning toward the inner self. However, this is also accompanied by a release from self-concern and redirection to a primary compassion for others. The constant need to protect the self is perhaps the greatest source of our involuntary servitude. As long as self-protection dominates our thinking, no man is really free from the demand for constant self-absorption and aggression.

If the self is its own prime object, it is impossible for us to let go of what is required to support its accomplishments.

Although the laws that govern physical existence differ from society to society and age to age, still there are fixed demands for anyone whose attention is centered on himself. The Christian experience is one of release and reorientation. Again: it means to be rid of the insatiable demands of the self and to turn both from outer circumstance to inner concern and from self-concern to a concern for others.

Yet, except under the most unusual conditions of a disintegration of the self, we simply cannot let go of what we have held on to so tightly without reaching out to grasp something else. This is the source of the paradox in the Christian expressions of freedom. It does not involve a release from all masters; it becomes a bondage to Christ and no longer a slavery to the self or to the outer world. The Christian cannot cease to cling to himself and then embrace nothing; the release comes simply because he is enabled to let go of what has obsessed him due to the fact that he now holds onto Christ. Why is this so, and how is this transformation able to take place? Such an experience of release must come because the individual finds, through his relationship to Christ, a power greater than his own and one that is also stronger than his previous attractions. This is why Jesus is not experienced simply as a man. The transforming power some have felt in their relationship to him has been so strong and overwhelming that it could only be described as a divine confrontation.

Release comes and freedom is experienced only if a God is encountered whose power is sufficient to neutralize any other force that presses its demands upon us. Paul and other Christians are not released from all obligation by this experience; they are only set free from previous obsessions. Now they are captives again, but it is to a higher power, one free from evil or destruction, hence divine, and they serve in a newness of spirit. One slavery has simply been exchanged for another, and yet this change is reported as "freedom." The orientation is new because the self no longer dominates itself. If this self-surrender actually proves to be to God, the self now has room to move freely. You can determine whether the release is divine or merely deceptive, because, in relation to just another human power, the self will not undergo such an experience of expansive liberation.

Perhaps the question we need to ask, in order to understand

how Christian freedom can simply mean "bondage to Christ" and still be experienced as release, is "Must the experience of being unexpectedly captured always precede the experience of freedom?" That is, can freedom be arrived at directly, or, if it is, would that not really be simply the attraction of the self to another power? This element of "surprise capture" needs to precede freedom, or else the attainment of any intended goal is not accompanied by the sensation of freedom. Perhaps that is why the achievement of a goal long desired actually often does not satisfy us as much as we expected it to when that moment comes. Success may be gratifying, but, when it is, it seems to be connected with a surprise in the avenue or in the unexpectedness of the way in which the results came about— that is, either suddenly or in an unanticipated manner. In short, we need first to be seized by an outside power in order to know what freedom means, but then the question becomes whether this power is alien and unfriendly or whether it might be God.

This necessity for capture to precede freedom may be connected to the fact that a man who knows no restraint on the self can never know what freedom means. We think, whenever we labor under a burden we would like to shed, that freedom should be defined as a situation in which no demands are made on the self whatsoever. Instead, total lack of restraint is chaos, and, when it happens, it quickly leads to the self being driven about wildly by whichever needs and desires are strongest at the moment. Lacking all control, we quickly fall victim of every pressure. Only by drawing on other restraints does the self seem able to devise any steadiness or power of resistance in order to hold itself back from all of the strange demands that would occupy it fully if they could. Thus, "bondage to Christ" may simply supply the anchor that men need in order not to have their freedom swamped by the thousand demands that set upon us, almost any one of which is stronger than the individual's powers of resistance.

This meaning for freedom, and its relation to the surrender of the self to God as the only means of release from obsessive demands, may also explain the traditional notion of 'discipleship.' If we follow the more romantic notion of freedom as the lack of all restraint, and if the experience of conversion actually brought about an explosive absence of all control, no

Christian would express his relationship to Christ as one of discipleship. Bands of roving, unrestrained, and uninhibited wild men might have resulted from meeting Jesus, but not a team of disciples intent on carrying their experience out to others. These primitive Christians felt themselves to be both free and yet bound to a master; they were captives because he had released them from themselves and then dedicated them to a new life and to a mission. They were not free to do anything they pleased. They were released from an old way but immediately bound to a new one. They became disciples, and yet they experienced freedom in their new allegiance. They became disciples because they surrendered themselves to God whose presence they experienced through Christ. This relationship to a higher power provided them with the only condition upon which the experience of freedom is possible.

Perhaps to set out to seek freedom as our primary goal, then, is impossible and will always be doomed to failure. If you demand freedom pure and simple, you end by coming under bondage to what you seek. The self must be seized from behind, taken by surprise, and shaken loose by the power that touches it. In this experience, men become disciples, and they are devoted to that which has given them a release from themselves they could not obtain by trying, because their very effort only tied the knots tighter. A disciple, as it turns out, must be someone who has experienced unexpected release. The need of others became clear to him only because he lost his own self-interest in this process. He is one who, in devotion to the divine power that accomplished what the individual could not himself do, binds himself freely as a disciple. Any other route to discipleship is either false slavery or a weak pretended submission. It can last only temporarily—until the self returns to reassert its own interests again.

If freedom cannot be achieved by an absence of all bonds, it still is possible that some powers are so different that to be a prisoner to them is not expressed as slavery but as freedom. How can powers differ so in their control of the self that one seems able to produce an almost opposite effect from that of another? This must be what we mean by the divine *vs.* the human and why, traditionally, men have insisted on giving to Jesus a divine status as God's son. We know that to encounter every other power is only to experience trading one form of subjugation of the self to drives that dominate it for another set of needs, and this is not to escape all slavery. When God is encountered, the self is destroyed; man's fear of divine confrontation is well founded. As the self's drives are met, stopped, and destroyed, the experience men have that converts them is that, actually, they are not totally destroyed as they feared they would be. Instead, they are transformed to new life. You would expect the loss of all your known powers to mean destruction, and yet, *in God's case alone*, the meeting of such overwhelming power is experienced as transformation—that is, after the first moments of religious panic have been suffered through and pass.

To such a power that is able to transform, man willingly pledges himself as a disciple and claims that his new bondage is, in fact, freedom. And it is a freedom from the powers that formerly dominated him, from which he could not release himself. If what should have destroyed him did not, that power is called divine. Human power is not like that, except perhaps, occasionally, when mercy and compassion restrain us. Such a man who has encountered God is free from normal demands; their grip on him has been broken.

Above all he is free from his own self's incessant demands. His intentions have been turned to others. He is free of human demands, because the power that has captured him he acknowledges to be divine. Of course, if he is mistaken in any of this, he can become a fanatic or else be religiously intolerant, and, in this case, he will destroy rather than preserve. The powerful forces that are loose in religion are hard to distinguish one from another, and a mistake at this point can turn a man into a monster instead of into a servant of man who is freely bound to God. But such are the risks of freedom, even when it is a divine freedom.

B. WHAT IS THE CHRISTIAN DISCOVERY OF FREEDOM?

Where 'freedom' is concerned, we are dealing with perhaps the most 'philosophical' of all religious questions. Yet, the whole theme of Part I was that religion is still something different in kind from either philosophy or theology. If this is true, before we can discover in how many ways a religious question can be structured philosophically, it is necessary to determine what is specifically Christian and unique about the convert's experience of his new freedom. Such a personal experience of change gives us our primary data, and it prevents philosophy of religion from treating the question on purely philosophical grounds. The theological answer given must be fair to the original Christian experience—and represent it with the force it had—that is our criterion.

First, we note how common and how important this experience of release and freedom is in the report of Christian conversion. The use of the term 'release' is correct here, for the account almost always takes the form of a removal of previous restrictions and burden. 'Sin' and the 'law' are the two most important factors. Thus, we really cannot know what form freedom will take until we know exactly how 'sin' is defined (see Chapter 20), since *that from which we are released determines what our freedom can be.* In fact, this release from the burden of sin is essentially what 'salvation' means (see Chapter 23), which points up the fact that almost all of the problems of philosophy of religion are interdependent in their conception. However, what is perhaps central to this experience of freedom is the discovery of "new life." Discovering freedom always seems to involve the removal of restrictions which have held the person down in the development of his full self.

The primitive Christian expression of his freedom as release from the 'law' involves a slightly more complicated question. Removal of the strict observance of Mosaic religious customs became a matter of deep concern for early Christian converts, as well as an item of contention. It was Paul who particularly identified his new Christian freedom with a release from the burden of ceremonial law. Except for the occasional convert from Orthodox Judaism, this is a problem that cannot affect anyone today in the way in which it absorbed the early Christians. Yet, if release from ancient ritual law seldom has a literal significance any more, it may still be that some form of freedom from ceremonial observance is central to the Christian experience of release. If so, we must begin by asking "What regulations restrict the growth of the spirit in our day so that our own contemporary religious ritual has become oppressive rather than liberating?" It is certainly true, for instance, that the first Protestants experienced this same release from a decadent Catholic code, so that perhaps an experience of spiritual release from archaic ritual restriction is, and always should be, central to the Christian discovery of freedom.

This, of course, raises the question of the meaning of 'the Kingdom' whose coming Jesus clearly announced. However, we know that his disciples did not understand exactly what form this would take or how it would appear. To this day, it is part of every Christian's task to decide in what sense he can proclaim that 'the Kingdom' has, in fact, come with Jesus' announcement of its presence. Some Jews of his time misunderstood this proclamation and took Jesus to be the long awaited Messiah who would lead them physically and deliver them from political oppression. They supported Jesus when they thought his announced kingdom might lead to this kind of physical freedom, and they crucified him when their political hopes were frustrated. Even his disciples were broken and dispirited when Jesus' physical leadership was cut off.

Evidently, then, if Christian history had stopped with the experience of a martyred political challenger, we would only have one more record of a revolt that failed. Whatever else the experience of Jesus' resurrection meant, it clearly told the disciples that his kingdom was not political and that it could therefore survive death. It actually had come, but in a different way than either his disciples expected or the Old Testament prophecy had predicted. In the experience of this revelation, when the true insight dawned in the midst of disappointed hopes, the early Christians found their release, and it came to them as a sense of freedom from the bonds of the physical world. In order to obtain their release, they had to expect it in one form, see this thwarted, and then have freedom surprise them by arriving in an unexpected form. For a Christian, perhaps freedom must always come in an unanticipated way, in a form not subject to prediction and control. Can this happen only after political ambitions have been disappointed and some risk is involved in our physical mode of existence?

In reading the New Testament, perhaps everyone since Jesus' time who would like to become a Christian must search to discover for himself the meaning of freedom. It is clear from the beginning that this will take some unexpected forms, ones not anticipated by our everyday ambitions to achieve power and the fulfillment of our desires. One scene in the Gospels always stands out in this consideration—Jesus' reading of the passage from Isaiah 61:1 in the synagogue: "The Lord . . . hath sent me . . . to proclaim liberty to the captives." After reading these words, Jesus commented that today they had seen that promise fulfilled. This shocked his Jewish listeners, for they knew that only God could accomplish this (as he had obtained their release from Egypt). Thus, Jesus' claim to represent this liberation could only be taken as a blasphemous claim to divinity. This was particularly true since the Jews of his time could not see any evidence that he had obtained their political liberation.

The question of 'freedom', then, in Christian terms, always involves a claim of divine presence, since the release offered is of such proportions that it requires God's action to break the natural order. The Jews could not see this in what they took to be Jesus' political claims, and so they crucified him for this blasphemy. In the midst of his political failure, those Jews became Christians who could recognize God's action in restoring this sacrifice to life. The kingdom had come, but its existence was within and not without, as the Jews rightly expected it to be according to their previous history.

The experience of Christian freedom is also dependent upon our notion of 'God' (see Chapter 18) and on our ability to discern his action to produce release in unexpected and often unobservable ways. This freedom comes upon us not as a result of our effort, since that is directed in different and often unsuccessful ways. It must be God's action that renews, and this involves an experience of the immediate presence of the divine (in later days, the Holy Spirit represents Christ). As a result of this divine encounter, life is restored in the face of otherwise inevitable destruction.

Freedom of this type becomes a present possession, and it cannot be taken away or confined by prison walls. It brings a power with it that can defy every restriction and even death, and it does all this in God's name. It is a bold freedom and yet it is intangible. Since it is a release of the spirit, it always requires a philosophical setting that does not identify 'soul' with 'body', and this is why the early Christians found Platonism such a sympathetic vehicle. The freedom of the children of God, as inaugurated by Jesus and the 'kingdom' that he brought, is a fundamental message of the Gospel. Thus, the experience of being released by such divinely given liberty is perhaps the primordial fact that first made Christianity possible and without which it cannot continue to be renewed. A new spirit comes and it gives vitality. Such renewal, however, is inward and unseen, even though it is related to overcoming physical death.

The Christian experience of freedom also always involves liberation from the determining factors of sin. In other words, it moves forward to prevent the continuance of old ways as well as backward to release our behavior from the burden of accumulated guilt. It always appears to be "outside the law," whether this is Jewish religious legalism or a Puritanical austere custom. As the first section of this chapter indicated, this does not lead to a lack of all restriction. Its essential feature is that the restraint is now interior and divinely imposed rather than externally demanded. The ordinary citizen is a slave to worldly powers, even if politically he is a free man, but it is his release from spiritual damnation that the Christian experiences. Powers present in the world (drugs, sex, or wealth) obsess man and bind him to their satisfaction. The Christian experience of freedom is a release from the dominance of all such forces over the individual, even though an alternating cycle of continued bondage and renewed release goes on.

At this point we must ask "In what sense is it ever possible to be totally free, to know no limits? What experience could yield a feeling such as this?" We have already pointed out that Christian freedom is not a lack of all restraint, but, if so, why should the experience of it take on this aspect? Those factors in the world external to the self that restrict and bind it are neither replaced by other restrictions nor overcome by force. They only become powerless as the center of the self's attention shifts inward rather than outward. The external forces become ineffectual, and, in that sense, Christian freedom is a lack of all (external) limits. Not that the individual goes promiscuously wild; these forces simply no longer apply or touch the self at its center. Because the self has come under the control of spiritual forces, its release from material bondage has the feeling of a total freedom and a lack of all limits.

In fact, of course, neither the Christian—nor any other individual—is ever free from the necessity to deal with external forces as long as the body must be protected and cared for. Realizing this fact often dampens the original Christian experience of release. However, this involves not so much an absence of all limits (although the experience can have this feeling at first) as it does the release from the dominance of one set of forces and the substitution of new governing principles. Yet, in this case they are spiritual and divinely given and have a power sufficient to break the normal limits set on humanity. This report, of course, is often accompanied by the assertion that the former individual subject to such dominance is "dead." It is not simply a repressed personality rising to consciousness to replace an earlier self, but God or Christ who now lives within the individual. This divine in-dwelling that replaces external bondage is crucial to the Christian experience of freedom. This is why such freedom is not simply an assertion of the self's full powers but is reported as a loss of self. God is capable of assuming direction for the self.

This does not mean that the self experiences a loss of power. The evidence of most conversions seems to indicate a greatly increased vigor. The dominating control is now thought to be an in-dwelling divine spirit, although the "mistakes" of Christians make it clear that this control is subject to certain lapses and uncertainties. Nevertheless, in spite of its precariousness, this divine direction as replacing that of the self characterizes the Christian experience of freedom. After all, the experience does not say that spiritual freedom cannot be lost or that it may not have to be regained again in the next instance. The coming and going of this divine spirit in a person constitutes that individual's religious history. The uncertainties involved do not deny the coming of freedom; they simply confirm its unpredictable nature. *To be transformed to live precariously in such uncertainty is Christian freedom.*

C. IS FREEDOM COMPATIBLE WITH OBEDIENCE?

In a sense, this question has already been considered in the discussion of the Christian's report that he becomes a 'prisoner' at the same time that he is free (see Section A). A further and partially independent question is involved here. It relates to the traditional religious notions of 'obedience', 'humility', and 'submission'. Humility may seem to be a strange idea to connect with freedom, since usually the experience of gaining freedom is accompanied by self-expansion, by a dominance of the ego, and by a concentration on the self's powers. Evidently, then, Christian freedom differs in some important respects here. Rather than fierce pride in individual accomplishment, the Christian experience involves a meekness due to the knowledge that the release, and all that it accomplishes, are not the result of individual power and self-assertion, but are due to God's unexpected intervention. When what the self cannot accomplish is done for it, it is set free, but then it also should become obedient to the power responsible for its release.

Submission, of course, is no longer taken as something that is due to any temporal ruler or worldly power. In this sense, a free Christian is not submissive, and perhaps he is even socially assertive in the name of God's purposes. His submission is inward, and it is to God alone (although here Protestants and Catholics differ over determining God's authorized representatives). The strangeness of Christian freedom, then, is the fact that outer release is gained only at the price of inner submission and obedience. A spiritually self-assertive Christian is a contradiction in terms. One who tries to control or to dictate the events of the inner life of another person substitutes spiritual domination for political release and distorts Christian freedom. The question becomes to ask: What must a Christian be obedient to in his freedom?—and it is clear that the first answer is, not to any external authority. His submission is spiritual, and, since only God had the power to grant him this freedom, his obedience also belongs to God alone.

If Christian freedom is release from the Mosaic law and sin and death, it involves a new order inaugurated by Jesus. Prior to his coming, man certainly was not free from any of these three forces, except perhaps momentarily and by dint of great effort. Those who still do not think we have been set free are non-Christians; those who think we have been (or can be) released are disciples. To be clear about the meaning of Christian 'freedom', we must know what the new order is that we take Jesus to have inaugurated. What it is will determine what our freedom is like. How we believe it to have been inaugurated will give us the key to our possible participation in it. A new relationship to God has been established for the followers of Jesus, and it is offered as a free gift. Since this relationship has been freely established, it should be enjoyed in freedom.

Now the question of 'merit' enters, for if you have freedom by your own right, you neither submit to any man, nor feel you must enjoy that freedom in humility. A rightful freedom leads you to subject yourself to no one, so that the surprising quality in the Christian experience is that of release as an unearned gift. It is not yours by right, as are other freedoms which are guaranteed by law, and thus its granting always comes as a surprise because it is undeserved. That God should act in this unusual manner, that he should disobey natural rights, all this tells the Christian a great deal about God.

The experience of the bestowal of freedom by divine intervention is the source of a new insight into an unexpected side of God's nature. That God would act in this manner, or could act, is only possible if God has certain dominant features. Freedom is never experienced by the Christian as a self-contained event. It is connected with a revelation of God's nature and his ultimate plans. As such, it is strangely found not to be incompatible with submission, obedience, and humility, although these are due only to God.

If the normal experience of freedom is not like this, then we have a theological test for determining whether the demand for freedom springs from Christian or from secular sources. No external restraint can ever be imposed as a Christian demand, whatever its natural justification may be. Similarly, any given demand for change in regulations may or may not be justified, but the protest can only be Christian if it is based, not on some supposed limitation on the individual, but on an assertion that God's own expression is being stifled. Christian freedom cannot be achieved by a fight or by force, since the core of its experience lies in our learning that it comes only by God's action. What God may be able to accomplish through individuals who are so released is another matter, but, in their actions in response to God, they will have to bear the responsibility for claiming to have heard his demands clearly. Since God's own actions do not come of necessity, any interpretation of them cannot be claimed with certainty either.

One question that suggests itself is "Does freedom actually mean 'to obey willingly'?" The limitations set on human powers are such that men can always be coerced. We fall under spells so easily that we often obey simply because we have lost all self-control. However, to obey without internal or external coercion may itself be the meaning of freedom. This involves both an independence and a power in the will that can direct it, but this might mean setting the will free from anything that inhibits its spontaneous commitment. When the will is unrestricted, it may commit itself by its own power. Perhaps, then, all we are set free to do is to obey willingly rather than to be forced to do so under pressure. All this, of course, says nothing about what we are to obey or whom we are to follow freely. For the Christian, either his following of God's will has not been free up to now or he has been rebellious; however, now he is released to obey voluntarily. If this interpretation is at all correct, freedom is not incompatible with obedience, although only in this one important instance.

D. DOES GOD'S FREEDOM DIFFER?

There are philosophical theories that treat God and man alike and describe them both under the same categories. To do that may still be possible philosophically, but the Christian experience of freedom tells us that the concept of God that accompanies this freedom forces us to attribute radically different powers to God. The Christian reaction to freedom is one of being released from natural bonds, even death, and all this is accomplished by God where human power could not free itself. God must be able to accomplish what men cannot; he must have control over the power required to break the natural order. In order to grant freedom, he must exceed in power those forces that are superior to men. This means that, whatever concept of God is adopted for Christian theological purposes (and more than one may do), *at least sufficient power must be attributed to God to explain the Christian experience of involuntary freedom.*

There are, of course, theories that' attribute necessity to the divine nature and consider freedom as an inferior quality insofar as it involves contingency. In order to explain the Christian experience of freedom, we must admit that freedom is a central characteristic of divinity too. Such a God is himself the source of human freedom, because he knows freedom and a lack of determinism in his own nature first, and this is a different God from many—for example, Plotinus' One or the Buddha.

God must first be free in order for man to experience freedom in encountering him, or else the experience of divine action would not be the release from natural bonds that has made the Christian proclamation unique. Of course, 'freedom' can mean many things, and Spinoza's God, for instance, is "free," and anyone who comes to know him experiences freedom too. Yet, this involves not contingency but necessity, so that what Spinoza really means by freedom is to be "determined from itself alone." In that sense only his God is free.

Although, according to Spinoza, man may, by improving his understanding, share partially in this divine freedom, his theory cannot explain the Christian experience fully. Spinoza's God does not break nature's restrictions set on man; he is Nature. Man is not set free from death and his own limitations; he is reconciled to them. The issue is, *What kind of freedom must be attributed to God in order to give him the power necessary to explain the Christian's experience?* Saint Thomas' God is also free, but his concept does not involve the contingency of choice between nonnecessary alternatives. The question is whether this kind of contingency is a central aspect of the Christian experience of freedom. If it is, then we must work back from this experience to locate in God's nature an attribute capable of explaining a revolutionizing experience. This does not mean that God's freedom must be identical to what man discovers. In fact, what we have argued is that God's freedom must be superior and not the same in order to explain its almost violent impact on man.

Could man experience freedom and might God still be necessary in his nature? The stoic advice to accept truth and unchangeable fact involves a kind of rational liberation and freedom. Yet this does not seem to exhaust the new Christian's experience. He feels the impact of a direct action by God which arrives in a manner not expected (for example, not a political rebel, but a spiritual leader). All of this indicates a God whose freedom is capable of the unexpected and who is able to intervene and to act directly in specific cases as a result of his own contingent decision. Freedom in God cannot be different in kind from man's experience of its nonnecessity when he confronts God, or else man is deceived in his freedom. Of course, it is possible that he and all Christians are deceived in their experience, but the force of their release from bondage supports their conviction (that is, their faith) that they are not. Freedom involves an association with the contingent and the unpredictable; it is a release of power not inconsistent with reason and knowledge, but still controlled only by will.

Our experience of freedom is not self-contained; it involves an understanding of God. It is not a fact of action and of release alone; but it comes to us in virtue of what we now understand God to be. In the sense that we do not achieve our own freedom, this new understanding of God's nature is an unexpected disclosure, a revelation. In fact, it would seem that *only the disclosure of God's activity can create freedom by an involuntary response to it.*

If God's nature is opened, freedom flows out as a consequence. If because we originally did not understand God's nature and intent we were bound by natural forces, only a new vision of God has sufficient power to release us from this failure. Such insight into God, however, is itself something freely given and not easily attained. To say this does not at all mean that men could not think about God before Jesus; they did. All it means is that the Christian revelation of freedom, contingency, interaction, and reversal is not a long expected view of God that emerged out of the previous theological discussion as such. *It required God's direct action to create a new experience of him.*

This raises the interesting question of whether man can become free without God. Nietzsche and Sartre both feel that God's existence actually inhibits man's freedom. Now the issue becomes "Does the elimination of God kill or create freedom?" Nietzsche and Sartre both oppose God in the name of freedom because they have a deterministic conception of God, and such a God, if he exists, certainly would dominate man. All that can be said to those who advocate the death of God in order to make human freedom possible is that a foreordaining God is not at the center of the Christian experience of freedom. 'Foreordination' in the sense that God can establish a goal and is sure that he can attain it, yes. Foreordaining in the sense that every human action has been established from eternity, no. Is God capable of self-controlled change? That is the crucial question. If so, he may accomplish his goal flexibly, and he need not determine individual human action in the process.

The loss of a God who himself is the source of our experience of freedom would then kill freedom too, since its source would disappear. To proclaim the death of a God who is incapable of change might open freedom as a human possibility, but the major argument is not over freedom but over how we should conceive of God. In answering that question, since we have more concepts of God open to us than one, the issue is what experience will we appeal to, to provide the basis for our selection from among alternative Gods? If it is Aristotle's impression of the ability of pure actuality to move others while itself remaining unmoved, that will lead to one kind of God. If it is Plotinus' overwhelming discovery of the controlling presence, on every level, of degrees of unity, God will reflect that psychological experience. But, if it is the Christian's experience of being released from the dominance of natural forces, that will lead to a God who does not restrict human freedom, but who grants it and is, in fact, the only power capable of holding contingency open to us.

The Christian experiences the vast difference between God's freedom and his own, and it is this that he must explain if he is a preacher or a theologian. What must God be like for his freedom to be so superior to ours? What must he be like that he would extend his freedom to man voluntarily and without duress? What must man's nature be so that he can be liberated by divine disclosure and not destroyed by it, as the Jews often expected to be?

Freedom, at present, means that our natural power extends itself until it is stopped or thwarted or exhausted. God's freedom does not move against established limits or superior powers, but it is such that, since God voluntarily establishes limits, he may break them if he wills. His power and his goodness are subject to his freedom. In fact, *it is 'freedom' that defines the relation of the attributes within the divine nature.* This fact requires the presence of contingency in God, an ability for controlled change and, above all, a capacity to restrict his own unlimited power in order to grant freedom to others.

E. HOW IS 'FREEDOM' DETERMINED?

In considering the Christian experience of freedom in relation to other theological concepts, it is clear that freedom has many meanings. The correct question for philosophy of religion is "How can we establish the meaning of 'freedom'?" For it is also clear that some concepts of freedom actually deny or move against the peculiar Christian experience. Were these interpretations of freedom correct, the experience could not be what it claims, or at least its interpretation would be altered drastically. Although not all concepts of freedom will do for Christian theological purposes, it is an amazing fact that, from Augustine to Thomas Aquinas to Luther, theologians have often worked within a metaphysical framework that made the attribution of contingency to God impossible, difficult, or undesirable. In this case, the primitive Christian experience of unexpected intervention is both altered and changed into some other form of freedom.

Perhaps it is just this question of determining 'freedom' that has been subject to the greatest fluctuations in theology. In philosophy of religion, it is 'freedom' that has been the most susceptible to domination by some particular philosophical theory. If one philosophical view interpreted freedom in a certain way, theology seemed bound to work within those limits. Yet, we cannot eliminate all philosophical interference here, for freedom is the most philosophically prejudiced question of all religious problems. The only course open to us is to learn in what ways freedom may be defined, to examine the original Christian experience of freedom, and then to see what can be done to construct a sympathetic metaphysical framework. It is clear from the examination of the historical theories in Part II that the interpretation given to freedom has been determined by the philosophical context used. Thus, our only question concerns our ability to provide a philosophical interpretation of 'freedom' of our own choice and construction.

For example, in his *Theological Dictionary*, Karl Rahner suggests that freedom means that man does not "exist harnessed to a universal natural order which totally determines his nature."[*] Clearly this is not so much a dictionary definition of the actual usage of the term as it is a suggested philosophical context within which a Christian doctrine of freedom can be set. This becomes apparent as Rahner describes man as "set in openness" to discover various possibilities and to realize his own nature. Freedom is human nature, and for man to abandon it is to abandon himself. The existential background of these definitions is clear when Rahner speaks of man being "summoned" to freedom and freedom of choice as an essential dignity of the person. These are interesting descriptions of the meaning of 'freedom', and they show, in themselves, how subject to philosophical variation this concept is. And this is true not just in minor ways, for an interpretation of freedom springs from the center of metaphysics.

In dealing with freedom, we face the full range of philosophical questions, since they determine its conception. We must understand not only what God is like in order to appraise freedom, as indicated in the last section, but also what man is and how he achieves human dignity. According to Spinoza or Hegel, for man to accept historical necessity is to evidence his greatest dignity, and, thus, that is man's freedom. Now, on existential grounds, man is said to determine his freedom and that is how his nature is fixed. Interestingly enough, neither interpretation fits the Christian experience perfectly. The existential interpretation Rahner prefers leaves freedom to

[*] Karl Rahner and Herbert Worgrimlar, *Theological Dictionary*, trans. R. Strachen; ed. C. Ernst, O.P. (New York: Herder & Herder, 1965).

human accomplishment, while Spinoza and Hegel rule out contingency. Clearly, fixing a useful meaning for 'freedom' is far from a simple matter.

Where we seem to stand philosophically on this problem is that it is possible to experience freedom as a Christian individual claims to, but it is not possible simply to express it as such. Although the Gospels are not philosophical investigations, in order to express the Christian gift of freedom, Paul and the Gospel writers first had to borrow known concepts and then express freedom in those terms—for example, release from the dominance of evil powers. In its expression as opposed its experience, freedom needs a structure, and this immediately takes on various philosophical shadings. It is not a concept that can be expressed in neutral terms. Its expression involves the term in theories that interpret it in crucial ways, just because it is so central to all philosophical understanding. For instance, if we understand freedom as Kant did (that is, as a physical impossibility but as a moral necessity), religious experience will be expressed quite differently.

Yet Christians are not allowed to be silent, as are followers of some Eastern religions. They are enjoined to speak, to explain their experience, and to proclaim its results. Because of this missionary injunction and the centrality of preaching and, thus, the necessity for Christian communication, Christian theologians are condemned to philosophical involvement. They must report on their new freedom, and it is impossible to do this without entering into philosophical theory. Any report of freedom is prompted, of course, by the experience of its being granted, but the manner of the report is molded by the philosophical context which is consciously or unconsciously selected.

Some religions may ignore philosophy. Christianity cannot because of its need to define philosophical categories in order to report its experience adequately in verbal form. Were freedom not so central to Christian experience and so crucial to philosophical outlook at the same time, or if the 'word' were not such an important aspect of God's nature, the situation would be less complicated. As it is, philosophy of religion begins by being schooled in the implications involved in philosophical definition.

F. FREEDOM AS FUTURE

In struggling to find a definition of freedom that will fit Christian experience and at the same time cover both God and man, one feature is central. Freedom in Christianity always involves a future mode, and that is 'hope'. Freedom is also announced as a present possession, although our problem is to explain how this comes about. Still, it is not said to be realized perfectly as yet. This must wait for a future day, which is the subject of Christian hope. Freedom, at present, exists only partially and as a promise of a future divine action and its consequent state. Whatever freedom may already have been granted, there is greater freedom yet to come. These future expectations are usually referred to as 'eschatology', and it is interesting to note that eschatology is not so much an independent question (although it is sometimes treated in this way) as it is the outgrowth of an attempt to explain the Christian experience of present freedom when this is coupled with its expected future perfect realization.

Thus, we would not face the question concerning what the future will bring if we had not experienced a present gift of freedom that is genuine but at the same time somehow not fully realized. What now is only partially known serves to raise the question of the future in our minds. Christians did not somehow suddenly begin to talk of eschatology and expect all kinds of things in the future. They experienced a present dramatic change and a granting of freedom, but it seemed to them still only partial and thus to be a sign of more yet to come. For this reason, in his new freedom the Christian lives oriented toward the future. He feels his freedom to be not yet fully realized, but, because of the amount that has been given to him in the present, he has come to expect its fulfillment. This future orientation of the Christian's experience of freedom explains why he does not feel he has the power presently to overcome all restrictions. His freedom is anticipatory; even in its present in-breaking it is dependent and also contingent upon future divine action.

The role of human action in this interim state becomes a crucial problem. The Christian has been granted a new freedom, but, in the meantime, just how much new power over natural forces has he acquired? How much is expected of him in virtue of his present gift of freedom, however incomplete it may be? Christian freedom has an eschatological structure, and this explains the temptation, which some give in to, to explain the new Christian freedom entirely as a future state and to picture man as currently in no improved position in relation to the world's powers. If Christian freedom were either fully formed now or left totally to the future, its explanation would be so much easier. As it is, we can never be completely sure what new powers and changes can or cannot be attributed immediately to post-Christian man.

What we need to understand about the Christian gift of freedom is why the experience of present change is very real and yet why it also must always involve hope and remain presently not fully realized. Perhaps men turn away from Christianity more over a failure to answer this question than for any other reason. They listen to the message and experience the conversion, with its accompanying sense of change and freedom, but then this all remains not fully realized. In that sense, it seems to them that they were mistaken in thinking they had experienced a change; Christianity appears as a hoax. The memory of the experience of radical opening grows dim, and they think nothing has happened because everything has not been altered all at once. It is difficult to shift from the experience of present freedom to a dependency on future hope, and those who cannot will fail to catch the essential meaning of faith. This in-between state is hard to live in, and, like the dialectic involved in the One and Many of Parmenides and Plato, we tend to move either toward one extreme or the other.

Perhaps we can express this dilemma over the contrast between present freedom and future hope by asking "Why did Jesus not stay with his disciples to lead them in their postresurrection community?" He certainly could have if he had wanted to. They had lived through their experience and passed their test, in the sense that they had failed (for example, Peter's threefold denial), and then God had acted to save the situation. In spite of all this, evidently those who were to become disciples had not yet passed all their tests. Listening to his teaching, attempting to preach themselves, experiencing the shattering of their plans in Jesus' crucifixion, or even the restoration of their hope in his resurrection—all this was not yet enough. They had expected a wrong form of the kingdom, one too overt and too political. They had anticipated a wrong kind of leadership from Jesus, a guidance too secure and too immediate. In the resurrection they could learn what the coming of the kingdom actually meant—and yet perhaps their understanding was not fully formed even there.

That is, had Jesus remained with them, they could have formed a community on the basis of their new understanding. They could have accepted his leadership on the proper terms then. Yet, their new freedom was not complete nor was their joy fulfilled, because their faith had not been given its final test. Having received a promise and an initial release, the question was "Could they remain loyal in an ensuing difficult interim period, one of unknown duration and without direct leadership?" It is easy enough to be a disciple when you have a leader to follow, even if he is not always understood. It must have been overwhelming to experience God's gift of power in Jesus' resurrection, but the hardest test of all is to possess a gift now and yet to be forced to hold steady indefinitely to wait for its fulfillment, all the while subsisting on only spiritual guidance. Having once received a gift of power, is it possible to live on for an unknown length of time simply in the hope of its final fulfillment? *That is really the question of faith,* not some minor problem over supposed logical paradox.

This is the way in which our understanding of freedom involves faith. This is also why freedom's definition requires a philosophical context. It is not real and fully evident now. As a Christian experience, it cannot be. It exists only as imperfectly realized, and thus its total structures are unknown. Christian freedom may be partially evidenced in present action (for example, acts of passion and humility), but it cannot be fully known or structured. Thus, to be understood it must be given form and expression, and this is precisely the activity of philosophy. That is, through the aid of technical terms, we structure for the understanding what cannot be immediately seen. It is the element of the future in freedom that involves it in uncertainty, and this makes it both hard to get hold of and to sustain. If it were not for this aspect of unrealized expectation, Christian freedom would simply be, and it would not need explanation. Its need for definition itself evidences the uncertainty involved in a freedom of this peculiar sort, but such a precarious situation is not particularly strange whenever freedom is the issue.

Freedom is not literally "seen" in any instance, so that a Christian concept of freedom is not inferior by being non-obvious. Its future orientation only complicates it in contrast to other doctrines which may refer solely to present experience. Freedom has always been a problem, because, although actions can be seen, what we do not see is whether they are done "freely." This hiddenness of the springs of action gives rise to the need for philosophy, and Christianity actually has some superiority (perhaps to counterbalance the difficulty of its future orientation) in that those who experience its power testify to its effects in their lives by forceful word and action (for example, Paul). Unfortunately, this is far from being a universal experience, and so even a number of unusual alterations are not enough alone to establish freedom with any certainty. We are dependent on the testimony of a minority and a partial realization within a few, and the issue is whether to believe this or not.

16

FAITH

A. FAITH AS A DERIVATIVE CONCEPT

'Faith' is a special word in that it has no complete meaning in itself. It is meaningful only in relation to the question "Faith in what?" Unless that can be answered clearly, it is not possible to say what 'to have faith' means. By its nature, it is a concept that can be applied to almost anything. In order to make its meaning concrete, the object or objects of faith must be specified. The problem here is that most matters that are said to involve or to require faith are subject to certain imprecisions. Faith, in the basic sense of placing confidence or committing trust, would not be involved if this were not so. Yet, just because of this fact, it is often difficult to specify the object of faith with very precise detail, and the meaning of faith is at least partially dependent on our ability to do so.

The fact that faith is a derivative concept means that its character as faith is determined by its object. It is not something in itself to be had or not to be had, to be rejected or accepted. That this is sometimes what is done does not prove that it is right. It merely proves that some individuals are unreflective about the meaning of faith and accept a certain formula as offered, or else they reject it and take this to define the limits of faith. Actually, faith is a much more complex affair and is subject to an infinite variety of forms; faith has as many forms as there are ways that an object of faith can be formulated. When one statement is offered as defining faith, the first question ought to be "Is there another formulation I could accept more easily or reject more clearly?" Or "Is there another form of faith that might be even more difficult to achieve?"

Take as an example the Christian problem of "faith in Jesus Christ." If it were clear beyond all question exactly who he was and thus what faith in him represents, the matter would be much simpler (perhaps it would not involve faith). This does not mean that we are without all guidance on this matter. Where faith is concerned, this is seldom true. Unless we were presented with certain material that in itself is inconclusive, the question of faith would never arise. Either nothing would demand it, or what is demanded would be clear beyond question. This is not the case with Christianity. Its own uncertainty is what raises the problem of faith. We begin, let us say, with the material of the New Testament, and we have some definitions of who Jesus is and thus what faith in him would mean, but all of these are not either clear beyond question or one in their formulation. These uncertainties in the objects themselves give rise to the need for faith.

Jesus' own words appear in several gospels. Our task is made more difficult because his own statements are not exactly the same in each of the four gospels, nor is a standard terminology used throughout the New Testament. It seems as if Jesus purposely left us with some uncertainty about his nature; he wrapped it in figurative and in indirect statements precisely in order that the question of faith might be involved. If the definition of Jesus and his role were clear and compact and consistent, it would not reflect the picture of faith accurately. He could be accepted or rejected as a whole, but it would not force on the individual the task of formulating the object of faith more clearly for himself. Creeds are designed to do this, but they also do too much. That is, they do the individual's work of formulation for him, and thus they can, ironically, actually make it more difficult for an individual to understand what faith involves.

As it stands, it is both the variety of statements about Jesus and Jesus' own indirectness that force the problem on the individual. He must himself decide who Jesus is before he can ask about the status of his own faith concerning him. It is not at all that the individual is without help here. If he were, the question of faith would never have been raised, for only when a problem is posed or a formula is presented does the question of acceptance or rejection arise. The would-be believer has the materials of the New Testament, the history of the creeds, plus the whole picture of the Christian church, to present him with an understanding of Christ. It almost seems as if the problem is that we have too much material, not too little. If that is the case, perhaps this also tells us something about the meaning of faith—that it is required, not in simple matters, but only where complexity cannot be eliminated.

Now the believer can see his problem and can understand how faith is defined. Faced with this complexity, he must formulate his own response to the question "Whom do men say that I am?" As he does this, then, as the object becomes more clear, so also can it be seen what "to have faith" in this case can mean, if in fact it is involved at all. That is, if the answer is a fairly simple and obvious one, it also can be accepted or rejected simply (for example, Jesus interpreted as a teacher or a prophet). If it gets more complex (for example, Jesus as the son of God or Messiah or Christ), then, as the accompanying difficulties become clear, it is evident what faith means in this instance and why it is required.

Even thus far we perhaps still have oversimplified the problem of faith. Sometimes if we knew in advance fully and clearly what would be involved or what would be required, we would not have the courage to begin the quest. Limited forward vision is sometimes an advantage and a protection against timidity and a shield against overwhelming a person with too great demands at the start. Thus, one seldom knows at the beginning either what faith is (that is, how its object is defined) or what it demands. At first, the simple meaning of faith involves starting out to settle these matters when the route is unclear beyond the starting point. Thus, a dialectic is involved. As you try to define more clearly the object of faith (for example, the attribution of divinity to Jesus), then, as you are initially successful, it also becomes clear what faith in this case may mean (for example, some trinitarian formula, or the belief in resurrection).

At this point, as the meaning of faith is defined by the definition of its object, additional problems actually develop. When faith is a meaningful question, the issues are usually not independent, but one question comes to involve another (for example, Jesus and the nature of God). Then, these connections must be explored. Since they are the unclarities of the beginning point, they come back at the end now compounded tenfold. Establishing a meaning for faith makes possible the opening of new issues. Then, as these are defined more clearly, a new and more complex meaning of faith can also be defined. Then, this either demands or makes possible further exploration starting from that point, and faith is redefined once more.

A venture discloses more of the object. That is, if you learn more about God by means of faith in a concept as you define it (for example, father of Jesus Christ), then, as more of the divine nature becomes clarified, the meaning of faith is expanded, and this demands a new affirmation or rejection. Take, for example, what happens in the encounter with evil. If you have a simple notion of God such that his nature is all-good, any encounter with the destructive power of evil will call this notion—once accepted in simple faith—into question. Now the concept of God must be rethought and expanded. If this effort is successful, the new notion will be more complex and will include both the sources of evil and its acceptance in the world. In the light of this, faith demands both a new definition and greater strength to fit its more complex object. *Faith increasingly becomes more difficult, not less, as its object is expanded.* The simpler the notion, the easier the faith, but it is also more subject to revision.

Or, we can put the issue in terms of the demands that faith makes. If the ethical commands of Jesus, for example, are accepted rather simply, faith seems like common sense, and it is not too difficult to follow. But if our understanding of Jesus is expanded, the demands on the individual are increased too, and then faith encounters a crisis. It is no longer what first was accepted in a very simple manner, and the reforms it requires in our conduct may be more extreme (for example, selling all you have and giving to the poor). Faith is a new thing in the light of its more complex object with a more demanding God, and its achievement is also made more difficult. The real problem is that, in this process, we do not seem to be able to reach a limiting point where faith can be defined once and for all. The life of faith never reaches a plateau.

If in order to be meaningful we must specify the object of faith, perhaps the most difficult question is "Is faith itself involved in determining the object?" From what we have just said about the dialectic of one level of faith making it possible to move on to a more complex level, the answer would seem to be "Yes." However, that is a fairly simple involvement of faith in specifying its object. The more difficult question is whether it is possible to apprehend the complex object itself without faith? To this our answer is a qualified "No." Faith is defined as a response to an object, and so the object must be apprehended before the response can be determined, although this can easily be a matter of increasing degree. In this case, faith does not determine the object but is determined by it.

However, a qualification must be introduced. However simple the level may be, if the person will not risk affirming faith in that object (for example, some simple description of Jesus), then he *may* (not must) be blocked both in any further development of that concept and also from reaching any greater degree of faith. Many men actually seem to be in this position. Unwilling to risk a simple commitment, they make it impossible for themselves to move on to discover a more adequate formulation, although perhaps at the same time this would be more complex and more difficult to believe in. When a simple object of faith is inadequate, it is always possible that a more difficult one actually would be more acceptable, but the way must be open to reach that level before the larger task can be considered.

B. FAITH AS OPPOSED TO REASON

The traditional opposition faith *vs.* reason can be very misleading if it is not properly understood. Reason and faith are involved with each other, but sometimes the statement of this problem makes it appear that each is one thing and thus that both are held together by some single relationship. This, of course, is too simple and actually not true. We have already indicated that faith has many meanings—as many as the definitions of the objects offered to it. What 'faith' involves as a response also depends upon the way its object is conceived. 'Reason' similarly has many meanings. If the task of theology is to define the object of faith (primarily God), and if the work of religion is to act in the light of this, then, classically, it is philosophy's job to define what reason can mean.

Although philosophers are by no means in complete disagreement about this, and, indeed, have an accepted tradition (just as Christians begin with common material about Christ), still the history of philosophy clearly demonstrates that the conceptions of reason are more than one and are not all mutually compatible. What reason is or can do depends upon what philosophical view the definition stems from. The description of reason is so basic to any philosophical theory and is so involved in the technical heart of the major doctrines, that it is safe to call any definition of reason a "metaphysical principle." In the light of such a first principle, much that is basic to the doctrine is developed, although in that sense 'reason' is not an initial postulate, but rather an end result of the development of the view. Very much like faith, however, reason may at first receive a simple definition which then grows more complex as different issues arise.

In order to understand how faith relates to reason, we must understand how reason operates. What does reason do? Of course, there is no one simple answer to this question, as we have just indicated; but, on the whole, reason is *the* philosophical tool *par excellence*. Its basic aim is always to understand, to render an object rationally comprehensible. Exactly how it does this or to what limits it might be confined, this is the task of the individual philosophical view to define (for example, impressions and custom for Hume, the necessary presupposition of experience for Kant, the given phenomena for phenomenology). Yet it is clear that, in this sense, reason is not somehow opposed to faith, but rather, and of necessity, always is involved in it. Since faith depends on having an object presented to it, this can only be done by reason. Reason renders its objects clear to faith so that faith is able to decide rather than to be confused. Reason makes faith's task clear.

At that point reason stops. For example, it may clarify the conception of Jesus' nature, but if this, in turn, involves some commitment beyond the simple task of definitional clarification, it is not for reason to decide whether this is to be believed—for example, that Jesus actually performed miracles. To ask reason to make such decisions is either to misunderstand its task or else to fail to realize what is involved in reaching a decision. 'Volition' is the element we need to add here in order to determine a response. Reason may decide what kind of volitional element is required (for example, very strong in the case of miracles), but it does not itself conclude whether any person will make that additional venture. That is an individual affair.

There is, of course, one exception to this picture. This occurs when reason is taken to be an exclusive test—that is, a criterion without need of any addition. When reason is said to be adequate to every task, then, of course, a certain view of the world (and perhaps of God) is involved, in addition to a view of reason's powers as commensurate with this picture of 'being'. This, perhaps, is the only case in which philosophy in itself renders faith impossible. For, if every situation has only one rational solution and definition, a simple reasonable rendering is enough to determine acceptance or rejection without addition. To such a view, faith must object in the name of philosophy. This is because such a theory allows no possible relation between faith and reason, since it leaves no meaning for faith in the face of reason's singularity and omnipotence.

If how 'reason' and 'faith' are related depends on how each is conceived, in some sense they mutually define one another. This is not unqualifiedly true, since reason may define itself so that faith is excluded (or it may specify faith's meaning), but faith cannot be understood until some conception of reason is offered to define it. If the definition of either were obvious, this might not be true, but it is clear that philosophers continue to differ in their conception of reason, and it is even more clear that faith has meant and does mean many things. In the face of such flexibility, it perhaps takes two points to define a line, so that neither concept can be clear when it is taken independently from the other. If the basic uncertainty in the world were less, their mutual dependence in definition might be less too.

What this may indicate is that reason cannot exist without defining its limits. Faith means the recognition of the limits of reason and the willingness to place trust beyond what reason defines as within its sphere of determination. That does not mean that any item of faith is altogether outside reason's grasp (for example, a conception of God), but it simply says that, at that point, reason renounces its ability to determine the matter with finality. Faced with a clarified definition offered by reason, but one pronounced as being beyond reason's final determination, faith takes on a clear meaning in being an affirmation at the point of reason's indecisiveness (for example, a clarified concept of the resurrection of Jesus). To be rational means to know the limits of reason and its sphere of competence. To be faithful means to know what in the area of uncertainty one is willing to affirm and to trust.

If a concept of reason is such that it demands that only what it guarantees as certain is to be trusted, then such a philosophical base excludes the possibility of faith. How are we to determine whether reason's demands for itself are excessive, since, if they are, reason cannot admit correction at this point? This is why faith must be defined as a concept, and in this light it becomes clear that other less exclusive conceptions of the power of reason are possible. Whenever the picture of reason is presented as multiple, faith is possible. Theology need not fear reason as such; all theology has to fear is a view of reason that claims exclusive truth for itself and total competence in every area. Otherwise, it is always possible to correct reason by contrasting the variety of its forms and thus indicating the options available to us regarding reason and its limitations.

C. FAITH AS DEPENDENT ON AUTHORITY

Of course, in its relation to the concepts that reason presents, faith does not act in complete independence. If it did, it might have to be by sheer willfulness. Instead, faith acts rightfully only under the recognition of authority. If reason cannot in itself determine the acceptance of a concept (for example, an end to time or a day of last judgment), something else must enter to allow our will to commit its trust. Otherwise, the task of the will would be too great, and it would tend to be paralyzed by the burden of open decision. Sometimes this provides the explanation of why there is indecision in religious matters. By itself the will may lack decisiveness, and it needs to look to other criteria for direction, first to a rational clarification of the issues and then beyond reason to some recognition of authority.

How is the presence of such an authority, one that can authorize belief, to be discerned? First, it appears as a command. It is easy to see in the biblical literature, for instance, the constant use of injunctions to certain behavior and to belief. The appearance of such statements, of course, is not sufficient in itself, for it is true that there are many such commands and not all are to be believed. For example, there is irreconcilable tension between the Old Testament belief that Yahweh will slay the enemies of those who obey his commands and the New Testament injunction to love our enemies. Both are demands, but both cannot be obeyed. Still, the existence of two such opposed commands gives us the problem of locating an authority for belief. If this does not determine faith, it at least makes the problem clear for the will: to find an authority that it is willing to trust.

Where faith is concerned, we are brought to the question of acceptance. If in considering faith we do not recognize at the outset that to reach a state of acceptance is our goal, the whole task of faith is transformed, and perhaps it is made impossible. If our attitude is one of self-assertiveness and of confidence in our individual ability to achieve and to be adequate in all matters, faith is little likely to be seen as the proper reaction to a concept that reason presents as beyond its bounds (for example, that God decided to become incarnate). When the exercise of authority in the sphere of religion is granted, then the acceptance of this may be seen as the desired goal. Now the pressure of deciding between a variety of recognized authorities is at least lessened because we know that an acceptance of one is our aim, and this relieves the tension.

Where faith is concerned, the issue may be one of the individual's willingness to submit. 'Submission' is a key concept in defining faith. This does not mean that, even if an individual can bring himself to this state, all problems are thereby solved. For since authorities are multiple, the individual must still decide both which version of authority he will agree to submit himself to and how he conceives of the source of that authority. Nowadays, this is less a problem in the political than in the religious sphere. Politically, the locus and operation of authority is basically defined. Religiously, even if some church structure has worked this out, the individual still has a more difficult time spiritually because his basic materials have nowhere near the clarity of a political constitution.

Insofar as faith is dependent on the acceptance of authority, it involves a denial of self-will. Perhaps this is the factor that really makes faith so difficult to achieve and to hold to, rather than some intellectual difficulty over the remaining unclarity of concepts. Insofar as reason alone is sufficient to determine what one believes, no problem of self-will is involved. The individual simply takes every rational conclusion as if it were the product of his own reason, or at least as if it were theoretically achievable by him too. Whenever the question of authority enters, we know that an unpopular concept is involved, but *this may account for the difficulty our age has with religion; a generation that cannot submit cannot believe*. Self-will is challenged by the concept of authority, because it is perfectly obvious that something is needed that the individual does not and cannot produce by himself.

The recognition of the possibility of faith as dependent on the acceptance of authority, then, places the issue on a new level. Self-will is not destroyed at the outset, since the individual must first locate an acceptable version of religious authority. It is always *his* decision to submit to it or not, and this is a decision he may, in turn, revoke at any instance. In that sense, self-will never disappears and is always important. No authority can be accepted without it, but, by its strength, our own will is brought into at least temporary submission through the recognition of authority in the religious life. Self-will has a crucial role and, if it is entirely lacking, faith is powerless. However, if self-will does achieve its own denial, it is subjected to an authority it recognizes as greater than its own, just as John the Baptist deferred to Jesus.

Perhaps this point can be made by contrast. If faith is treated as a completely voluntary affair, it may not be able to exist. That is, if the uncertainties of reason in considering the material of religion are left simply to the power of the will to affirm or to deny, then either no decision will ever be reached or a decision will be achieved simply by accident. Granted that reason does lessen the task of faith by specifying some definite concept (for example, Jesus as possessing authority to forgive sins), the individual will need to find some grounds simply beyond the concept itself and his own desires if he is to be able to act decisively. Or, when the will simply follows its own desire in these matters, the instability of such a ground for decision becomes quickly manifest in our inability to sustain that faith over any period of time—because desires fluctuate.

The area for volition must not be of an unlimited range or leave open every option as possible. Rather, volition is simply *the ability to follow an authority of its own choosing in an area of competing authorities and loyalties.* To say this changes the picture of faith, and it explains why faith cannot be identified with absolute volition. That is extreme self-will, to be able to believe simply what one wills and to accept no norm higher than that. In such a situation, commitment becomes either impossible or so momentary and unstable that it does not deserve the name 'faith'. Actually, it is close to its opposite, willful desire. Faith implies a steadiness that sheer volition never has. In this case, faith may depend on the will for its force, but it also involves the voluntary submission of self-will to a recognized authority.

If, for its existence, faith has this dependence on the acceptance of authority (for example, the Bible, a Pope, individual Christian witness, or some theological rendering by a council), how is it possible for these two ultimately to be compatible? 'Faith' means voluntary trust and commitment to what reason can present but cannot guarantee (for example, the spiritual presence of the kingdom now). Authority means the power to command and to require obedience to its rulings. These two would certainly seem to work against each other.

The answer to this problem is that both of them do not fit together neatly; they do oppose one another somewhat. This defines the life of faith and explains its uncertainties (see Section F). If this were not so, faith would not be either so difficult to achieve or so hard to maintain. This inescapable voluntary aspect tends to withdraw its acceptance of authority (for example, obeying Jesus' commands), while the authoritative element tends to rigidify and to become arrogant and insensitive to the uncertainties involved in any assertion of its power.

Faith is destined to live within the range of these incompatible elements. It is not that they are totally inharmonious or cannot be brought together, but by nature they tend to pull apart. If either voluntary acceptance or authority is taken in independence as defining faith, it actually disappears either into caprice or into dogmatic rigidity. Thus, for the sake of the health of faith, its sensitivities should be increased by forcing it to deal with two elements that can never be reconciled once and for all. Otherwise, faith loses its element of trust and commitment and becomes merely an obviousness that contains no stimulation. The constant opposition of authority and self-will guarantees that faith, if properly understood, will always be a challenge and full of life.

D. FAITH IN COMMUNITY CONTEXT

If we are right that 'faith' is a concept that does not have much meaning in itself and about which we must always ask "In what?" it follows that the secret of understanding what faith means, and of determining whether it is possible, lies in our ability to discern those contexts that give it meaning. The concept of 'reason' is one of these defining points, and faith's relation to the acceptance of a locus for authority is another. Next we must consider whether faith is strictly an individual affair or whether, perhaps, it most often gains meaning in a community context. It is, of course, the individual who must decide to accept or to reject a proposed item of faith, but the question is whether this issue takes on significant meaning only in a community setting.

To be a fierce isolationist where matters of faith are concerned, then, may be to handicap yourself, because neither do the issues become quite clear nor is the full force of the meaning of faith made plain except in some community. Particularly where faith is at issue, there is a tendency to think of this as a matter to be worked out and decided entirely on one's own. Rugged individualism in religion has certain admirable qualities, particularly where it is contrasted with thoughtless and perhaps even deceitful acquiescence to group opinion. Where faith is concerned, the central burden does fall on the individual, and all important thought goes on in the areas of the mind that are essentially private. In any valid decision of potential long-range durability, the origin of the volition must come from the center of the individual, but, in this process, what role does his community context play?

One way to approach this question is to ask "Can we only learn what faith means by sharing it?" This is to turn the question around and to view it, not from the standpoint of the origin of faith, but from the question of its employment once it is achieved. This is important because, if faith has a certain necessary aim, then to decide the issue without that in mind is perhaps to misunderstand it or to prejudice the outcome. Where religious faith is concerned, one has a tendency to think of it as strictly a private matter. As far as the origin of the decision is concerned, this may be true. In its employment, it may not be, and this should affect the way in which faith is considered from the beginning.

If you think of religious faith as a matter of benefit or harm to yourself alone, all attention is centered on the self, and this actually makes decision more difficult. Of necessity, the question of faith focuses on the individual; but, if it leads to excessive self-preoccupation, this makes the issue impossible to solve. In the case of Christianity, particularly, it would seem that faith has an external orientation and is meant to release the person from himself and to turn his attention instead to the service of others in self-forgetfulness. If this is so, the question of faith must always be posed with this release from the self to a service-for-others goal, or the question of faith will be wrongly posed. In such a situation, the community context cannot be ignored, since it is crucial to decide how faith will or can express itself in order to understand what faith involves.

In this case, it may be necessary to determine the work of a community first in order to see concretely what faith involves. Otherwise, the issues remain nebulous; and, if faith is not an abstract but a practical matter, it remains incapable of valid solution on that level. *We must see the work a given community proposes to accomplish as its expression of faith, and then we can understand what an affirmation of faith involves besides words and concepts.* To say this does not, of course, solve the problem entirely, for one always retains the basic choice of which community to place himself within in order to give substance to his thought. Even within Christianity these communities are more than one and quite diverse. Yet to place the question of faith within the context of a particular community's proposed work at least puts the question in its proper context, even if later on that particular community does not prove to be the best one for any particular individual.

The questions of faith (for example, the nature of God or Jesus' inauguration of his 'kingdom') require careful conceptual formulation and intellectual clarification, and without this the questions may never be posed in such a manner as to be capable of any clear solution. This is the theologian's task—that is, to give a clear, contemporary formulation to the traditional questions. However, when it comes to any individual's attempt to resolve these issues and to determine his own faith by them, even the theologian must find a context of some community work in order to give the questions a nonelusive form. To leave the questions on the plane of intellectual formation, once this has reached a point of sufficient contemporary clarity, is to fail to see the only way in which faith can achieve a concrete form.

Another way to put this question is to ask "Can faith ever be simply a one-to-one relationship—that is, between man and God, as some have suggested?" Where religious faith is concerned, it is true that the individual often feels that he is left alone struggling with God, as Job was, perhaps even without the benefit of comforters. This element of "lonely struggle" is essential for all questions of religious faith, particularly to shape their correct formulation. But for their solution, perhaps we can put the problem symbolically by saying that Job made the question of faith more difficult by sitting on a dung heap and anguishing. What if he had risen and gone to join others in some religious-community service work? As a servant in an active and concrete and constructive context, he might have found it easier to solve the problem of continued faith. When the mind is religiously troubled and oppressed, idle hands do indeed become the devil's workshop. The self turns in upon itself and festers.

On his own, an individual can discover this context of a work that aims to relieve the suffering of others, or it may come from some secular organization. For the sake of religious clarity, and so that the question of faith is not obscured by the good works which a faithless person might engage in too, the religious community (a minimum of two or three gathered together in God's name) is the preferred context for deciding a matter of faith. The individual joins with them in their work which is oriented to alleviate suffering. Now the direction of attention is shifted from a concentration on the self, and, apparently, it is even turned away from the opposition of self *vs.* God in religious struggle. In this community setting and in this service orientation, the questions of faith may come back again in a context concrete enough to make an answer possible.

The person no longer is isolated, but is defined by a group; he is no longer self-concentrated, but is turned outward in attention, not to his needs, but to the needs that group proposes to serve. When this happens, the one-to-one relationship is broken and the issues may be solved, not necessarily affirmatively, but at least firmly. Jesus' repeated injunctions, those regarding the necessity both for loss of self and of service to the needs of others, seem to indicate his own clear instructions to place the question of faith in this context for its solution. The setting is to be the religious community united in its allegiance, but the orientation is outside the group toward those in spiritual or physical need. Now the question of faith receives significance, and individual decision must involve more than intellectual assent.

Kierkegaard has told us that no man can give faith to another, that in this matter each man stands alone in absolute isolation no matter how many examples of faith surround him. This core of isolation in matters of religious faith which he describes is undoubtedly true, but perhaps his account plays down the sense in which faith equally involves a matter of learning by imitation. Of course, as in any apprenticeship, unless the novice becomes independent and finds his own unique style, the imitation has failed. Yet, it still might be true that a man can easily be disoriented where religious faith is concerned unless he has examples around him both to observe and to imitate if he so chooses. These need not be all contemporary models, and many examples may have to be tried before any success comes. Still, it is a community of believers who are most likely to provide them.

In this case, religious literature offers us a context too. When we talk about faith as requiring the concrete setting of some community work, this need not mean only an actual organization in the present day. If we begin by the imitation of a model rather than by free self-expression, the models and the communities and the examples of serviceable work—all these can be found in the literature and tradition of the community too. In fact, the example is often clearer there, since the literature has been selected for the purity of its examples and not for its dubious cases. Every tradition tends to preserve the best of its models freed from their nonmodel behavior. Thus, religious literature is more definite in its leadership than any present community can be, except the most outstanding.

A group is needed for purposes of orientation in matters of faith, but each has its own problems. In this case, the one who reads or hears about the model will find that no present community is as pure in its written or spoken representation. Then, if he cannot compromise and join in the most fitting community work, he may end by frustrating his good start and by inhibiting that concrete expression necessary if he is to preserve the meaning he first grasped. This tendency is all the more true because the literature and tradition give us a report, not only of the results of interior intellectual struggle, but also of the work of individuals and groups who, in actual fact, probably were not as clear in their work as the selected reports preserved about them are. In matters of faith, the models to be imitated may be read off the printed page, but in order to be of any real assistance to the individual who is now troubled by questions of faith, he must place them back in the context of some present but less than ideal community work.

E. WHAT FACTORS WORK AGAINST FAITH?

In attempting to accomplish any project, one is blind if he does not proceed in full knowledge of the powers that move in opposition to him. This is particularly true of religious faith. We need to know in what context to set faith in order for it to make sense, and we also must know what forces are at work that aim to make it impossible. In this matter our first question is "Do certain philosophical views make faith impossible?" The answer to this is, without going into detail, certainly "Yes." However, the problem is actually more complicated than this, since different philosophical views will cast the question of faith in different ways. Some make faith more difficult or at least less desirable, and all philosophical views slant the question in certain ways according to the formulation they use. When Hume, for example, sets the question of miracles in the middle of a theory based on the democratic accumulation of immediate impressions plus custom, the question of belief is given a very special setting that it might be well to challenge first.

How can it be that theology might be self-defeating where faith is concerned? Theology has as its task to formulate the issues for religion present in any day, although it does not do this in independence from philosophy, as we have learned. Still, if theology sets excessive demands for itself, if these are out of line with actual experience, the theologian is only left with his proud goal. However, the individual may be left with a definition of faith it is impossible to achieve. Kierkegaard, for instance, places such an intolerable burden on the individual in isolation that no human being has the strength to achieve such "absurd" do-it-yourself faith. Or, the theologian may be intellectually ambitious and demand either that theology be a rigorous science or that its propositions be characterized by certainty and necessity or historical verifiability. Then, if, in fact, the material of theology (for example, God or a religious community) does not lend itself to such finality, the theologian may insist on his goal and refuse to revise it. However, the individual will recognize the discrepancy and find it impossible to commit himself to faith on these grounds.

It is, in one way, a laudable goal to try to induce a greater stability and certainty into this situation. Yet, if the material of Christianity simply does not lend itself to such treatment, faith finds itself opposed by being made to depend on goals that cannot be achieved. Where a changed future is so heavily involved (rebirth and a radically revised future existence), such assertions cannot be verified in the past, and they can, at best, be only partially evident from present experience. Stability, in this case, is difficult, and any demand that ignores this will actually work against achieving faith.

God must be conceived in order for faith to have a basis, and this fundamental requirement works to faith's disadvantage. History indicates our extreme difficulty in reaching one agreed conception of God even within Christianity. This is not the place to go into the problems connected with the formation of an adequate concept of God, but, where faith is the issue, it proceeds blindly if it does not recognize opposition stemming from this enormous problem. Faith cannot simply come into existence. It first meets the opposition of the ancient problem of conceiving of God. Not that this is impossible to accomplish. Many people, including philosophers, have reached an adequate solution for the conception of God. But this does give the problem of faith an opposition it must meet first, or at least the individual should proceed knowing the extreme difficulty involved.

The problem of conceiving of God in a manner concrete enough to give faith a context actually works against faith, but that is not the end of the matter either. For almost a majority of people, the problem of the widespread power of evil in the world also works against faith, and for many any commitment is impossible until that issue is given an acceptable resolution. Thus, it is not simply a matter of somehow being able to conceive of God. Once this is done, the force of evil opposes him (and also the individual's faith), and now an unresolved theodicy blocks trust. Can his conception of God account for evil's presence and its wide scope, and how is the way God has chosen to treat men to be justified and explained? No matter how the question of faith in the person and authority of Jesus is framed, it is either opposed or subtly undermined by the constant force of the presence of evil and the problem of its reconciliation with God's nature.

If the world now were clearly as faith describes it, the opposition between God and evil might not be so harsh. But, if we are told either that God loves us as children or that we should love our enemies, when we compare this with what we see in the world as it is presently designed or with what we know of man, the truth of these religious sayings is not at all obvious. This does not mean that such a classical Christian assertion cannot be given an acceptable meaning, but it does indicate that faith must always work against the fact that the world seldom appears as religion describes it, or at least not as we see it on the surface. Thus, religion always begins by convincing us that something can be understood differently when we see beneath its surface. This is not impossible, but it does require a certain kind of nonempirical philosophical context.

The world in which we live is not clearly unified into one thing. It seems quite multiple and full of loose ends, with divisions and decentralizations that tend to multiply almost as fast as they are overcome. A religious picture always treats the world as if it had a single plan and had resulted from one God with a unified goal in mind. This may be the case, but the burden of proof falls on the religious view to prove this as the more profound interpretation. The would-be believer is always opposed in his faith by the fact that the world, on simple inspection, does not look as he describes it. If this is coupled with a philosophical view that insists on surface impressions and simple facts as the basis for truth, a nontranscendental philosophy and the appearance of the world will combine to make faith exceedingly difficult.

Only a few of the forces that work against faith have been outlined, the strength of whose currents must be taken into account in plotting our course and in estimating our religious speed. One important question next suggests itself: "Can or should faith be understood in terms of those forces which oppose it?" If we take some simple affirmation that is offered to faith (for example, God is willing to forgive sins without exacting retribution), what we must account for is why this is so difficult to accept and why it never seems to remain a simple proposition but becomes increasingly complex. Perhaps faith is not to be understood by a simple inspection of the suggested belief alone, but instead is best grasped when the forces that oppose its acceptance are outlined, calculated, and understood.

Any item of faith that is not considered in the light of the strength of its opposition faces trouble when it is affirmed. Therefore, to turn immediately to try to assess what stands opposed to any belief (for example, an unverifiable future day of last judgment) is to give the item of faith its real definition. When all that surrounds faith favors it and harmonizes with it, then it is understood least, just as Christians may have wealth and success but not strength except in days of persecution. This fact may seem to point to the danger of considering faith in the context of community, but really this is true only if it is a community internally oriented to pacifying its own religious concerns. If that religious community is externally oriented and engaged not in simply talking to its own kind but is attempting to serve the needs of an alien if not hostile world, then faith will meet plenty of opposing forces. It need no longer fear introversion or the lack of sufficient opposition to define its task clearly.

F. IS FAITH BY NATURE TRANSIENT?

In any attempt to achieve faith, to misunderstand its nature is to fail to decide. Beforehand, it always appears that, if only one could decide for or against one point (for example, to accept Jesus as a mediator with God), the issue would be settled. In advance, we may think that any decision regarding an item of faith should be a permanent one. Such is not the case, and to fail to grasp this is to lose all decisiveness in these matters. Why is it that faith cannot be one thing or remain unchanged? The answers to these questions cover the whole philosophical-theological-religious range, but at least to understand the answer in outline is to grasp why faith must be transient. Then, if we treat it as such, it will not be mistreated, and nothing will prevent its continued residency on an itinerant basis.

Take the example of the acceptance of Jesus as a divine mediator. Faith in this assertion is obviously dependent on what conception of God is used, which obviously is subject to change and requires constant renewal if its vitality is to be maintained. Since the response to the question of who Jesus is lies at the very heart of Christian belief, and since the biblical documents and tradition do not speak with a single voice on this matter (not that we are left without orientation, but simply that the terms used certainly do vary), the reappraisal of Jesus is a constant necessity for a Christian. These variables make faith a variable matter also. However, if this is understood, one may learn the art of maintaining at least a certain stability and control over these volatile elements. To expect faith to hold steady is to lose it by misunderstanding. If its nature is to be a transient, it requires the exertion of constant effort to maintain its present level, and relaxation for even one moment means that faith will move away without realizing it.

Look how quickly Peter's faith moved away from him between the single affirmation ("Thou art the Christ") and the triple denial ("I do not know him!"). This should stand as a constant warning to every Christian successor to Peter that the loss of faith stands as near to us all as the failure to repeat the effort needed to maintain it every day. What we must understand is why faith requires constant reaffirmation even after a moment of insight. Perhaps one factor is the discrepancy between verbal assertion or intellectual insight and practical implementation. Peter saw and affirmed ("Thou art the Christ"), but then denial came in the situation of practical implementation—that is, at the trial, when Peter's life was at stake along with Jesus'. Verbal affirmation and intellectual grasp may be too easy. Unless they are implemented in a context of action, faith fades, since it is not wholly a verbal affair.

Perhaps this is the significance of Jesus' parting threefold injunction to Peter (to match Peter's threefold denial): "Feed my sheep." To see and to say are one thing. However, unless words turn into deeds, faith cannot sustain itself, but instead is lost in the inevitable intellectual confusion that always surrounds it. When actions are taken and practical stands are assumed, faith is on solid ground, and its verbal phrases have concrete substance to test themselves against so that they may be further defined. Otherwise, formulas lose their precision, since they lack any practical reference to hold them back from their natural tendency to shade into a thousand concepts similar in kind to the original. The disciples were sent out to work, to preach, to heal, and to serve. *That activity formed the only possible basis for their continued faith and ours.*

To form a cloistered religious community may have been a

second tendency of Christianity, but it was not its first ("Go forth unto all nations"). Perhaps this accounts for the early, and sometimes still strong, vitality of faith. It did not close in upon itself but turned instead to ground itself in practical outreach. This early power is important because of the nature of faith. Terms shift in their meaning and do not always remain the same. Even in one age, no term of importance has a single meaning. Thus, to rest the constancy of faith solely on our ability to achieve fixity in intellectual formulation is to base it on material that by nature is subject to constant shifts. Every day demands a new context, and crucial terms must continually be revitalized and stabilized. Faith, however, must never be more than partially based on this verbal enterprise.

When we place our faith in formulas or in creeds or in theological doctrines, we do give it a kind of temporary mental stability, and the mind needs such intellectual fixity in order to orient itself in the midst of complicated material. Yet entities of this kind (that is, words and concepts) are at best an unstable medium. Faith must be formulated there first of all, or else it cannot be communicated by preaching. However, to try to hold it solely within this medium is perhaps to seal its doom, and certainly it will commit the believer to an endless intellectual struggle in which the odds are against him. In understanding why faith is transient and moves on unless held, we need to be clear about the medium in which it is formulated. If our material is words and concepts, these can have staying power, but only rarely and not without constant translation. If the medium is practical action, this too can go astray but at least it provides a more concrete test.

Now the importance of philosophical theory becomes clear once again. Philosophers differ about language as a medium and about the power and the status of words. Since faith always exists partially in this form, to deal clearly with the status of language as a medium is decisive for outlining our approach to faith. Language may disclose unchanging entities, and when it does it seems to be a less transitory medium. But all this depends on only one theory of the status and use of words, and, according to other philosophical interpretations, faith would have its greatest transitoriness when placed in verbal form. At this point, the philosophical appraisal of action is important too. Unless action is on a par with intellectual formulation, faith revolves in a circle in the mind. It may find intellectual completion, but perhaps it also never rests.

On the other hand, if action has an ontological status different from that of words, and if the goal of faith is not simply intellectual vision, then in its translation into action we might understand faith by seeing it receive a practical test. A baptism with words perhaps is necessary for an intellectual understanding of faith's meaning. A baptism with water may more graphically symbolize the significance and the object of faith as it exists in the mind. But a baptism of fire (physical action) either burns faith away or else ingrains it into the mind and body more unforgettably. Say a word, and you may get some reaction to it that will guide you. Act or work in specific ways, and opinion will quickly solidify around that clear target. Action cannot be thoughtless, if it is effective, and it cannot be without aim, if it intends to test Christian faith.

G. CAN FAITH BE HAD BY TRYING?

If due to its nature faith cannot be had or be held without exertion, it is time to add that, unfortunately, neither can faith be guaranteed by any amount of exertion. We must face the fact that many try desperately to achieve faith and yet fail, while others seem to obtain it and to hold it without apparent effort. This indicates that faith does not come in direct proportion to expenditure of effort and that yet, ironically, it may be lost without it. At other times, faith comes and a person is enabled to believe, but this arrives only as a delayed reaction. That is, it makes its appearance at a time long after the actual thought has been put forth and the exertion has been made and both have ceased. We must work on faith, then, with great care, and we should understand that it must never be forced. Faith does not operate in perfect harmony with our efforts but maintains a certain independence of its own.

Without analyzing this phenomenon of faith's lack of direct responsiveness to effort, let us pause and ask what kind of God this failure of all coercion would seem to lead us to. He must be capable of holding onto a certain independence from the ways of the world, and this is a discovery that would shock

Spinoza. A God of our type is not unresponsive; the return he gives is not out of all relation to human events. It is just that his response is never forced by human thought or action. Instead, it comes from his own nature and in accord with his own decisions, and this may or may not correspond exactly to any given man's effort, thought, or action. Thus, since faith certainly depends on establishing a satisfactory concept of God, unless God is visualized as possessing this aspect of detachment and independence, faith may be misplaced and thus be subject to disappointment. God can be compassionate and loving, but clearly he displays this neither instantaneously nor on demand.

How is it possible to understand the fact that faith may be "freely given"? Everything in this examination now has indicated that faith can be achieved and has laid down guidelines for its understanding. But, if faith must be attempted within this framework and yet if it does not automatically come from this, no one can demand or even expect it as a result of his labors. Since it has no guaranteed formula, its arrival always has the aspect of being "given." Even when faith in some item (for example, the descent of the Holy Spirit) is present, its continued appearance is subject to no assurance. Thus, it must be received and held as "given" and not as purchased by exchange. To hold faith in this loose and unpossessive grasp is to give it some independence. In this case, the person does not come to depend on something that is merely given and thus is not under his full control to detain.

Our freedom in the face of the uncontrollable arrival and departure of grace is like our freedom to control our own major behavior patterns. We cannot always act or not act in certain ways by sheer force of will. Yet often we can place ourselves in a context most conducive to what we desire, although we cannot guarantee a certain action simply from our own energy or control. And, what sometimes is more important, we can work successfully to stay clear of those contexts in which our control is either weakened or overwhelmed by superior forces. This maneuverability can enhance powers in the self which otherwise might not be strong enough to be successful alone. The right choice of circumstances, not clothes, makes the man. Therefore, community, the right response to authority, and so forth, all of these are a proper context for faith. To work in these favorable conditions and to avoid an unconducive setting, this sometimes is man's only control over faith.

This does not necessarily lead us to the formation of exclusive religious communities, as has sometimes been supposed. To gather in communities is, of course, the right way, but the individual need not withdraw entirely into these protective environments in order to preserve a weak faith. To move out from this base into alien circumstances sometimes is his best context, and without doing so faith may be lost, as has been indicated. To withdraw into the desert to fight the devils that beset the individual who is alone may be an admirable feat of daring and a test of strength, but it also may be a context within which faith is seldom given before exhaustion arrives. Such a situation may be too self-centered to be the proper context in which faith can be freely received.

Actually, the way in which faith arrives is better treated under a different concept—that is, spirit. In other words, what 'grace' means depends upon how faith is conceived, what sort of thing it is taken to be, and how 'spirit' is thought to operate, since that is the current mode of God's presence in, and relation to, the world. Grace can be subject to misunderstanding if it is thought to be a concept that is fixed in itself. Since we have already discovered how much variation 'faith' is subject to, and since we shall discover how difficult it is to discern the presence of the 'spirit' in the sense of the holy spirit (see Chapter 21), it ought to be clear that what 'grace' is and how it operates is totally subject to how these two basic concepts are defined and related. If we attempt to approach 'grace' directly in order to understand it, it will be misunderstood if its subsidiary nature is not first recognized. 'Grace' is not something that exists in itself.

If grace does mean a gift divinely bestowed, how can God be said "to give"? By asking this question, we learn, just as we have discovered with the concept of faith, that from the peculiar behavior of subsidiary phenomena (for example, "giving grace") much may be deduced about God's nature that we might not discern directly. He must be good in the sense of being ungrudging and outgoing without regard to self, or else he would not 'give' away anything man does not directly work and bargain for. He must be a generous and an outgoing God in this sense, not a mystical One who withdraws and only draws others into himself. Of course, balanced against this is the cruelty and destruction permitted into the world by divine authorization, and this is why the 'giving of grace' requires a complex philosophical setting if it is to be understood at all and not simply dissolved into contradictions.

Where faith is concerned, if philosophy is classically defined as the search for or the love of 'wisdom', this is a goal that the self sets and achieves for itself. Does this self-achieving aspect of philosophy interfere with faith, particularly as we have expressed its uncontrollable quality—that is, that it is not obtainable by sheer effort? In considering this question, many parallels might be drawn to show that philosophical insight also seems to come accidentally and without directly intending it. All of this softens the opposition of philosophical acquisitiveness vs. our lack of control of faith, but it does not deny the fact that wisdom is the result of human struggle and that faith has an element of a divine gift not always the reward of effort.

We see again the importance of philosophical theory, because some theories of knowledge can allow for such a phenomenon as 'gift' and others either cannot or make it appear quite strange. From the other side, we can soften the opposition by making faith a mode of knowledge along some sliding scale with philosophical achievement, as Thomas Aquinas did. This removes some of God's initiative and freedom, and it is tied to a certain view both of faith and of the divine nature, as we might suspect. Here again we see how much 'grace' is dependent for its interpretation on a prior series of concepts. The shifting relations possible between various theories of philosophy and a variety of religious questions come together in a focal point when we ask whether faith can be had by trying, since the answer to this depends on the exact interpretation given to 'philosophy', 'knowledge', 'faith', 'freedom', and 'God'—to name only a few central concepts.

H. THE TEST OF FAITH

Now that Christians have inherited nearly twenty centuries of creedal affirmations and a church structure to accompany them, we tend to think of any "test of faith" in terms of our ability to affirm certain propositions as true. In the early days of Christianity, the situation we faced was not completely different, but at least it was a simpler one. In the Gospels and in the early church, men were faced with the problem of defining verbally just who Jesus was, but it is also true that in the primitive church actions were much more clearly at the forefront as being basic to any test of faith.

As Kierkegaard has pointed out, to affirm Christian belief once might have meant to risk your life and to suffer constant persecution. Now it is a matter of privilege; some college charters allow no man to hold their presidency unless he is a member of a Christian church. In a day in which Christianity is not a suspect minority but is itself the Establishment, it becomes easier to think of a test of faith in simply verbal terms. Now no sacrifice is required in order to be Christian, and certain rewards are even likely to be yours in return for at least a verbal acceptance.

Of course, Christianity is not only this outer form, and it may be that we have already moved into an era in which Christianity no longer is so accepted and respectable. If so, to continue within a church may involve some pain and struggle and sacrifice. In any case, our point is to ask what can, in fact, constitute a "test of faith" and in what ways some ideas about testing faith may involve a fundamental misconception. In most cases, it may be sufficient to work out a verbal formula and then gain either an adherence to or a rejection of it. But, if we deny this to be true where Christianity is concerned, this may tell us something important about what 'faith' means.

What I want to suggest is that, in the case of Christianity, the test of faith is 'pragmatic'. That is, the test is neither verbal nor structural, in the sense of belonging to an institution; instead, it lies in practice. There is, of course, much evidence to support such an interpretation of Christian 'faith'—for instance, Peter's threefold verbal affirmation of his loyalty to Jesus and the threefold reply, "Feed my sheep." Jesus also tells us one thing about his kingdom: not everyone who says "Lord, Lord" shall enter but only those who *do* the will of the Father. Verbal adherence certainly is not sufficient in itself. In the description of the mystery surrounding inclusion in the kingdom, it is clear that some who might seem to belong by virtue of appearance and word will not be admitted, while others will be because of their actions, in spite of all unlikely appearances.

The intention of the individual may definitely count in determining this—that is, his attitude of faith. Yet, in addition to this, act and deed are clearly involved and perhaps are the most important. Like philosophical pragmatism, the real test does not come in theory; it is located in actual practice. How a person behaves toward others and toward God is the test of his faith. And precisely what the actions are that define Christianity, this is the job of the New Testament to illustrate. Thus, we find Jesus frequently using parable rather than strict and consistent formulation.

If a simple definition would suffice, Jesus could have achieved his purpose much more easily, and certainly he would have escaped persecution and crucifixion by his willingness to issue clear philosophical statements. What we learn from the Gospels and the actions of the disciples in the early church is not simply a correct creed to recite; it is a way in which to act. Both our actions and ourselves require radical transformation to meet this goal. Basically, it is not so much a matter of words, although they have their place and even their divine use.

To note this nonintellectual basis of Christian faith is not necessarily to deny all function to creeds and verbal formulas. Rather, all this raises the question of faith in a more delicate way by asking "What is the relation between definite formulae and physical action?" For, if action were that clear in itself, Jesus could simply have lived and worked and that would have been enough in itself. Instead, the centrality given to preaching the word in Christianity indicates how important words are to bring about a needed change in routine. If Christian life did not involve such a radical reversal of normal action (for example, "love your enemies"), words might not be so important in shaping action. As it is, we must first somehow come to understand this nonnatural way of acting (for example, loving God with all your heart, which certainly is neither easy nor natural), and also we need to grasp how words are a way of presenting and enabling that change.

It would seem then that words and creeds and institutions

and affirmations are all related to actions in that they can direct activity in new ways, although the test of faith itself, strictly speaking, lies in the resulting actions themselves and in nothing else. If the actions are not changed, then the test of faith has failed. Does this mean that, against Luther, one is saved by works and not by faith alone? This is true in the sense that faith can only be tested pragmatically by action. We need not interpret "faith as works" in the sense that faith is not any action itself, or even a series of actions, that "earns" salvation. That is a divine gift, but it can be true that the *evidence* of faith is found only in action. This does not at all make faith a quantitative matter, but it does mean that faith is only made known by its fruits. Only faith has the power to save. Words may guide and form that faith. Only action can evidence what that faith is and test its validity and its strength.

Why, then, do we struggle to find fresh verbal definitions of faith in a new day? If only actions count pragmatically, why will not any old former creed or definition of Christianity do? In a sense it will, in that if one is converted to Christian life it does not matter much which words, new or old, are associated with this redirection of his spirit and action. But, since we have agreed that it is not easy to reform actions along Christian lines (for example, ceasing to try to save one's own life), the question is: Which words and formulae have sufficient power and effectiveness to accomplish such a reformation? It is not only Roman Catholicism, either in Luther's time or today, that demands institutional reform. Each individual needs a basic redirection to his life and action. How is that to be achieved? An old formula may point the way, but, on the other hand, it may be so beautiful and familiar that its words only please the mind and do not move us to action.

No matter how accurate the classical phrase may be, then, where Christian faith is concerned we require a series of constant redefinitions of faith precisely because it is not entirely a matter of intellectual agreement. We need words effective enough to convert behavior, and this may require a constant novelty of approach and the incorporation of certain contemporary idioms in our phrases. This situation is the hardest of all to deal with, for old creeds are not wrong and Christian action is not something quite new. It is just that it is difficult to find a form of statement that is sufficiently forceful to control and to direct action, since what you want to avoid is intellectual consent that lacks the actions needed to prove the solidity of the faith.

17

REVELATION

A. THE ACCEPTABILITY OF REVELATION

It probably is true that, unless a religion can establish a meaning for 'revelation', it is little likely to prove either its own usefulness or its validity. For, if there is no genuine revelation from God, men can gather everything they need to know on their own, and then natural and humanistic forms of organization are all that we need. A 'church' is formed by receiving some new revelation, so that, unless it can be established that God has actually made some disclosure, churches are unnecessary organizations.

'Revelation' means "action which discloses intent." Thus, it must be that God's intentions cannot always be discerned by ordinary observation and that they are subject to being disclosed by special events not observed by all men at all times. This being true, revelation requires a special background in order to be either understood or accepted, and here the role of philosophy in shaping theology becomes crucial again.

It becomes clear, on consulting any given series of philosophies, that some can permit revelation to occur and others rule it out as impossible, or at least as not intellectually acceptable. It is interesting that modern philosophy is, on the whole, unsympathetic to the idea of accepting a claim to revelation. On the other hand, with some classical theories of knowledge (for example, Plato or Plotinus), the idea of revelation is at least admissible. For instance, if one demands 'universality' as a criterion for all valid knowledge, revelation is ruled out from the start as an unacceptable and provincial source. Or, if the epistemology in use denies all transcendence of either natural modes of knowledge or existence, revelation is excluded, since it is meaningful only as a communication from a higher order and as a form which exceeds natural modes. Fortunately for theology, no one epistemology is forced upon us, but it certainly is crucial to determine first whether any given theory of knowledge does or does not rule out revelation.

More than this, it is not even so simple as an "either/or"— that is, either a given theory of knowledge admits revelation or rules it out. On this question the most obvious case of "shaping" takes place, since the philosophical basis used to work out a theology will "interpret" revelation and shape it in its form and source. For instance, with Kant we know that all certified knowledge is mediated by the categories of the understanding and that no validated knowledge can reach us from outside these forms. This places an unavoidable time and space limitation on all that is communicated to us. But, if knowledge were not subject to these Kantian limitations, it might be much more possible to have revelation come from outside the conditions most knowledge is subject to. Moreover, before anyone can admit that he accepts a certain revelation as 'divine' and 'authoritative', he must know what revelation means. Otherwise, when the communication comes it will not be understood for what it is. It will both go unrecognized and remain unresponded to.

If revelation is "action that discloses intent," this definition also applies simply to the human and the natural level. Clearly, at least in the case of religion, this action must be God's, and the intention revealed should be a divine one. This means that the theoretical base we operate on must be such that it will permit a divine action to intervene in the natural process and evidence itself. This also means that God's intention is not evident and cannot be read off either from the historical record or by a projection made solely on that basis. His intent must not have been "built in" to the original construction if it requires special and extraordinary action to reveal it. For revelation to be meaningful, we must assume a God who does not expect that all of us should always know his intentions. An element of surprise goes along with this; such a revelation, it follows, will be unexpected no matter when it comes.

In recent times, it has been customary to treat 'revelation' in conjunction with 'history'. This tendency, of course, reflects certain special theories about the nature of history. According to its literal meaning, revelation must be different from simple historical knowledge. If we view man as historically and as temporally bound, revelation may come within history, but certainly it is not a part of the historical process. Revelation is that which sets history aside. In fact, as the first and last chapters of Part I pointed out, religion is closely connected, not to a study within historically recorded time, but to considerations that are outside of all time—that is, creation and eschatology, or the radical transformation of the present natural order. Of course, all religions involve historical understanding in the sense that their revelatory events are remembered and not forgotten. They can have commemorative repetition—for example, the eucharist, which recalls the first event and connects all those who are later in time with it once again.

Where revelation and history are concerned, the issue arises of God's control of the process. In order for revelation to be an action that breaks into the natural order, God must be thought to be in undisputed control and to be able to exercise his power to alter events. Sometimes it is said that God's plan "progressively reveals itself in history," but this cannot really be the case if the possibility for revelation is accepted. That is, precisely because God's intent is not clear from a study of historical events, revelation or a special in-breaking is required if his purpose is to be known at all. If it is viewed as being present in all of history, then God's intention is at best unclear, and so it will not be known unless it is extraordinarily revealed. In this sense, 'revelation' is opposed to 'history' and is not a part of it. In the normal processes of development and change, God's aims remain concealed, and 'revelation' becomes their extrahistorical disclosure.

Revelation, of course, cannot be considered in isolation from the concept of 'authority' (see Chapter 13). Just as revelation will not be granted validity under certain philosophical assumptions, so likewise, unless we can see that authority is sometimes vested in strange places, we are not very prone to understand revelation. That is, revelation involves the admission that authority can be granted by God at times and places not fully anticipated. God is the ultimate locus of authority himself, so that revelation means the placing of his authority within a particular circumstance on his own conditions and initiative. The formula for any revelation is, at the same time, a formula of authority. This lodging of authority in something human and limited always involves the paradox that divine authority comes to rest in something by nature imperfect. Thus, revelation really depends on our ability to accept the granting of divine authority to something immediate and limited and human in our lives. If we can accept that, we can accept revelation.

It is also true that revelation involves the concept of the 'word of God'. We must be able to admit the fact that God can communicate to man and that he does this not generally but specially and through some group (for example, the people of the covenant), or else through an unusual individual whom he raises to special status (for example, a prophet). As a part of this, we must consider whether particular words of God can be unusual—that is, whether they can have a strange inherent power of their own which the same words would not have when uttered by man. This explains the idea of a blessing or a curse, but it also involves the power revelation is said to have. That is, if such words of God have no more inherent power than comparable human words, revelation will not be taken very seriously. However, if the word of God possesses inherent power of its own, it can reveal just because it has extra energy to do what ordinary words are impotent to accomplish.

One major question concerns whether the word of God comes generally and impersonally or whether it is personified. In general, the word of God in the Old Testament takes impersonal form, although it may be uttered through the medium of a person. The claim present in the New Testament record, on the other hand, is that the power of God has become a person. God's word is not said to be mediated by human emissaries. It actually has taken the form of a person, and this is why the question of the attribution of personal characteristics to God is so crucial for a Christian theology.

'Revelation' comes to mean the Christian message in particular, and this is precisely the announcement of the appearance of God's power in human form. This is the revelation: God has appeared and his power has been present in a specific, limited person. There is a genuine difficulty here, for not everyone will agree either that a fallible human person is capable of bearing such authority or that the divine nature is such that it can be contained in human form.

What this tells us is that revelation discloses a presence we would not ordinarily expect to find at that time and place and in that form. This being the case, its unusual quality is not easy to accept even after it has been announced. It cannot be something that genuinely is 'revealed' if, after it has come forth, it then is taken as either natural or obvious. It must retain its nonnatural quality even when it becomes a familiar assertion. We must not ever expect to encounter God in human form or else such an appearance discloses nothing. What is revealed need not be "unreasonable," in the sense that it defies understanding (although it may), but it simply cannot have been what always was expected or suspected. This being the case, the issue always is "On what grounds will we either accept or reject the revelation once it has appeared?" This depends upon the context we create for it.

B. HOW CAN WORDS REVEAL?

On most occasions, words yield only ordinary knowledge and sometimes not even that. How can it be, then, that on some occasions and in some circumstances words can have such extreme power as to be revelatory of God himself? What remains an ordinary meaning in one context must be capable of becoming revelatory in another context. If this is so, what we must try to understand is under what conditions words can become revelatory. What happens that adds such extraordinary power to what usually is so prosaic? Of course, we may not be able to decide about how this happens in every case. It is possible that the conditions under which revelation takes place are themselves unusual and incapable of being pinned down to one formula. If this is so, it is more difficult to understand how words come to have such unusual power, since no irreversible formula for this transformation can be set down.

Of course, along with this problem, we also have to ask about human sensitivity to words. Even in an acknowledged revelatory situation, not all persons who hear the same words understand the same thing or even experience any sense of revelation. If this were not true, Jesus could not have been misunderstood. As it is, perhaps the strangest and most controversial fact about revelation is that the same words that reveal for one do not possess the same power for everyone. Part of this fact may be explained by the "deafness" of some individuals or perhaps by their lack of willingness to recognize what is said. Still, it must be that the power of revelatory words is not such as to force an equal understanding on all.

In considering the ability of words to have revelatory power —but not such that they either disclose at all times and places or to all men equally—we also must ask "What experience might be a necessary prerequisite to enable a man to grasp such extraordinary meaning?" If a group of words always led to only one meaning, our situation would be different, but words exist on many levels—or rather, their power to convey meaning does. This being the case, under what conditions do actions that otherwise are simple become revelatory? In answering this, we all know that words we have heard many times on various occasions can become very different in their affect on us at another time. Often this novelty is due to an intervening experience that has opened us so that we grasp these same words on a new level of understanding. Revelatory words must fall on ground receptive to their meaning if their potential power to reveal is, in fact, to be experienced.

Our question about how words can reveal, then, hinges partly on the condition of their being received by a listener who is capable of grasping the power inherent in them. Therefore, one answer to our question is that words do not have the power to reveal if the person hearing them is unreceptive. Yet another answer must also be that words in themselves do not contain this power internally. In the majority of instances, they direct the listening mind in only ordinary ways. It must be, then, that words have the power to reveal when they are used by a being powerful enough to give them such needed additional power. The revelatory quality in words, whenever it is present, derives not from the word but from its source. Words, then, reveal when they lead a willing listener to the source of their momentary borrowed power.

C. THE OBJECT OF REVELATION

If the power of words to reveal depends upon our ability to attribute authority to them, and if to have the necessary authority means to possess both power and an ability to make that power effective, then the issue becomes whether and to whom God might delegate such decisive authority. This may be given to persons, but it can also be vested in words that, once uttered, are enabled to give evidence of the power of their source. In this case, 'hearing' and how we approach it are serious matters and involve, not only the mind, but also the whole being of the one who hears. This is particularly true since to report a hearing of such words is to speak of obeying them. The whole personality is brought into play in facing such powerful words. Ordinary men are dependent on prophets, for only a man inspired by God could utter words with such force.

Still, this power must be deployed if it is to reveal an object, since 'revelation' means to unveil or to remove a covering in order to expose to view what had not been seen. Therefore, in order to understand revelation we must ultimately be able to specify what hidden objects were opened to our view by its intervention. Of course, although there may be minor objects, the major subject of revelation is always God himself, and the assumption is that otherwise God would remain hidden. We also assume that all action and initiative come from his side. If so, we know that God must be such as not to be accessible to direct observation and natural prediction. Otherwise, such elaborate means would not be necessary in order to allow a self-disclosure.

We learn a great deal about the nature of its object from the mere fact of the occurrence of revelation. In the first place, an encounter with God is achievable only by "waiting upon him." He is not accessible if he does not wish to be. Since the initiative lies with him, unless he initiates the motions of revelation, he cannot be approached directly. God has interpreters (for example, prophets), and they are necessary to counteract normal human blindness. Yet, it is not easy to relate to an object such as this. If we can see what we are up against and approach it at our own option, we could control the situation much more easily. As it is, we are dependent in this relationship and must act accordingly. Somewhat like children, we must learn to speak only when spoken to.

When God speaks, his words amount to actions, since they seem to be the primary means by which he acts even when his words are carried by a spokesman. If it is man who is addressed, God seeks to elicit a human response. Otherwise God has no reason to speak, for, if he remains silent, he also remains unobserved and then man is free to act independently. His purpose in speaking or in revealing his nature is to establish a relationship between men and himself. In this case, the relationship is literally caused by the words spoken, so that, for all communication between God and man, words are indispensable.

What we learn from the appearance of revelation is that, if man is to know God, God must accommodate himself to man's creaturely capacity. As things stand, given God's initially concealed nature and the limits set to man's knowledge, the two could not meet. No effort on man's part alone could overcome the gap. Given the initial lack of full compatibility, man and God cannot join on a level of mutuality unless God acts first. His "actions" may take the form of powerfully revealing words, but, of course, they may also assume more concrete modes of presentation. Whatever form God's action takes, it must be such as partially to close the gap that is naturally present as a consequence of the lack of openness between the divine and human natures.

Where a prophet is in question, fulfillment or nonfulfillment becomes our criterion for the truth of his words. That is, the prophet reveals God's nature or his intent by predicting certain future events or the consequences of some intended action. In this case, if the future event, in fact, confirms his words, he is still not a revealer beyond all doubt, but at least we are moved to inspect his words more closely for greater signs of their authenticity. If the action when indulged in does, in fact, lead to the predicted results, at least we are put on our guard to follow the lead of the prophet's words to try to determine the source of their power.

If revelation is to reveal an object that otherwise is not accessible, it must be a unique event. For, if it were an ordinary and repeatable event like the rising of the sun, it could not be said to reveal or to need revealing at all. Its meaning would always have been obvious and it could not lead beyond itself. Such an event must evidence a special relationship, and its revelatory quality comes precisely from the unusual connections. This, of course, makes it not subject to check by repetition. It can be authenticated by no simple external sign. Thus, a revelatory event or word depends for its effect both on the power carried within it to overcome barriers and on the individual's ability to sense its uniqueness and to accept such unusual circumstances.

Revelation, then, can only be understood by coming to discern its object. Otherwise, its intention surely fails, since it is not meant to focus on itself and on its function as an instrument. If revelation does not relate us in new ways to an object not before completely accessible, its words or acts will lack power. Their power, of course, is derived from the object toward which they direct us, and the extent of their power is determined by their ability to break through human barriers and to place us in direct contact with their source.

D. THE POWER OF MIRACLES

The uniqueness of the revelatory event is similar to the problem involved in the description of a miracle, and in a certain sense all revelatory acts or words have the aspect of miracle about them. Beyond this characteristic, however, revelation is usually attested to and surrounded by miraculous events. In the New Testament, for instance, the reported miracles are not isolated events; they simply serve as an indication of the revelation being enacted. Unique as revelation must be, it requires signs that point to its significance so that this can be grasped, and miraculous events are a large part of this testimony.

Miracles, of course, are the result of the operation of the power of God, so that disbelief in any reported miracle actually stems from the disbelief that God is the source of power, including this unusual event. It is not miracles that certify God's existence; it is more an awareness of God's locus of power that makes miracles acceptable. Miracles can be believed in to the extent that God is understood, and they tend to be rejected when no such source of unusual power and action is admitted. In the case of Jesus, the problem is to acknowledge his actions as a demonstration that God is the source of that power. The rejection of Jesus' miracles is based on a refusal to accept him as containing God's power authoritatively.

The power of God is revealed in decisive action, and the observable effect of this is a miraculous event. Since we cannot see God directly, it is only through the things he does or makes—or the words he utters—that we have any knowledge of him. Thus, if there were not miraculous events, God could not be revealed. Yet such occurrences are not accepted as evidence by everyone. The miracles of Jesus are simply signs. Only those who have the eyes to see God's hand can grasp the purpose of the interruption or the reversal of the natural processes. With Jesus, the miracles are signs that a new age had dawned, and, if any new eras are to be inaugurated, it will certainly take some unusual interruptions to accomplish such a difficult breakthrough of nature's structure.

The effect of miracles involves another question. In the eyes of some, any unusual or unpredictable event simply evokes wonder. However, miracles can also signal the call for a change. If repentance is to be induced in men, perhaps only the confrontation of a startling event can enable this to take place. Even when the individual may desire a change, his own resistance to this may be so ingrained that only the kind of shock that accompanies a miracle can produce the force necessary to induce the needed basic alteration.

Whenever miracles occur, they indicate the presence of divine power in that individual or in that group. Thus, they are a seal of authority, a sign of approval, a notice of the presence of the power of disclosure in that place or person or word. 'Mystery', of course, is another concept connected with 'miracle', for the appearance of both the power and the change it induces always involves that which is mysterious. This means "that which cannot be fully disclosed or known." The miracles accompanying revelation partially indicate its nature as well as its power and its authenticity. Any given miracle may be plain enough (for example, water *vs.* wine), but it indicates the presence of that which cannot become transparent to man.

Of course, if miracles are divinely connected, they are not isolated occurrences, but are intended to reveal God's purpose or plan of salvation. They cannot be understood as single events, but only as an indicator of the direction of God's movements. In the account of the 'transfiguration', Jesus is transformed by a heavenly radiance. This marks a turning point in the gospel narratives in the way in which the writers describe Jesus, or in their final recognition that this miraculous appearance indicates divine intent. Those around Jesus shared in this experience, so that a once familiar event was given new meaning. Miracles indicate the presence of this transforming power.

E. KNOWLEDGE OF THE FUTURE

If the concept of revelation includes a prophetic element, it also involves a fulfillment of those forecasts. If Jesus is accepted by his followers, it clearly is because they feel that, in him, all prophecies have been fulfilled. In other words, we become conscious of receiving revelation at the moment we are aware that what we have expected—what has been predicted—has come and is concentrated in one experience or in one person. If prophecies that refer to future events always remained just that, we would not necessarily have any sense of experiencing revelation. That comes when what was expected only at some future time is experienced as a present fact.

We count as revelation what seems to tell the will of God in our own day. Since all days are not the same, obviously the experience of revelation cannot always be constant. Religiously speaking, we continually try to experience God's will for the present and the future. Only when our relationship to the future is cleared up do we understand revelation. The prophets stood in the midst of the stirring events of their time, and there they discerned the character and the purpose of God. 'Revelation' makes the future known in this perspective, and as a consequence it yields a religious basis upon which to act. "The day of the Lord" means that things only partially seen before are now accepted as revealed and fulfilled.

Apocalyptic writers are always more concerned with the future than with either the past or the present, and such writing has always had the characteristic of revelation. The future is opened and known, not, of course, in detail but only in relation to God's purpose and intent. A 'seer' is one who can interpret signs and unusual circumstances, so that revelation of this type always involves an ability to translate and to clarify that which seems significant but is not yet clear in itself. 'Ecstasy', of course, is characteristic of prophecy, so that revelation involves the taking of a person outside himself. Then, detached from his own existence, the future becomes clear. Insight of this magnitude does not come in ordinary moments.

If the future needs to be discerned, the question involved is whether God can change or modify his purpose. If his action is fixed from all eternity, there seems little need for more revelation than one. If, however, God is capable of a change to meet the times, continued or at least renewed revelation might be necessary. Here is one clear illustration of how philosophy shapes theology. It is quite clear that your notion of God (particularly as related to change) already contains the ways in which he could or could not act in revelation. What is revealed and how it is accomplished will depend on the nature of the God being revealed.

If every book of the New Testament, for instance, declares or assumes the resurrection of Jesus from the dead, what does this tell us about revelation? The resurrection may be a present event in time, but its revelatory quality comes as an eschatological sign—that is, it must be understood in its reference to the future. It reveals God's future purpose; it is a symbol for the ultimate consummation of God's intent. There is duration or measured time which surrounds a present event, but there is also time in the sense of 'fulfillment' and 'opportunity'. The resurrection is a revelation in time only in this latter sense. It opens opportunity and offers fulfillment as ordinary existence in duration cannot.

Fulfillment is a matter of seizing an opportunity opened to us by expending appropriate action. Revelation enables us to see what that opportunity is. The resurrection is God's opportunity—that is, it is his action that either provides for his own purposes or opens up possibilities to us that heretofore were closed. This is God's relation to time, so that what revelation is must always be understood on a future oriented basis. The mission of the prophet is to show us what it is that God demands in the way of certain responses to his action and to direct us toward the future and away from preoccupation with the past and the present. If we try to understand God and his action only historically, we miss the characteristic orientation to the future that is the substance of revelation.

In order to receive revelation, we must direct our thought toward the future or else its meaning will not be discerned— that is, it will not reveal. 'Time', in this sense, often refers to future events in which God will restore his people, and nothing is evident in the present that requires that such intention be revealed. This may need to be projected forward to a day of righteous judgment, but this is not demanded in an unqualified manner. Jesus actually came to reveal forgiveness, and this is a revelation of the future in itself, since it changes our impressions about what God's actions may be like at the end of time.

In any revelation, the true nature of present time is seen as well as the future, so that those who receive this revelation (that is, Christians) must live in the future as well as in the present moment. However, the characteristic orientation now is toward a future victory. Whatever their present state, all those oppressed will eventually gain recognition, but only through the action of God's power. The resurrection is taken as a sure revelatory sign that such a victory has been won, or that this overcoming will be recognized at some future time. Any such victory is eschatological, however. That is, it signals a final triumph of God not now generally recognized. The present revelation simply opens this sight to those who can, in this event, accept a forecast of the future.

Revelation, nevertheless, concerns more than some future time or end of time or change in time. By virtue of focusing on the future intent, it also opens up a participation by man today and at once in that which is yet to come. There would be no need to forecast future events if the information were purely theoretical. Instead, what revelation accomplishes is to make a future event also a present reality. Therefore, a grasp of the revelation at the same time means to enter that future relationship in the present moment. Obviously, such participation cannot be in full, since the future is not yet solidified in its uncertain detail. The contemporary moment tends to restrict us to the present, but the acceptance of revelation means to break the bonds of that grip and to bring something of the future into present existence.

In this case, a "knowledge of the future" cannot mean its absolute possession in detail. That is not possible. To know what the future will be like, however, is to grasp it already but not as fully realized in explicit form. In order for this to be, the future must invade and be contained within the present time. Revelation uncovers what now is latent but that cannot be discerned as such without aid. If such revelation is accepted, we agree to that forecast and relate it to the present situation. From now on we will see the present primarily in terms of what is yet to come in fact.

F. A TIME OF OPPORTUNITY

Kierkegaard, of course, is famous for his use of the concept of the 'moment'. He does not think of it particularly in regard to revelation, and yet it can have a very definite meaning in this respect. Kierkegaard considers the moment both in connection with the incarnation—that is, God's entrance into time— and as defining the point at which the individual believer makes his commitment in faith. When revelation is our concern, the moment refers to God's transcendent power which can accomplish great things in a little time. In order to accept revelation, it is necessary to grant this possibility first, namely that God can break into time's steady and slow process and accomplish much in an instant. Of course, even men do something like that, not when they are acquiescent and dull but in their finest hours.

In some traditional religious literature, we hear of the moment in another way. God is depicted as "angry," but his anger lasts only for a moment while his kindness endures forever. If this is true, such moments of anger are not revelatory; they indicate almost the opposite about God. Yet, if what we know are moments of anger, it will take a certain amount of revelation to make the idea of God's kindness seem possible. We experience anger; if kindness underlies this, it certainly needs to be revealed. Revelation means a balancing of our perspective, so that what one might infer about God from the natural order can be counterbalanced and yield a different picture.

'The moment', as an item of revelation, also refers to the culminating point looked forward to or predicted by religious prophets. The moment of Jesus' birth is emphasized because it was accepted as revelatory. That is, the time looked forward to by the prophets now was believed to have arrived in that moment. Jesus' ministry is treated as an affirmation that the expected time has arrived. The difficulty of belief is to accept the fact that so much awaited for so long has actually arrived and is concentrated in such a small space of time. Revelation involves fulfillment; the time foretold or expected has entered in at that specific point.

If revelation involves such moments of significance and concentration, it also tells us where to look. It announces the right moment, and it points out the opportunity not available in every situation. Revelation is directional. All times are not alike, any revelation declares; but only if you understand what is opened to you will you be able to grasp what otherwise might not be available. If revelation points to a time of opportunity, it always carries a warning with it. To neglect the moment of opportunity is disaster; to embrace it means salvation. The idea that revelation is connected to these moments of opportunity indicates both that we need to be told where they lie and that, usually, we cannot figure this out for ourselves.

The issue that revelation presents for us is how are men able to discern the opportunity of a given time? How can the signs of the times be read? Those who are able to do this uncover the revelation and are able to participate in it. Those who do not are prevented from sharing, and participation in these revelatory occasions, which involves the creation of a new entity. The Exodus revealed God's plan in a moment of action, and it created Israel. Jesus' appearance revealed God's future plan and formed a new people. Clearly, the opportunity for a new creation actually present in a moment cannot be discerned from the surroundings, since they are old. Revelation enables man to see the possibilities present in a new moment which historical study is bound to miss.

Yet, even when these opportunities open up, revelation also involves a quality of 'waiting' as a part of its meaning. In any revelatory moment, it is God who acts, not man; and, if man is too active and is not silent enough, he may miss the chance to discern the opportunity present. To receive revelation requires a waiting for or upon God. You await or expect God's promised activity, but, without this mood, the revelatory moment may be misread. The time of opportunity arrives, but it is of limited duration, and man must be quick with his attention and response. If this is so, we have to ask "What are the conditions in which we should place ourselves in order not to miss a revealed opportunity that remains open only for an instant?"

G. HOW IS TRUTH MADE KNOWN?

If we are to understand revelation, let alone accept it, we must first decide what 'truth' is and how it can present itself. At this point, philosophy underlies theology and shapes it, particularly if the theory of truth used is such as to prohibit any unusual disclosure, concentrated presence, or restricted access. Revelation is said to uncover truth, but, in order to know what this means and whether it is even possible, we must first know what we take 'truth' to be. Only then can we tell whether truth is such that it can be "revealed." If truth, for instance, is a property that belongs primarily to God, perhaps it cannot be disclosed directly or in any ordinary manner but only in unusual ways.

If 'truth' is taken to involve reliability, dependableness, and an ability to perform what is required, this gives it a different meaning. It becomes not something easily uncovered, and perhaps it can only be grasped as it is subject to disclosure. If consistency and faithfulness are thought to be qualities of truth, no first glance will make this evident, but only some convincing experience. In reverse, truth, in this sense, may be what God demands of men, in which case this demand is not evident in nature unless it is disclosed. If truth is that which has validity and stability, it is primarily something to be done and not only thought about.

Revelatory truth considers itself as taking precedence and as superseding all other human apprehension. If so, truth must be such that it can be provisional and then be passed beyond in later times. If truth is what God has made known of himself, it would correct or replace all other concepts. In this case, many truths are not ultimate but only temporary. If this is so, truth of this ultimate kind is a stimulus to conduct. It is something to do and to obey—once it is disclosed. Insofar as men see this truth, they live acceptably, and this means that what formerly they knew and accepted passively now becomes of such power as to form and shape their action. A truth such as this is more than simple apprehension.

Realizing how special the concept of 'truth' is that makes revelation a possibility, we need first work out a theory of truth in order even to consider revelation. If such a theory does not include revelation as a form of truth, it is not the facts of revelation which are in contest but the acceptability of one theory of truth over another. In this way, revelation is philosophically dependent: that some theories of truth exclude it while others at least open its possibility. No philosophical theory of truth can establish revelation; the question is whether its appearance is even permitted. In determining this, our first question is "What philosophical options do we have for defining truth?"

18
MEDIATOR

A. THE INDIRECT APPROACH

It seems perfectly clear that the Christian approach to God admittedly is indirect. God did not speak directly; he revealed himself in Jesus of Nazareth, and the acceptance of the Christian claim depends upon one's ability to admit the fact of such divine indirection. In order to do this, however, we first must resolve one question: Can any approach to God ever be direct? If the answer is "Yes" (or if the possibility of any approach is flatly denied), the Christian claim is undercut before the assertion is made. Of course, whether the approach can be direct depends upon what kind of God one is dealing with men, but Christian assertions clearly are in between these prohibits any direct appearance. Others do and can mingle with men, but Christian assertions clearly are in between these extremes. God is not such as to confront man directly, but he is such as to be able to be present via the office of a mediator.

Thus, one's feeling about the need for, or appropriateness of, God's use of indirection will depend upon what description is given of God's nature. He must be such that the appearance of a mediator is not a step out of keeping with his nature. This may help explain why the Trinity is not treated separately in Part III as one of the issues facing us, in spite of the fact that it is certainly a major Christian doctrine. That is, you never begin with a trinitarian doctrine. You start with the aspects of the divine that are real to you, and then attempt to fit them together into an interpretation of the nature of God. In Chapter 20, we shall consider what leads to the belief that the Holy Spirit is a reality, but, in the present case, we have to ask what might make men accept Jesus as God's mediator. Then, when the various aspects of divine presence are contemplated, an attempt can be made to put them together, possibly into a trinity. However, we cannot go on to consider God's nature as multiple until we can establish whether we need a mediator in divine things.

If we do not accept this need, we might be able to approach God directly. If so, we would structure our church and our worship quite differently. This indirection on God's part also explains why neither Jesus nor Jesus-as-the-Christ (to borrow Tillich's term) is treated as a problem in a separate chapter in Part III. Jesus, or the attribution to him of the title "Christ," is not an issue until we first establish our need for, or our lack of, a mediator in approaching God. The Jews took indirection for granted, and so they could at least see how Jesus might function in this role. Their question was not if men need a mediator, but whether Jesus fulfills the requirements for this role. But this is no longer an accepted premise; some men approach God directly and some not at all. Unless we consider the necessity for a mediator as our fundamental question, the issue over how to define Jesus' nature and his work will remain confused.

Of course, a theory of human nature, as well as one of the divine nature, is involved in an appraisal of Jesus. Depending on how we assess man's powers, we shall see either more or less need for the services of a mediator. It is true, then, that one of the major problems facing philosophy of religion is to develop a doctrine of human nature, an "anthropology," as it is sometimes called. In trying to appraise Jesus, we see the primary influence of philosophy in shaping theology. For, although some characteristics are assigned to man in the biblical record, the development of a full theory of the nature of man is a philosophical enterprise, and it varies greatly from one metaphysical theory to the next. We must be clear what man's powers and limitations are before we can be sure how it is possible for him to relate himself to God—or whether he can do this directly at all.

The nature we ascribe to man also affects how Jesus' divinity will be outlined. If we begin with Jesus' humanity, how it can be related to divinity will certainly be partially controlled by our view of human nature. The concept of the mediator also contains the issue of human nature: to be a mediator involves sharing in both the sides to be bridged. Here is the center where our view of man and our view of God are jointly worked out; and, in a Christian theology, it seems impossible to work out either side first or independently. This fact partially begins to answer the question about our inability to follow any route except an indirect approach to God. If God and man's nature must both be defined within the context of their relationship, this already indicates that man cannot be understood alone and that God cannot be defined in isolation.

B. THE NEED FOR ASSISTANCE

Our first problem, then, is to determine whether and in what ways any man is in need of assistance from outside himself—and even from outside man. Furthermore, this involves setting the goals it is appropriate to expect a man to achieve before we can determine whether all or most men can do this alone. Some goals (for example, Stoic acceptance) are perfectly achievable without anyone's help, let alone that from a being who is nonhuman. If Stoic acceptance is our goal, we shall never see the necessity for any divine aid. Disagreement over Jesus' role as a mediator with God arises, in part at least, because we differ over the goals appropriate to man and about his own inner ability to fulfill these. This need for ethical definition again brings home the involvement of philosophy in determining theology. The kind of ethical system worked out will almost in itself either make possible or eliminate man's need for assistance from anything like a divine mediator.

Before we can determine whether Jesus answers any need or serves any function in relating us to God, our needs and our goals must be outlined. It is at this point of philosophical definition that the religious and the nonreligious man split.

They differ not so much over the nature of religious experience as over the fact that the religious man accepts certain needs and then defines his goals in terms that involve the ways God can enter in, while the nonreligious man so defines his philosophical definition of needs and goals that God is excluded at the outset. If man's needs and goals are such that he requires no assistance beyond himself, it is pointless to raise the issue of God. For there is no role open in the drama in which God could be cast.

A case in point is provided by Kierkegaard's treatment, in *Philosophical Fragments,* of the Socratic notion of the teacher's task. Socrates believed that man already knows essentially what he needs to learn, and that the teacher's job is to stimulate him to recall it, to draw up into consciousness what essentially he has grasped already without the teacher's aid. Hence the teacher is needed as a catalyst and as a prodder, but he does not seriously change the student in the learning process. Kierkegaard, however, argued that man needs radical reorientation before he can even be taught at all. This is a basic point of philosophical disagreement between Kierkegaard and Plato, and its resolution determines the type of theology that either can or cannot be built on this basis. If men need prior radical readjustment, we must ask what power can accomplish this, and it is at least possible that the answer might be God rather than the human teacher.

The question of man's need for assistance is tied in with the issue of 'sacrifice'. Jesus came to people accustomed to the idea of sacrifice, but he eventually changed its meaning, and that was the problem. A Jew believed that he could not atone for deliberate sin simply by offering up a sacrifice in the temple, but Christians quickly came to view Jesus' crucifixion in terms of the notion of religious sacrifice so familiar to the Jews. However, now it was asserted that Jesus could and did do what temple sacrifice could not do; thus he opened a new era of freedom. Christians were forced to break with Jewish custom as they realized the radicalness of this claim. Today, of course, the idea of religious sacrifice is not a part of everyday thought, and so it must either take on new meaning or have none at all. The question for us is, in overcoming the damage due to our errors and misdeeds, do we need assistance other than the restorative work we as individuals can ourselves provide?

If we see the need for someone else to make a sacrifice so that we can be released from our bondage, the idea of a mediator can take on meaning for us. If we feel that our situation as man against man does not require someone else to make a sacrifice so that good relations can be restored, the function of a mediator—whether divine or human—will have little meaning. A mediator voluntarily intervenes between two estranged parties although he is not responsible for the estrangement. By intervening in order to reconcile, the mediator is offering a gift, and thus making a sacrifice. Without the mediator's service, the breach is such that it could not be healed by our own effort.

In its Jewish setting, sacrifice was needed to span the breach between God and man as well as between man and man. Now, unlike the days when God was directly encountered, we seem to need a mediator even to find God at all or to consider him real. Actually, our present situation is not too far from the original Christian notion, since Jesus did more than provide a sacrifice to restore a people to good relations with a traditional God. He revealed a new God, and the God whom he revealed was such that sacrifice in the traditional ceremonial sense was no longer necessary. Jesus' sacrifice, as Christians came to interpret it, took the form of revealing a new concept of God with whom we could more easily unite. Jesus' mediation filled the role of sacrifice by revealing a God who no longer demanded it.

Our problem today is neither the inhibiting effect of rigid ceremonial practice nor a notion of God that estranges man from him. Our difficulty lies more in the absence of a clear conception of God, so that the mediator we need is one who can make God real again. Thus, the modern question of sacrifice: Is it through sacrifice that God becomes real, and what do we require as mediation in order to discover a new relationship to God? Our sin is not so much to have disobeyed God's rules in the way in which the Jews sinned against their law; it is to have lost all sense of the reality of God.

If this genuinely is our situation, we must, first, determine whether man feels the absence of God to be a loss or a need he cannot himself supply. If a loss is felt, the function of a mediator—one who will help men find God by leading them to where he is to be found—can once again take on meaning. Then, in the light of this need, Jesus' role can be appraised and each man can decide whether Jesus can accomplish this. If so, if he discloses God so that man can be related to him again and if without him men could not accomplish this discovery, there is a real and contemporary significance to the concept of a 'mediator' between God and man.

In Jewish law atonement was achieved by sacrifice; the wrath of God was turned away by the sacrifice and man was reconciled. However, if men have no sense of God's reality, they cannot feel his wrath over their actions or even understand what this means. Therefore, 'atonement' in times such as these must first take the form of a reparation for man's loss of God and his total turning away from all divinity before any sin can become real enough to require reparation, or before God's wrath can be felt strongly enough to cause us to avoid it. If no divine wrath is felt, there is no force or reality to Jesus' office. Before we can decide what Jesus might accomplish, we have to understand what man needs today.

A mediator, as has been noted, is anyone who establishes or maintains between two others a relation that neither could nor would exist without the mediator. Since our estrangement from God is not over sin, it would seem clear that no relationship to God will exist unless someone establishes it for us. When left to themselves, men do not establish a close relationship to God; rather, they tend to lose it. The question of Jesus' mediation, then, depends on whether he can establish and maintain a relationship to God that could not exist without him. In this case, establishing a relationship means first of all showing us in which direction to look for God and then disclosing God as really present where he was not expected.

The "death of God" in recent times would seem to indicate that we do need assistance in finding God. Without outside help God does not seem to stay alive for men through their own efforts. Is this a function that Jesus can provide? If so, he will establish himself as a mediator and as one without whom God cannot stay alive for men. Does the meaning of sacrifice now lie not so much in atonement for previous sins as in the fact that only in sacrifice is God revealed and made real? If so, this would be sufficient to establish Jesus' function as a mediator. Man learns that both the way to heal his estrangement from God and to gain any sense of the reality of God's presence also lie through his sacrifice of himself. To reveal an unsuspected route is the function of a mediator.

C. THE NAMES OF JESUS

A study of the various names used by and attributed to Jesus is a task for a biblical scholar. However, in trying first to determine the need for a mediator so that we can then better understand Jesus in this role, it is important to note that no single title is used consistently either by Jesus to describe himself or by his commentators to report his accomplishments. What might be the reasons for the lack of consistency? What is the significance of this fact in our attempt to understand what it is that Jesus accomplished? One thing is clearly evident: No one of the then existing titles or religious offices fits Jesus perfectly. His own contemporaries had trouble understanding his claims, and the exact nature of his function escaped many, or at least it was unclear enough so that it was differently appraised. His own proclamations and actions were not so clear that they removed all doubt. He seems to have intended to place on others the burden of describing him.

In such a situation, any uniformity of conclusion about Jesus on the part of all men is excluded due to the uncertain beginning. Thus, any 'revelation' will always rest against a background of some residual uncertainty. The names of Jesus will never be reduced to one. Apparently, it was never intended to be otherwise, for it is silly to think that God could not have spoken more clearly had he wanted to and that he could not have removed all doubt had that been his desire.

It is obvious that Jesus is variously understood and variously misunderstood, that in all our records he does not openly proclaim any one identity, and that the claims and names originally used are not one with the ways in which his followers came to understand him after his death. Without much question, this places the burden of decision on those who experience his presence. The writer of the Gospel of John reached a conclusion about these questions, and he publicly proclaims his discovery of Jesus' identity by becoming an author. That is his privilege. In fact, it is an example of the kind of resolution that everyone who deals with Jesus should come to, whether the decision is as positive as the fourth Gospel writer's or more negative. Lack of uniformity in the record does not prevent a verdict being reached that gives Jesus one title. In fact, each Gospel is itself the record of a process of decision and gradual clarification similar to what we all must pass through.

'Christ' and 'Messiah' are perhaps the two most common titles we think of in connection with Jesus of Nazareth. Although there is nothing to prevent anyone later from declaring him to be the expected Messiah, it is clear that he did not openly and directly claim this title. Of course, there is no uniformity in interpreting the role of the Messiah in Jewish tradition. But whatever the degree of disagreement, in times of oppression hopes spring up for the coming of a Messiah who will liberate the Jews. Jesus appeared at such a time, but he did not fit these expectations exactly. Indeed, disappointment over his failure to be a political liberator accounts, in part, for his crucifixion as a false Messiah. If Jesus fulfills this role as liberator, it must be in an unexpected and nonpolitical way.

Today we more commonly title Jesus as "Christ". This means that the interpretation of his role as mediator has come to be identified with the function of 'Messiah' to the extent of blotting out his given name or tying it to, "Jesus Christ." This concept will be discussed more fully in the next section. The point to be clear about here is the indecision and the tentativeness Jesus' name involves, and the sometimes bold assertions we make in spite of this. We must comprehend the variety of names used by Jesus about himself, and by his followers, to express what his function is to be. 'Jesus' itself is derived from 'Joshua,' which was a common name of the time meaning "Jehovah will save" or "the salvation of the Lord." Joshua led Israel across the Jordan into the promised land, and later others were quick to see the parallel of Jesus leading the new Israel through the waters of baptism into their inheritance. But, originally, the name 'Jesus' clearly was not interpreted in this way.

If Jesus had simply and in single concepts defined his own function without reservation or obscurity, we would not have to approach his interpretation indirectly. There are many affirmations, some of which come from his own lips, but even his disciples did not quite understand them clearly at the time. They did so later, however, and perhaps this indicates that an understanding of Jesus' role is the result of a process through which every individual must go and is not a matter that can be decided beforehand simply from the given data. The data provide the starting point for the interpretation, but do not of themselves yield a single affirmation. Whatever else we can say, there seems to be present in the biblical record a certain hesitancy about either direct statement or explicit self-interpretation. Jesus is not unaware of his own powers, but his attention most often seems to be directed elsewhere—that is, on others rather than on himself.

The concept of 'servant' also is now commonly used to describe Jesus. In the limited but important reference to this role in Isaiah, the servant is one who fulfills his divine mission, and this is to the world and not to Israel alone, but it comes through suffering and a death he bore for others. Although this image is present in Jewish literature, it is not a common one, and it is opposed to the concept of the savior who will restore the lost monarchy. Actually, it was more as a political and as a religious leader that he was first understood—that is, as one who would overcome oppression directly by his power. The picture of a God who suffers may be the most profound way in which Jesus reveals God's nature and mediates between God and man, but it certainly was not the only way in which he was understood and categorized at the time. Nor is it a role claimed exclusively by Jesus himself, in spite of his reference to the necessity for him to suffer in order to accomplish his mission.

D. THE ISSUE OVER AUTHORITY

The issue over Jesus' 'authority' is perhaps the primary concern, which is just the way it seems to be in the Gospel accounts themselves.

In some ways, Jesus did claim a divine authority, and it is the attempt to appraise this claim that causes the confusion over his proper title, and rejecting this assertion leads to his crucifixion.

'Authority' is the key issue in the New Testament, and it still is today. What is Jesus' assertion in this regard, and can it be accepted? Neither question is, or ever was, easy to answer. He did not claim simply to be a certain clearly expected person, but, unmistakably, he asserted his authority to act for and to represent God. In one form, this claim is accepted and embodied in the doctrine of the trinity, which establishes Jesus firmly within the divine nature. Although this doctrine was unknown in its explicit formulation in biblical times, it is nevertheless one legitimate way to deal with and to account for Jesus' appropriation of authority. It is precisely this claim that offended orthodox Jewish ears as blasphemy, because a Jew felt that he possessed God's law. To presume to stand above it was to claim an authority reserved for God alone. A Jew believes in one God, and thus he could not accept Jesus. A 'Christian,' however, is one who acknowledges Jesus' right and thus is forced to a theory of multiple divine expressions. Accepting Jesus' claim to authority means that God has multiple facets.

Jesus' disciples were unsure how to interpret his authority, and those who expected him to lead them politically and physically were dejected by his crucifixion. Their interpretation of his authority was shattered by his death, but this is also the meaning of the resurrection: The sign of God's authority was, finally, manifest in Jesus' triumph over death; and this became the central factor around which Christians gathered and in terms of which they interpreted his now confirmed divine authority. *Any rejection or radical reinterpretation of the resurrection is, in fact, a rejection or reinterpretation of Jesus' authority, and around this the whole question of Christology revolves.*

Both Jesus' miracles and his new rules regarding the Sabbath could be accepted within any one of several concepts about a religious leader or seer. His asserted resurrection, however, requires a more radical and extreme authority, and

Christians became Christians by accepting this manifestation of authority and by attributing to Jesus a nature powerful enough to match an execution of power able to reverse the most unavoidable natural limits.

The idea of suffering and of assuming the form of a servant adds a complication to the idea of a blatant display of divine power and authority in the act of resurrection. In fact, one can speculate that it might have been something like this that caused Peter to deny Jesus three times at his trial after he had sworn that he would not desert him. That is, if Peter had originally accepted Jesus' authority when he became a disciple, then to see his Lord mute and humiliated and powerless in front of his accusers must have shattered Peter's faith. The prophets had been more bold than Jesus. Facing this sad fact, Peter could only have thought he was denying a righteous man, not God himself.

How can suffering and the change involved in becoming a servant also represent God's power and authority? That God might send fiery leaders to rouse the people against a tyrant—all this a Jew could understand; God had acted this way in the past. However, that one who represented God and acted with divine authority should be humiliated, suffer, and submit, that is a very hard concept of 'authority' to accept. No wonder Jews rejected it by and large. The Christian approach to God always involves the puzzle of trying to appraise Jesus' 'authority', for he does not act as we might expect an all-powerful God to behave. The God who led Israel in battle and destroyed its enemies would not manifest his authority in reverse —that is, by serving quietly and suffering without defense. If one is really "sent by God," he should conquer. If he did, it would not be too hard to understand that kind of divine authority.

The question of Jesus' 'authority' is the issue of his 'divinity', of course. Is he the one "sent by God," and, if so, how is this power tested, and how would you expect it to be manifest? He may suffer and still be divine, but it will take a new and a more complex notion of God to account for this seeming paradox. His death does not disprove his divinity; it only indicates God's willingness to suffer for a time at man's hand—

that is, it does if you accept the resurrection and the over-coming of death as God's final sign of the full presence of his authority in Jesus' words and deeds. If you do, then to what degree must divinity be present to account for the breaking of the bonds of death, since this certainly is man's most powerful and unavoidable natural enemy? The response to this question is usually to assert that Jesus must be fully God in order to overcome death and yet fully man because he is able to die in the first place. The degree of the acceptance of divine author-ity in Jesus determines the question of his divinity *vs.* his humanity.

If 'Christ' is an English version of 'Christos', which means "the anointed one," and if 'Messiah' is simply derived from the Greek form, the issue over accepting the title 'Christ' for Jesus turns on whether we accept him authoritatively as God's spokesman. Israel's kings were anointed with oil as a sign that God had chosen them for their office. When they were anointed, the spirit of Yahweh came upon them mightily. The title of 'Christ' came to mean "the king of Israel," and so the issue clearly is "In what sense and to what degree is God's seal of approval placed on Jesus?"

Some expected him to become a king, but his crucifixion, which involved a ridicule of that title, put a quick end to such an expectation. Now, if Jesus is not literally to be king of Israel, in what sense is God's seal of authority still set upon him? It was thought that it might be found both in his teach-ing and as evidenced in his miracles, but these were abruptly halted too. Thus, the issue comes to center around the resur-rection. Is God's raising up of Jesus a sign of the authority in his words in spite of their early misinterpretation and his fol-lowers' misexpectations?

The Gospels vary in their representation of Jesus' claim to authority. With John, his extraordinary power is admitted from the beginning, but we really must ask "From the begin-ning of what?" The answer seems to be "Beginning with the resurrection." Even after the resurrection, however, it is clear that some disciples took this event to mean that, now, he would act like the Messiah—that is, restore the lost kingdom of Israel. They must have been just as disappointed by Jesus leaving them on ascension day as they were in his crucifixion.

After that second departure, if he is to restore a kingdom, it surely must be different from a physical state. And, it is in puzzling over how a new kingdom has, in fact, been established that Christianity first began and always begins. Peter realized that God had made Jesus into 'Christ' by raising him from the dead.

The only thing absolutely clear about Jesus' authority is that it was not manifested in the ways in which even his followers expected it to show itself. Perhaps every later person must first go through this trial of disillusionment and of misunderstanding what Jesus will accomplish before, in disappointment, it is possible to find God's authority present in new and unexpected forms. To fix the mode of divine authority in rigid ways, then, may doom its appropriation to failure, if in fact its experience is tied to the necessity of prior disappointment and misunderstanding. Again, it seems that God cannot be understood directly but is to be found only after an initial attempt fails. To stop too soon or to accept defeat may be to deny oneself a possible discovery of God, *if, and only if, his nature is, in fact, such that it is revealed in suffering and known only after initial disappointment.*

We have to ask "In what position is it necessary to be in order to discover and to appraise authority properly without ruling out in advance every chance to sense the presence of such divine authority?" It is not true of all religions, but it may be characteristic of the Christian understanding, that God's power and authority are never directly seen, but are manifested only indirectly. If this is the case, it fits with the need for a mediator. It also means that a recognition of divine authority never comes before the fact, and perhaps not even with the experience, but only after the fact. In order to discover authority in trying to account for what has happened, you first experience death and loss and suffering. You expected that to be the end of the matter, and then it is not. Out of it life comes back again; and, in attempting to account for how this could happen and how the natural order could be reversed, you are forced to assert the presence and action of divine power. The discovery of authority in God's case must be *ex post facto.* Human authority can be directly manifest. It is God's necessary indirection that is both so characteristic and so difficult to explain.

E. THE FULFILLMENT OF EXPECTATION

You cannot accept Jesus as the divine fulfillment of a long-held hope unless you begin with some expectation. If the Jews, or at least some of them, expected a Messiah and so could deal with Jesus on those terms, it is just as clear that non-Jews did not then, and do not now, live in that expectation. Even Jews usually feel a strong Messianic hope only in times of persecution. However, if it is true that the Messianic hope does not exist among all Jews but arises only at times and under certain conditions, it could be that these same conditions will give rise to certain expectations to which all men are subject. We need to consider this possible universal-expectation-in-times-of-adversity-and-exile if Jesus cannot be understood except in terms of a fulfilled expectation.

Clearly, the Messianic hope springs up among the Jews when they are being oppressed and persecuted, whether in Egypt, Germany, or Poland. Ancient longings arise again when they are not their own political masters and when it is difficult to practice their religion or to preserve their lives. They hope for a redeemer who will fulfill their pleas for life and freedom. Into these conditions Jesus first came, and perhaps similar situations must always be involved if his role is to be understood at any later time. Favorable religious and political circumstances may not be the right context in which Jesus can be comprehended. Whenever we are free and in control we are bound to miss his significance. If our cries are not those of the Jews of his time, or at least if they are not phrased in those concepts, what longings do we have, what expectations still persist, that Jesus could be considered as fulfilling?

It is interesting that the Old Testament does not refer to a future Messiah—a king who will rise up and restore the lost glory of the kingdom of David. Messianic hope is expressed in the Psalms of Solomon, but these blessings are expected for Israel only. The expectations of how God would visit them and redeem his people varied greatly in biblical times, and they still do. Sometimes it was thought that God himself would intervene, but at other times his action was not considered to be that direct. In any case, 'Messiah' is used only to designate the human 'son of David' whom God would raise up. On all of these counts, Jesus either does not fit the picture or, at the very least, he fulfills it much differently than expected. To expect literal and direct and specified action from a Christian God may be a very wrong expectation—one that leads to religious frustration. If you insist that God act openly and always according to a previously written script, you may find such a God, but evidently he will not be Christian.

The Jews did not expect the Messiah as a future promise, and Jesus' contemporaries did not interpret him in this way. They expected certain things of Jesus, and these expectations were not forthcoming. Even after his resurrection, which might have been interpreted as a present fulfillment, he leaves his disciples again without securing them against their enemies. He postpones his promise into the future, which is where things stand today. God's presence is still expected, but it is only offered as a future promise. The expectation is fulfilled, but only in terms of an as yet uncheckable future radical rearrangement. Both Jews and Gentiles expect the blessings of any divine coming to evolve only to our own community. Instead, they are showered universally, which undercuts their strict control by our organized groups. God extends himself—but to people whom we had not expected him to include. And this frustrates our efforts to control the distribution of his mercy by exclusive regulation.

We want divine favor to rest on a specific group, and he extends it to no visible boundaries. The expectation is fulfilled, but the tight little inner group is dispersed in the process. If our anticipations for how God may visit us vary both then and now, it follows that the way in which we experience and express this fulfillment will always change and can never be subject to a single formulation. Since we expect very different things from God, the mode of the fulfillment, whether it is positive or negative, cannot be one. A hope differently fulfilled will always be somewhat differently expressed than when it was first voiced. It is true the disciples agreed on Jesus' resurrection as the key to their expectations, even if they had not expected it and could not have predicted this turn of events. Still, they never gave this a single final formulation, and even the immediate witnesses expressed the unexpected fulfillment in a variety of ways.

If good Jews sometimes expected God himself to intervene, you can understand their failure to recognize this intervention in the form of a carpenter's son. If, later on, any Christian comes to affirm that indeed God himself did intervene directly—and if he even goes on to call Jesus 'divine' in order to explain this—it is understandable why this could not have seemed obvious at the time, no matter what special powers his contemporaries might have been willing to attribute to Jesus. In spite of the miracles and the authoritative teaching, it is not so much *in* what Jesus did that God is clearly manifest as it is in what God did *to* Jesus—that is, to raise him from the dead after his humiliating defeat. If 'Messiah' designates only the human 'son of God' and if 'son of man' is, in fact, Jesus' favorite title for himself, we will never accept him as divine if all we expected in the first place was a human being of unusual power. We grow in understanding only in terms of what we originally expect.

In saying all of this, it is still true that God did not fulfill the expectation men had for Jesus at all in the way in which they anticipated these acts. Still, if you expect nothing from God you have no basis on which to appraise his supposed accomplishments. Before Jesus can be understood, we must come to exist in a mood of expectation, and, like the Jews, these longings may only arise under disappointment or oppression, whether physical or psychological. Then, if our expectations are not fulfilled as we demand, we are in a situation where we may either misunderstand or else regroup our thoughts and try to grasp how unexpected events may still be counted as fulfillment. In order to fathom Jesus' role, we have to ask what we expect from him, and then we can ask in what way he either can or might or did fulfill this longing. Of course, he might do this by upsetting our whole scheme.

If, at this point, we bind God philosophically by fixing in advance the way in which he must respond, we may prejudice our ability to see an unorthodox response to our expectations. If we insist on conformity to an advance philosophical formula, we may miss God when he proves less philosophical than that. The unexpected ways in which Christians discovered that God had fulfilled their expectations or else promised to do so in the future should lead them always to refuse to confine God's actions within preestablished limits. Philosophizing is not irrelevant, but it should come after our own experience. Evidently, reason alone does not determine how God will act, and so we must be careful theologically not to impose a particular philosophical scheme on God too quickly. He may be like that and he may not, and we can only tell after we have seen how our expectations are either fulfilled or changed by disappointment.

F. THE FORM OF GOD'S PRESENCE

Any concept of the existence of a mediator between God and man rests on the assumption that it is possible for God to be present among men. Before we can appraise any such claim, it is necessary to ask how God might actually be present among us. What forms can divine presence take, and, in the light of this, how can divinity be recognized definitely and perceived clearly? Of course, it is impossible to answer this question once and for all, since that would mean to exhaust all of the possible concepts of God and to know which particular one existed in fact. We may, certainly, look at it from the other side and begin by claiming God's presence in Jesus. Then, our problem becomes to construct a theory of the divine nature such that it is possible for God to be present in that way—that is, in a human form. This really underscores the fact that we must work from both sides simultaneously. We must look for evidences of divine presence, and, at the same time, we must work to construct a concept of God philosophically. Then we can move on to determine his possible presence.

If we begin with Aristotle's 'Unmoved Mover', clearly it cannot assume human form. It could only relate itself to men by causing them to desire its own condition and to strive for it. If we accept Plotinus' 'One', it can be present everywhere in the sense that unity is, but, of course, this is only in an inferior way (that is, through greater multiplicity) and never fully. In order to be present with a God like this, a man must abandon his own nature. It is unthinkable that the One should yield his position to come to man. What kind of God will fit the Christian experience of unexpected presence and a breaking of natural laws? Spinoza's 'Substance' is never unexpected in its actions. For Substance to break a natural law would amount to a destruction of its own nature. Before we are able to decide how and who can mediate between God and man, we must reach a decision about what limits we should set on the possible modes of divine presence.

Perhaps today we are in a better position to appraise the presence of divinity precisely because we have ceased to believe in it. That is, whenever we take God for granted, his presence seems to be only a matter of routine. Whenever God is missing from the scene, then to experience any form of divine presence certainly would be surprising. The important point is that God's presence in Jesus was not originally an expected event, and this is true in spite of the addition of the birth narrative to the Gospels, which makes that event appear in a way in which it did not evidence itself at the time. If it is the case that God's action must come as a surprise, and if its form is usually unpredicted, then, in a day in which God is not expected to act because he is not widely believed in, we may be in the best possible situation in which to judge a question of divine presence. When he is not anticipated, he may be the most easily apprehended, but this is true only by contrast and after his entrance has taken place.

The disciples did not expect God to act as he did, and, when they felt the action of a power they could only describe as God's, they attributed divinity to that upon which this power focused—that is, Jesus, later called Christ. The attribution of divinity is never simply acknowledged as the result of a routine consideration, but it comes only as the result of a response to an unexpected and powerful action which breaks in upon us with such force and upsets normal expectations so totally that it comes to be called "divine." Whenever we seem to find God's action all around us daily and in a routine fashion as if we had always lived religiously, then it is hard to experience anything so unusual that it warrants being set aside and labeled "divine." If God is considered to be everywhere, it is difficult to place the locus of his action at any one point. Fortunately, we no longer live in a time of intense divine presence. For this reason, perhaps it will be easier for us to understand any unusual in-breaking when it occurs.

Do we experience any manifestation of such power in a moment of crisis and change such that it instinctively draws from us the label 'divine'? Are we in an age of any Messianic expectancies or oppressions or frustrated hopes so that we look for any divine intervention? *Only in such a state of expectancy, plus divine absence, is any fresh understanding possible.* Perhaps Kierkegaard is wrong in thinking that extreme anticipation distorts, at least where God is concerned. If we expect nothing but what we find, then, of course, we look for nothing beyond our present lot, and we could not recognize anything new if it came.

We should not decide about what is and what is not divine simply abstractly. Such an appraisal can come only after a powerful in-breaking and reversal. Not that every experience of power is divine. That would eliminate the power of the Devil and the Antichrist if true, and it would make God's location too simple a matter. The intervening power may be demonic and destructive, but, as Plato noted in the *Phaedrus,* some powerful disturbances are heaven sent and some are not. The problem is to learn to distinguish between the two.

Still, we are not able to distinguish the divine from the demonic in-breaking unless we experience some manifestation of power. It is not possible to decide whether our expectations are false until we understand what it means to live in a state of constant religious expectation. What divine interventions would we like to see today so that we can later decide whether they may yet happen or have already occurred when we were not looking? *The form that God's presence can take is set by what we expect.* Even if it does not occur in this way, at least this provides the starting point from which we can next ask whether what we have experienced is in fact a new form of God's presence, in spite of his apparent rejection of the specific mode of our expectation.

What the Christians assert is that the mediator who is necessary to bring this experience to us must be able to represent God perfectly and still be flesh and blood. In the Christian context, this tells us that the form that God's presence takes should be concrete and immediate and not far removed from the base level of human existence. This form of God's presence is not too expected when we consider human nature *vs.* divine perfection. And yet is it impossible?

In asking whether a mediator can provide a form of God's presence, our issue is something like this: "What must one be in his nature in order to be able to serve this function?" Traditional Christology has answered this question by propounding doctrines of two natures and one substance, fully God and fully man, and so forth. Our issue is not so much to decide on the total acceptance of one expression over another as to determine what must one be like in his nature in order to serve in the capacity of a mediator between God and man. Since not every attempted mediator succeeds, any acceptable answer to this question must represent both sides fully and powerfully enough so that the mediator cannot fail to accomplish this bringing together, this needed reconciliation. If we experience an overcoming of estrangement as stemming from God, the issue is solved: the power that accomplishes this act will be labeled fully divine.

If by the means of the mediator's office his people are able to come into the presence of God, we next need to ask "What is required in order to bring us into God's presence, or perhaps God into ours?" However, the problem is that we cannot answer this before the experience of its accomplishment. In order to determine the mediator's status, we must feel the force of reconciling power—that is, the coming of God's presence. Then, in response to this, it is possible to say something about what the mediator must be in order to achieve what he did. He who does not benefit from such mediation is simply not in a position to decide about the source of its power.

19

GOD

A. THE QUESTION OF GOD

'God' is not a question that can be asked without preparation or support, and all of the other major issues in philosophy of religion provide a context that helps to structure the problem more concretely. Of course, the other concepts do not in themselves determine an answer; the exact way the problems in philosophy of religion relate to each other is not that simple. Nevertheless, to learn how to ask the question about God properly certainly is at the center of the whole issue and determines our success or failure. If this question could only be raised in one way, it might be a different matter. As it is, half of our perplexity comes over wondering how we should put the question of God at the outset.

The trivial problems of life are easily asked and just as easily answered. Our quandary over knowing how to approach God itself is an initial warning about just how difficult the question is and just how precarious our chances for success are. Surely, we must research the problem, and we have access to endless data. It is not because we lack material that we do not solve the question of God. It is that we cannot be sure of any one of our various answers, and so we are forced to keep on reformulating the question.

Sometimes "the question of God" is taken to mean the question of our uncertainty about his existence. However, we want to begin this inquiry on a more fundamental level than that. We start with both a dilemma about how to approach the question and a problem over how to begin to think about God. All this arises before we even get to the point of considering our certainty or uncertainty about his existence. *The question about God always begins at the point where all questions are still under consideration.* We have to know how we should start out before we can argue over our success or failure in following a certain line of argument. To say this is not quite to begin with Descartes' "method of doubt," which is a dilemma about how to achieve certainty with regard to any proposition. Since we question the goal of certainty itself and its applicability to the question of God, we do not so much begin with various doubts about God as we do with a lack of understanding about how to start thinking about him. The basis of our uncertainty concerns how and where to begin.

Descartes and others somehow do not seem to have begun with any doubt as to how God should be conceived. They were sure that he was infinite, unchanging, and the like. Now, we are no longer sure how God ought be thought about, and we often begin with absence rather than with Anselm's preformed concept of God. We also know that there has been a great deal of change about God (even within Western thought). Thus, we have inherited no one agreed upon or guaranteed way to conceive of such a being. Every traditional concept has been challenged, and every option is available for consideration. The openness of the question today is refreshing, in a way, but it is also disconcerting, since it means that we lack the initial orientation we sometimes have had when the framework of our thinking was more settled. If we live in an age of anxiety, we perhaps are more uncertain about God's nature than our own.

Of course, the question of God differs from some in that, for a few people, it is their most urgent concern, an issue of life or death. For others, it does not seem to matter or to affect their lives. For still others, even to raise the question arouses hostility and resentment. 'God' is an issue the response to which runs the whole gamut of possible positive and negative attitudes. This phenomenon both helps and hinders our consideration. It helps us in the sense of marking the issue as certainly being important, and it is an advantage to have so much zeal and intensity bent toward the solution of an inherently difficult issue. Indifference does not hinder consideration of the question, except in that it treats the matter lightly; only a serious effort is likely to yield any significant results on so opaque an issue. Hostile and negative attitudes thwart consideration in the sense that they block the reformulation of the question, and this is the most important requirement for success. Even a strong hostility marks the problem as important. In a negative way, it contributes energy to the project, not to mention a healthy reason for us to begin by reformulating the question itself, if possible.

We might even go so far as to say both that anyone who has had success in answering the question of God has done so just because he has found a new way to ask the question and that those who have failed have done so because they could not raise themselves out of the rut of old forms. The histories of philosophy and theology seem to be a series of discoveries of new ways to ask old questions and thereby to find avenues to fresh success. Unfortunately, there perhaps is no problem older than that of God, and there perhaps are few about which it is harder to gain a fresh perspective. However, success is not ruled out, and puzzling over the question of God itself continues to drive some to make new attempts. How can we find a way to ask the question of God that is not simply embedded in ancient, and thus unprofitable, quarrels?

B. THE PROOF OF GOD

As far as philosophy of religion is concerned, the question of God is most often put as an issue over the possibility of 'proofs' for God's existence. Since the origin of philosophy, a series of proofs (and disproofs) has been offered, so that one way to approach the question of God is to consider the various proofs that have been put forth. It does not matter whether this is done via Augustine, Anselm, Aquinas, or Spinoza. The point is that any one of these can provide a context and thus initiate thought about God. Hopefully, this even guides thought toward discovery. However, the multiplicity of these proofs itself is a problem, since this situation indicates the lack of agreement over avenues of approach that might be helpful. This absence of an easy simplicity also suggests that the philosophical context that surrounds it, and the assumptions upon which it depends for its force, are more important than the formal proof itself.

Of course, the first issue that arises is the question over the meaning of 'proof'.* If we were all agreed about this crucial criterion, there perhaps would be no need for philosophy at all and there might no longer be any uncertainty about God. As it is, our differences over 'proof' indicate the heavy dependence of the question of God upon a series of philosophical assumptions. We cannot decide about God's existence until we find out how many meanings of 'to prove' there are. Since there are more definitions than one, we can never conclude this matter once and for all, and God remains involved in the difficulties of establishing the criteria for 'proof'. Clearly, a decision over whether God's existence can be 'proven' rests on a prior agreement over the meaning of proof. Centuries of argument have failed to provide unalterable uniformity here, although we do have a number of now classical suggestions.

In addition to the variety of meanings possible for 'proof' itself, we also have to ask "What are the conditions and characteristics of a valid conviction?" Whenever we talk about 'proof' where God is concerned, we must keep in mind its effect upon the attentive mind, just as much as we consider the logical and technical details of the formal proof itself. With some questions, it is not so hard to determine exactly how the mind becomes certain about a conclusion. Where God is concerned, the matter is more complicated. Because his nature is so unusual, it is harder to determine just what it would mean in this instance for a mind to become rightly convinced. We have to decide about our possible relationships to such a being before we can know whether it is possible to reach conviction in God's case.

* As a working definition consider this: "A proof is a valid argument, where 'valid' means that the premises are all true and that the premises logically entail the conclusion." Where God is concerned, does this seem to apply in any simple fashion and solve our difficulties?

The various proofs are not themselves neutral, so that the argument revolves around the ability of the conclusion to bind anyone who follows the proof. Instead, what happens is that each step of the proof raises its own questions, so that one must first turn and argue about assertions that are not part of the proof itself but are assumed by it as a theoretical context. We are involved in controversy even before we start the proof. For instance, in Anselm's formulation ("that being than which none greater can be conceived") we must either argue about, or else agree with, this definition before we can consider whether existence must be attributed to it necessarily. Or, in Thomas' argument from causation, we have to agree what 'cause' means and how it operates before we can decide whether it can lead us necessarily to the existence of a first cause itself uncaused. Since we have to determine whether we can accept the way in which the proof is set up, conviction always rests upon prior assumptions.

Some treatments of God in philosophy of religion spend most of their time arguing pro and con the various 'proofs' which have been given. Any of these proofs can be presented fairly simply, if you extract them from their various philosophical contexts, but the actual fact is that to do this distorts them. It may very well be that the greatest source of support is lost when the argument (say, Anselm's ontological proof) is removed from the philosophical setting that gives it its power and in which it arose. By the time a proof is set out, it would seem that the issue has already been decided. That is, the first principles of that philosophical view either support or move against the argument, and so they cannot carry to God a mind that is either unwilling or rejects the premises of that philosophical context.

Before following any proof can work or fail, we must decide on the philosophical context for its consideration. Hopefully, we begin by understanding the author's own setting (for example, Anselm's Platonism) and then either accept or reject, modify or substitute, in order to reach the framework that gives it its force. For instance, if we believe that all knowledge must be reduced to custom and to immediate impressions, as Hume does, we shall be very limited in what we can say about God, and we know that any God resulting from an argument based on his assumptions cannot be transcendent.

However, the effect achieved by the proof depends equally upon one's view of man's mind, on what arguments can accomplish psychologically as far as changed attitudes are concerned, and on what degree of conviction we can expect any mind to achieve, for how long and under what conditions. 'Proof' itself seems to be as controversial as God, and thus God's existence is hampered as much by continued uncertainties over 'proof' as it is by the special qualities of his nature.

C. THE KNOWLEDGE OF GOD

When we ask what knowledge we have about God's nature, the responses some men make assume that we really are without any source of information. When you stop to consider all of the data relating to God (see sections D, E, and F), it becomes clear that no one really can claim that we are without substantial information about God. That is, he cannot unless he has a certain definition of 'knowledge' according to which the mass of material available has somehow been ruled out as unacceptable. What this situation tells us—a vast array of reports about God simultaneous with denials that we know anything—is that God is locked in the middle of the central philosophical controversy: What is knowledge? If we did not continue to be uncertain about what to accept as meeting the requirements of 'knowledge,' philosophy probably would not persist. We have many arguments, theories, assertions, and vast quantities of information. Yet philosophy exists because we cannot accept all of these, and because we still try to establish satisfactory criteria for evaluating what is and is not 'knowledge.'

In this sense, God can never be free from philosophical controversy. Those who accept or reject certain 'evidence' for God will do so in the light of some accepted criteria for knowledge, but we can never force all men to accept one standard, in spite of the efforts of some philosophers along these lines. Thus, in any discussion of God we must establish the criterion for knowledge on which we agree to operate. Otherwise, we cannot decide what to admit and what not to admit as evidence. Unless we do this, we will not understand why some philosophers accept data others reject when it is clearly available.

Of course, the same problem that gives rise to philosophy troubles religion too, so that even the religious life cannot escape the philosophical dilemma over establishing a clear test for knowledge. That is, not all the evidence for God is uniform or in agreement. He has not always been described, or his activity reported, in the same ways. Thus, every religious person, as well as every philosopher, must decide to rule out or to reinterpret at least some of the reports concerning God. The religious person may follow the simple expedient of accepting an already defined tradition, but that does not do away with the fact that the problem exists. In any case, the theologian cannot ignore the difficulty, since it is precisely his job to purify and to keep consistent what a given religious tradition reports about God.

Perhaps the most important issue over defining 'knowledge' is the traditional demand for 'universality'. Philosophers do tend, although not always by any means, to think that whatever can be called knowledge ought to be universalizable, at least in principle, and be acceptable by all men. When enforced, this requirement hampers most religious sources of information, since by their very nature they claim to be the discovery by a few of a revelation not given to all. In fact, it is probably the unargued assumption of the test of universality that from the beginning rules out of consideration most of the reports from a religious tradition about its experience of God. If data that appear to some but not to all could be accepted as 'knowledge', our sources of information about God would be considerably richer.

It is true that in modern times we have been more inclined to demand universality as a test for knowledge because it seems to be a part of modern science and its impressive methodology. Without arguing whether, in fact, scientific theory always operates on an implicit assumption of the universalizable quality of all that it calls knowledge, the crucial point to determine is whether in the case of God and religion 'knowledge' ought to have any special characteristics that would distinguish it from other situations of knowing.

At first glance, this difference should not seem so strange if it is true, since God most certainly is not an object of knowledge in any ordinary sense. Thus, he might very likely be open to a way of knowing different from that in other fields. The unconditional demand for universalization as a criterion for knowledge and the demand that knowledge conform to the same standards in every instance—these two philosophical questions are perhaps crucial to our search for knowledge of God.

At the same time, we have to ask whether God is really different from every other situation where the criteria for determining 'knowledge' are a continual issue? 'God' may very well present special difficulties not encountered with other objects. Still, the important point is that, in every area, our uncertainty over the criteria for knowledge remains constantly unsettled beyond any possible final reformulation. Thus, our conclusions about any question in that field are no more certain or uniform than the area of acceptance for the implicit standards of knowledge. Physics may have wider areas of agreement regarding 'knowledge' than metaphysics, but still our conclusions always depend upon prior acceptance of some standard and test.

Let us, then, begin by asking first what sources of information we actually do have about God, without ruling any of them out in advance as either conflicting or unacceptable. Then, after we see what the raw data are, we can try to establish a criterion according to which we shall admit certain information as evidence for the question of God, or else rule it out as not conforming to the requirements necessary to be counted as knowledge. Whenever anyone asserts in blanket fashion that no information regarding God is available, he has simply taken over some epistemology. Then, according to its criteria, he has ruled out a large body of data as inadmissible. Kant knows we can and do think about God. Thus, when he says we are not able to think about God, we realize what he means is that, according to his accepted standards of knowledge, most of the quantitatively enormous thought about God is to be ruled out as illegitimate.

Our problem where God is concerned often is to keep the door open for consideration and not to have it slammed shut to further thought before all of the possible approaches to the question have been examined. In order to do this, our relationship to philosophy must always be kept both open and flexible. It should be such that the philosopher does not rule out the possibility of theology before he has considered different definitions of 'knowledge' that might allow it, and the theologian does not consider certain data as 'knowledge' just because it is important to him before he questions the conditions under which others might or might not accept such a claim. Whenever the philosophical context within which God must be thought about is assumed and not argued to, both affirmation and denial are in danger of having their basic assumptions rejected without conscious appraisal.

"Naturalism *vs.* transcendence" is a good illustration of the issue here. According to the majority of accounts, God has at least some transcendent qualities, even if he does not transcend nature in every respect. A 'naturalistic' position, one that rules out any acceptance of transcendence of the natural order, practically determines the question of God before it is considered. Yet those who speak as if qualities and beings that transcend nature are clearly acceptable run the risk of not being understood by someone who neither experiences these qualities nor accepts such reports because transcendence violates his naturalistic premise. Clearly, on a naive glance, without philosophical assumptions, nothing about the natural order itself prevents the existence of a being or beings that transcend it either partially or completely. It is only when 'nature' comes to assume the role of a norm that it can be used to rule out of existence what does not conform to its particular mode.

There is, of course, an easy tendency to take what we see before us as the criterion of existence for all that is, but there is no self-evident reason why all of reality should conform just to satisfy our love of simplicity. Reality may, in fact, be more subtle and complicated than Ockham's razor allows. It is not at all clear that scientific theory has succeeded by assuming that what immediately appears to be true is, in fact, the best criterion for ultimate truth. If we find a more complicated, intricate, and fascinating world of science behind the simple appearance of things, and if understanding nature requires vast complications, unsuspected premises, and quantities of speculative theory and abstract mathematics, there is nothing to prevent this from being true even if inconvenient. Likewise, God need not always be approached by using the most obvious and blunt standards.

On what basis, we ask, are the evident sources of information about God rejected by those who say we have none? We must answer this question, in part, by considering what these sources of data are like so that we can understand why some men establish rules in order to reject as evidence what seems to others to be so clearly before them. Our sources tend to take the following forms: (1) religious documents which record the encounters various groups and individuals have had with God, their conviction about a divine presence in such events, and the determination of the authors to set this down in writing so that others might know about this divine experience plus their conviction; (2) the actual history and effort of religious individuals (disciples) and groups (churches) as they work to carry out the divine injunctions they have received and celebrate together (worship) in order to preserve this relationship and to honor the divine presence; (3) the technical writings of philosophers and theologians who, sometimes using this religious data and sometimes simply following their own reasoning, have worked out more detailed and systematic doctrines regarding the nature of God and his actions.

If we consider these sources of information and ask why some reject them, we find that each contains a negative factor that, if it is selected out and stressed, serves to undermine the credibility of the source: (1) Information that is an account of God's activity is not something universally and directly verifiable by all, and often it contains reports about God's action that some find either offensive or unbelievable (for example, that God should order the slaughter of innocent people). These reports, then, lack a universal quality, and they contain conflicting or questionable aspects. Thus, they usually need refining before they can be accepted. No one can believe all of the reports about God simultaneously. You are forced to make a choice from among the various accounts, and this means that such evidence always lacks uniformity and verifiability beyond doubt.

If we turn to (2) the work of the people who represent God

and consider their effort, we find some very compelling cases (for example, saints) and some impressive work (for example, Albert Schweitzer), but, again, their record is far from uniform. As the history of the Jewish people illustrates, a group can be disloyal to its divine injunctions. They can fail to live an exemplary existence, and they can indulge in practices either forbidden by their religious belief or reprehensible by humanitarian standards. The evidence that "God is at work" is present in religious groups, but, taken as a whole, it is a very mixed and inconclusive picture. In the face of this, one can feel the presence of the devil in religious fanaticism almost as often as the presence of God. Since the evidence is not uniform, to achieve credibility we must select only the best from among the total behavior of religious people. Such mixed evidence will always produce mixed conclusions whenever religion is judged. The question is whether it is possible to treat this selectively and to accept only some of the record while rejecting other parts.

The (3) work of the philosophers and theologians represents a slightly less chaotic picture, since their primary function is to take this mixed evidence and to refine it into a more consistent and coherent picture. The effort of philosophy is always to establish criteria according to which a reader will know what to believe and what to reject. What is actually amazing is that so many philosophers have found enough material to be able to construct rather detailed accounts of God's nature. All of these do not agree, but at least they provide a very rich source of material for training us to think about God. In recent times, philosophers and even theologians have seemed less sure about their ability to describe God directly. However, the work of those who have, although variant and sometimes rejected, still forms a considerable body of material.

In spite of the difficulties inherent in each of the major sources of information about God, all still are available to us, and they form a potential source of evidence. Since in no case is the evidence universal or all of its parts entirely compatible and without objectionable aspects, we must ask: "Who is willing to put forth the individual effort always required to sift through this mass of material to see if one creditable case can be found (that is, to encounter God through a combination of the material plus the effort expanded in sorting it)?" Perhaps even more fundamental is this question: "What primitive assumptions does the individual have that either lead him to accept or to reject any or all of this data, and will he become metaphysician enough to try to uncover these assumptions and to question their validity?"

All we know in advance about answering these two questions is that (1) certain individuals have made this effort and, as a result, have found ways to think about God again. They have been able to form rules according to which they select some of the material and reject other parts as inauthentic—or at least as not pertinent to the view of God they have developed. Although all men will never accept and follow only one account of God's presence and thus are not likely to come to full agreement, single individuals have never ceased to be able to relocate God in the midst of this material. Furthermore, (2) we have no one set of primitive assumptions we all must accept in every field, even if in some areas we come close to universal agreement (for example, mathematics). In religion, can we accept this inevitable continued disagreement over the assumptions we should employ? Are there areas (for example, religion, ethics, politics) where universality must be abandoned and where insight comes more on a selective and individual basis?

If we turn to ask whether there is anything special about the information concerning God contained in the available documents, in this case, the Bible, we discover some interesting features about our "knowledge" in this area. That is, God is most often reached in the everyday business of living, in social relationships, and in current unsettling events. The people to whom God's presence and words become real are only occasionally priests and saints and kings. God does not discriminate against the noble classes, but, on the whole, those who know God—and the events in which his presence is manifest—are not the esoteric or the intellectually gifted; most often they are ordinary men. Of course, miracles are not "ordinary" (for example, the exodus event for the Jews or the resurrection for the Christians): these are climactic and contradictory events. Nevertheless, on the whole, the circumstances that form the setting for the accounts are familiar to everyone (for example, eating a meal, marrying, dying). God has sometimes been said to appear in temples, but usually he has been experienced in more ordinary surroundings and among more humble people and in familiar events. By virtue of his experienced presence, these events often do take on enormous significance (for example, breaking bread and drinking wine). However, in their initial occurrence, they were not thought to be unusual—until God's presence was made known through them (for example, the Passover meal).

We learn one important additional factor from our religious documents: God becomes known by seeking and doing his will as this is revealed by the prophets, the religious tradition, and individual conscience. If we learn and accept this fact, it means that knowledge of God cannot result unless you are willing to become involved. Such information cannot be demanded in advance; it comes as a result of an effort to follow the divine will as represented. Then, perhaps, the individual who shapes his action in this way may either confirm the reports about God or gain his own first-hand and fresh encounter. It is interesting that knowledge of God, in this sense, is not speculative but practical. That is, it comes as the consequence of an intense effort to direct your manner of living in certain ways. Both action and effort seem to be a precondition for seeing.

D. THE CHRISTIAN GOD

If both the sources of knowledge about God and our avenues to him are as just described, all Gods cannot be approached at once. Rather, we have to accept some particular context, and, in doing so, we gamble that our original choice will be fruitful and not restrictive. Of course, nothing prevents us from trying more than one context, but it does seem that we have no choice except to select one setting at a time in which to try to pin down some knowledge of God. Thus, we begin by asking what is unique about the Christian experience of God, and, particularly, what special sources and circumstances do his followers report as surrounding their knowledge of this God? If we are successful, it may be that such specific conditions will become unimportant, but that does not mean that they are not crucial at the outset.

In what ways is the Christian experience with God distinctive; how does it alter the problem and focus it differently? In order to answer this question, we must look to the specifically Christian sources of information and see what is unusual about these reports. First, the most striking feature of Christian belief is that God has not himself appeared directly, as he did at times in the Hebrew literature. He becomes known in the person of a mediator, Jesus, and often he is represented by the presence of a Holy Spirit. There are, then, peculiarly Christian forms of God's presence, and these are the basis for the Christian claim to possess information about him. It would seem that these distinctive features will always characterize Christian knowledge of God, since it is in this way that God first became known to them and is still to be encountered.

In order to understand the Christian experience of God, we need to know why we should not approach God directly and what this restriction tells us about any mode of God's presence? Of course, Christianity is not alone in saying that God is not to be apprehended directly, but the special conditions attached to the restriction define the Christian. In the first place, 'spirit' is the mode of God's presence in the world after the time of Jesus. In the original era, God's presence was experienced more directly in the work of a person and by what happened to him. Even so, this was not a direct divine presence; it was indirect in the life of a person. However, from then on God's presence is less definitely located; it now resides in the direct action of the Holy Spirit. Except for those who knew Jesus personally, all who live later can only know God through his presence as spirit. Of course, this encounter takes place by recalling the events of Jesus' life and death which are accepted as evidence of God's presence such that he can be made known again even at a later time.

In some ways, all this indicates that the traditional conception of a "beatific vision" of God is not a particularly Christian experience or mode of approach. To be caught up in rapture, or to prepare for this possession by an ecstatic vision, may be highly religious. It may even be authentic in a more general sense, but it is not the early and specifically Christian mode of approach. According to that way, God is encountered in the life and work of a person who is fully concrete and visible. The means to recover this are associated with performing the duties he enjoined and seeking to obey the divine will in specific actions benefiting other people. Our attention is not directed at God himself with ecstatic rapture as its aim. *The Christian experience of God is involved with a specific outer direction, to the service of other people in need, rather than inward to the individual who confronts God alone.*

If it is a Christian encounter, the irony is that knowledge of God immediately directs us away from God. It is outer rather than inner directed. It is more centered on action than on contemplation, since its assertion is precisely that God is to be discovered in the midst of action and not in circumstances that outwardly are particularly 'holy'. It is illuminating to note that any attempt at a direct approach, although it may lead to some God, does not lead to a very specifically Christian God. According to Christian reports, God's discovery must be made indirectly, just as his approach to man was covert and came in the form of a human person. When we understand the reasons for this indirectness, the features of the Christian God begin to stand out with some uniqueness. That is, one of the first things we learn is that we deal with a God who is capable of keeping his presence hidden. More important than this, however, as a God he appears quite different in kind than we might have expected.

Thus, knowledge of God will have a somewhat startling and unexpected quality about it. Since he acts in unpredicted ways, his projects are always subject to some controversy and misunderstanding. He could have acted neatly, decisively, openly, and in a manner beyond dispute, but, according to the Christian encounter, this is not the way God chose. His appearance in human form always leaves open the possibility that some will recognize only human and not divine activity. Given his indirect appearance, there is no way to force anyone to admit God's presence who does not want to. The burden of proof is, thus, left to man, since God did not himself choose to clear up the situation beyond all doubt. Those who do discover the presence of a Christian God will see one who appears and acts in human ways. Of course, he does not adopt

every human way, but specifically certain actions of Jesus—
that is, healing the sick, freeing man from sin, and proclaiming
God's forgiveness. Now the problem is "Can we too see God
acting within these works even at a time long after their happening?"

Even more important, however, the Christian experience is
one in which God condescended and came to man. As we
know from our own experience over the difficulty in swal-
lowing our pride, this is not easy to do. Unforgiving men who
hold power demand that we come to them and meet them on
their terms. The most powerful men can force unconditional
surrender. Strange that God should not do what his power
enables him to do better than men. Human beings, it seems,
are more bound by the pride of their superior position than
God is. The Christian experience of God, then, is one of the
surprise of being sought out and visited by God. "He has come
to us!" is the Christian's startled report. The way up to God is
not long and narrow, because he is close at hand, although,
unfortunately, not in a manner unmistakably recognizable by
all. "How to discern his presence?" is the question, not "How
to find a way to leave our place and find his?" 'Condescension'
is a key Christian term where the experience of God is concerned, since the early Christians were sought out in unexpected ways and found in unexpected forms (for example,
servant, suffering).

It is true, of course, that his contemporaries used all kinds of
divine titles for Jesus and expended vast efforts trying to fit
Jesus' coming into a history of God's expectation. In religious
circles, God's visitation is in some sense always expected, and
the basic form of Christian religious life is to act and to work
in such a way that you are prepared for God's unexpected
visit, whether in the next instance or in another lifetime. The
important point is that this expectation (that is, the birth narrative) was added *after* Jesus' mode of divine presence had
been revealed to a few, and it is most of all an evidence of
man's tidy rational sense. We want to tie in God's presence to
traditional expectation, and so we rewrite the script and
supply the missing elements. What at the time was surprising
and an unexpected revelation of God now, in the telling and
retelling, borrows traditional formulae in order to find a way to

express its message. God's presence was not discerned in advance (He is a carpenter's son; crucify him!). Only in retrospect, after the power of his action is felt (for example, forgiveness; release from death), does God's presence become overwhelming.

Yet there is one more surprising quality about the experience of the Christian God. Not only does he come to us, instead of forcing us to leave our houses in search of him, and not only is his presence always indirect in its human form or action, but also he shares our life and its burden. This no God need do. He is not forced to suffer; Aristotle considered this the most ungodlike thing of all, and Spinoza certainly thought it the opposite of what one experiences in knowing God. Yet Christians report a sharing in suffering by God such that it carried him to the limits—that is, to death. In the acceptance of our human fate, they still manage to discover God's most revealing and significant quality. This is not possible in all approaches to God, but it is characteristic of the Christian. Of course, divine suffering is dramatically different from human, since the experience of God's presence first comes, not in witnessing him suffer (for example, in Jesus' crucifixion), but in the experience of finding that, by entering in, he opened a way to overcome the limits of human life. This overcoming did not have to be accomplished by such an unusual personal appearance. It could have been done by divine edict issued from aloft; but the Christian God chose a more dramatic means, and in the process he submitted himself to rough treatment and to a possible misunderstanding of his intention.

The traditional biblical name for God has been "he that is," but, in the Christian interpretation, this means that he is ready to manifest himself as a helper. God is he who has made himself present, although not through necessity or to everyone, but only to those who are able to discern his presence in certain homely activities. In a sense, this gives God's discovery a "pragmatic" meaning. That is, God is seen and known in his actions. If you understand God, you testify that you have experienced his movement personally. You are a witness to the divine movement which produces change. There are theories that divinity means to be an "unmoved mover," but this is not the Christian report. It is not even one of necessary and universal action, but rather of personal and individual activity. The results of this are said to be available to all, but they are by no means recognized or accepted universally.

However, the experience is not one of complete individuality and isolation. The concept of the 'kingdom of God' gives evidence of the Christian sense of God's openness to experience within a community. His action to bring the Hebrews out of slavery bound together those whom he rescued into a nation. God's action forged the bonds of community. For Christians, the experience of God's presence among men in Jesus, and in God's action to save Jesus from death, now becomes the divine activity to which Christians testify, and in doing so they become members of his kingdom. The form this kingdom is to take has been a matter of some dispute since Jesus proclaimed its inauguration and then left, but it is clear that Christians are to know, to discover, and to work for God within the group of those who share this kingdom. In this sense, the Christian knowledge of God always has a communal aspect and association.

The concept of the kingdom expresses God's rule over the minds of men, but of course he cannot rule over those who do not acknowledge his power and intent. Since the divine kingdom is not a physical state, its presence can neither be seen, nor its laws politically enforced, nor its authority made clear beyond all dispute. In fact, the opposite is true. The presence of God's kingdom and any individual participation in it are always matters of question involving some uncertainty. If God is experienced as ruling over all the relationships of man to man, this is hard to account for, since very little of any divine touch is evident in most of the political and commercial relationships we observe. Evidently, if God is to rule in the relationships between men, it will not be in a visible kingdom but in a union of spirit formed between those who acknowledge both his presence and his decisive actions. In the Christian sense a kingdom of God is not found and then occupied. *It simply consists of all those who have come to know God in his Christian manifestation and are bound together as a community when they testify to their peculiar experience of God.*

If, for Christians, a real knowledge of God derives from their experience of his action and his presence in Jesus, this assertion is always complicated by the fact that God must also be more than the actions we find in any one life, however revelatory. We need to have a wider and a more transcendent notion of God before it makes any sense to say that we find the full attributes of divinity concentrated and present in what to all outward appearances is a purely human form. In other words, divinity cannot be experienced in Christ unless we have some prior notion of its nature; nor can its presence be unexpected unless we knew enough about God beforehand to expect him to behave differently and more majestically. One way to express this is to say that the Christian religion did not begin with Jesus, nor can it begin again today without some prior background. We must become familiar with the general literature and lore about the behavior of Gods and about their natures. Then a specific experience of divine activity can take on meaning by crystalizing a large body of ideas and by standing in dramatic opposition to existing notions of God.

In other words, Christians first had to be Jews (or pagan worshipers today) before they could (or can now) discover what it means to conceive of God in Christian terms. This dawn of a new conception of God and its difference from the Jewish tradition leads to the struggle we read about in the books of the New Testament. The early Christians had to understand the old 'covenant' between God and man before they could come to realize that a new covenant had been made. It was necessary to realize how a people had been formed around God's action in earlier days. Then they could put together the idea of his new activity in forming a new people and yielding a particularly Christian God. Thus, our present rampant paganism may provide a necessary backdrop for discovering God anew—if we know something of the history of divine appearance.

E. THE CONDITIONS FOR DISCLOSURE

If we must come to be aware of the peculiar circumstances that the early Christians discovered to surround the divine disclosure, this ties the concept of God to the idea of 'revelation,' because some Gods do not make any effort to reveal themselves. In this case, whatever discovery is accomplished will have to be done by man—for example, as in the case of

Plotinus or Spinoza. Some Gods see nothing to be gained by engaging in any extraordinary self-disclosures. If the Christian (and Hebrew) God is not of this type, in order to understand him it is crucial to grasp both the conditions for his disclosure and what it is in his nature that leads him to take this step when all Gods would not.

On most occasions, as men we know that it is to our benefit not to reveal our true intent or our real nature. "Never let the other man know what you are thinking" is the successful politician's motto. Hiddenness and camouflage are common human techniques. Thus, if God breaks this hiddenness in any action or revelation, this ought to tell us something about his nature. We cannot know God any more clearly than we can understand the conditions under which he is revealed and the reasons for his revelation in this manner. Sometimes it is said that God is seen and known "in crisis and via prophets." If this is true and if these conditions surround revelation, both are decisive regarding our grasp of God. We can conclude that normal conditions are not likely to reveal God, but that it often takes a time of crisis. Not all times are equally informative but only some, and thus "common" human experience may be unfruitful or even misleading where God is concerned.

Furthermore, if prophets are his instruments, only a few persons are suitable as vehicles for understanding God. Proof in this case cannot be universal; Anselm is wrong. Given this situation, the problem is to understand what kind of men or women these extraordinaries are and to learn what distinguishes the false prophet from the true. It would have been so much simpler if God had allowed all men equally to serve as divine vehicles; but, if the Jews and the Christians are to be believed, this is not the case. If all men are not to be trusted alike in divine matters, the problem becomes to discover which men are so attuned to God to be able to represent him adequately. The complaints of many that they cannot understand God ought to be anticipated. Most men should not expect to grasp God, and, in this case, the common man's problem is to learn which leaders he can trust in religious matters.

Anyone is a 'prophet' who deepens, clarifies, and articulates a knowledge of God's character and purpose. Traditionally, these are men who stand in the midst of a great historical crisis in the life of a nation or a person, and they interpret to the people or to the leader what God is doing in the events of their lives. Shattering events seem to provide the condition for revelation and the place to look for the appearance of proph- ets. If neither God nor prophets appear everywhere, we have to know when and to whom to look if we are to expect any divine discovery. According to reports, there are more mis- leading situations and false prophets than there are true; God has intentionally made the situation difficult. In the case of Jesus, more often we are told to look within us rather than without, but this only increases our difficulty because the inner world is so much less structured to begin with than the outer. Here no one can guide with certainty, although we should accept as prophets those who can sensitize and increase our powers of spiritual apprehension.

If we consider the 'suffering servant' as the image of God's appearance in the New Testament, it can tell us what perhaps is the most important Christian condition for revelation. That is, not all people by any means can be expected to see God but only those who are able to humble themselves and who can voluntarily assume an inferior role. Pride may be the crown of the virtues ethically, as Aristotle described it, but it is a block to any Christian apprehension of God. If humility is a condi- tion for the revelation of God, this means that many, perhaps a majority, are blocked here, and it also indicates something interesting about a God who would set up such a requirement.

In contrast to most important human personages, God must be able to overcome an understandably vast pride in his powers and move to set this aside in dealing with others less powerful and fortunate. He must be capable of assuming the level of those with whom he deals. Many human beings cannot do this, and some do not even feel that it is the right thing to do. If only the humble and the meek in spirit (which says nothing about the outer circumstances of men either pro or con) can see God, certain difficult preconditions must be met before it is possible to focus on God.

In Christian terms, of course, God can be seen in the pas- sion of Jesus, and his power is felt in the resurrection. As is clearly evident, not all will see or feel God's presence in these actions, and yet it is equally clear that some have—that is, those Christians who form God's kingdom, who preach the word and carry out his commands. In a certain way, *this makes the experience of death a necessary approach to God.* The natural human self is proud when left alone, so that humility may mean the death of the master self and its transformation into the life of the servant. *Without living through such an experience of loss—that is, the death of the self in obedience—it may not be possible to understand God, at least as Christians experience him.* This raises the crucial question "How should one live who would understand God?" Evidently, some ways of life block this vision until they are set aside, while certain other modes of life are conducive to discovery.

The idea that there are conditions for God's disclosure, and particularly that this may involve a way of life or even a radical reversal in the normal orientation of the self—all this presents grave difficulties where philosophy is concerned. Philosophy involves the use of reason as an instrument of understanding, but the Christian demand seems to place a limitation on how far reason can go, and it certainly sets certain practical and nonintellectual conditions on the achievement of understanding. As antiphilosophical as this may appear to be at first, any teacher knows that the major blocks to understanding actually do lie deeper than reason. In a pre-Freudian age, it might have been less easy to accept the fact that the attempts of reason are sometimes defeated by powers superior to its force. However, in an era of the unconscious, we have a greater sensitivity to the limitations of reason and to the restrictions placed upon it. We know that it is not quite such an affront to reason to set nonrational conditions for its ability to understand. This is more a recognition of both the difficult world in which we live and the often superior forces from which reason must first be set free, although this can seldom be accomplished by its own power.

As strong as reason may be in God, we must conclude that it does not completely control his nature, or else the use of human reason alone would be a more certain path to understanding divinity. Emotion, which often blinds us, must also characterize the divine life. Perhaps it is just his ability to set his ego aside, to condescend and to suffer that indicates God's lack of bondage to emotion, since he can pass to a lower state freely as we sometimes cannot. This fact Spinoza could never deduce from his use of 'reason,' but the Christian experience does point to an unusual God of this type. God must have a power of control we lack, or else he would not risk the loss of himself in moving downward. It is just this fear of loss that holds us back from offering assistance to others and makes us seek to be secure by enlarging the self's experiences and its own domain. Strange that the opposite route should be a condition for disclosure where God is involved.

F. THE NATURE OF GOD

If we just discuss the problems that face philosophy of religion rather than construct a systematic theology, it is impossible to give a complete description of the divine nature. In fact, it is the theme of this book that no single description is possible, and that many philosophical assumptions enter in to shape any theological doctrine, particularly where God is concerned. This fact becomes even more clear as we discern the special qualities of a Christian God, and particularly when we suggest that there are personal and human conditions for divine disclosure. Not every philosophical view can accept the Christian description of God. Neither Aristotle's nor Plotinus' Gods act in this way. Similarly, not every philosophical view can admit the fact that certain dispositions must be met and specific actions performed before a knowledge of God becomes even possible. Some types of knowledge are incompatible with such special restrictions from the start.

There are many philosophical suggestions for what God's nature is like and what his attributes are—for example, infinity, pure act, and so forth. Now, on which basis can we accept or reject certain suggestions when we try to think about God? Obviously, there are many ways to go about this and not all allow us to reach the same kind of knowledge. Can this be done simply dialectically, by the abstract consideration of various concepts, or must some experience precede this and become a basis upon which the concepts are either accepted or altered? Some suggested descriptions of God come to us out of the philosophical tradition. It is possible to learn rather early what kinds of metaphysical assumptions each is associated with, but upon what basis do we then move toward adopting one set rather than another?

If we take 'time' as an example, there is no reason in itself why time might not characterize God's nature, but this depends upon philosophical conceptions of time and metaphysical assumptions about the factors associated with it. Aristotle thinks motion and change are always connected with time and that this indicates an inferior existence. Whenever you talk of God as a 'cause,' on the other hand, this meaning is very deeply imbedded in the kind of metaphysics you construct. If 'necessity' is considered of prime importance, God can act as a cause in only one way and not in others. It seems very much as if the description of God's attributes is like the working out of a set of first principles or the primitive concepts for a metaphysics. There is no sufficient reason internally given to select one set over all the others—that is, unless you are trying to account for some particular experience. If so, this experience can provide a controlling force which leads you to prefer either Aristotle's stress on 'pure actuality' or the way in which, in the accounting for the world, Plato keeps the power of self-motion in the soul as a first principle not subordinate to any other.

If we consider the way in which God's actions are described in the biblical record, we have some idea of the special experience to which Christians appeal and which might be used as a touchstone to form a description of the divine attributes. God's acts of power are grouped around three great crises: (1) the deliverance of Israel from Egyptian bondage, (2) the acts of divine judgment and mercy in the exile and restoration, and finally (3) sending Jesus, working and suffering with him, and, at last, raising him from the dead, an action that brought the new Israel into being. If the Christian always focuses on these events, whether or not they all enter into his particular individual experience, he knows that any description of the nature of God that he develops and accepts must be such as to allow God to accomplish the acts attributed to him freely and of himself.

Unfortunately, even if this much is accepted, it does not

make Christian theology a simple task. All this may shape theology in one direction more than another, but it does not yield one and only one theology. More than one metaphysical view can accept and interpret these statements of God's action, and so more than one theology can be formed from them. However, it now becomes a question of which description of God's nature gives the best or the most adequate account. The answer to this question may vary with the times. That is, metaphysical schemes tend to lose their effectiveness and to need reworking. What was once a powerful framework within which to describe God's attributes need not always remain so. All this having been said, there are still some affirmations everyone can make about a Christian God, even if they must be phrased in different ways and continually need to be set in the midst of new philosophical contexts in order to be effective.

For instance, in his own nature the Christian God is invisible, which is not the case with all Gods. However, he becomes visible only in Jesus, and he alone knows God directly and without mediation. This is why it is said that everyone else must come to see God in Jesus. Furthermore, God is now recognized as love, and Aristotle could not have described him in this way. This attribute becomes evident in his self-communication in Jesus. That is, he has come to man in the person of a son and out of his love for man. Any Christian God must be characterized by these feelings, and he should be left capable of acting to express them without restraint. However, when we begin to describe God as 'infinite' and 'incomprehensible' to human thought, we are on more questionable grounds religiously, and clearly we are more philosophically dependent in our basis for these assertions. If by 'infinite' we mean that he is not thwarted or ultimately opposed or fails in a lack of power to accomplish his purpose, it may not be useful to attribute that to him. However, for Spinoza this would require a necessary relationship to the world, and such involvement is more questionable for the God of Christians.

'Incomprehensible' clearly cannot be used in relation to God without depending on a previously accepted theory of knowledge, and so that doctrine must be stated first. For one thing, Christians assert that he became comprehensible to man voluntarily by appearing in Jesus. Thus, if he is in some ways incomprehensible, he must be such as to be capable of changing this situation when he wills. Infinities are understandable on the basis of some theories, and so that attribute alone need not prevent God's comprehensibility to men. His mode of action or hiddenness may make him incomprehensible more than his infinity. Thus, it is clear that only a union between a theory of knowledge and a description of God's nature can determine whether and in what ways God is 'comprehensible.' This involves the combination of a developed theory and the relevant experience.

When a theologian, for instance, says that God "never enters the realm of human knowledge as an object," we face a case of the pure philosophical determination of a theological conclusion. Nothing in the biblical account prohibits God from becoming an object. He is not a natural object, it is true, but a large part of the Christian assertion is tied up with the fact that he became an object and assumed the consequences of that action. According to certain theories of knowledge, to be an 'object' is to occupy an inferior status, just as to suffer indicates the same thing for Spinoza. If God cannot become an object, this will change the Christian conception of the 'incarnation' quite considerably. In discussing God's attributes, we must always ask whether making one statement rather than another depends more on the assumption of certain metaphysical principles (for example, it is inferior to be an object) or on an attempt to find a way to express certain religious experiences.

20

SPIRIT

A. THE INNER LIFE

When we come to the concept of 'spirit,' we arrive at the center of the religious life and also at that which, philosophically, is the most controversial. This is because, if man does not have an inner life different in kind from his outer actions and circumstances, religion of any type is much misguided. Not all philosophers deny all forms of life except the physically visible. Thus, there is room for a concept of 'spirit' philosophically, although there have been philosophers who would not admit this. More importantly, however, because of its nonphysical nature, 'spirit' is not easy to define.

Whenever the structure of something can be grasped overtly, the philosophical approach we use is not quite so important. Clearly, in the case of spirit we are dealing with something not fully formed or structured from the beginning. Thus, how we approach and describe it, and the terms we decide to use, are themselves formative in how we finally come to conceive of the spirit. What can be seen is less subject to unintentional distortion, but we can adopt attitudes that prevent us from discovering how the life of the spirit might exist and yet differ from our outer life. We must begin by asking why some philosophies either deny or make possible a conception of the spirit as constituting the inner life of man.

If the inner life is sometimes silent and invisible, how can it be discerned? Can we discover ways by means of which what does not easily show itself can be revealed? Even if this can be done, it will obviously take time and care and patience, and this always means that it may be overlooked by anyone who will not make the necessary effort. If man's spirit is so difficult both to discover and to make solid or visible, think how this problem multiplies where God is concerned. His mode of presence in the world has been said to be by means of the "Holy Spirit." Atheism results unless you can make God's presence meaningful and his action in the world understandable in the form of a spirit. If God is to be discerned, then, it will have to be from partially invisible rather than from fully visible phenomena.

Even for those who claim to believe in God's presence as spirit, the same problem crops up in spiritual *vs.* ritual worship. Any sense of the presence of God usually leads to worship, but, if God is taken too concretely, the worship becomes a mere repetition of ritual forms. If, however, God is to be worshiped as a spirit, our attitude toward ceremonial forms should change considerably. You need not abandon all ritual, but it will be meaningful and important only for its spiritual significance, particularly insofar as it is able to make God visible *qua* spirit. If the inward spiritual element of worship is given primacy, as Jesus intended, we become less attached to the particular ceremony for its own sake and begin to see it only as a means to increase our sense of God's presence as spirit.

The body, of course, still remains the medium of all communication, and nothing is said that prevents us ultimately from seeing the body as inextricably involved in the life of the spirit. The person as a whole man involves a body, and yet this does not preclude our belief that the spirit might be related to an order of physical life other than its present constitution in flesh and blood. Again, our ability to conceive of spirit is dependent on the way in which we conceive of 'body,' and especially on whether we think that its present form is the only possible one or whether 'body' is capable of a wide variation in forms. Whether we think that the spirit can communicate itself through the body, then, depends on how flexible our philosophy is in allowing us to define 'body.'

In order to understand the inner life, we may have to grasp what it means to be "poor in spirit" and why this might be a good condition to be in. Physical success can lead to pride, self-esteem, contempt for the unsuccessful, and it often ends in lust for even greater physical power and possession. The humble in spirit, as contrasted with the arrogant or the rich, are those who trust in God, not in their own physical control. Jesus was concerned with men's motives and inner attitudes, and often these are obscured or distorted by the physically rich and successful. Those who are humble do not put their ultimate trust in their own political schemes, so that "poverty of spirit" might be a necessary condition for the discovery of both God and our own inner self. Of course, such spiritual humility is ultimately independent of a man's external conditions of life, although it can perhaps be prejudiced by them.

B. GOD AS MEDIATOR

In order to make sense of any concept of 'spirit,' we must first ask whether God can be approached, be known and be related to, directly. If so, any concept of spirit as a mediator of God's presence becomes superfluous; if not, we must ask through what means God can be approached and related to at present. We are forced to consider a concept of 'spirit,' because we must decide in what form God can be present if we are not related to him directly. As Jesus described it, our relation to God may be as a 'father,' but obviously God's presence in this relationship would be in a form other than what we think of as God-in-himself.

In considering this question, the force that lies behind the idea of God as a 'Trinity' becomes clear. If God has various functions and forms of presence rather than one only, the Trinity is a means to formulate the variety of ways in which men either find God present or discover themselves to be related to him. If this divine approach is not always in one form, or if God is experienced as being 'here' as well as 'there,' we have to reformulate this experience of dealing with God in such a way that it does justice to the known aspects of God. We do not, we cannot simply begin with the concept of a trinity within the divine nature. We must first face irreducible diversity in relating to God, next find ourselves in need of a mediator, and ultimately make sense of this by a theory that brings together all the various aspects into one nature.

If God mediates his own presence to us, if he relates to us in such a way that his essentially transcendent nature is, in fact, brought to us and made known, this can only be done through something like 'spirit.' If we have various experiences of God, and particularly if the central Christian experience is that of God's action to make himself immediately available, our problem is to tie all these experiences together. We need to build a concept of God that will do justice to various modes of existence and presence, and the concept of trinity is a way of preserving God as one and yet accounting for the diversity of our experiences of him.

One possible reason for much of the prevalent atheism is a failure to formulate a contemporary doctrine of the trinity adequately. Our failure to unite our diverse experiences in one concept leads us to reject any idea of God that is single in its statement. An atheist cannot grasp a far-off God who yet interferes—unless exactly how a God can be both transcendent and yet imminent is made intelligible once again. Can a creator God, one who once was active, also remain detached and not constantly interfere in the process?

Biblical scholars agree that the concept of the trinity does not appear as such in the New Testament documents themselves; it is a later development. Yet the real question is "What experiences of God are there that lead to a trinitarian concept that reconciles God's apparently diverse forms of presence?" God is said to be incarnate in Jesus and to remain with his disciples after Jesus' absence through the descent of the spirit. If these forms of imminence do not exhaust God's nature, we need a trinitarian form to unite and to hold together the diverse modes. If we cannot provide this, we drift toward atheism; we reject all forms of God in the face of a failure to find a way to hold together an experienced variety of modes.

In the Bible, God is continually said to be known through,

or to be present in, his 'word.' Yet, since all who hear these words do not believe in God, we need another factor—that is, a spirit whose presence enables man to understand the word—if we are to see God revealed in it. Exactly how the trinity is expressed does not matter; its function as a concept is clear. For instance, although Jesus is taken away from the disciples, God's continued presence is still promised to them. He is said to have overcome death, and yet the final stage of the battle has not been reached. *Spirit is left as our guide "in the time in-between."*

This provides a way in which the 'ascension' of Jesus can be understood. It is to be grasped, not so much as a taking away of Jesus, but rather as the coming of a new presence of God in the Holy Spirit. The ascension inaugurates a new and yet provisional relationship to God for those who enter into it. In spite of the definite promise of salvation, it is clear that this new stage has not yet fully come. The Lord has been withdrawn from our senses, and thus the victory, on faith, must be hoped for in the future. If the consummation of the world has really commenced, still the process is a secret one not to be discerned by all. Thus, a sense of the presence of God's spirit in the intervening time bridges the gap between the promise and the waiting.

If ascension means "going to where God is," the doctrine of the 'spirit' surely means that God remains present even though withdrawn from sight. Since no one can ascend to God unless God first comes down, ascension involves the double concept of God's presence and absence. To be with God is to be exalted. Thus, if any man on earth is ever transfigured like that, God must be capable of a spiritual presence. To participate in the sovereignty of God over all things is to be "at his right hand." Thus, if men are to share in this rule and its resulting kingdom, this can only come about because God is spiritually capable of presence at *their* right hand. If the biblical documents often do not distinguish between ascension and resurrection, possibly it is because both simply are ways of indicating God's spiritual presence and action.

If the body of Jesus is said to have been raised and glorified—that is, passed to a mode of existence akin to spiritual body—this simply indicates God's ability to be present in spirit and to enter into corporeal life in order to transform it. If the Israelites could recognize God's presence with them by the appearance of a cloud, what Christians need to ask is "What signs now indicate that God's presence has been continued after Jesus' departure?" If the visible intercourse between Jesus and his disciples was brought to an end, and if this is said to involve a prelude to a new manner of relationship between them, we cannot understand what this is or participate in it until we grasp how God can be present as spirit.

If all things are said to be under Christ's sovereignty, and yet if he has been taken away from sight, there is no way to understand how he can rule now without a knowledge of how spirit operates. If the ascended Christ is to intercede for men, he must have a continual spiritual presence as the only way in which we can unite man with God. 'Spirit' is as good a term as John the Evangelist can find to express what God the father is like essentially. As spirit, he is also said to be truth and love. Thus, it is easy to see that, as the aspects of spirit are understood, these form a basis upon which God can be understood when he might not otherwise be approachable directly.

In Christian terms, the understanding of 'spirit' is closely tied to the concept of 'father,' and this points again to the necessity for a multiple approach such as the doctrine of God's ultimate trinity (*vs.* Plotinus' use of unity alone). If God communicates himself, he is a 'father,' since that is what fatherhood means. Fatherhood also requires a family context within which it is understood, so that the use of fatherhood in approaching God requires something like the multiple and mutually related concept of trinity (as a counterpart to family). If men are to be of the same fundamental character as God, just as children are of one flesh with their father, this must require a presence of God as spirit and the possibility for physical men to relate to him now as spirit.

If a Hebrew writer often speaks of a family whenever he wishes to define a community, both 'father' and 'trinity' and 'spirit' are all ways of indicating God's essential not-aloneness, his involvement with men. *Men who feel themselves completely alone have not come to understand God as spirit.* The existentialist stress on aloneness can be religiously self-defeating. Yet 'father' involves not only kinship but also authority, in which case God as spirit cannot be discovered without a preliminary willingness to acknowledge the presence of authority. A son not only bears his father's character, but admits his authority. Accepting this common authority of those who acknowledge God's spiritual presence unites all who do as brothers. The standard name for a Christian is a brother, precisely because he shares a common spiritual authority.

C. CAN SPIRIT REVEAL AND GUIDE?

If spirit is "the agent of revelation which makes it possible," before we can understand spirit we must discover how it is able to reveal. As far as Christianity is concerned, it is clear that spirit is not the first means of revelation (Jesus is, by his assertion of sonship). Rather, spirit is the agent of the extension and continuation of revelation. In order to fathom how Christian revelation can continue in the face of Jesus' absence, we must understand the mode of spirit's presence and how it can operate to continue to reveal God's immediacy. A 'prophet' is a man said to be specially fitted to be a channel of communication between God and man, but that is so only if he possesses—or is possessed by—God's spirit.

Spirit must be *a mode of God's presence in the world such that it is capable of forming a community;* otherwise it cannot reveal. Thus, the forming of a genuine community, one not dictated by nature or by common background, is a sign both of the presence and the work of spirit and of its ability to reveal. Such is the origin and reason behind all monastic communities—and all Christian churches. Yet, all of this depends upon recognizing how and in what sense spirit can guide us. We can be led by a visible presence, but it is not easy to see how we can be led by anything not physically apparent to us. Of course, the question of the interpretation of scripture is at stake here too, for we must discover how we can think of spirit as guiding our biblical understanding, since reading the same recorded words does not inspire everyone. At this point, we encounter the concept of 'grace' too, since that is the form which God's guidance takes after the shift away from Jesus' physical leadership.

It would seem we cannot understand grace, or brotherhood, or the kingdom, or the implications of Jesus' ascension and yet continuing authority—none of these can be clear until we grasp how God can be present and operate as spirit. Jesus preferred the title 'son of man' which indicates his membership in the human race. Yet the same title in *Daniel* refers to a mysterious heavenly figure with an apocalyptic role. To reconcile these two divergent meanings, we must come to understand how a Holy Spirit could be present and even take control of man so that he would be human and yet spiritually possessed of God. If the kingdom of the saints is to be established, it can exist in this era only as our communion via the spirit and in God's continued presence as spirit among physical men.

If a holy community comes into being when people respond to Jesus' teaching, this result is the work of the son of man. If it is to be observed, it must be discerned spiritually and not by any observation of the general life of men. The title 'son of man' suggests at once the likeness of the prophet as man and yet the greatness to which God calls him in service (for example, Ezekiel). Through him—man though he is—God speaks to us and carries out his purpose. Thus, the creation of a holy community can only be seen if the eye discloses one thing and the spirit another. Even if one day the physical form may be transformed to mirror the spirit, still in this age everything depends upon our ability to discern the life of the spirit as present but not physical.

This does not mean that spirit cannot at times create visible results even now. The expansion of the early church is to be understood as an outpouring of the spirit on the eyewitnesses to the resurrection. New structures are sometimes created by the movement of spirit. It is just that such structures can neither be identified with spirit nor be counted on always to contain it. Spirit is more independent from visible structure than that. The beginnings of the church were characterized by a constant presence of the spirit as a supernatural power, so that such a sense of its continued presence is a required sign for any church's authority. The whole church is the sphere of the spirit's work, it is true, but unfortunately it is not always equally evident in all parts or at all times.

Spirit can withdraw, and our spiritual health depends upon our ability to detect this absence. However, its presence is often taken as a sign that the "last days" are at hand. The activity of spirit in reshaping men need not signal the immediate end of the present physical life, but it does transform what it touches. The Holy Spirit fashions a community, so that love comes to mean simply love of those who are brethren in that community. A new spiritual order has arrived, whether everyone can discern this in the outer circumstances (for example, miracles) or not. Membership in the community, or church, is not dependent on whim but on the real influence of the Holy Spirit. Only those whom it has changed are brothers in fact.

When we speak of 'spirit' we mean to characterize "immanent deity." We are trying to say how God, who has withdrawn visibly for the time, can nevertheless be with us, reveal himself to us, and offer guidance. As we have already noted, this is the idea behind the notion of the trinity; Christians have, in fact, experienced God's real and full presence in three aspects. This leaves us with the problem of how to tie together these operations to meet the Judaic demand "Behold the Lord our God is one God."

Religious experience presents us with a difficulty that only philosophical structuring can solve, but then our problem is not to mistake the resulting theological doctrine for the original experience that first made it necessary. For example, we can speak about God as "divine Wisdom," and this is the Holy Spirit that spoke to the prophets. Then, for Saint Paul, this is equated with the new powers that flowed from the resurrection of Jesus and transformed all those who came to share in the belief. In Paul's time, power changed men in new ways and took on new forms. They were aware that it was not without historical precedent, and yet neither was their experience identical to its earlier forms. In order to make God revelatory now and yet variously present in earlier forms, a philosophical concept is necessary that can unite variety—for example, the trinity.

When we ask how and whether spirit can guide and reveal, at least part of our answer lies in the structure of the community that emerges. If it is a distinctive and a unique society (as the primitive Christian church was), the formative action of the spirit can be seen in its visible results, and the community becomes a present form of revelation and guidance. Those who enter it share a new and a common life because they have been moved by a new and a common love. All this they feel is possible only because God has fulfilled his promises and Christ his. Thus, in order to discover revelation and guidance as present, we need a concept that unites God's promises, Jesus' actions and the present power of divine change—in spite of any momentary nonpresence of any of those forms of divinity at any given time or in any given group.

In order to understand how spirit can be God's presence and how this can reveal and guide, we also need to consider the power and the function of 'names.' In whatever way names are related to other objects, a name has always been regarded as part of the being of divinity. Thus, God can be present and potentially powerful in his name, but our question is "Just how can a name signify the presence of God?" When scripture speaks of a "chosen vessel to bear my Name," it is clear that the writers feel that he who can bear the name of God can also represent his mind and purpose. The difficulty, of course, is that there can be false prophets, so that not every claim is to be trusted. But, if in any specifiable situation God's name can signify his presence, we discover a mode by which he may continually guide and reveal.

To "believe in the name of the Lord," then, is no small matter, for it means that you regard the person who claims to come in God's name as, in fact, a man worthy of such immense trust. You believe that he can perform that which his name or title implies, so that to accept the title 'Christ,' as it was given to Jesus by his disciples as a result of their transforming experience, is to recognize in Jesus a source of divine presence and guidance equivalent to God's being present in his name. Those who feel the power in this name band together for the common task of carrying out the commands that have come "in his name." In this way, a name can form a fellowship or a communion. Such binding together of persons comes because they share in something; in this case, it is an allegiance to the real presence of God in a name.

Christians become such by their name—that is, by their sharing together in the transformations which Jesus' presence accomplished and in response to which they gave him the name of God. Such naming drew them together first, and it still may in the present affirmation of the transforming presence of God's power. The whole community of Christians is the "body of Christ," because the power of this name has brought them into common fellowship. Here is spiritual solidarity without distinction of race or social position. The allegiance to the name of God has the power to break these natural barriers that separate men, or so they affirm. The use of God's name testifies to their experience of his transforming power revealed as being present now to guide us.

D. CAN SPIRIT BE UNDERSTOOD?

Whenever we tend to treat Jesus as being primarily human, we ought to detect on our part a rejection of all mystery, for how God can be fully present in a visible man, while being himself invisible, is surely bound to remain something not fully understandable. Our attempts to comprehend this take the form of developing a doctrine of the spirit as a mode of divine presence and operation, but this will be either enhanced or inhibited depending on our philosophical position regarding the acceptance or rejection of 'mystery.' Of course, 'mystery' is not one thing. It takes many forms and is defined in many ways, so that first we have to sort out the various meanings of mystery and decide which if any might be philosophically admissible. Religion deals with mystery, but it is up to theology to define an acceptable philosophical form.

That God should be present in human form does defy normal logic. Thus, if all mystery is rejected and normal modes of knowledge alone are accepted, taking Jesus as representing God's presence is ruled out from the beginning by a philosophical norm. For instance, the writer of the Book of John clearly feels that it is possible for the gospel tradition to come alive in new generations. For this to happen, an invisible spirit must be able to move to transform later individuals, although not always in regular or predictable ways. As opposed to the ordinary procedures of nature, such continual but uncontrolled rebirth of spirit is a "mysterious" operation. Accepting the ultimate presence of mystery involves admitting forms for the understanding other than natural rationality.

God as spirit is active in the world, unseen but not unknown. Clearly, the movements of spirit can be "understood," but only if understanding is conceived of in ways that allow for a broad variety of forms. "As the Word became flesh in the man Jesus, so the Spirit is incarnated in the church which calls on the name of the risen Lord"—such a statement can be meaningful if understanding is broadened to include unusual forms. Mystery must be compatible with understanding in this case, for both God's presence in the man Jesus and his presence in the community that calls on his name are unexpected and also not fully explainable phenomena.

In order to grasp such a special meaning of understanding, which includes the operation of spirit but does not eliminate all mystery, understanding must be accepted as including an as yet unrealized future reference. We must accept the notions of 'to fulfill' or 'to accomplish,' so that present understanding includes mystery because the work of the spirit is expected but nevertheless presently incomplete. It cannot all be seen because it is not yet. There is a space of time (indeterminate) that must elapse before something happens finally. The completion of the work of God's spirit involves an unspecified period and, until then, understanding of spirit is possible but not without all mystery. Spirit's operation will be brought to completion, its full intention will be made plain, but not now.

Can our present idea of 'understanding' include such an unfulfilled future reference? 'Mystery' involves an experience of an interior meeting and a union of man with God's infinite power. Thus, in the inner life, the union of God with man can be experienced at least for a moment. However, since any altering of the external nature of man involves an unrealized future time, this discrepancy between outer facts and inner experience keeps mystery present in the understanding. By interior movement and change, we can 'understand' the power and the nature of spirit. By interior meeting, we can understand how God might encounter and unite with man, but the external facts always remain slightly opposed to this. Thus they inhibit full understanding now.

Mystery may be capable of being eliminated in the understanding of the past and the present but never where the future is involved—that is, *if* the future is to be changed in any fundamental ways from a continuation of the past record or the present experience. In Christian terms, the operation of spirit always involves this future reference. Its work has begun, but it is not complete. Those who 'understand' spirit must first understand that they accept the mystery involved in a future hope not presently fully visible.

E. CAN SPIRIT CHANGE US?

When we pose this question, we are essentially asking about the effective power of 'prayer.' If prayer is "the loving response that accepts God's will regarding what to do," the fundamental mode or theme of prayer is thanksgiving. If this is true, thanks is only given in response to effective change, so that to be able to pray involves a prior recognition of the change produced by spirit's presence. Furthermore, prayer assumes an ability to deal personally with a personal God; so that, since God as a person is not easily evident, this recognition must be a change effected by spirit, which in turn enables the acceptance of God as personal. If prayer can cause change, it is only because he who prays has already been changed in certain basic ways by the action of divine spirit.

In order to understand the relationship between change, spirit, and prayer, we perhaps need to consider the meaning of 'exile' first. When the Israelites were exiled from the Temple and unable to engage in the proscribed Temple sacrifice, prayer became their only effective means of worship. Thus, it may be that Christians who are presently excluded from both their kingdom and the promised new life can only give thanks in prayer for the change already effected in them. At the same time, *they use prayer as the only means presently possible to relate themselves to a future from which they must continue to live in exile.* Psalms represent corporate *vs.* individual worship; and, for Christians, the Lord's Prayer begins by requesting the coming of the kingdom for the community in full. Their present unity depends upon a future promise, and so it is not possible to achieve that desired unity without giving a future orientation to the group. No congregation can locate its unity completely in the present or in history; to attempt this is to spread disunity and to lose the future in which our only hope lies.

If all prayers by Christians are offered in Jesus' name, it must be because the name represents God's presence and because it is through Jesus that man's will can be changed and brought into line with divine purpose. If all such prayer is an act by a person within a group, the communion sought with God must both change the individual and develop the bond of Christian brotherhood, because those who unite in prayer have all experienced a similar change. The prophets had special power as spirit-filled men. Now, through prayer, all Christians have this same spirit and thus the same potential power. The ultimate proof that the prophet uttered God's word was the manner of its fulfillment. In the case of the Christian, his presently changed inner disposition and his charitable acts are at best partial proofs; final confirmation, of course, awaits a completed future change. Thus, our prayers continue as the only way to relate to such a future and bring it into the present.

The spirit of God is said to be bestowed on those who did believe and repent. In the first act of creating and maintaining human life, it was the spirit that was sent forth by God to accomplish this, so that all future transformation of human life must take place by virtue of the spirit's presence and power. Whenever the body is extraordinarily endowed, or when God's people receive a powerful leader, this is accomplished by the "invasion" of the spirit. Spirit means *divine power immanent,* and the presence of such a foreign power is bound to alter the human recipient. Great prophets rarely speak on the basis of their own inspiration, since prophecy is the characteristic mark of God's presence among men in the form of a spirit.

In the case of Jesus, supernatural powers descend on him at the critical hour when his ministry begins. Without such an invasion by divine spirit, his work would not be possible. John the Baptist had foretold the coming of the Messianic age when great gifts of the spirit would be bestowed. Jesus received these in full, but only for a short period. His followers now are given them in part; their faith rests on a future full descent. In this sense, a new age of the kingdom has come within man's reach, since the work of the spirit in Jesus is part of its reality.

Jesus believes that the moving spirit is God's and that, as immanent in him, it is effective to conquer evil. If so, this certainly is a major change which is brought about by spirit's presence.

In the New Testament, the doctrine of the Holy Spirit depends on two sources: (1) the fact that Jesus died and is alive again due to the power of the spirit to reverse nature, and (2) the experience of the spirit's presence in Christian lives as verified by the fruits of their new actions. Those who are faithful have, thus, been regenerated by the activity of spirit, but they should be meek and quiet in spirit, since this change has not been accomplished by their own spirit. They are enabled to love one another now but *not by trying*, and suffering still is very much a part of this vocation. Their transformation is only partial. Those who remain loyal have a promise of eternal life in a transformed mode, and this is confirmed by the spirit's presence until that future time of accomplishment. Saint Paul had seen a demonstration of spirit's power to transform, and, thus, he believed in its future fulfillment.

In Jesus men experienced God as present and as powerfully at work renewing men. After Jesus' withdrawal, spirit performs this same renewing action without a visible focus for its activity. Because the gift of the spirit came to Jesus from heaven (that is, God's dwelling place) as an act of God's love, so when anyone feels God's transforming power he is aware of a new freedom to love produced by the spirit's presence. Jesus received the spirit as the divine pledge of immortality. In him it was accomplished, except that his withdrawal has not yet been reversed. Nevertheless, the spirit's less tangible and obvious presence among those who accept its promise is a pledge of the immortality yet to be completed.

Saint Paul is convinced that the presence of the spirit is the only condition upon which individual Christians can be holy in their actions and intent. If their new life is to be different, this must be because it is governed by divine love. If man's nature is to be changed—wholly in the future but now only in part—this is impossible without the spirit's presence. If the life-energy of God has flowed or will flow into the lives of the believers, this is the meaning of the power of the spirit. By this action alone, men are reconciled to God and are enabled to be new creatures, always in part now and only later in whole. Thus, without the spirit's presence no essential change is possible, although minor and transitory changes can be made by our own sustained human effort. If such change is not yet complete or always lasting, the presence of the spirit is also the ground of man's confidence in a promised future where it will be.

'Wisdom' means skill in making thought issue in appropriate action, and as such it is different from simple 'knowledge.' Skill, then, as an addition to knowledge, requires the presence of a moving spirit without which knowledge is ineffective. The wisdom of God is manifestly operative in what Jesus was and did. It is at this point that those who accept Jesus as Christ discover the most visible and powerful effect of the transforming power of the presence of God. Folly is the opposite of wisdom, and it implies a knowing without doing and without any change. Wisdom, thus, can be regarded as a gift of revelation, since it means not only to see what must be done for men but also to receive the power to accomplish this. If the status of any man is changed by membership in the church, it is because the community evidences to him the presence of God's transforming spirit which he now comes to share in union with them.

'Thanksgiving', then, is not meant to be represented merely by words, but it is the very mainspring of a new form of Christian living. It is the right motive for all service. That is, it is a recognition of the change produced by the spirit's presence, and all action is now a response to this, a thanksgiving. We express our thanks by presenting our former lives as a sacrifice. Our obedience to Jesus' commands is not a way of earning our promised future renewal. It is simply the expression of gratitude to God for those transformations already wrought, as well as for those expected, by the action of the Holy Spirit. Our obligation to Jesus is now rendered to our neighbor who has come to represent him.

A 'eucharist' is a celebration; it is the thanks of one who has received spiritual gifts not of his own accomplishment. This is the recipient's awareness of grace, of unearned renewed power. Consequently, he is grateful; he celebrates. Thanksgiving also means to praise or to confess. We praise God because of his generous use of power to free our love from its self-confinement. We confess in order to give thanks, since purging the hold former sins have on us is necessary to open the human spirit to praise. A sense of indebtedness to God is found throughout the Old Testament, and the Christian feels a similar necessity to respond for his new indebtedness, even though most of his thanks still must look forward to a promised future consummation.

When we remember all of God's mercies, and when we consider his future promises in spite of present evil or bondage, praise is called forth in the one who has faith. God, of course, is the ultimate ground of all thanksgiving, because we attribute all the transforming actions of spirit to divine gift. Those who give thanks testify that spirit can transform us and to their confidence that it yet will complete its promised and once manifest renewal of life. Since the majority of spirit's present action is inner, the evidence of its ability to change is glimpsed only indirectly in acts of love which seem to flow from its inner presence. Any individual can affirm his awareness of its inner power to change, but this is still connected to an expected future presence when its presence will be more overt.

F. THE FORM OF THE SPIRIT

Since understanding spirit presently involves mystery, and since its power to transform is only partially and indirectly in evidence, any real grasp of spirit depends upon our ability to discern and to embody the forms it can or ought to take in human life. In considering its possible forms, perhaps the first thing to ask is whether in this case the word and the thing are one and the same. That is, if the spoken word is charged with the personal power of the speaker, it has objectivity; it is the person made audible. In God's case, the utterance of his name, or of a new name, is a creative activity. If so, we need to discern the movement of the spirit in those few words that seem to be from God.

What is revealed through the prophets (or by Jesus' life and death and life) is the word of God. That God has become incarnate in the flesh is tantamount to making all men priests and prophets of God. Now this does not take place just through the special few; every man may become a vehicle of the divine word—that is, he may feel and respond to the movement of the Holy Spirit in his actions. Wisdom and the power of discernment are the special gifts of the spirit, so that whoever can put knowledge into creative play is an instrument of the spirit. Wisdom and the divine spirit are closely related, since the ability to employ knowledge constructively is not a natural property of all men but a divine gift to a few. There are many now who either cannot act or else who act destructively. *To be released fully either to love unselfishly or to act charitably requires divine assistance.*

We learn the forms in which spirit can be present from its accompanying signs. Gifts of the Holy Ghost, powers and wonders, accompanied the early preaching of the apostolic witnesses. The word is formed in preaching, and the presence of the spirit in it is testified to by the signs which accompany it. If actions follow that ordinary words could not invoke, God is taken to be the donor of these gifts, although only if the actions are helpful and are healing rather than selfish and destructive. Every Christian may become a partner in the spirit now that it does not fall on only a few men. The God who once spoke by prophets now can enter into the lives of all Christian believers. Love, of course, is the supreme and all-inclusive gift of the spirit, so that whenever love is able to break out of self-concern, to overcome obstacles and to communicate itself in spite of barriers—then we know that such love is the divine gift of the spirit and not of our own making.

Jesus is called divine because he is the one upon whom the spirit rested and remained, which is why he is called Christ. Christians are those who have experienced rebirth—that is, the birth of a new spirit within. Almost more indicative of the forms that the spirit takes are its result in the missionary movements of the church. This is an essential activity in the life of the community. Outreach for conversion is not simply misguided zeal, because the sign of the spirit's presence in transforming power is an uncontrollable desire to communicate that life-giving spirit to others freely and without requiring anything in return. Power, life, glory, joy—these are the characteristic marks of the Holy Spirit's influence. God grants

Christians the powers of his spirit to accomplish in the world the transformation of others that men could not do on their own.

For every Christian, Jesus was the visible form of God's spirit as present to us, and the events of his life indicate the full presence of divine power. That is, death can be overcome by no less a force than that which first created life. Although Jesus has withdrawn, the token and pledge of his real and continued personal presence with the community during the long days of the ensuing separation is the gift of the Holy Spirit in its various forms and powers of transformation. Due to the existence of spirit, Jesus can remain with men as present although unseen. However, God's spirit can continue to represent him only if Jesus first was its embodiment. The memorial meal Jesus enjoined upon his followers offers the form of a real presence that is personal. The symbols are not Jesus, but they are the forms of the spirit, which is what we now realize Jesus essentially to have been.

To worship means only to labor and to serve in the mission of God. In the Old Testament, the true worship of God was regarded as the dutiful ministration by sacrifice and obedience to the Law. However, service not rendered heartily and freely is not true service. The inward, spiritual attitude of the worshiper becomes an increasingly important factor. Thus, *the forms we expect worship to take indicate the forms in which we think spirit can be present.* The authority and power of Jesus confer, by commission, on those who openly invoke his name the real power of that name to testify to him and to minister to those in need. This involves both men with physical needs and those who require a prior inner renewal before they can serve a new function.

True service is perhaps the primary form of the spirit's presence. This springs from a love of God, but it comes only from a love that exists because God first opened himself to us without prior demand and not because we opened ourselves by force of will. This service in the time of God's absence is directed to one's neighbor who now is to be viewed, by the aid of the spirit, as God's child. In most cases, one's neighbor would not be accepted in this way at all, but would be seen simply as a man, so that any man's appearance in this divine light depends on the form spirit takes. Every action entered into in this spirit of God's outgoing love is, for the New Testament, an act of worship. The location of worship, in this case, is indifferent to Christians, since *God is worshiped where men are healed and life is renewed*. Such a spirit is with men always and everywhere, and it cannot be tied to a single locality, although it can be discovered in one.

The expectation of a second coming by Jesus discouraged the early Christians from building special places of worship. Like Abraham, they were sent out on a pilgrimage. Marking time, they did God's bidding (spreading the transforming and healing power of love) until they expected to be called together by Christ's literal return. Each Christian still lives and works in this state and under this expectation. Their fellowship is a present sharing with him in his glory, but, *in the intervening time, the spreading of healing love must be strangely mixed with unavoidable suffering*. Just as Jesus could not escape it in responding to God's love, so likewise no disciple of his can live without pain; the form of the spirit willing to undergo suffering gladly is its truest manifestation.

21

SIN

A. THE WORLD INTO WHICH WE ARE BORN

Sin without God is meaningless. God without sin is inconceivable; the two go together and define each other. If we lose our sense of the presence of God (as repeatedly happens), we cannot be aware of our 'sin', although we may be conscious of error or even of wrongdoing. This is because "to sin" means to fail to obey a divine command. Thus, if in our actions we do not know what God asks us to do, we cannot be aware of any intentional disobedience. Just to the extent that we are able to form a clear picture of God's 'will', to that extent we can be sorry if we fail to live up to it. However, it is sometimes hard to discern what God's will is, just as it is often hard to be sure which of our actions are really 'sinful'.

Can we ever be clear about God's will? Christians and Jews can be, but just to the extent that they understand the focus of their religious faith. Other religions also are defined by their particular formulation of the actions God wills for them. The Jew is faithful to his Torah, or the Law, and it is this allegiance that makes him Jewish. Of course, Jews differ in exactly how they understand what the Law requires, but no Jew ignores the fact that it is the seal of his relationship to God. To break the code, to which he feels God has obligated him in return for delivering him as a people, is to sin against his covenant with God. Christianity split off from Judaism precisely over the Christian assertion of freedom from this Law and his obligation to a new law.

A Christian is defined by his willingness to center his understanding of God's will in the actions and teachings of Jesus and in what he understands God to have done in Jesus' death and resurrection. These actions by God, and Jesus' presentation of them to man, define a new code. Allegiance to them shapes his picture of God, and it also sets the notion of sin. Specifically, Jesus redefined the Law and the Prophets in the great commandment "Love thy God with all thy heart and thy neighbor as thyself." In understanding this demand of love, sin is fixed for the Christian as any failure so to act, and this requirement of love also gives a center of focus to the Christian's notion of what his God is like. He forms a picture of what God must be if he would do and say what he did in the person of Jesus and also define sin as he did in the double commandment.

Not to love God above all, then, is to sin. Yet, this is not the natural direction of man's affection; it must be learned. Nor is God an easy object to love, since so much of his nature is, at least at first, hidden, and so much has been and still is subject to such a wide variety of interpretation. Clearly, we have to train love in a special way where God is concerned. And, if love's first intention is toward its own desire, to convert love into an emotion that is equally concerned with any person who happens to be set down next to you without your choosing, that is to be forced to change love and to re-form it. Given love's raw nature, sin is natural, and obedience to God is a virtue very difficult to acquire and to hold. Sin becomes *whatever blocks our central affection for God, as well as any action or word that keeps love from learning to subordinate its own desires to the needs of others.*

Given this picture of 'God' and 'sin' and natural 'love', it is quite clear that the conditions into which we are born are less than ideal for keeping us from sin. For that matter, little in life prevents us from denying God in the first place and thus losing all sense of sin. If we take as a model the Christian conception of God's commands, it is clear that both the nature we were given as men and the world in which we were placed predispose us to turn in the opposite direction from such compliance. It is true that various sets of divine commands have also been introduced into the world at various times and places (for example, the exodus and the incarnation), so that we do have forces that oppose love's untrained direction; we have been given some guidance. Nevertheless, since God is never easy to discern and his commands are not above dispute and misunderstanding, love is hard work.

Placed in a situation in which it is possible and even easy to deny God, we find ourselves in a world in which sin also can remain unrecognized. If the first man (Adam) was not even free from rebellious desire, at least he is pictured as knowing God's demand clearly. In spite of this, the world in which he lived (the garden) and the people with whom he dealt (Eve and their sons) made it easy for his vision to be blocked (Adam may enter a plea of temporary insanity). A desire in itself natural becomes rebellion against God. This war, once launched, cannot be voluntarily halted. If the first man was exempt from death, this made it difficult for him to see what harm might come from satisfying desire. Once death blocks his path, man naturally only increases his desires and the furious activity to satisfy them before time runs out. He feels the pressure of the limits within which they must be satisfied or else go unfulfilled.

Our participation in the common situation of humanity can at times give us a sense of collective guilt over sins not specifically our own. 'Original sin' is the name for such a feeling of human solidarity. Guilt is original to our situation and to our human nature, and sin results unless we can reverse the tide, or until God is lost from our sight. In the latter case, we get rid of all sense of sin, but we also take on a sense of common guilt without being aware of having broken any commands (free-floating anxiety). To go against God is terrifying enough, but not to have a God or any sense of a clear demand —this is almost more terrifying due to the burden it places upon the individual. A sense of unease is the unavoidable companion of being unsure about either our crimes or our accuser. Kafka's *The Trial* is modern man without a sense of God.

Adam is Man, because in him we see clearly the paradoxical character of human nature. Like Adam, we are all given a nature capable of high destiny but also of wretchedness. Not falling into sin would be more possible if our own nature were more ideal—that is, less capable of dividing into warring factions. We can know God and his commands because we have God's image. That is, we share with God the power of understanding, of grasping truth, of creating what is beautiful and the ability to will what is right. We are not, however, given God's power always to resist sin—that is, his ability never to contradict the best in his nature. God knows temptation, but his power to refrain is not threatened beyond his ability to resist and to control. Our power is always threatened and subject to failure, misdirection, and miscalculation. The divine image in us is not complete, and its inadequacies push it toward destruction.

In addition to disobeying the divine commands of love, man can sin by aspiring to be God. This happens when we claim for the self a power or a glory or an honor really applicable only to God. To fail to recognize our own inadequacies, or our potential to fail, is to sin by not understanding our precise relationship to God. As a result, we desire or attempt what can only lead to destruction, because it exceeds human power to achieve. Adam passes on to us an earthly life which always is born out of our failure in paradise. Because we are confused about our place, we sin by disobedience. We join Adam as slaves to death, because its constant threat, as well as the limits it sets upon what we can accomplish, drives us to exploit self-centered love rather than to redirect our affection. Whether for a long or a short time, to succeed in convincing love to obey the commands of God and of others is to achieve at least momentary sainthood.

If the world into which we are born offers us less than optimum conditions, Jesus returns us to Adam's starting place. That is, he claims to open the possibility, through him, to reenter a relationship of justice with God. What this means is receiving the gift of an ability to obey love's divine commands, to curb its natural flow, to discover God as its object and every other man as its recipient. In such a situation, spiritual life is restored, since what destroys it in the first place is the complete absorption of the self in its own demands. Constantly to seek self-fulfillment is to block spiritual life, because no outlet is left if every attention is centered inward. Strange as it may seem, an inner spiritual life grows only after our energy has been spent external to the self. Then, an emptiness is created as a result of which we are no longer an object of our own attention.

Each man faces an adversary, which is himself, because the unreconstructed self insists that it focus only on its own demands and on their satisfaction. We are our own worst enemy, as the saying goes. Thus, Satan represents every man just as Adam does. There are devils and demons in the world, but they are simple to deal with in their seduction as compared with the inner Devil's suggestion that we center our attention constantly on our self. If the kingdom of God is within, it is equally true that our foes are internal too. The battle rages where it cannot be seen and where the powers of darkness require no external assistance. If 'Christ' means "he who saves us from ourselves," the Antichrist is equally easy to define. His goal is insidiously close: He advocates that we save ourselves for ourselves alone, which appears again and again as a theme with each new generation. No aim could appear more natural to, or cause more catastrophe within, the inner man.

Malignant spirits suggest that their destructive work is what apparently preserves and insures the self against harm—that is, they urge primary concentration on self-preservation and self-satisfaction. Actually, malignancy spreads because such a stress turns love in upon itself and blocks it from going out to either God or man. These powers are "of this world" insofar as our setting in nature leads us to deny God or, more likely, to fail to see him clearly. Such a spirit constantly tempts us with the idea that self-satisfaction is natural and healthy, rather than ultimately destructive of the self and others. Anyone who causes internal distress is a Devil, and we sin against the divine command of love whenever we are our own Devil. Satan is the name for our accuser, and no one who brings charges against us publicly can cause so much internal damage as when we accuse ourselves.

In spite of Jesus' injunction to forgive others their sins, it is almost easier to do that than to forgive ourselves, and it is also far more destructive when we cannot. If our self-directed flow of love has harmed someone and we know it, we block our own attempts to turn our love out toward others because our guilt keeps us focused inward. Who can turn us inside out? That is our question if our efforts at restoration only drive us more deeply interior to the self. Is the human personality open to invasion from the spirit of God as well as to being besieged by devils? Demons lock us within ourselves where love can only do damage to itself. How can the self be made equally vulnerable to divine assault, so that it can be captured from itself and then released?

In Genesis, Adam's story is simply told, and from then on it is reenacted by each one of us. Looking back either on our original state or on his, we call that action a "fall" by which we first begin to block either love's outgo or God's command. We lose our balance, and, once we do, the recovery of equilibrium is difficult. More than that, damage to psyche or body always leaves a scar which it is either difficult or, more likely, impossible to remove. Once love errs, its virgin state is lost, and it cannot make itself fresh and unspoiled again. An irreversible barrier has been crossed; we can date our fall only in looking back to our own genesis story. At the time, it simply seemed like the natural satisfaction of love's demands. If we once knew God, or if we take God to mean the unnatural demand that we place every self on a par, a decision to turn away from this radical demand is the loss of any hope for achieved holiness. It is the beginning of the soul's death which is willed in the attempt to satisfy first its own demands.

B. SOULS IN PRISON

Pride is always said to be a source of sin, since it is pride that encourages love to focus on itself and on others only in their relation to the development of its virtues and that self's demands. Pride holds the attention of the self upon itself and unwittingly blocks the outward flow of love which is our only source of spiritual health. Pride in itself is not wrong, as some of the Greek philosophers have said, as long as it is not unwarranted or, as Spinoza saw, as long as it leads to a full expression of the self's powers. Earned pride is not inherently a sin. In order to see the damage it can do, we must look at its effects on the self's ability to love and at the direction pride gives to that flow of affection. God is blocked and his commands are silenced as long as pride holds control of our attention.

There is nothing good about humility if it decreases the self's effectiveness or if it blocks its power to act. However, there is nothing bad about humility if it helps to shake down the barriers the self throws up around itself. Such barricades lessen the possibility of being hurt, but they also block us from venturing out to the assistance of others, although it is quite possible to have a "happy" facade all along. Just to the extent that humility keeps the self open, to that degree it is not bad. Sin, as the failure to obey the commands of love, places the individual in a situation of inward alienation from God. When love obeys only its own inclinations and is inner directed, such sin estranges us from those around us. This is true even when we are not conscious of its opposition to either God's will or the direction of his love. Some sin is conscious and voluntary. 'Original sin' is not so much a voluntary personal act as it is an instinctive natural response.

Without a consciousness of sin, it is impossible to accept the renewal Christians proclaim to be available. Only when we see that man's original situation needs reorientation (if not complete reversal) before love can find completion, only in this condition is it possible to understand any offer to break nature's bonds. The essence of original sin is the absence of 'grace'—that is, of love as freely outgoing without consequent demand of repayment. It is this kind of direction to love that initially is lost. This privation in man, whenever it occurs or is deepened, separates man from God. Or, this privation makes it difficult for man to locate God, because the natural direction of his affection leads him to himself and not outward to others. Sin is not a total turning away from God toward nature, and neither is salvation exclusive absorption with God. Lack of relation to God turns us to ourself. Grasping the divine command enables us to turn from God, to bypass the self's centripetal pool, and to love others selflessly.

'Hell' is not "other people," as Sartre has said. Essentially, it is to be left blocked within the self and thus to be unable to go out to others without first demanding that their attention be focused on our self. To live in society with God is to be able to find him, to know him, and to love him, and as a consequence to love others without regard to rank. To live out of society with God is hell, because we can never be free for a moment from self-concern and attention to our slightest needs. To be forced to listen constantly only to the self's demands upon itself and others—this is certainly to be locked in hell with no exit. Hell is a state of final personal alienation from God, because only in our ability to respond to his commands can the self be free to live and love anything other than its own self in a self-defeating manner.

Human life is constantly threatened with the real possibility of personal shipwreck. To lose the power to move and to navigate is for the self to be becalmed and powerless. Such personal incapacity is hell, and, if the condition remains unremedied, that is to live in hell for eternity. Christians have announced their reception of the message that God intends all men to be saved. Yet, if some retain the possibility of remaining in eternal perdition (permanent self-estrangement), God's will, in that sense, is thwarted in spite of the range of his power. The problem is that, regardless of any offer of help (even if it is from God), only the individual self has the power to accept. We cannot be forced to turn, or else the self would be destroyed by having its integrity violated. God could have created less fragile and less independent souls, but then they would not be in his image. Like true sons, we inherit God's inability to be forced. What in him is a virtue in us, if uncorrected, can be our downfall.

'Paradise' means constantly to be responsive to God's commands and to be able without effort to set the self aside in love. Such a state is 'righteous', because our mode of love is instantly responsive to command, and our self is both constantly open and able to bestow assistance and affection without entangling obligation. Jesus constantly warned us against unrepentant sin. It is impossible to soften these warnings, and there is no reason to do so. To refuse the offer of restoration in response to God is to damn the self to constant self-absorption and inner struggle. The wages of sin are death, since to be blocked from life is certainly to be locked in hell and to suffer the mental tortures of the lost. 'Fire' is a natural symbol of such a state, for the self consistently destroys itself by consuming itself endlessly.

Judaism knows both the same bliss of responsiveness to God and the self-inflicted punishment that results from disobedience. Christians have associated this problem more with the direction and the mode of love and less with the performance of ritual, and they claim that their hope has new ground for the renewal of ravaged souls now made possible by Jesus' ministry and sacrifice, followed by God's action in response to this. For them, Jesus's resurrection signifies the release from the bonds of self-inflicted death. After his crucifixion, Jesus was pictured as descending into hell and as preaching to the "souls in prison." Perhaps only if the self's incessant demands are first crucified can we learn how to say anything effective to those who have locked themselves in hell. Many inflict death upon themselves who do not know that it is possible to gain release from themselves and from their self-bound love. Their prisons must be descended to before their souls can be touched or moved to reverse direction.

'Hate' is the opposite of love; that is, it signifies love blocked and now unable to gain release from the self. In retaliation, the ego is likely to strike out furiously, hoping to destroy what it cannot love. Yet 'indifference' is even more deadly where love is concerned. Hate is a strong passion, but at least it possesses power. Although dangerous, some hope remains that hate's energy may be converted (for example, Saul into Paul). Indifference is a love afraid of itself and held so in check that its power turns neither to good nor to evil, neither to assistance nor to destruction. The salt has lost all savor. Those who have sealed themselves hermetically in indifference and isolated themselves in a vacuum of detachment are the most difficult to reach. They have learned the dangers of hate and love, and they have vowed to spare themselves agony by avoiding all risks. They may end by breaking all contact with others, and what hell is worse than to be left totally within one's self?

To hate the self is to deny the self, and it may lead to a willingness to remove the self, even a readiness to be crucified. Thus, those who hate themselves, while this is not a healthy situation if left alone, actually are closer to becoming free to love. Their extremes may drive them to abandon the self in desperation, to let go at least spiritually if not physically. The soul that languishes in the prison of indifference has less chance of release than the self that fights with itself, even when it turns its natural self-love to hate. Such a soul may, in rage if not in knowledge, at last in desperation abandon self-love and self-attachment and stumble into God's command concerning the prior loss of self.

The metaphor of light vs. darkness is always associated with sin, and it provides an appropriate symbol. To be bound by sin, to be unable to hear or to respond to a divine command, to be closed inward in self-love, this is certainly to lose the self in darkness. To respond, to move outward un-self-consciously in affection, this is certainly to bring openness and freedom to the soul and is rightly associated with light. Prosperity and happiness, the abundance of inner satisfaction if not of outer materials, all these certainly go with freedom from sin and the inner presence of light. The opposite of such self-transparency is adversity or sorrow, and the soul may weep within itself invisibly and be unable to prosper. These states are seldom identified with ignorance vs. knowledge, for the lack of intellectual sophistication may make the coming of light in the soul easier to accept. By contrast, too much knowledge can actually burden the soul and slow its movements.

The ignorant can be just as free from sin to the extent that they can communicate selfless love. The power of evil is associated with darkness, and the soul that cannot release itself from self-attachment does live in darkness. Everything associated with God is seen in terms of light, since the refusal to turn in upon oneself creates a situation of openness and ease. Yet all associated with God and light is not free from dread, awe, and fear, since darkness is his intentional creation too. When God is known, the fear experienced on our first encounter with divinity is transformed into a loving reverence. The divine in contrast to man is unnerving, at least until we discover that *his extreme difference from us is based upon his openness to love without self-involvement.* Yet, in spite of this, God's constant and inescapable demand is for a similar love by man. Even though this demand is the condition for man's ability to convert his natural love, our first encounter with it still properly inspires dread.

The "fear of the Lord" dominates the Old Testament, and it clearly is one of the basic responses of man to God's demand upon him. Whenever God is found, his contrasting sinlessness fills man with a sense of his own unworthiness, even when this experience is the necessary preliminary to cure. Thus, fear is a permanent element in man's relationship to God, since it exists wherever sin remains and might be exposed. The discovery of the divine has an effect on man's consciousness, and the first reaction usually is not a pleasant one. 'Wickedness' means to seek evil in contempt of God or man, and putting oneself in knowing opposition always sets up the situation of fear. When we realize that an action motivated by selfish love is bad or displeasing or harmful, we know evil as that which causes pain, unhappiness, or misery, and this includes the discipline and punishment involved in knowing God.

C. THE UNREALITY OF DEATH

If sin results both from God's absence and from its terrifying consequences, it is still true that neither Christian nor Jew has, as the Epicureans, ever thought of death as total extinction. Death at the very least is conceptualized as a continuance of existence in an underworld, a region of shadows, misery, and futility. In this case, it makes perfect sense to say that we live in the midst of death, for the lives of many are characterized by such an obscured form of existence. It is easy now to make sense of the expression "hell on earth" and to understand Sartre's assertion that men create hell for themselves. To the extent that shadows cover their lives, while misery and futility haunt them and love is thwarted and turned in upon itself, to that extent there genuinely is hell on earth constantly and of our own making.

If we think of the dead as living in a land of silence and forgetting, as unreal and half-material shades, it is not hard to see how much of our present life also has these characteristics. As the central character in Sartre's *The Devil and the Good Lord* expressed it, our problem is to become real. The experience of dread always accompanies our approach to the dead, and now we can understand why. Death involves a meaningless and desireless form of existence, as depicted in Old Testament poetry. When death is near, we become too much aware of the presence of these characteristics in the midst of our own life. Life and death are not far enough apart for comfort; they are not sufficiently separate to enable us to take nearness to death calmly. We already live there too much.

In religious terms, the real horror of death has always been said to lie in the fact that all intercourse with God is at an end. In itself this might not seem to be so bad, if it did not signify that we are left entirely to ourselves without recourse whenever we are unable to release love from self-involvement. This is the horror of death: to think of the future as the total internal confinement of the self. The Old Testament literature suggests little about our ability to find release from such a deadly condition. But, by New Testament times, belief in resurrection is held by most Jews, except the Sadducees. Christianity is based on a hope in our ability to be set free from such confinement. This, of course, depends on an apocalyptic point of view. All suffocation of love has not been ended now. Such death-by-excess-love is all around us, but now at least a joy is possible in the promise of the final availability of release.

Death would be strange if it freed the soul from all connection to the body. Plato's theory notwithstanding, death may not be the end of all physical involvement. The body both hampers us now and at the same time is the instrument for love's expression. We do not necessarily need the particular physical form we have now, but 'life' means physical involvement, and this makes the problem of death and resurrection more complicated. 'To resurrect' need not mean to piece an old body together again, but it may mean to free the self to communicate itself in love and to provide it with a responsive and nonimpeding physical instrument. The goal of resurrection is the breaking of the power that all physical bodies have to frustrate the self.

'Heaven' is always associated with heights, and, whether or not this is interpreted as literally "up," to be in heaven certainly always means to rescue the soul from its confinement to its own depths. If heaven is the abode of those who are saved, to be saved must mean to be free of that which drags us down both internally and externally. If 'heaven' is also sometimes a circumlocution for the name of God, it is easy to see that to be in heaven would be to be able to speak God's name—that is, to be responded to and to be able to respond as we are not always able to on earth. In hell, we cannot locate God's word; in heaven, we are able to relate the self to divine command. To be able to speak God's name is to be able to love our neighbor, since to know God is to accept that demand upon our love.

On earth there are many partial and temporary salvations. There are moments of bliss and elevations of the soul, but they cannot be sustained. To be in heaven means to have been given full release from that which drags us down and turns us inward. To be partially released is not salvation; to be fully free is to be in heaven, to live uninterruptedly on the heights. The existence of heaven—that is, of such a plane of existence—depends for Christians on Jesus' conquest of death —that is, a victory over those forces that compel us to live in an unreal half-world. All of us would like to live an existence such as 'heaven' implies, and we would gladly emerge from the shadows by our own efforts. But, momentary as our successes may be, we cannot escape fully the bonds that hold us in constant threat of loss. Jesus' subjugation of all deteriorating forces is the precondition for our ability to enter a life of openness with the divine, with others, and even with ourselves. Which is worse: Never to have known a better life or, having tasted it, not to be able to sustain that level of existence?

D. THE POWER OF DECISION

In order to deal with sin, 'confession' is a necessary ability. Those who cannot learn to confess, to speak their weaknesses openly, cannot be cured beyond momentary relief. In order to confess, a certain power of decision is needed; more often it is this that is missing rather than the lack of desire to confess and thus be rid of guilt. Confession involves the declaration of a personal decision, and to utter contrite words without this quality of personal decisiveness is a trivial matter. This, of course, cannot be done by the individual alone, so that the existentialists who stress man's essential aloneness also thereby condemn him to an inability to confess with any hope of pardon or change. A community must be formed or exist within which the confession can be heard. Occasionally, God can make up this community, but, unless there are also tangible members, the lack of specific persons makes it very difficult for the potential confessor.

'Concupiscence' is sometimes said to be "how sin manifests itself." However, rather than treating this simply as unrestrained desire, it is better to understand it as a lack of the power of decision. You persist in pleasure when you lack the decisiveness to say no, and confession requires first the ability to stop by telling yourself "No." Saying it does not always bring it about, at least not permanently. Yet, without this quality of decision, pleasure runs on unchecked and confession is impossible. To confess involves first to admit one's guilt. More importantly for Christians, it also means to admit to and acknowledge God's saving gifts of power. Jesus' constant demand that men "confess his name" is simply a condition for their ability to open themselves to admit the power of change.

'Asceticism' is not much in fashion in an age of excessive indulgence, and yet such austere practice has a genuine connection to confession and decision. The term is late in its origin (circa 1646); the idea came much earlier. We cannot love properly without training, and confession is idle unless it is preceded by renunciation. Asceticism is valuable, if not taken in itself or done in excess, then for its testing and training of the power of decision. For the Stoic, this means deliverance from all ties with this world in order to obtain the free imperturbability of the 'wise man.' Both Christians and philosophers have given up the goal of becoming wise men; they only claim to love wisdom, not to be able to possess her. Ties with the world always remain, and one who loves cannot hope to be free of disturbance. Nevertheless, renunciation is still a test of our power to decide and even to exclude natural pleasure if necessary.

If confession means the open acknowledgment of sin, its first requirement is that we be able to open ourselves. If our individual power is not sufficient to accomplish this, at least we must acknowledge, confess, and remain loyal to the power that in fact entered in to open us out from ourselves. To confess is to be assured of God's forgiveness, since it involves both our discovery of God's lack of self-centeredness in his love and our ability to relate to him and to accept his demands just because we have been released from our self's demands. 'Confession' means to acknowledge, to admit, to declare that something is so, and, in this case, it is to respond to the unexpected selflessness of God's love which has power sufficient to move and to forgive.

If we come to recite a 'creed,' it is only as a form of confession—that is, of admitting publicly our release by a power not our own. This is not a freedom from all restraint; but instead, it comes only by the acceptance of demands. A creed publicly admits our 'debt'—that is, that we have someone to whom we owe release. The debt of love, of course, is the only obligation that cannot be paid in full, and so we recite our creed over and over simply because we are unable to forget love's debt. Because, unlike human love, divine love is limitless and selfless in its orientation. It knows no limits, and thus it can never be measured in order to cancel it by repayment. It knows no depths to which it will not reach. Our bondage is the fetters sin places upon man, but it is also the bond that is the legitimate uniting force that keeps us together in community. As all of us were held immobilized by sin, so we all share a common debt for love's release which makes us one.

'Lust' is always an intense emotional assertion of the self. To envy or to desire only becomes wrong when it is ungoverned or entirely selfish. In that case, our power of decision is tested, for upon that rests our ability to limit desire and to keep it from binding us in sin—that is, blocking us from love and from God. Ruthless self-assertion is the very essence of idolatry, so that, when prophets warn against idolatry, their aim is to turn us from the extremes of self-assertion that always block us from God and create gods out of our own desires. If existentialism recommends salvation by self-assertion, we know it to be a dangerous path along which it is hard to distinguish men from idols. Lust makes an end out of its own desire and permits no higher gods.

'Temptation' is whatever incites us to sin. That is, it means to turn our attention entirely inward and thus to lose all momentary regard for the interests of others. Temptation also means to prove or to test, so that it is not all bad unless we succumb to it. In fact, our power would remain undirected, unformed, and merely latent unless some test drew it forth and gave it purpose. The crucial moment in temptation comes in our reaction to it—that is, whether all else is obscured and action is determined only by our self-concern. Jesus' supreme temptations were spiritual, not physical. It is possible to tempt or to test an individual physically, but the great battlefield involves an unseen spirit. Benefits can come from struggle, but only if the result is a victory over temptation. To lose is to give in to only self-concern, and then the vicious spiral has begun.

'Conscience' is that element in man's experience of freedom that makes him aware of his responsibility. He who acts out of inner conviction is a man of conscience, whereas he who allows external concerns to determine his action is not such a man. For the religious person, the final authority for conscience rests on God's will, but this gives him an additional problem because his conscience must first determine what God might will or not will in this instance. A man of conscience is one who is able to enact and sustain his own power of decision. To sin is to lose this control, and to act against conscience is to be unable to act in accordance with one's inner conviction. This discrepancy is the main source of sin and the primary breach that needs to be healed.

E. THE LACK OF AUTHORITY

Sin can only be understood in relation to both a commandment and the power to command. In a day in which commands are either little accepted or even openly rejected, one result is the paradox of widespread sin and a general consciousness of it. All the while there is little clear sense of what specifically is being violated. For Jews, the commands are clear: those decrees that the God of the Covenant announced to the people of the Covenant (although it is true that the precise way in which these are to be interpreted has been under dispute ever since). In defining his commandments, Jesus appeals not so much to this tradition to support his own authority as to his messianic mission and power. To understand a command we must recognize its source, so that we have been left with the problem of trying to discover what new source of power might have appeared in Jesus' person.

If God does exercise an authority over all things by a personal activity, it is possible to recognize his commands and yet to feel a sense of sin in any failure to comply. This requires that we have a prior understanding of God's personal nature and of the mode of his activity. Therefore, whenever our sense of God's presence is obscure, our sense of sin is also vague. Yet we may fail to recognize commands because we do not understand their purpose. Commands are not simply an exhibition of authority—that is, they are not if they are divine. Their intent is to build a community, a people of God. Thus, sin is meaningful not individually (as modern man has tried to make it) but only as a violation of those commands that establish and hold together a community under God. If we lose this sense of community, or if we cannot accept the efforts of God to establish communities loyal to him, sin will never be more than vaguely felt.

'Promise' is a necessarily complementary word to 'command.' If we are not dealing with a tyrant God, his commands are always given for some purpose, and it is the result of this aim that we accept as a promise. The effect of a command is to bind men to God and also to their neighbor (following the Great Commandment), and this is done in a relationship of love. In order to understand the element of promise in any command, we must grasp how 'command' can form the basis of love and also how sin not only violates a command but also frustrates any loving relationship. Nevertheless, a command is meaningless as an edict or a decree unless we acknowledge that that person who is its source in fact possesses authority. The primary question in considering sin is to ask "Whom do we acknowledge to have authority to command us?" Of course, this cannot be God unless he has first become real to us in his nature.

'Covenant' is almost synonymous with Torah or Law, but its real importance lies in seeing it as the instrument by which the Prophets tried to recall the deserters in Israel back to faithfulness in the covenant. Thus, sin cannot be felt until there is a preexisting agreement which we can admit has been violated. Jesus does not speak explicitly of a "new covenant" until the institution of the Last Supper, but now this becomes the means by which unfaithful Christians are recalled to serve their new law. Spirit poured forth with dramatic effects after

Jesus' promise, and this stems from fulfillment of his covenant. Spiritual renewal goes with new covenants, and thus a withdrawal of the spirit characterizes sin. A covenant is an ordinance of salvation from God, since it alone makes sin clear and can serve as a norm for repentance—that necessary precondition to salvation.

If 'law' is synonymous with the will of God, a question arises with Jesus' 'new covenant': Did he have the power to set aside the old law? The same question arises every time we violate an existing code. However, in Jesus' case, it is also the test of his divinity, since the law he sets aside was accepted as based on divine authority. If the law reveals the will of God, to replace it is to claim a new disclosure of God's will, and sin is redefined as a result. The heart of any religious law is the personal relationship established between God and believer, so that any new law sets up a different relationship, and the absence of all law means the disappearance of all communion between God and man. Law includes ritual observances, but, at least for Christians, sin is redefined because these acts now are given less weight.

The question is whether God provides guidance or instruction. If we believe this, we will not lightly dismiss the oracular utterances of priests and prophets. Instead, all our effort will be bent to try to locate and to accept these sources of guidance. This 'law-giving' must be taken as the whole revelation of God's nature and purpose, and our test of Jesus' divinity is whether we accept his teaching as authoritative. If we are in a new dispensation of law, old ritual observances may be set aside, but not all instruction is absent. Man can enjoy God's communion regardless of past activities, and he need not discharge any formal debt or perform any special rituals. However, a new commandment is acknowledged which replaces the old one. In Jesus' teaching, all men universally are brought into the field of divine activity formerly occupied by Jews alone.

How is any new law put into effect? This question is crucial —that is, it is if Christianity is not the absence of all law. As with the old ways, it can only be accomplished by an efficacious speaking of God's word. The test of our respect for the law, and the sense of our personal acceptance of sin, depend upon acknowledging that source as divinely authoritative. Religious law is not essentially restrictive, but it is an offer of life according to a prescribed and blessed pattern, so that our sense of sin will depend on what pattern of life we take God to have enjoined. Of course, to anyone who cannot accept this way (for example, either loving one's neighbor regardless of his merit or serving the needs of others before your own), all such prescription appears as a stern command. A people was created by Moses' leadership, and it came about because they acknowledge his teaching as revealing the character and the commands of God.

If 'pride' is the root and the essence of sin, this can only mean to attribute to yourself or to some man the authority of guidance which rightfully belongs only to God. The proper attitude of man in the presence of the Lord is self-abasement and trustfulness, so that to indulge in self-assertion is to let pride block the service of God. However, with Jesus, respect for God is to be shown more by your life and deeds than by mere words. The Christian virtue of 'humility' is introduced, and it is based on the wonder of divine humility as evidenced in the suffering of Jesus. Pride has its origin in self-concern; humility has its origins in a willingness to allow the self to suffer for the sake of others. Punishment is the divine reaction to sin. God is violently hostile to it, because it destroys the mutuality of the divine-human relationship and makes it impossible for man to carry out God's commands—that is, to be saved from himself.

F. THE WATERS OF DESTRUCTION

What is 'unclean' must be washed and purified. Jesus, however, abolished the prescriptions on ritual or ceremonial purity in favor of purity of heart. This makes it harder to detect what is defiled and also less easy to be certain of its restoration. If 'holiness' is a condition of approach to God, it is useless to speak of finding God until we have found a way of purification. In accepting and following that way, God alone can be observed and not before, although it is the sense of his presence that induces us to follow a way of life that will destroy old habits. What is 'profane' is what does not pertain to God. That is hard to discern, and it depends partly on one's understanding of God, but it is crucial to discover what such actions and ways are, so that we do not expect to find God in the wrong places.

Unfortunately for us, uncleanness is more contagious than holiness, so that it is easier to go astray than to find a path leading to God. Uncleanliness is closely allied to sin, and cleansing usually means miraculous healing. Ethical purity is the mark of those who have been restored, not that their every action actually exemplifies this, but only that their bondage has been broken. The Antichrist becomes simply the man of sin. Formally, in Christian terms, it meant those who deny that Jesus is the Christ, but this involves all those who do not accept his new commands as divinely authoritative. In the present age, all the forces of evil are unleashed to do their utmost, but that only precedes the final victory of God. In the midst of contagion, then, the believer holds fast to the final rightness of divine cleansing and restoration.

Water is often the symbol of destruction, but so also is it, interestingly enough, the symbol of God's activity in the world through the Holy Spirit. Biblically, there are waters of destruction that are also the instrument of salvation—for example, Noah's flood and the Exodus through the Red Sea. The destructive force of water represents both God's judgment on sinners and also the salvation of a faithful remnant. The overwhelming waters of trouble cannot appear to be anything but bad at the moment they arrive, and yet they may very well be at the same time the living, cleansing waters that proceed from God's presence. This is not to say that all destruction is good or that only the bad are destroyed; that is not true. It is just that not all destruction is always bad.

God saves his people from sin by a washing of regeneration and a renewing of the Holy Spirit. However, it may well be that some destruction is necessary before any such dramatic change is possible. Traditional symbolism also depicts God as providing water in the desert for his people to drink. Does he only provide for spiritual thirst when the body is vulnerable? That is our question. This need not mean that all privation is good or that all spiritual thirst is automatically satisfied, but it may mean that beyond judgment lies salvation and the

promise of water to quench thirst. A certain amount of destruction is necessary and some harsh pronouncements must
be accepted before you are ever prepared to stop and turn.
Water is also part of the imagery of spiritual fruitfulness; that
which can drown and destroy also seems able to restore and to
satisfy. Not all that is annihilated is bad, but there is no apparent way to overcome sin and ardent self-attachment except
by tearing the self open or causing it to drown.

This connection of the intensity of evil and destruction
with salvation perhaps explains the prediction that, when evils
of all kinds have reached their climax, deliverance will be at
hand. A new age is born only out of travail and affliction and
persecution. Real suffering is not local but universal, and it is
necessary in order to usher in the Messianic Age. This may not
be such a strange action of design on God's part when we
realize that suffering is the essence of the mission of the
Messiah. Thus, anyone who follows him will also participate in
that affliction. It is the ultimate test of a disciple, and it may
very well be the only means to acquire discipline too. Those
who obey and accept are offered, not immediate relief, but
only an ultimate reward following an intervening difficult
time. To be able to persist in such a state requires discipline.

Vengeance, however, is traditionally reserved for God, and
its presence indicates the religious confidence in the moral
order of the world in spite of apparent success of flagrant
violations. God takes the role of the avenger upon himself as
well as that of the suffering servant. However, such full accounting is never promised as possible within either our time
or the structure of this world. It is reserved for an age to come,
which requires for its possibility the destruction of the present
order. Apparent loss and unjustified wrong cannot be accepted
easily, nor can the present order simply be abandoned, since
the future exists not in fact but only in promise, except perhaps spiritually. *Perhaps the greatest sin is to lose confidence
in God's command in the face of the waters of destruction.
Perhaps to be freed from sin is to be able to trust in such an
uncertain situation.*

"The good suffering" is that strange concept with which the
religious individual constantly wrestles. To accept it is not
easy and tends to slip away, and its misunderstanding has

probably caused more pain than it has relieved. What is 'good' is usually thought to be what is pleasant, joyful, agreeable, of benefit, and prosperous. This is the description of God's original creation, and it is hard to reconcile this with the suffering that follows, as Job knows. Yet what is 'good' is also what is 'right,' and it might be that this brings us closer to suffering, since it is not attained apart from God. Sorrow is a part of mankind from the first, so that suffering is traced back to the beginnings of the human race. If the Old Testament did not shrink from attributing the cause of evil to God, why should we?

Suffering has a punitive or retributive character, and sin or self-attention always brings suffering. It is the visible sign of the wrath of God. Nevertheless, particularly when it is undeserved, we have to ask what good divine wrath is intended to accomplish. A consciousness of afflictions does awaken a desire for deliverance, so that, without suffering, we might very well be content to live in sin and remain estranged from God. Sin has a disciplinary or purificatory effect, and yet that does not account for all of sin or even for the majority of suffering. The righteous suffer too, and so the great religious question is to account for "the good suffering." Obviously, like sin, it is not good in itself but simply for what it intends. In sin's case, at least, the results can be seen; with suffering, its goodness can seldom be located in the present.

22

GRACE

A. THE RECONCILING WORK OF LOVE

The problems we face in trying to understand Christianity come to a head in any attempt to deal with the concept of 'grace'. This term has in many ways come to be uniquely associated with Christian doctrine, and in itself it does represent what Christianity claims has been accomplished. In order to understand what 'grace' means, perhaps what is most important is to grasp what has been so decisively changed that it radically alters our previous condition. The unique and revolutionary work of Christianity focuses on an understanding of 'grace', and yet for this reason it cannot be understood simply on its own terms but only through a result achieved. What is commonly spoken of as 'grace' is only the end-product of an activity that somehow has yielded radical change and an alteration of status. Yet in order to understand this, we first have to step backward and ask "What is it in us that first needs to be overcome?"

If men are sufficient in themselves, and if they feel no need for any change other than those readily achieved by human activity or some evolutionary process, the assertion of a divinely accomplished change is not likely to be taken very seriously. If men feel no bonds restricting them from the relationships they would like to achieve, freedom from these bonds will seem either not very real or at least not severe enough to require God's action. Grace, then, becomes meaningful only in opposition to the feeling of a need for release by the aid of an exterior power in order to be able to complete life as we would like it. This does not have to be defined in an identical fashion for each man. The only important point is that, before grace is understood as a theological concept, a personal assessment must be made and a decision reached as to whether it is possible for us to free ourselves to achieve desired relationships.

After determining the necessity for a reconciling power (those who feel this need are religiously disposed; those who do not are not), we must understand what 'reconciliation' accomplishes and how it does its work. 'Reconciliation' always means that a previous hostility of mind or estrangement of spirit has been put away by some decisive act. If we accept this definition, it is clear that we often accomplish such a result for ourselves among our fellow men. The issue is whether anything more is required where God is concerned. Furthermore, are there also crucial and decisive situations in which this cannot be accomplished by us on the human level effectively enough to overcome what stands in the way of man's fulfillment? In Christian terms, it is clear that this reconciling work, this changed relationship between God and man, is taken to be the result of the death and resurrection of Jesus. However, this in turn is only understandable in terms of the nature of love, both divine and human.

According to the Old Testament, love in God is represented as his continued faithfulness to his Covenant people in spite of their apostasy. His determination is such as never to let them go in spite of their betraying action. In the New Testament, God's redemptive love is always active to save those who have sinned and to maintain them in a relationship to him. However, even conversion itself is represented as a work of divine grace, so that God's love reaches out and turns around those who are no longer able to redirect themselves by their own will and power.

Love always implies a conquest by God of man's self-

centeredness. This cannot be the work of love as desire; it must be a love willing to place its own demands second. It moves first toward one who might otherwise never turn outward from himself away from his own desires and concerns. What needs to be done is to redirect the natural inward flow of man's affections, but this requires a love that moves by a different principle from ordinary love and also. one that is willing to act first without being solicited.

It is clear, then, that grace can be understood to the extent that both love and man's needs are defined, not to mention an insight into God's nature such that we realize what his responses are. Each of these may be conceived of in so many ways that, until these concepts are philosophically clarified and defined, grace remains ambiguous. This does not mean that Christian assertions about how God has acted are somehow the result of philosophical refinement. It does mean that these proclamations cannot be understood until the human context into which they are said to have come is first made clear. Since both love and man's needs are subject to a variety of interpretations, this is not a simple matter but rather one that tends to shift from day to day as theories about nature and man change. Thus, God's action may be consistent; it may even have been just exactly as Christians describe it. However, what it accomplishes and how it will be effective can only be determined by stabilizing what is otherwise basically a flexible intellectual situation.

If love and man's needs were not subject to such a variety of interpretations, the situation would not be so severe, but it would also not be so susceptible to divine action. *It may be only because love is very unclear that room is left for divine grace.* The uncertainties regarding man's needs may in themselves be what bind him and keep him from more independent achievement. Our possible differences of opinion are a main factor in opening disagreements and in developing estrangements. If love took only one form and if man's needs were uniform and consistent, we might not feel the desire for reconciliation so continually from our disagreements. We become estranged because our situation is indeterminate enough to allow us to take differing paths. In this situation, the reconciling work of love can be understood and it also becomes necessary. Recognizing this may at the same time make clear the relationship in which man stands toward God.

B. THE KINDS OF LOVE

If love were all of a kind, life would be much simpler, and the wounds inflicted by it would be less severe. Love takes many forms and not all of them seem beneficial. It would be nice if love were not so complicated. However, in order to understand 'God' and 'grace', we have to place both of them within an understanding of the types of love and how each one operates. We live in a confusion because love is constantly felt, and yet its kinds and its objects are not always clearly distinguished. Religiously speaking, among all the forms of love, how is God's activity to be discerned? Maybe if we can become clearer about the results of love we can see more distinctly whether God's action is anywhere present in our world. In the Old Testament, love simply means kindness and graciousness in general. Evidently, if you change your view on love, you also alter your conception of God's nature. *God will be understood as love is interpreted and then either accepted or rejected on this basis.*

As Plato points out to us so clearly in the *Symposium*, love usually means some form of desire, and often it is our desire to possess so firmly that there is no threat of future loss. In this case, love seeks to be as divine as the gods and to have its objects guaranteed to it. Such a need to possess draws the soul on and leads it to many virtuous acts, but this is always within the context of love's desire to possess an object in its own firm control. Love of this kind responds to the attractive qualities it finds inherent in an object, and it appreciates its objects for what they are.

On the other hand, love can also be not possessive. In this case, it is neither drawn out by the value nor by the attractiveness in the object; instead, it creates worth in its object because of its own presence. This is a love that shows itself by helping its object rather than by a need to possess and to enjoy it. It has become selfless. In doing so, it bestows value on its object as a result of its discerning interest and presence. In this situation alone, affection can flow outward freely without demand or restraint.

Although grace is often described as a "gift," whether it is will depend on the kind of love that lies behind it. There are many kinds of gifts, and some are not all good. Any gift that seeks to control or to possess or to enjoy is not the result of grace. At this point, we also begin to learn something about God and man. Since he is limited by his power in life and this is subject to need in his vulnerable incompletion, man is not easily led to give himself freely. Usually he gives out of need or at least out of recognition of a superior quality in the object. To bestow value on an object not clearly desirable in itself is more the action of a divinity, and it springs from God's superior power and lack of concern over preserving or enhancing his present position. This does not mean that God may not be appreciative or even have desires under certain circumstances. Nor does it mean that men are not on occasion capable of giving without demand. Such a division of love recognizes simultaneously both the unlimited source of the one and the restricted needs of the other.

The other issue at stake here is whether man is of himself capable of releasing such selfless love, or whether its presence is always the result of divine initiation. It is probably impossible to determine this beyond dispute, since all we see are the comparatively rare appearances of that love which does not seek its own enhancement. Love like this does appear in men; the issue is over its origin. Perhaps its presence is a result of the divine example, whether reported in Christian literature or in other religions. Yet even if it were of human impetus, it still seems to require something other than human effort to increase the effect of its presence very significantly. Desire to possess and to enjoy still is the predominant human form of love. This does not condemn it in itself. Everything depends on how it is used, but it should be distinguished from a divine love bestowed as a gift.

Love knows a variety of forms in human experience, but most of them involve a passion arising in response to a need or at least the recognition of intrinsic value or beauty. In these forms, love seldom is an unmixed blessing, since, of course, it is dependent on its object for sustenance. Because this cannot be an independent relationship, it may very easily become a competitive one. In these circumstances, we seldom can enjoy it without complications. Thus, we refer to the "pain of love," because the lack or the need involved often is painful, which is what Plato pointed out in the *Phaedrus*.

Love's complexities can get us into trouble that either partially or wholly destroys its pleasure. This does not mean that love is bad or not worth having, even though some men become so disappointed as to think so, but it does mean that love seldom comes pure and simple. Often the problems that accompany it spring from our limited human power which is not able to sustain either itself or the objects of its love. Love fails by being burdened with demands for a power that simply is beyond human capacities.

Love not given or granted for possessive reasons is free from such complications. Unfortunately, this can come only from a strong and a secure person who is able to give without fear of loss and who can offer himself without demanding security in return. Such a surplus of power men seldom have, for the object can be enhanced only if the giver is not diminished in the process. If his own stability is at stake, the gift cannot be offered without strings, and then the focus of attention shifts to the act of giving itself. This is ironic, since the whole aim of an enhancing love is to lift up the recipient without regard to prior merit and to make no demand on the part of the giver for his own return. Such love is both rare and difficult, and it demands reserves of power seldom in man's control. Such surplus and generosity are associated more with divinity.

C. THE FREEDOM OF LOVE

As Kierkegaard pointed out in his *Works of Love*, the paradox where love is concerned is that it tends to be commanded and yet, by its nature, it can only be given freely. On the human level we face this situation constantly, either when others try to find ways to force love or else when we try to act in ways that elicit it as an uncontrolled response. That this situation should obtain between men is not so strange. Being limited and always dependent on others, it is natural that we seek the support of those around us and that we should want this support to be emotional as well as physical. Such physical support as we need can be seen, but the emotional support we

require is harder to estimate and to control, and it is also more
difficult to be certain about. What can only be given freely and
without coercion, that we try to regulate simply because we
need to and are unsure of ourselves. Where God is concerned,
however, you would think that the situation would be
different.

God has commanded love ("Thou shalt love thy neighbor . . . "), and yet you would think that he would be so self-
sufficient that he would not need to do this. However, there is
an important difference to note. This command is given, not to
everyone in the sense that it is an inborn instinct in all, but instead only the few who accept the authority of those chosen to
represent God (for example, Jesus) are subject to command.
Thus, it is quite possible not to recognize any commandment
to love, since the binding force of this injunction comes only as
a result of having previously accepted some word as divinely
authoritative.

Furthermore, the most important difference is that human
manipulated love follows the normal channels of need,
whereas *divinely commanded love seems bent upon diverting
love into new channels*—for example, "love your enemies."
God also seems to command what can only be freely given,
but in his case his directive is for a different purpose. It is not
to protect and pad his own secure position. Rather, it is designed to teach us to relax our protective instincts and give.
Divine love has the peculiar quality of trying to convert us
away from ourselves.

Such commands as religion makes do not extend to all. Instead, the acceptance of these demands defines the community
of believers. That is, if we accept its authority, the pronouncement is designed not to bind our love but rather to push us to
experiment. Then we may discover that an obedient response
to this command to give is precisely the condition for the
freedom of love. This fact is, unfortunately, perverted by
Christianity at times (and by all men too). In this case, the
precondition of the acceptance of authority is made into an
excuse that tries to bind men to all sorts of actions and beliefs
which they might not otherwise engage in or accept. For instance, certain ritual performances and explicit actions on the
part of believers are treated as not symbolic of this new direc-

tion of love but as actions demanded in themselves. Yet, in spite of all the abuses of religious authority, it still remains true that the precondition for the discovery of both the freedom of love and its release from the human tendency to clutch at it and to hold it close for fear of loss is the release of the self for submission to some divine authority.

In order to understand this strange situation, one so subject to perversion and abuse, we perhaps need to ask "What binds us so that love alone can offer release, and what natural tendencies does love have that must be cured before even love can serve as the instrument of freedom?" To begin with the second question, love in men tends to conserve itself and to hold itself in. It reacts in this way the more it discovers its limited supply and the more it experiences a few rejections and losses through expending itself on unworthy objects.

Life, at least for most of us, teaches us caution and not expansive distribution, so that we tend to restrict our expressions of love rather than to increase them. After being hurt in unsuccessful love, we can hardly bring ourselves to give it to family or to friends, let alone to offer our affection to wounded strangers or acknowledged enemies. Mental hospitals are full of this inhibited love no longer able to express itself even when it would like to. Love becomes increasingly bound and restrictive in its scope, and, until this natural tendency is reversed, neither it nor we who possess it can know freedom.

To return now to the first question, we ought to be able to discern the vicious circle in which most men and women become caught. We are bound up tight as persons to begin with, and we cannot release this knot by increasing self-concentration, self-protection, and restriction. Even the love we seek to soothe our frustration and to satisfy our needs only increases this rigidity—that is, it does as long as it seeks only to secure itself and to command. Love is paradoxical in that it simultaneously contains within itself the desire to dominate and the generous impulse to give freely.

Within these alternating cycles, most men are caught, and only love in its aspect of freedom can release us. Yet, love in the sense of self-centered desire must itself first be set free. And in order to be free—it turns out surprisingly enough—it must be commanded. Otherwise it will simply yield to its self-protective side and end by strengthening the fetters that restrict us rather than working to release them. Unless love first is directed away from itself by responding to a command, it cannot detach itself from its selfish desires, and it cannot be released nor release us to turn outward to give without reservation. The person who rejects all commands ultimately cuts off love.

Due to its dual and mixed nature, love must be separated into its parts by something other than itself. Love as self-giving cannot be released from love as desire-for-protection-and-satisfaction unless it is commanded to turn away from itself by a power superior to the self—that is, by a divine authority which it respects. That is why introspective concentration upon self-knowledge is potentially so dangerous. Unless it can yield, the self will exhaust itself in trying to satisfy insatiable demands by limitless pleasure. When love recognizes and responds to a commanding presence, it can venture and trust itself to be held secure from loss. If left alone, it circles around and around inside itself and cannot break the magic spell of self-absorption. *The cords that bind the self to its own desires must be cut from the outside.* On a human level, this can be accomplished by the response to love and care whenever it is spontaneously offered by another. On a religious level, complete release is secured only by the response to a divine command.

'Grace', as the giving of love and thus as the enabling power for others to be released from a self-love of desire, has a special quality. This distinguishes it from its human counterpart, the outgoing love of one man for another, which can secure only limited release. That is, in God's case the Christian discovery is that both the love and the command are "unmerited." If this is true, of course, it is a reversal of the natural law which we discover in our experience of human intercourse. If we overlook the unfairness of some systems of economic and social rewards, even on the intrapersonal level where love is concerned, affection usually is given in proportion to the merit and desirable qualities of the individual in question. As Plato points out in the *Symposium,* love is love of the beautiful, and in this sense it is instinctively aristocratic and conscious of a hierarchy in value. If we simply follow love's emotional guidance, we learn where beauty lies by observing our instinctive response to it, but this tendency certainly is the opposite of bestowing love where it is not deserved.

We have even sometimes thought that the natural ladder of value discovered by love will lead the mind toward a God who is the source of all value and goodness himself—for example, Saint Augustine and Saint Anselm. If it does, it is not the Christian God whom we reach by this process of response to beauty and goodness as we discern its presence in the world and its hierarchical structure among men. This is why Christians speak about a "revelation," because the message is a surprise and not what one ordinarily would have suspected, or even discovered for himself: we hear that God is *not* represented by the normal value structure of the world and that he, instead of giving his love according to the merit of the case, offers love equally to all without regard to value.

In a world strongly oriented by aristocratic and selective norms, one would not expect to discover such a democratic God. It is, then, not possible to discover him in the world's process. It must come in spite of the way in which men naturally behave and respond to what is placed before them. The world's value structure tells us much about how men behave but little about God's more unusual actions. In this sense his love is "unnatural."

Of course, this divine way of love, one that commands those who accept its revelation, is not totally opposed to human instincts. Human ways are too complex and diverse for that to be possible. Thus, within men's emotions, we find already present a strand to which this command to reverse love's direction can find both a response and a means to penetrate further into man's nature and alter his structure. No conversion can be accomplished without some interior basis to work upon. The conversion of love to new ways must be accomplished from within; it cannot be imposed by force from without. That within man that responds to the divine command of love, which is to surrender its self-concern and thus discover its release, might be called "compassion." 'Passion' is its correlate, and it is this that involves and dominates the self when it seeks its own satisfaction, no matter whether its results are pleasing and satisfying or simply frustrating.

'Compassion', on the other hand, can have the force of passion, but it differs by being built upon 'sympathy'. We do at times lose our self-concern momentarily, and, when we do, we find our emotion involuntarily directed outward because it is caught up in the distress or the suffering of another creature. However, why does this very human instinct of compassion for those less fortunate, for those who are trapped in trouble or threatened with loss, not in itself convert love away from the self and direct it outward? Because it is one thing to *feel* the emotion of compassion in response to misfortune and a very different thing to *act* upon this instinct.

Occasionally we do respond to need without thought of our own jeopardy, but more often this instinct is prevented from passing into demonstrative action by the other side of love, one which fears involvement and risk and any exposure of the self's vulnerable powers. We do not always assist human beings in distress, and most often we become involved only when we can do so without risking our own protected position. We give easily only when we are aware of our superiority and sure of our prerogatives.

Only with the support of a divine command, it seems, can compassion really pass beyond momentary instinct and convert the self to an outgoing demonstration of love. Yet, in separating love as desire from love as outgoing gift, a divine command does have the original human instinct of compassion to build upon. Self-giving is not entirely alien to man. It is just that this instinct is seldom strong enough in itself to work a total conversion of the direction of love and thus gain the release of the self. The 'unmerited' quality of God's love as it has been announced—that is, that it comes by gift and not as reward—this has the power needed if we are to build upon the human instinct of compassion and release love by controlling it. The freedom of love is found only in an involuntary response that carries the self outside of its own restrictions, but this happens only when instinct is sufficiently strengthened externally to gain the power to become action. Love, since it is based on emotion, cannot be free if it exists only in thought. It must be released if it is to be love—that is, to act that way in fact in human involvement.

The concept of 'grace' centers around the discovery, one

made by Paul and Luther and all who are converted to Christianity, that God's favor is entirely free. That is, it comes nevertheless when it is wholly undeserved. There is no obligation of any kind that God should be compassionate in this way. His love is not distributed according to merit but according to need and to the responsiveness it requires.

Israel benefited by God's special protective relationship over them in gaining their deliverance from bondage and in establishing them as a nation. By way of contrast, the Christian's discovery is that all the wealth of God's Covenant love is now available to every man and not only in proportion as the Law is fulfilled. Righteousness is not achieved as an effort and as the result of a long project to which God then responds with favor. It comes as God's free gift, and, thus, those who receive it are amazed because its availability is not commensurate with their merit. God's freedom extends to enable him to reverse the normal conditions of love. Thus, his action in this regard is never without the quality of surprise.

God's love is intended for the world in an unrestricted fashion in a way true of no human intention or commodity. We men are always plagued with the condition of a shortage of supply and an abundance of need. This necessity to conserve our resources, both personal and social, is perhaps the greatest single factor that leads to love's tendency to turn in upon itself and to become desire rather than to move outward in compassionate self-giving. Yet, even though this is the Christian's discovery of God's unrestricted intent, such love can only work through a mediator and a chosen body of disciples.

The discovery of the freedom of divine love does not eliminate justice, and it is this struggle to keep compassion in balance with a strong sense of divine fairness that has always perplexed Christians. This revelation of the outgoing quality of God's love requires Christian believers and theologians to turn immediately, not to celebrate a lack of all restraint, but to reconcile this generosity with a sense of justice. The freedom of love does not involve an overthrow of the demands of justice, but a divine outpouring of love itself justifies.

In spite of the Christian announcement of this unexpected

quality in the divine nature, all restraints and requirements are not broken. What is discovered is that God both demands and himself offers to satisfy these demands, although through a means not always seen or accepted. We insist on performance from ourselves and from others. Sometimes we lack the means to fulfill our own demands, and often we even demand more than it is possible for others to give. Sometimes our demands are accompanied by offers of assistance, but more often they are not.

We do give our own services when our love is compassionate rather than made up of desire, but we restrict this kind of support to a very few persons and circumstances. Even if we were more generous, our resources to give are limited so that we could not extend our offers of help very widely or freely even if we wanted to. This is the source of man's ultimate frustration over the attempt to seek social justice. It is this discovery of the unrestricted freedom and limitless power of God's love in the face of the demands for justice that men call "grace."

D. THE RESPONSE TO LOVE

Faced with unexpected divine immensity, the question becomes "Does such love require or determine its own response?" If it does, we have the amazing circumstance that what is freely given in the process also restricts or cuts off the freedom of the person to whom it is given. Of course, this is quite understandable, since it is a very human complication that our love is often a two-edged sword. What someone gives generously overwhelms or obligates us, and this restricts the freedom of our response. Many a child lives the life of a psychological cripple because he is blessed (and cursed) with overly generous and too-giving parents. A superabundance of resources is not always what provides the greatest freedom, as Americans have learned to their horror in the midst of the greatest luxury ever known to man. Of course, the world God designed and selected offers that problem to very few, and the love he gives is not always demonstrated materially. Nevertheless, even in spiritual and emotional matters, excess can stifle and inhibit just as much as material overabundance. Therefore, the question of the determining force of God's offered love is still a serious matter for human freedom.

Perhaps one answer to this can be found in the indirect method chosen for God's manifestation of his grace. The direct confrontation of man with divine power would paralyze all human effort, but, according to the Christian account, God presented this offer of justifying love in a concealed and an indirect form. The offer is genuinely open, but it is not heard or recognized by all. Because the forms in which God chose to manifest his outgoing nature are unexpected (for example, via a carpenter's son and crucifixion, among others), it is always possible for any man to reject such power because he does not recognize it for what it is. Man can fail to respond to its presence and thus remain unmoved by what, if directly confronted, has the power to deaden or determine all response. What happens as a result of the discovery of this freedom of love in God's nature is a serious question whose answer remains uncertain. However, fortunately for man's freedom (and also for his obstinance), its disclosure is unorthodox enough so as not to force the recognition of its presence.

The exercise of divine forgiveness and the disclosure of the Gospel's message, both are intended to elicit a response, but this reaction does not involve a prescribed and an overtly determined behavior. It is dependent on faith on the part of the hearer. That is, since the gift of love is not blatantly evident to all, and since, in fact, the freedom of God's love moves in ways counter to natural expectations, it requires great trust on the part of a believer that this is the truth about God's nature, his actions, and his intent. *Any manifestation of God is nondeterminative, because it is clothed in such nonobvious form that it is both easy to reject and hard to accept.*

Those who see through this and who respond may build up a new divine community by the activity of the Holy Spirit. Then the sphere of reconciliation becomes an experienced reality. The source of the reconciliation is God's manifest love, but, since its presence is not controlled by externally fixed signs, it most often is experienced before it is known to be real. It is often recognized only later by what has been built as its result.

Love that is commanded, since God's message takes the

form of a demand, involves the response of a man in whole and not in part to the prior love of God. However, this is a difficult offer because of its nonevident character. It has to be discerned or heard (for example, when preached) before it can be responded to. 'Love', as it exists in God, and 'faith' largely overlap, because man would have nothing to have faith in unless something had first been offered. *Faith cannot mean hurling oneself into nothingness; it takes on meaning only as a response to love offered but not coerced.* 'Faith' in a Christian sense is trust in the disclosure of the freedom of God's love and its power to convert the direction of our own love, even when these facts can never be evident to all.

Given such circumstances, love becomes the mark by which those who are truly disciples of Christ may be recognized. It is not by their words or verbal pledge but by their *actions* and the direction of their affection that Christians are made evident to others and to God. This conversion of the natural self-centered desire into outgoing compassion is the sure sign of God's presence in Christ—and also in men. When the direction of a man's affections have been converted (which is the only true meaning of 'conversion'), then he has become Christian. When they have not been, then he lacks the only genuine sign, no matter what office he occupies or the strength of his external professions.

Love is also the mark of the church, since that community is created by God's reconciling love, and all those who are converted by this love in the direction of these affections become members of that group, whether they know it consciously or profess it with their lips. Christianity is a pragmatic affair; it is not, in its operation, an intellectual matter. Those who have been reconverted by the manifestation of God's love, and then have had their own love reoriented, are disciples by their actions and members by their condition. After the change has been experienced, of course, they may reflect on it with their minds and also express it to others in their words.

In a sense, the response man gives to love may involve entering into God's life, in the sense that our reconstituted human love has now been shaped by the divine example. Men come to participate in the divine nature by being made to be like it through the action of God's compassion and its radical surgical effects on their desires. God communicates himself to us in his own being because his nature is discovered in the freedom of his love. Insofar as our love is released to be free, we have also received God's communication. We cannot share in God's nature (that is, be one in the body of Christ) until our inner directed desires have been broken and turned outward. This we seldom can or even want to accomplish for ourselves. Thus it depends upon our response to a prior disclosure on God's part. *Men understand the divine nature in being changed by its outgoing love so that they learn to love like that.*

Under such circumstances, the response to love can itself be free and not coerced. Granted that it is not free in the sense that man is unable to achieve this total conversion of affection by his own power, it is 'free' in that God's action is lost unless it is responded to. Love is commanded by God, but that demand can be repulsed. Most often this is because it remains unrecognized or is ignored, but sometimes it is thwarted by vicious counterattack. This ability to resist God is man's most fearsome power, both for himself and his own welfare and also for his actions toward others. He can reject all solicitation and enclose himself within himself; he is perfectly capable of refusing to break out to respond to any offered affection. He can become catatonic. Then he is truly untouchable, and even God's outreaching affection cannot break through.

This power to resist God is man's greatest weapon just because it can repel the greatest possible force. God could smash such resistance, but that would crush the spirit in shattering its protective shell. Unless man is willing to venture out from behind his improvised shelters, even God's love is lost on him. The greatest question of religious preaching is "How can man be induced to venture so that he might experience what otherwise he is cut off from ever realizing?"

Love is such that it can be offered, but its response is free, as free to reject as it is to accept. We often do not allow others to do for us what they want to do. Then they are helpless if their good intentions are not properly received. Of course, to venture is to risk damage, to run the danger of being hurt if the intentions of the other person should prove to be false. We are afraid. We hide our responses or cloak our feelings for fear that they will be wrong or their honest expression will leave us exposed to damage. To respond to love requires a sensitivity that all too easily is bruised and lost and then is beyond recall. The first move of compassionate love is to reawaken sensitivity and to inspire trust again, like the "growing of wings" Plato describes in his *Phaedrus*. This depends on human initiative, and for that God is always dependent on men. God's love is divine, but the preparation for its reception is always a human act. If it were not so, we might neither see nor be able to receive such immensity without being overcome. Our freedom is to accept change while remaining both ourselves and human.

E. THE REVELATION OF LOVE

What we need to understand most is how anything regarding love not normally visible can be brought to light. There is so much that can be seen and felt about love. Yet, it is a curious fact if, in this special case, it cannot be grasped until it is disclosed. Sometimes a woman has a hidden lover who admires her from afar with his eyes, but on the whole the presence of love is usually all too evident, even if sometimes we are confused over what to do about it.

The Christian claim is remarkable in saying that divine love is the most hidden and the least suspected form of all and that it cannot be fully known until it is revealed. The time and form and place of this revelation waits on God's pleasure, and this evidences the fact that he has a stronger control and restraint over his love than most men are ever able to exercise. It is strange that the greatest passion of all should be subject to the most powerful control, particularly when our world is recorded evidence of the damaging effects of uncontrollable little passions.

In the case of Christians, they claim to know this love of God through the self-revelation of this fact in Jesus of Nazareth. To be a Christian means to see and to have felt the transforming power of love in that location, wherever else others may claim to have found love too. Jesus reveals God's love by what he is and says and does, even in his death; and God evidences his love by what he does to Jesus—that is, to release him from the bonds of death. Human love as desire causes crimes of passion that rain death down upon our heads daily. The divinity of God's love is evident in its restoring qualities and in its strength not to increase death but to overcome it. Love is known in its life-or-death qualities.

In the case of Jesus and his disciples, it is only after Pentecost that the full significance of his person and his work become clear. Here again, the indirect and noncoercive quality of divine love is evident. At Jesus' death, the Disciples felt the end of love and not its beginning. Even in his encountered resurrection they did not grasp the full significance of the revelation. Only as the power of the Holy Spirit possessed them on Pentecost did they come to realize either God's presence or his accomplishment.

Evidently, God's love must do its work first before its power or presence can be grasped—when we look back to report what has happened to those whom it touched. In spite of God's amazing action (for example, against death), it requires possession by the Holy Spirit to stir us sufficiently in order to recognize and respond to what has taken place. What stands in constant need of revelation is precisely that which our natural expectations do not predispose us to see and what they actually inhibit us from discovering.

Thus, God's love would seem to have an unpremeditated quality about it. That is, it is so disarming in its action that it is hard to recognize as it moves. We are usually alerted to the direction of men's desires, because these begin to be evident even before they lead to action, although we are not always as sensitive as we should be in discerning this direction and preparing for it. Whenever our love seeks its own purpose, it is most easily found out. However, if it genuinely seeks the good of another, this is hard to grasp because the normal interests of the self deceive us in this case.

Love can operate most freely when it is not expected and when its action is not anticipated. In this situation our defenses are down; we are off guard and vulnerable. They had no reservation for Jesus' mother at the inn. Such unorthodox behavior by God, his appearance under strange circumstances, this has to be seen in order to be believed or understood. Therefore it requires revelation for its disclosure. What is indirect and selfless cannot be anticipated but only known after its presence is revealed by being felt and then reflected on.

That is why we use the expression "to fall in love," because love's presence as selfless (vs. desire) always takes us by surprise. We had not expected it to be there when it came to light, and our response is to lose control in such unanticipated events. We fall in love and we fall in sin. Love always seems to come up from behind to seize us—that is, when it comes to us vs. when our desires reach out to grasp their object. In God's case the most startling fact is his personal condescension. Men are often too proud to evidence their need or their love; but the strange fact is that God, who has no need to do so, comes to us, rather than demanding that we conform to him.

God's appearance in human form is startling because it is so unaristocratic. It often goes unrecognized because we cannot understand such a strange reversal of order: that we who need to do not, while he who has no needs yields without pressure and moves first. This condescending quality is perhaps what is most unnerving, and it could not have been grasped without being revealed. We use love to force our way. God uses love to accommodate to ours. Surely we could not be expected to believe such an incredible story if it had not actually happened to us—or to our friends.

As Freud clearly demonstrates, 'love' is a controversial concept, and its philosophical interpretation is a subject for a variety of interpretations. This is perhaps the most important way in which philosophy can shape theology. For, as love is understood, so the Christian message will be interpreted. This means that if love is misunderstood, we remain blind to the Christian revelation. Clearly love's ways are not obvious but become clear only by the aid of definition. Thus, *philosophy has the job of constructing the intellectual context within which love can be defined and grasped and made known.* As love goes, so goes Christian theology. Even if love is given to us, it is still true that it must be philosophically shaped before it is definite enough to form a part of any doctrine.

23

SALVATION

A. THE MOST PHILOSOPHICAL DOCTRINE

The deeply religious person may consider strange the announcement that what is probably the central religious doctrine, 'salvation', actually is the most philosophical of all theological concepts. In fact, he may want to deny that it should even be considered as a concept; he might argue that it is more an event or experience and not an intellectual matter. Yet the importance philosophy has at the center of religion is due to the uncertainty that is always involved. New Testament documents are neither completely clear nor agreed as to what salvation consists in. Of course, we are not left guideless, and much of the rest of this chapter will try to put together the meanings that can be given to salvation as it is derived from those documents.

However, of all the central Christian concepts, the greatest uncertainty surrounds salvation. This may be just as it should be, but still, in order to understand what 'salvation' means, we must first settle our context of interpretation so that all the material can be brought together in one focus. Furthermore, and perhaps more important, before we can know how to receive any assertion concerning salvation so that it may either affect or not affect us, we have to clear the way by removing any attitudes, outlooks, or beliefs that might block the reception. Thus, the philosophical disposition of the person to whom the doctrine is presented is crucial if we are to know how he will interpret 'salvation'. It is the most controversial concept just because it is subject to such a wide variety of interpretations and requires so much preparation to be received.

The most important concepts seem also to be the center of the most controversy. Notice in this text how many important theological terms are necessarily involved in order to define 'salvation'. Simpler and less important terms might require a less complex philosophical context, but salvation evidences its centrality by the way in which it serves as kingpin in the network of interrelations among important religious concepts. In fact, it is hard to say whether salvation is the result of the manner in which these subordinate theological terms are defined, or whether implicitly it guides the way in which other theological terms are interpreted and brought together.

As we proceed, it will be easy to see how holding certain philosophical views will either block or shape the acceptance of the meaning of these concepts, especially salvation. We must fight fire with fire; only a philosophical analysis can either unblock the resistance or open the individual to hear the meaning of salvation, and only a philosophical context can give salvation clarity enough to make its meaning forceful. Salvation borrows ideas from the current philosophy of any age in which it becomes powerful. The only question is who dominates whom.

B. A RESCUE FROM WHAT?

If, in considering the possibility of salvation, every prejudice is touched and every philosophical nerve is activated, perhaps we need to begin by asking "What is it that we need to be rescued from, and in fact do we all want to be extricated?" If other religions offer various forms of salvation, for Christianity salvation is connected intimately with the escape from *death*. It is impossible to treat the report of the *resurrection* in any other way. Death is considered ultimate for man, but now the report is that even this restriction can be broken. If the existentialists have taught us that the thought of death is instructive because only in such a boundary situation can we understand our limits (that is, our nature), resurrection as indicating an escape from death is equally illuminating about our *human nature* and what it can become.

Forgiveness, of course, is involved here: if man has earned his death, only an act of pardon can relieve him of this burden. The consequences of life have to work themselves out, forgiveness or no forgiveness, and so death cannot literally be avoided. We cannot accept facing the death we deserve as an end to life, so the question becomes one of the possibility of *restoration*. No life is perfect; thus, punishment for failures must be accepted in order for forgiveness to be possible. Where *God* is involved, the question becomes "How to preserve the fellowship between a loving God and a faithful people?" At this point our notion of God becomes central, since we must come to think of him as capable of such a relationship and of engaging in such action or else the notion of salvation will fail.

If 'death' is central in trying to understand what it is we might be rescued from, *life* must be understood before we can know what to be restored to life could mean. Given certain notions of what 'to live' means, it would be difficult to think of any such state being restored from death. For one thing, unbelief can be considered as a literal death even in life. If *belief* or *trust* is central to the meaning of life, to live without it is to exist in the midst of death, and this is a death from which we might be rescued. Even *Jesus* can be understood on these terms, since in his presence some men have felt themselves confronted by the living God. In this case, life takes on its meaning as an awareness of *divine presence;* death is its absence and a state from which we could be rescued only by being placed in God's presence.

If men discover this in Jesus, he can legitimately be said to *redeem* them. That is, by contact with him death is overcome through divine presence; men can live again. Of course, to say such things is to fly in the face of much empirical data and to go against some theories of man's nature. Before we can decide whether man's condition can be overcome, we have to agree as to just what this condition is and what powers can be applied against it. *Sin* is also involved, for only if it is taken as a block to man's nature does it make sense to see redemption as a cleansing from *guilt* and a release from the power of sin. If these conditions do bind man in servitude, they at the same time *alienate* man from God and create *futility*. If Jesus secures this release, he is the medium of redemption, and men belong to him in virtue of this action.

Only one who is threatened or oppressed needs salvation, and then this consists in deliverance from danger and tyranny or rescue from imminent peril. Given this situation, we can perhaps see the importance of a philosophical context for interpreting 'salvation', since we must first admit that human nature is in this much peril before the idea of release becomes meaningful. Unfortunately, our views of the human situation vary widely. We must decide what man's worst enemy is. Is it sin, and is man capable of self-deliverance? A *savior* can be accepted as such only when we first agree to the need for one. Before a people can be rescued, they must first feel themselves helpless. Then salvation can take on the aspect of passage from darkness to light, from alienation to a share in the divine life.

Slavery is the term prior to salvation, for men do have other problems and not all of them imply bonds that cannot be broken voluntarily. *Freedom* is the result of such salvation only if the bonds holding man amount to an involuntary servitude. Fear must be involved, and the hostile powers should be such that man is restricted and inhibited by their presence. Now salvation means *liberty* and an assurance of power sufficient to maintain man against what he fears will enslave him. We must ask "Rescue from what?" before we can decide to accept release or to believe in its possibility. Salvation is not a term that is clear in itself. It becomes clear and powerful only when the forces that restrict man are agreed upon and felt. Then their dispersion can be reported as release, as freedom, as salvation.

Since death figures as the primary power that binds man, we cannot understand what salvation from it could mean until we know what forms *immortality* might take. If this means only continued existence, that is one thing, and it is not a very likely prospect. It involves the Platonic concept of the survival of the soul after the death of the body. But, if life is not taken as fulfilled in a disembodied existence, immortality will have to take another form. In how many ways is life possible? This must be our question. One possible theory about this, which is determined by our philosophical perspective, is that immortality involves a renewal of body and soul together but under new conditions. In any case, it seems clear that man does not possess this quality of deathlessness from himself, and so he must either receive it by some new relation to God or not at all.

If sin separates us from God, death appears to have this same quality. Any reversal of this, certainly, is an incredible happening. According to the Christian account, God did not simply will a reversal of a natural law. Being himself not subject to death, he nevertheless tasted and submitted to death; but, unlike us, in doing so he destroyed it, or at least he made its destruction possible. For this to be the case, God must be thought of as the sovereign disposer of all that is. His *control* is constantly assured and nothing falls outside of it. At this point, it becomes clear that a theory of the divine nature is not secondary, but all important. Can God be so conceived as to possess both *power* sufficient to this task and a control of natural forces sure enough to accomplish it?

C. THE NATURAL PATH OF LOVE

Love seems naturally to involve the self at the center, so that, if salvation is said to be a free act of grace given without restriction, this might involve a *conversion* from the natural paths of love, a reversal of its normal patterns. In this situation, what happens to the person subject to such conversion? Clearly, the self would cease to be the center of every action and the person would be unconscious of himself. He would be free from its demands and now oriented outward. Love, even when it is conceived of as self-giving, can have the self at its center. All communication to others is not selfless, so that the salvation of the individual means his release from constant self-orientation. Then he is able to give himself selflessly.

In order to forgive, the self must first be overcome and be eliminated, since it is the self that has been affronted. Love is not enough to enable forgiveness to take place. Even in outgoing love, the self clings to its own; in desiring love, the tie is simply that much stronger. The self obtrudes itself between man and God—that is, the self that is locked in sin. Only if the flow of love is altered can the block between man and God be removed. Repentance involves a change of mind or intention, and this cannot take place as long as the natural direction of affection remains the same. We must ourselves forgive before we can hope for forgiveness from God. This condition cannot be met unless forgiveness is made possible by removing the self from the center of all affection, even the affection given to others. He who does not forgive cannot repent, but the normal self-centeredness of love blocks this.

To deliver, redeem, or free is an activity of God's, because man cannot by himself reverse the paths of nature. Our troubles concern our inability to forgive, and, for that to be possible, love must be redirected from its course. Love is an unknown enemy because it binds us to ourselves, and from such a naturally attractive enemy only a power greater than our own can deliver us. Love hands us over into the power of someone else whenever its flow is unchecked. If we are to be freed from our own oppression, Jesus must be stronger in attraction than love and capable of giving it an unnatural direction.

Divine *grace* has often been taken as an act of love, but in God's case, love clearly operates differently and even affects us unnaturally. Love in this one instance is not demanding; it does not tie us to itself or make us unavoidably and constantly conscious of its source. For good or for bad, affection normally binds, whereas divine love frees because it is not self-centered. In that sense, we do not learn more about God directly even by experiencing his love. Augustine said that sin meant to turn the mind from eternal to changing things, but he was wrong. It does not matter whether the objects are changing or unchanging, divine or human; sin comes, not fom the objects to which we turn, but from our inability to free love from its self-attachment.

As a matter of fact, many New Testament injunctions tell us to pay close attention to changing things and to their needs. The direction of our affection does split us into the City of Men *vs.* the City of God, but this is not because it is good to attend solely to God. *Goodness* comes through salvation which

frees us to love both God and man without the constant involvement of self in the flow of love. The difference lies not in
the direction of our attention, but in its *motivation* in the self.
As long as love is self-connected, forgiveness is not possible.
Only a change in the direction of love could allow us to become vulnerable in forgiving those who have not forgiven us.
Only divine love can overlook a threat to the self.

Conversion involves religious or moral transformation and
especially the radical adventure of trusting oneself to God.
This cannot come about as long as the self protects itself or
calculates its own safety. Only a change in the manner of one's
life could produce such a willingness to venture. The normal
routines of life dictate caution except for the thrill of momentary risk. Contrition is needed in order to break these holds,
but it really can only be powerful enough to accomplish such a
task when it develops as a response to God's forgiveness which
evidences his own lack of self-concern.

It is interesting to note that, in the Old Testament, it is God
primarily who is said to *repent*. As he is presented there, he
must be able to reverse his former direction and to change. A
rebellious subject who revolts, repents, and returns to serve his
rightful king, if God is taken as a model, might indicate man's
present wrong orientation in the *rebellious* way in which we
use love to feed ourselves. If *faith* means to return to God,
perhaps it is connected to sin, not as Augustine imagined, but
in the sense that to turn to God is to discover his selfless love
directed outward to all things. If we discover this to be true,
love of God can never rest in him as in another self. It exists
strangely as turned away from itself. Sin is not to fail to love
but to love self-centeredly. Faith is to trust God's vulnerable
and un-self-concerned love.

D. THE OPEN CRISIS

If we are a generation who have trusted love's natural direction as good, we may have closed ourselves to *salvation* as a
result. If salvation involves a rescue from bondage, we may
not even be open to receive such a change if love's direction is
left unaltered. In discussing the natural paths of love, we
noted the tendency of raw love to absorb us in self-concern. If

we trust love's instincts uncorrected, the last thing that seems necessary for love to do is to change direction or to engage in radical reconstruction. It may very well be that an open *crisis* in religion always results when love is not examined critically. Then we are closed to any goal but love's expression and satisfaction, and religion requires more movement toward a lack of self-centeredness and a desire for basic change.

If we consider the meaning of *judgment* in relation to salvation, it is important to note its connection to crisis. In this sense, natural love may be connected with, and upon occasion even prepare us for, salvation in the sense that so often it is unsuccessful. If love were never blocked but remained always successful in its expression, it would seldom produce an open crisis. As it is, love is so rarely fully expressed or entirely successful, which makes it the greatest producer of human crisis. Freud's whole psychoanalytic theory takes its lead from this point. In this case, the natural direction of love may open us to salvation when love's frustration makes it clear that we simply cannot go on as we are.

Religiously, we speak of judgment as the consummation of the world and of history as a whole. However, personally, judgment appears when love's inability to express itself brings the individual's whole way of life up for reappraisal. A great day of judgment may come in the life of nations from time to time, but, for individuals, this turning point often arrives when life forces a crisis upon us and threatens to bring natural progress to a halt. Religiously, we speak of a day of judgment when the righteous shall be restored and given the success and reward they failed to achieve under natural laws. Individually, our own attempts at righteousness may fail, and then a crisis can open us and make righteousness possible again. For Christianity, the character of this judgment is determined by the nature and the work of Christ. Because they are opposed to him, natural ways are brought to a crisis when it is clear they eventually will be judged adversely.

By *righteousness*, of course, we mean that which conforms to a norm, and, in a religious setting, this norm is God himself. In the case of love, then, in order to be righteous human love would have to discover divine love, perhaps in Christ. In the crisis of judgment that is induced, love can discover its ways to be deficient and come to desire a change in its basic mode of existence—that is, salvation. If we tend to think of righteousness merely in ethical terms, we miss its central religious significance. If we consider it to mean performance according to some established norm, we also fail to catch its significance as involving radical reorientation. Righteousness is not something that will naturally happen. It concerns the helpless and our benevolence toward them, but it is natural forces that produce the poor in the first place.

If there is to be salvation, God himself must be active as the father of the poor and the helper of the helpless. Left to normal ways, men do not achieve a radical reorientation of values. If God is to vindicate the helpless, his benevolence can only be shown by changing the usual self-centered direction of love. As a result of any such action, a new standard of conduct may be produced, but this will be the outcome of the transformation that salvation represents. Considering Christianity, then, we might ask "In what way did Jesus' coming, his presence and his conduct, induce a crisis through his judgment of natural human ways such that he opens us to a radical reorientation? Love's tendencies, when they go unchecked, constantly lead toward crisis, but does Jesus judge us in a way that produces crisis openly?"

Strangely enough, in order to understand the crisis produced by love's ways, it must be connected to *joy*. Joy is the emotion of release and particularly of release from self-attachment. In this case, unreconstructed love cannot yield joy for, however satisfying, love binds us to its object and to ourselves. For this reason, the beginning and the end of an affair of love may be characterized by joy but not its full flowering. In its initial stages, a new love frees us from our old attachments, but at that point we do not always expect simply to get a new bondage as a result. At its origin, we are released from love's demands and the expansiveness of joy can be felt. If, then, joy is said to be a part of our relationship to God, it must be because love in God has lost its human limitations.

Here again we discover part of the meaning of *grace*. No matter how exciting, love never produces joy at its height unless we are freed from self-concern by something outside ourselves. If joy is an integral part of any relationship to God, it must be because God sets us free from our own desires, whereas without him we cannot throw these off. God's presence, of course, has traditionally been associated with the *Holy Spirit,* so that the power of the spirit must be that it can cut the bonds of self-attachment. When love cannot complete itself naturally, a crisis is introduced. If God's presence results in joy, it must be because the crisis is broken when the Holy Spirit's presence shatters the confines of the self's concern and opens it to go out freely and yet without loss.

E. THE FUTURE INHERITANCE

Since salvation clearly involves coming to possess what now is not within your grasp, it also involves the idea of *inheritance.* More than that, this must be a future possession that comes to us as a gift rather than by our own efforts or powers. Otherwise, we would simply claim it now and satisfy our wishes. It is perfectly clear that Jesus considered himself as God's son at least in the sense of being his heir. In this case, it is through Jesus that later Christians themselves inherit the right to a life different from their present existence. Due to his action, they feel, they share Jesus' claim and are on a basis equal to him, although this is not a status they have achieved for themselves. However, whatever Jesus' position may be, their sonship is not physical; it is based on their faith in him as the means to new life.

In its orientation, all such talk of inheritance is *future.* It is not yet; any follower has no more than the downpayment that seals an agreement. The maturing of the contract is set for an indefinite future date. And this promise of a new future takes on a strange form in the present, and this unusual quality is what demands faith if we are to believe in it. That is, humiliation and suffering accompany its present state and indicate that we are not yet in possession of new life. This is particularly strange because the present sign of a future inheritance takes a form that would seem to deny it. We are not allowed to celebrate fully too soon. In that case, it is easy to understand why others cannot see what is not yet manifest and whose coming signs are almost a reversal of the predicted future inherited state. It should be hard to comprehend what such a "new world" can be like if humiliation and suffering are its present manifestations.

At this point, we discover the *eschatological* significance of salvation. Clearly, if a new order of life is to come, the present order must pass away. If the new order in any way is already breaking in upon the old, *this might create the upheavals that would explain suffering and humiliation as its signs.* New ways that require the death of old orders are greeted with resistance and inflict pain, just as we learn in our own revolutionary times. If salvation in its completion is always future and never present, and if the new age has already broken in upon the present without yet being able to replace it, its presence will be accompanied by violence and *pain* and the resistance that causes suffering. We may look forward to a full and complete realization of new life, but that is possible only when this age has been brought to an end and broken apart.

Perhaps this is the reason why saving work can only be carried out by *suffering*. Salvation has remained essentially an object of hope ever since the dawn of the Christian era. It means to have victory in the battle, but, if decisive victory lies only in the future, its partial presence now, ironically, only causes suffering. We need to possess the strength to act upon hope so that salvation can become manifest, but today we may have only sufficient strength to cause suffering in the midst of incomplete change and the chaos it involves. All that comes into being suffers, as Kierkegaard noted, so that the unrealized presence of new life in the midst of old ways will induce suffering in the struggle for a not-yet-successful radical change. New life does not come smoothly.

Yet if suffering alone characterized a partially present salvation, it might not forecast a very attractive new life. *Hope* is the other essential characteristic involved here, since some suffering is due to unrecoverable loss as well as to attempted new birth. The suffering of the Christian is strangely connected to hope, since he puts his faith in eventual victory and new life. In the stories of the New Testament, the theme of hope is not found prior to the Epistles, since Christian hope is founded on the resurrection. Here too its strange connection with suffering can be seen, since the passion and the death of Jesus put an end to the Disciples' hope for a restored kingdom which would be led by their Messiah. His crucifixion clearly put off any new age until some future time, since he had lost his bid for present leadership. Yet, suffering this loss somehow came to be connected to hope in a future new life.

Hope indicates a future *consummation*, and faith must mean our trust in God's power to accomplish this in time, in spite of all adverse present conditions. Since salvation is not yet apparent, it requires a patience with *waiting*. Our prospects for this world and its life are not necessarily improved at all by any action on God's part. Thus, if we possess such hope in an unseen and radically different future, it is a virtue that must be of God's making and not ours, since it is against the present natural state. Hope itself must be eschatological—that is, it always has reference to the future accomplishment, and it is not tied to any necessary complete present transformation. Much, of course, may be changed in the present day, but the basic human and natural framework remains as yet unbroken.

Whatever is to be true of the future cannot be totally missing in the present. If this is so, what present fact is hope based upon, and where is this new structure to be found? Traditionally, we have expressed this as a "change of heart." What before seemed impossible (for example, a changed human nature), we now hope for as a result of God's action, not ours. Such faith expresses itself, not only in confidence and hope, but also in believing that it will be true and in confessing this. This is why faith results in *preaching*. It is not self-oriented but other directed. Such hope cannot be contained within the self; it must be announced.

If justice means conforming to God's mode of love, such transformation must be a divine gift (a grace) and not a human self-annihilation and transformation. We do not, however, simply come to possess this future hope. It comes as a result of what we hear; it is based on the testimony of *witnesses*. Faith is the beginning of human salvation, but it remains faith because the confirmation of its inheritance is always future—that is, as long as the present age remains. We may see contemporary evidence of a new life not based on present principles, but we can only see this in part and by fragmentary glimpses. Our trust must be in those who have witnessed some present effect of an in-breaking power sufficient to transform life. This must both have the outer appearance of destruction and even be accompanied by destruction, but joy remains in the hope for a new life yet to come out of the transformation.

F. THE CONVERGENCE OF BEGINNING AND END

After he has struggled with the meaning of Jesus' life and work, perhaps the main question that remains to haunt the convinced Christian is "In what sense is the *kingdom of God* present whose coming Jesus announced?" It seems clear that our answer lies somewhere in-between denying its full and complete presence and ignoring the sense in which it may have arrived, even if it has not come so as to exclude the present natural order. We live in an age in-between, and our understanding of this suspended mode of life will depend on our ability to state and to realize in what sense the new order has come and in what sense it remains unrealized or postponed for the future.

In this case, our understanding of salvation is always tied to the doctrine of creation and to our view of last things. (See Chapters 1 and 6.) *The extent of our ability to allow ourselves to consider creation and eschatology will measure our degree of understanding of salvation.* Our grasp of the problem of creation tells us what part of the new order can be present now and what aspect of salvation must remain for the end of this age. We have to ask ourselves "What is the 'new way' of God's rule which can be discerned now?" Certainly any such kingdom will have to be germinal rather than complete. God's drawing near always first has the effect of breaking us. That is why salvation cannot come without a prior crisis, and that is why suffering (of the kind accompanied by hope and not despair) is, ironically, the first evidence of the presence of a new way. The coming of the kingdom announces itself in suffering that becomes meaningful and is not simply senseless loss.

Such an approach provides us with an understanding of *prayer*. Prayer, for the Christian, primarily takes the form of a plea for the completion of the kingdom, whether this is asked for in the spiritual life of that person or for men in general

("Thy kingdom come"). If men possessed what they wanted, they would have no need to spend time in prayer. Yet, Christian divine petition is distinguished from other forms of address in that it is not self-concerned ("Thy will be done"). It strains forward to the day when the gift of new life can be completed and when men can be released from love's selfish demands. Prayer is necessary to accomplish this, since salvation is something God performs and gives, not what men build naturally by themselves.

The initiative to break (*vs.* to combat) the power of evil is up to God's decision. We struggle with varying degrees of success for various periods of time, but we do not, we cannot, break the present natural order, not even to save the obvious good in it—except partially and at special times. And if we are in doubt as to whether the kingdom of God has come near to us, we can discern its sign in the obvious crisis it has provoked. When we despair of the church's constant internal turmoil, we ought to remember that crisis within the kingdom is unavoidable in this transition stage. Just as any proposal for a new order provokes crisis in the everyday world, so God's proposal involves individual spiritual panic, since the first effect of the kingdom seems to be destruction of present life. Man's acceptance or rejection of this kingdom, when it comes near, is shown in his attitude toward Jesus, who is the initiator of the crisis.

The basic meaning of the 'kingdom' is "God's reign," so that in order to test its presence we must ask "In what sense can the natural order really be under divine rule at this time and in what sense does the world presently seem alien to God's nature?" God, of course, governs the world from creation without ceasing, but the meaning of the "coming of the kingdom" is that he has changed now and rules in a new way. If, according to visible political sight, no change is apparent, his new way of ruling must be less than overt ("The kingdom is within"). Perhaps the coming of the kingdom, thus, is characterized more by a change in God than in man, at least initially. God has altered his relationship and thus has opened himself to rule in a new form—eventually.

In this sense, God's kingdom can be said already to have arrived. God has taken a new position of control, and, if so, any new orientation in man is merely a response to God's change. In another sense, God's full reign, his externally renewed order, is yet to be established, and we pray for that. His kingdom's coming has not produced much noticeable outer revolution so far, because the first initiation was internal to God and thus did not force itself on the natural structure. In this situation, man's response to nonphysical laws can only be voluntary on his part. No man need conform to them in the way in which he would have to alter his behavior in the face of a new form of the law of gravity. If man is to discern any change, he will have to locate it in, and then respond to, nonvisible signs.

Of course, there have been some visible signs (for example, the life and death and resurrection of Jesus), but they are no longer in front of us. *Creation* is involved in understanding salvation, since the coming of the kingdom opens once again the possibility of achieving the original purpose of creation. Thus, if there once were visible signs of the coming of the kingdom but if these are not now present, then in order to comprehend what the presence of the kingdom could mean, we must first go back and understand the intent and purpose of creation. The coming of the kingdom is undoubtedly a central theme of Jesus' teaching, but today our first question is to understand what this could mean. *It can really only be grasped as a coming together and as a convergence of beginning and end.*

If the natural order has not yet been restructured so as to allow the achievement of the purposes of creation, can the presence of the kingdom be understood today as the establishment of a new authority in preparation for a new age yet to come? Jesus set himself up as a rival authority to that rule upon which Judaism is based, the Mosaic Law, and it is this claim to authority that both argued to his divinity (as the only source strong enough to overrule the law) and brought him to death on charges of blasphemy as a result. Jesus made it clear that he was interested in nothing less than the renewal of the world along the lines of God's original purpose in creation. In order to do this, especially when externally it is difficult to see much evidence of such transformation (for example, death now still has control), it can only be as a new authority for man that the kingdom has come. Beginning and end have not yet converged in a visible sense but only by the creation of a new invisible (spiritual) authority.

Perhaps this becomes more clear if we ask why the coming of the kingdom was announced as "good news." This meant that God had taken action to put straight the evil plight into which the world had fallen. Traditionally, this is thought to be the function of eschatology, or of a radically transforming last day. If such an event has come and renewed the purpose of creation, it can only be in the form of an announcement of a new authority. If God opens the way to rule directly himself again, this must mean that at first he put off some of his sovereignty by allowing evil to cause such deterioration. Then, later he asserts his creative sovereignty again, but only as a spiritual authority and not as a transformer of physical nature (although the resurrection is the sign of his intention to operate there too ultimately).

Jesus' fundamental message is that the day of God's reassumption of sovereignty has dawned, and, if so, our response ought to be to look to see in what sense this has occurred. If God's reign is here, or at least if it is so near at hand that the signs of his activity are already manifest in crisis, men must make some response to the claim this places upon them. Jesus' *miracles* are primarily one testimony to the return of a divine authority directly present. The appropriate response to this is repentance and faith, or trust in the continuation of God's kingdom until its authority is manifest in physical change as well as in spiritual impact. We cannot see the last day of judgment, and the day of creation is never directly visible. Nevertheless, in the announcement of God's present authority, the issue is whether in those words we can see and hear the convergence of first and last things.

G. THE POWER TO ACCOMPLISH

Crucial in the question of salvation is who, if anybody, has the power to accomplish the fundamental transformation required. The feeling that only God can accomplish radical reconstruction does not deny power to man or prevent him from achieving what he can in his day, but it is central to the religious attitude to feel that only God is strong enough to effect a basic change in nature's structure. Where salvation is concerned, everyone else relies on him. This is a distinctively divine accomplishment, and all understanding of our relationship to the divine is colored by such a realization. The theory of salvation does more to determine a doctrine of God for us than vice versa. If he is strong enough to save by radically reconstituting the natural order, we certainly learn a great deal about divine power from this.

We discover other qualities too. God must be ready to help those in need, at least in the future if not now. This indicates a divine *compassion* for man in his weakness, all of which tells us that God's nature must be such that compassion can be a decisive characteristic. God is capable of love such that, even against waywardness, his love continues as ours does not always do. Salvation, of course, involves a *healing*, a restoring of man to wholeness. In Christ's resurrection, salvation is experienced as having been realized, but as yet this is the only place to experience its complete presence. Otherwise it remains as an expectation. Sanctification and a renewed *holiness* can be experienced now. Since these qualities belong properly only to God, their appearance is always a sign of divine presence. Things are not by nature holy. By God's action they can become so.

If holiness is acquired only by nearness to God, we can be sure of God's presence by any experience of holiness. Or, if we are used by God as an instrument to accomplish some purpose, that action can take on the qualities of the holy. Such divine presence and transforming power is an action and a *sign*. From one point of view, salvation is complete—that is, it has been assured. From another—that is, insofar as natural forces and tendencies remain unaltered, it is still to be accomplished. The Old Testament has a lively sense of the presence of God from beginning to end, which is mostly couched in simple, anthropomorphic terms. Whatever God's ultimate dwelling place might be, he could be found on earth among men. The New Testament is equally full of such a sense of God's immediate presence and the effects this brings with it. However, it is focused more on the difficult concepts of the kingdom and of a salvation that is both present now and yet to come.

Glory is a term associated with God's appearance and thus with his actions. This phenomenon surrounds the way in which men apprehend God's presence on earth. If this glory is not so much here and now, but is a characteristic of the Messianic Age, it has become eschatological—that is, it is associated with a future event. However, glory also is experienced in the person of Jesus, and this is the sign of his divine power to accomplish. The vision of Jesus came in the same form that all visions of God have come; his presence produces change. For the New Testament, God's presence and its accompanying manifestations are localized in Jesus, whereas in the Old Testament it was in the ark and the giving of the law, among other circumstances.

Not all, of course, can see this power of God to accomplish, as it is made visible in the glory surrounding Jesus, but only those whose eyes have been opened to see. That is why salvation is spoken of as the *gift* of an ability to see God's presence. In the passion and in the resurrection, God's glory is more clearly revealed, but only to those who believe and place their trust in the witnesses to these events now past. God offers to bring men into relationship to him by giving them a share in the divine nature. That is why this new relationship requires that men be transformed.

Faith is involved in this action, since one must accept Jesus' announcement of the presence of what cannot be directly seen and have confidence in the person proclaiming this. The difference here is that it is said to be God himself in whom we believe. We become confident that he has the power to achieve a fundamental reconstruction of the natural order. Our faith stands or falls on the credibility of the person believed, but, since in this case it is God, our trust is such that it lays a claim upon all our subsequent life. We respond to a complete trust in his power by obedience. The deeds he has done (for example, Jesus' resurrection) testify to his ability to perform. Faith is demanded in order to recognize the signs of the new order now present and also to discern the inauguration of the final dispensation already begun by Jesus.

We need to discover the criterion for our right relationship to God. A direct personal relationship is essential, since the conviction and trust required are of a kind that normally come only from such direct encounter. We are asked to accept Jesus

—that is, his words and God's action upon him—as the direct basis for this relationship. We are to become obedient to what God prescribes; he must abandon self-reliance and self-interest and trust God completely. To do this requires faith, for as yet we only have the signs of God's power to accomplish and not the direct action of God to restore. Jesus asks men for a faith wherein there is the conviction that he will do what he has promised to do through the Prophets. Our trust rests in the unseen reality of God's help.

If salvation meant that God's action was thought to be already complete, the question of his power to accomplish might not be so paramount. As it is, our whole ability to accept the present reality of the transforming action of salvation depends upon our confidence in God's power to accomplish what is offered. In the New Testament, this confidence centers in the signs of the events surrounding Jesus' life, but it is also true that, behind this, there must be a view of God's nature such that he retains the power to control and to transform radically. Not only in the understanding of a crucial set of terms but in its picture of God's nature, philosophy again is central to a full understanding of salvation. If God's power is restricted philosophically, salvation may become an impossible action for him to perform.

H. THE NEW INDIVIDUAL

Whatever may or may not happen to the natural order as a result of God's saving action either now or in the future, it is clear that its central aim is the creation of a new (or a renewed) individual. In Jesus, in Paul, and in many others, the power of the kingdom of God to transform is already manifest here and now. Even if death still has control over life until the sign of the resurrection is fulfilled, it is still true that God's kingdom may be present and salvation effective in the radical transformations it can effect in the life of an individual. The kingdom, then, is made manifest in changed, powerful individuals whose whole lives are bent to overcome *evil*.

The kingdom of God can be seen neither in nature, nor in history, nor in nations, nor in institutions as such. Individuals are the locus of the kingdom and, if it is to be realized and seen as now present, this will be through a changed individual. "My life has been changed," that is, its disruption healed—this is the central Christian testimony to the kingdom's arrival. God is present only in persons, which means that Christianity requires from philosophy a concept of deity compatible with his possession of *personal attributes*. "Resurrection" may have natural connotations, but primarily it involves the raising up of new individuals. *Whenever men arise who are obedient to God's commands and who minister according to his will, there the kingdom is present and salvation is effective now.* Such re-formed individuals are not totally new, of course; it is simply that their original ability to promote God's creative purpose has been restored.

This, of course, is why *baptism* will always be a central Christian sacrament. It signifies rebirth, and this announces the message of the coming of the kingdom. The persons who go through this, certainly, do not either achieve their new status individually or operate alone. They work only as part of "the body of Christ," which is the same as to say that their baptism incorporates them into some church or community. Baptism in itself, of course, does not bestow new life, but it is the outward symbol of the hoped for and ultimately expected transformation. First, however, there must come repentance before the individual can be properly prepared, just as John the Baptist preceded Jesus. The Spirit, of course, is the divine instrument in the experience of conversion and baptism, so that all of this requires God's activity and presence.

Baptism also symbolizes a sharing in Jesus' death and resurrection. God's action and presence were visibly manifest at that time, and now we are invited to be united with him and thus to join in that divine act. The origin of the doctrine of the *trinity* rests on this point too. God the creator is said to have acted for salvation. His action expressed itself in man's adoption to sonship, and it acts in the future to baptize individuals through the powerful presence of the spirit. Baptism represents the descent of the Holy Spirit to effect change; it represents God's resumption of his reign. Thus, in order to explain both the coming of the kingdom, its contemporary presence, and the joining of the believer to Jesus in baptism, the full doctrine of the trinity is necessary.

Jesus most frequently healed the sick by the laying on of hands. In that day, just as in baptism now, that is the means by which the Holy Spirit is given. New birth gives the individual a deepened interior life. Grace has overcome his bondage to sin (self-centered love) which incapacitates him. There is need for radical renewal, but, if the new life is to be spiritual, it can only be originated by God. We can restore the color of our hair, but the healing of the spirit requires the mediation of a spirit itself already touched by divine renewal. All entry into a new interior life is intimately associated with the action or presence of the Holy Spirit, so that it is this presence that must be discerned if we wish to understand how an individual can be renewed.

Jesus is finally accepted as the son of God by those who become Christians; he is the Christ, the expected Messiah and the deliverer of his people. Israel became God's son through the events of the Exodus. In a later day, God has established a new relationship of sonship which is available to those adopted by Jesus, who is God in the form of the son. Such adoption into the body of Christ is only potential, however. It awaits fulfillment; it is a reality at present hidden, except for the transforming presence and healing actions of those men whose inner life has already been reconstructed. Baptism confers the status of participating in the sonship of Jesus, or rather it is the outer act and symbol of a sharing in the divine life which either is hoped for and expected or, in some cases, has already begun.

In any creation of a new individual, the key concept, which cannot be overlooked, is *obedience*. Developing a willingness to be obedient to God's will and seeking to understand it are the first steps toward salvation. Although the next phase will follow, but at no definite time interval (one may have to wait on God for some time), the new individual is changed precisely because his spirit has become obedient to God's will. He no longer fights. He follows God's injunctions as he understands them in the life and teaching of Jesus. To obey is to hear and to respond. Saul hears a voice on the road to Damascus, and he follows it. The right response to the word of

God is central, and thus the preaching of the gospel is always at the core of Christian work.

Jesus became himself obedient to God, and on his work salvation rests. By believing, men come to participate in the accomplished obedience of Christ. What God prescribes in present claim or future promise—that is what men are to conform to in humility. This *humility* and obedience need not be expressible by concrete terms in our relation to other human beings, but its orientation to God is unmistakable. The obedience of one has opened the way to counteract the rebelliousness of many. To be reconciled to God implies an act of submission of the self in which past sins are expiated. 'Obedience' becomes a technical term for those now joined to Christ as one body. In spite of our constant objection to restraint and all our talk about freedom, to become a new individual is only possible by obedience to God.

I. THE PHILOSOPHICAL BASIS OF SALVATION

Consider, as a final question, the importance of philosophy in defining the whole web of 60 terms each of which has been indicated above to be necessary for an understanding of salvation: death, resurrection, forgiveness, God, life, belief, trust, Jesus, redeem, sin, immortality, conversion, love, grace, free, faith, judgment, crisis, righteousness, joy, inheritance, eschatology, suffering, hope, kingdom of God, prayer, power, compassion, healing, glory, repentance, spirit, trinity, baptism, obedience, and so forth. If so many difficult concepts were not involved in a grasp of what salvation means, or if each were not subject to so many wide and debatable interpretations, salvation might be able to escape philosophical interpretation. As it is, a philosophical theory can block theology at every turn unless it is worked out carefully.

This certainly is not because salvation is a purely philosophical matter. Not at all, although according to some definitions of 'philosophy' it might come close to being this (for example, for Plotinus or the Stoics). The problem is, as Plato put it, that most of our crucial terms are subject to wide debate and to a divergence of opinion. 'Salvation' certainly is one of these. When such a variety of definitions and meanings is possible, the term (and the phenomenon involved) can only be understood by first clearing up our understanding of the wide variety of questions involved. Philosophy either prepares or blocks the way to our approach, and so it is neglected only on pain of the frustration of our aims—in this case, nothing less than the restoring of human life presently blocked.

24

WITNESS

A. HOW CAN THIS BE DONE?

For a book that claims to study how philosophy shapes theology, it may seem unusual to end by considering the concept of 'witness'. This would appear, and probably is, about as far from a proper philosophical concern as it is possible to go. Yet, if such concepts as 'God' and 'spirit' require philosophical structuring because they do not deal with immediately visible materials, and if the philosophical approach used to these concepts is crucial, it is interesting to note that philosophy is even more important for a notion such as 'witness'. Why, you may ask? With 'God' or 'spirit' it is easy to see the way in which the philosophical doctrine you adopt influences the shape of the concept. With 'witness', it is a case of whether we allow the very idea to enter religion as legitimate.

That is, if certain philosophical views shape theology, that activity may become a purely intellectual affair and thus be antithetical to such action as 'to witness'. Philosophy's influence actually is much more subtle—and also potentially insidious—when it simply excludes from the beginning certain notions as being outside the scope of its consideration. However, some philosophies (for example, pragmatism and existentialism) are much more connected to action in their basic concept, and thus they can be extended to include 'witness' without being forced to brand it as "unphilosophical."

Thus, when we come to consider the question of 'witnessing', we must ask both how it can be done and whether it can be done. Is this aspect one that is crucial to religion and, if so, how can it be provided and accounted for in any theology? In some instances, to arrive at a clear idea (for example, Descartes' notion of self-existence) is enough; but, in the case of religion, more than thought is involved. If so, how can a proposition that finally is affirmed as true be transferred to the realm of action or made evident in the nonthought world? Moreover, is it crucial to the very idea of religion that it should never remain unmanifested but must move outside thought? If it is, working out a connection between belief and action will be crucial to the very truth of the idea. *It may be false unless its presence can be felt as well as thought.*

This problem involves the way in which thought is attested to in action, as well as affirmed in the mind, and perhaps central to this are the traditional notions of 'vocation', 'call', and 'work'. These seem to indicate that the person who accepts the truth of the idea recognizes that doing so also involves a particular mode of life corresponding to it. In accepting religious proclamations, men have usually felt either that their lives have been changed by this intellectual fact or that they should be. A 'call' involves claiming a person for your own and appointing him to a particular destiny. In this case, the one who calls is felt to be God, and he gives a new name to the person that indicates this shift in his life's work. In many cases, of course, this may involve periods of waiting. Change may not be immediately evident, but, in due time, the person or the people expect to be called to their divine destiny.

To do a particular work as a result of accepting certain religious ideas includes the idea of a 'calling out'—the notion of separation in order to accomplish a mission. This means that no witness is possible without being separated. He must stand apart and live and work in ways not quite like everyone else. Such a calling, of course, is thought to mean to enter into God's kingdom and eventually also into his glory. In this case, it is crucial to see that any present separation from the ways in which other men live is not an end in itself or intended for present purposes alone. It is a preparation for and an anticipation of new ways expected to be inaugurated by God in a new age. It is really primarily to this expectation that men are called to witness. If the promises of Jesus were fully actual now, witnessing would be unnecessary.

Of course, we must ask upon what basis some are called out to be so separated, and the answer involves understanding 'grace' and how God's nature allows him to act in selective rather than always in general ways. If God is capable of such special selection, the medium for this communication is crucial; and, in the case of Christianity, such a call reaches certain men through the preaching of the gospel (see Section E). It is important that men should feel that such a call to separation and to a special life is actually "of God" and that it will not be withdrawn. To realize this involves a fairly intimate knowledge of God's nature and some sense of personal confrontation. Yet perhaps the most crucial element in all of this is 'hope'. Such a call is not a sentence to a life of drudgery. In order to be authentic, it must be filled with joy and with the expectation that, through such a vocation or work, this hope will be spread to others by your special instrumentation and the transformation begun in their lives now—even if in minimal ways.

In trying to understand how a witness can be made, how it can be done, at this point we come to the concept of 'ministry', or 'office'. An office is power in and for a community, so that one can minister (or be a minister) only in a communal setting. His power comes from and is exercised within that group, although it can reach outside its present confines to bring others in by its effective work. The ministry of priests in New Testament times was confined to sacrificial worship in the Jerusalem temple. Prophecy of the kind familiar in the Old Testament had ceased. Thus, it seems clear that Christianity is connected with a new prophecy, a new divine calling, which is intended to direct the office of ministry to a more active scope than temple worship. From its very start, Christianity necessarily involves the idea that ministry to others outside the sanctuary walls is a divine calling.

'Apostleship' is the answer to the question of how witnessing can be done. Originally, apostles were men appointed and sent out by Jesus with authority to continue his own mission. To understand apostleship, of course, we must first understand what we take Jesus' mission to be, but, in any case, it is fundamental to the idea of Christian ministry that men and women be sent out. The idea of mission is to participate in and to continue that movement of God toward men, which Jesus began and for which the early community called him "Christ." It is clear, then, that witnessing cannot be accomplished for the Christian simply by worshiping. Although this may be a necessary part, witness is not exhausted here. Witness involves being called, being separated out, and then drawing power from the community in order to speak out to others. The aim is to continue God's movement to man, his offer of aid to those who suffer, and our mediation too.

B. OUTER AND INNER ACTION

Perhaps the greatest confusion about the meaning of genuine 'witness' has come from the fact that action has two forms: inner and outer. Religiously, one must first be moved internally. Falsity in religion has always meant mere outer form, or action without inner conviction. This being the case, the inner change produced by religious belief can seem to the individual to be its own witness. If so, the slightly external form of religious ritual observance can appear to be genuine witness simply because it is an external act. Worship is a midposition. It is either the event trying to effect inner change or the inner change searching for its own form of external witness. Except in unusual circumstances, religious worship is not itself external witness, but simply the preparation for it and a necessary intermediate step.

There is an inner life that knows its own changes, but there is also decisive physical action. The idea of witness in Christianity always involves the concept of appropriate 'work'. When Jesus asked Peter if he loved him, Jesus indicated conclusively in his reply to Peter's protestations (and by the repetition of the question) that to be a Disciple involves more than to feel love. It requires work to feed the physical *and* the spiritual needs of those who are hungry. "Feed my sheep."

'Labor' must be involved and cannot be avoided in any genuine witness, and it must concern the needs of others, not merely those of the individual who feels moved. The Jews regarded work as a divine command from which no man was exempted; and now, for Christians, this labor must involve the relief of suffering if it is to be a divine witness.

If we are tempted to think of the religious life as one in which a man is supported by others, we might remember that each rabbi in New Testament times had to learn a trade to support himself. By requiring this, labor and witness were connected in an unavoidable way, whereas to allow physical ease in a religious life is to rob it of its quality of witness. According to the biblical story, it is only due to sin that physical labor, which should have been congenial and pleasant, becomes a hard discipline and a task. Thus, for the Christian, whose major inner change is a feeling of release from the oppression of sin, hard labor should appear to be a natural result of his conversion and the automatic form for his witness.

If in Christianity the person is made into a new creature, daily work should cease to operate as a curse, but become instead a glad and a free service. We should, then, be able to tell a genuine witness by the dedication of his energy, by its ease and lack of self-centeredness: it flows out freely to others and does not dwell upon himself. 'Service' is necessarily a part of witness. This always is accomplished partly by worship with the community, but it is equally involved with works of charity outside the walls. Just as life includes both inner and outer, so witnessing includes both worship and the hard work of translating outgoing love into action. Service is rendered not only in prayer but in life, in deeds as well as in rite. *A witness that is genuine can be discerned because it is whole, because it lacks neither side.* Action can be interior; the spirit is real and therefore powerful. It is just that witness involves more: action with a double intention and direction.

C. WHO IS AN APOSTLE?

From its very beginnings, Christianity has been closely connected with the apostles' witness, so that, if we want to understand what a witness must be in order to be authoritative, we need to be clear about who is or can become an 'apostle'. Of course, such a concept would be meaningless without the idea of being 'chosen' or 'elected'. If one could become an apostle by his own will or effort, it would be a quite different matter, and so we must always inquire as to where the call to apostleship comes from. In the Pentateuch, it is clear that God chose Israel rather than Israel choosing God, so that apostleship must involve the idea of original divine initiative *vs.* simple human effort. The choice is ultimately with God rather than with man; to be an apostle is to evidence this divine dependence *vs.* self-reliance.

To be either 'holy' or a 'saint' is to become—in that respect —pure or inviolable, but this can only happen by participation in the holiness of God. Thus, the genuine apostle has a sense of sharing in the divine life. He has become aware of that characteristic of God whereby men can be exalted. Those who are kind or godly or pious are so because of their duteous love for God, which reflects itself back in their actions toward others. Some element of their inner life or outer action has become associated with deity. As a result, it has been separated and cut off from profane contact or use. An apostle's work will contain this unusual quality which is not present in its secular counterpart in the secular city. To be affected by such action is to feel touched by God's nature and to be made aware of his presence.

Holiness, of course, is often associated with forms of ritual practice, but to treat these as anything other than symbolic is to be mistaken as to where holiness is to be discovered. Holiness is not found in ritual performance in church or synagogue, but is located in the spiritual transformation it represents. The New Testament times witnessed no considerable growth of new ritual practices; the idea of holiness is associated with inner change divinely wrought and with the outer charitable action that is its evidence. To be a Christian is to feel consecrated to God. To profess Christ and to be sanctified by the Holy Spirit is to become holy in that respect. All three members of the traditional trinity are necessary for discipleship. To be a 'priest' means to be one who may enter the presence of God. Since by Jesus' work every man may be sanctified and justified by God's grace, every man may be a priest—that is, become acceptable in God's presence.

To be a 'prophet', however, requires a special calling, one other than the priesthood of all believers; the prophet must be one who declares correctly and publicly God's self-revelation. Thus, it may be true that there is no special priesthood but only a few who are set apart from the community as prophets. If he is an accredited witness, he experiences God's self-communication, his coming to man, in such a way that through him this is expressed in a true and acceptable form. Many may experience God's activity in themselves, but few are chosen to represent this publicly by word. One can be a "silent prophet" who testifies, by his merciful actions, to his own lack of self-concern and his own correct possession of God's movement toward man. To give this a verbal form is strangely more subject to distortion and misunderstanding than is its presence in physical actions. The witness who is called to be a prophet must also have a rare philosophical skill and sensitivity. As Kierkegaard said of Saint Paul, he was not only religiously moved but also he had "a very good head."

Very simply, 'apostle' is the name that the New Testament gives to the twelve whom Jesus called to be his disciples, but it is also assigned to other missionaries and messengers of the Christian community. To be an apostle means to carry the message of God's decisive actions out to others and to recognize a special calling to such activity. Because of this, apostles have a unique function at the foundation of the church both in its development and as continuing witnesses to Christ. "Apostolicity" means the essential identity of every Christian community with the early churches formed by the apostles' activity. Any church is 'apostolic' if the word of God is preached in it, as well as from it, in conformity with the teaching of the twelve and Jesus' original commission to them rather than to any one individual.

Yet no one can be an internal apostle, since the office simply means "one sent forth." He is a messenger, and thus one especially authorized to act in a particular manner by the one who sends him. A sense of mission is essential to Christianity whenever it is in good health. If the sender is said to be God, his actions should represent the Christian revelation of God's condescending love and overcoming of death. It is interesting that Saint Paul's own right to be an apostle was challenged by his opponents; he had not been directly (that is, physically) commissioned by Jesus.

Just as Paul struggled to prove the authenticity of his apostleship, so must every one after the original twelve prove by word and deed his right to that title by the conformity of his actions to the original norm set down. Apostleship clearly was the highest office in the primitive church, but, within apostleship, it is clear that Paul was not prepared to recognize any further distinctions of rank. *To become an apostle is certainly not so much to be elevated as to be lowered and made equal.* This is the primary Christian office and experience to which all other offices and structures are derivative and subservient.

The chief work of an apostle originally was simply to preach the gospel to those who had not yet heard it, which means that an apostle can be identified by his preaching mission. At first, the true apostle had one necessary qualification: he had seen the risen Lord. Since that became no longer possible after the passing of the original group, today we must first ask what it means to "see the risen Lord" and what changes result from this experience? Here Saint Paul is the classical norm, so that every later apostle must use Paul as his standard more than the fortunate Peter. Paul's struggle to define and to prove his apostleship represents a trial every subsequent man must go through, and it is also the norm by which every claim to leadership is tested. This aspect of Paul's work no Christian can reject, even if his theology has debatable points.

In considering the biblical references, it is not possible in every case to tell whether "his disciples" means a small group who lived in close fellowship with Jesus or the larger body of all those who accepted him as their teacher or leader. Since the end of the pentacostal era, discipleship probably must mean both. It refers at the same time to the original group and to the change in their manner of living (that they shared everything together), which is a result of Jesus' call. Similarly, anyone who now comes to live in such proximity to 'Christ' becomes a disciple in virtue of that change. The later disciples can be discerned in the same manner as the first. Like all men, they are capable of misunderstanding and of error, but they are moved by God's effort to save Jesus' mission from failure. They respond to this divine action by communicating it to others in word and in deed.

D. TO WHOM IS THE MESSAGE TO BE GIVEN?

Since the full content of God's revelation did not become clear to the twelve until after Jesus' death and resurrection, no disciple lived in close physical contact with Jesus at the time he was a disciple in the full sense—that is, while preaching the whole gospel. Every disciple has had to live for a time separated from the presence of Christ, and thus the question arises to whom should his attention be directed in the meantime? The traditional answer to this question, of course, is "toward one's neighbor"—that is, the man in need. Yet, even this can be done for selfish reasons. Nonetheless, there is a true personal generosity that seeks out need for its own sake and not as a means to securing a private advantage or pleasure.

Neighborly love like this can only come by virtue of divine love. Left to himself, man is not capable of such selflessness. To be a witness in this sense means to share in the divine life and, in virtue of this, to be able to respond to need without self-reservation. In the Old Testament, one's neighbor meant a fellow member of the covenant people. It had moral associations and implied a reciprocal obligation and right. In Christianity, these same characteristics hold true, except that now the community is potentially extended to every human being regardless of race, creed, or background. This widens the obligation, and it also alters our conception of God's intent in the process. In a sense, who the recipients of this witness are to be is more clearly defined (that is, anyone), but this vastly expanded application also requires something more akin to divine love rather than human tendencies.

The question of to whom the witness is given involves the question of 'ministry'. This is not easy to solve, since the idea of 'authority' is inherent in such a mission. In any case, it is coupled with the concept 'to serve', especially in a personal capacity. We cannot be clear about how to minister until we can resolve the tension between one who is divinely sent to call others and one who is instructed to call by rendering personal assistance. *The paradox is the union of authority with the call to service.* Greatness in the community of disciples, it is clear, is to be measured by the degree of willingness to serve interests other than one's own. In the early Christian community, any conspicuous office, position, or work was essentially a ministry and a service to God and to the brethren. It might culminate in a total sacrifice, like Jesus', but essentially it begins by filling a need within the group.

All the various ministerial functions by which both the life of the church is maintained and its mission extended are essentially gifts of the Holy Spirit, and their proper performance is a sign of the Holy Spirit's presence and of its operation from within the structure. The gifts or functions in the Christian community were essentially three: apostle, prophet, and teacher. Thus, to carry out any one of these functions would be "to minister," except that originally these practices were confined to no specific locality and were simply recognized where they appeared as manifestations of the presence of the Holy Spirit. One man might exercise all three functions. Again it is clear that, originally, none of these involved either a strict form or a rigid separation.

If we consider 'witness', then, to be an 'apostle' would be to embody only one of its forms—that is, to be sent to convey the message to others. Prophecy involves edification, comfort, and consolation. The 'prophet', by inspired utterance, renews and deepens conviction, repentance, and hope, and all three of these are necessary qualities in the life of the community. Without them Christian life falls apart, but here the role of the apostle is not too helpful because of its outer orientation. Thus, the 'teacher' is vital to community life too, since he builds up the daily thought and life of the group by expounding points of belief and conduct. Thus, it is clear that the message can be repeated internally as well as communicated externally, since these intramural functions are necessary to the church's health. However, it is also equally clear that no genuine witness can be completely internally oriented.

The tension within any ministry that must be resolved, if it is to be successful, is the combination of ruling with preaching and of teaching with pastoral service. This is made more difficult by the refusal of 'ministry' to conform to any precise official lines. From the beginning, while the general control of all activities was exercised by the appointed minister in each church or community, a considerable contribution to spiritual life and neighborly service was also made through the ministrations of spontaneous prophets and teachers who held no official office. A 'church', and therefore a 'ministry', is simply a spirit-filled body able to produce, vary, and adapt its ministerial organs under the guidance of the spirit. This opens up everyone to be both potential recipients and donors. Of course, in searching for the proper recipients of a Christian message, the idea of 'sin' cannot be overlooked. For, unless there has been some "deviation from the right way," there is no point in delivering a message of either recall or of hope for a restoration. A continuously arrogant attitude which inevitably leads to strife or to disharmony affects us all, and the conveyor of such an attitude is the proper recipient of a message offering renewal. If, as the result of his attitudes and actions, his status has been changed, such an individual must be reached with a message if he is to be restored. Anyone who rebels against a spiritual superior, or anyone who is unfaithful to an agreement, is another candidate to receive a message of change.

Sin also means badness, violence, destructiveness, trouble, worthlessness, vanity, folly, and senselessness. In this case, no one is untouched by these qualities, and, as such, everyone can profit from hearing a message that offers restoration to a state in which such actions do not corrupt us. Since all life is upheld only by some covenant relationship, the essence of sin is the breach of a covenant, so that every deed that injures the community is a sin. The more deeply rooted such sin becomes, the harder it is to remove and the more destructive is the violence that erupts from it. To be at all effective, the message of restoration will have to be very forcefully preached. And since all sin who, whether consciously or not, are separated from God, anyone not immediately related to him is in need of a message from God. However, the content of such a message, in order to be at all effective, will have to be such as to reveal God's immediate presence powerfully.

E. WHO IS WITNESSED TO?

If too much thought goes into determining the meaning and forms for witness, we forget that the person or fact being witnessed to is central to our understanding of 'witness'. This question is involved in the concept 'Lord', since this idea means to rule or to command. That is, the one witnessed to must have authority, and it was precisely this issue that split the Jews of Jesus' time. The one announced is witnessed to precisely because the presence of authority has been recognized. The "scandal" Jesus gave to the Jewish expectations of an earthly Messiah, and to the self-righteousness of the Pharisees, was that he did not conform to the current religious norm and yet claimed authority for himself. By his behavior and announcements, Jesus offended the reigning authorities because he claimed a greater authority, and every later Christian disciple becomes one because he witnesses to the truth of these extravagant claims.

To accept such a notion involves admitting the presence of a secret. It is, above all, the privilege of the prophet to be admitted to the secret of God, so that the one witnessed to must be the person whom you accept as bearing God's secret. The great secret, of course, is God's purpose regarding *the future*, since it is not possible to discern any ulterior motive simply from a scrutiny of the past or present. We witness to the one who, we believe, represents the disclosure of God's intentions for a time to come. Thus, witnessing means a confident expectation that those secret disclosures will be made true—that is, in the case of Christians, the overcoming of death.

Our understanding of all this defines what the 'gospel' is. The term simply means "good news," and it expresses Jesus' own claim for the content of his message. As such, the message is essentially addressed to the "poor man," but this involves the spiritually impoverished just as much as the economically handicapped. The "news" is that the gracious reign of God has now become present and efficacious in this world through Jesus. This has become true in spite of the fact that it seemed already to have been rejected (for example, in Genesis or in the crucifixion story). What is to be communicated is simply that which occurred in Jesus' words and actions and that which was seen and heard by his disciples. Of course, "seeing" cannot be too narrowly interpreted in this case, since it is clear that the disciples did not comprehend the meaning of Jesus' words until *after* God intervened to reverse his death.

"To preach good tidings" is to witness to the belief that Jesus is the fulfillment of the promise of the scriptures, or rather that God's action to renew his son's life has opened the promised renewal to all. Jesus believes that his own preaching to the poor is the messianic fulfillment of the scripture's promise. The content of the gospel is that the kingdom, or reign, of God is at hand. Since it is not fully clear in what sense this has or can come, any such gospel also involves faith in the promise that a new order now only partially inaugurated will be fulfilled in due time. The difficulty which remains to plague us is that the reign of God does not come in the way expected (for example, by a political leader), and the announced new order is visible only at times and seldom is spiritually fully present now.

During the actual time of Jesus' ministry, the term 'gospel' has a slightly different meaning; but, after the death of Jesus, it is clear that 'gospel' comes to mean the assertion that Jesus is the expected Christ. It is no longer simply the message of the kingdom of God; now it involves the conviction that the promise has in fact been opened by the resurrection. Any church or community is itself built upon this gospel and is actually formed both as a result of its preaching and by the fellowship that is discovered. Saint Paul claimed a personal apprehension of the gospel which both authenticated its truth and constituted him as an apostle, and this is exactly what it does for every later believer. For those who receive this gospel, it is always "news." That is, it continually breaks in on them afresh and convinces them anew.

Interestingly enough, what is formed as a result of this action is not a militant, triumphant body but a 'remnant'. The members of the community are survivors of a disaster; they are those who escaped or were delivered. Men who accomplish a victory for themselves are militant and triumphant, but a remnant can only be called by God's action and is established only as a not-yet-realized future entity. Their minority community offers a place of deliverance for others to turn to in time of destruction, whether the decay is internal or external. A remnant is blessed by God's presence and not every organization can claim this. As such, it will have a holy character which secular life in general cannot have. It will be a nucleus of renewal, a little group whose life is maintained through crisis in order to become the founders of a new humanity. For this to be true, the idea of divine election must be present. The remnant survives, and is therefore saved, by God's action and not by its own, just as it later seeks to save others. In adverse and disturbing times, the church should rejoice; its only fear for its life lies in its own institutional success.

F. WHAT FORMS CAN EXPRESSION TAKE?

We cannot understand the meaning of witness unless we ask a prior question about what forms it can take. If its expression could be limited to only one form, its meaning would not be so controversial. Just because it has multiple forms, each finds its own advocate, and the would-be disciple is initially confused as to which direction to take. 'Worship', of course, is one traditional form that witnessing takes, although in a time of activist concern this is likely to be either depreciated or overlooked. If the Christian witness is to God's primary activity and not man's, one form of witness is to preserve this memory, to remember the divine action, and particularly to give thanks for it in a service of praise.

We need to find new life out of the surviving past. A name is made alive and constantly effective by remembering it. Thus, Jesus' life remains continually powerful by recalling it and what it stands for. A church is defined as those who belong to the Lord, and such a people will discover its holiness especially when they assemble for worship. They need to come together for such memorial services; if they do not, their identity and their holiness as a group will be lost. *Without worship, the needed common power for action fails.* The full development and interior inspiration of any group is the work of the Holy Spirit, but the community must meet together in common exercise or else this increase cannot occur. The word goes forth from God to create a community of believers, but their response to this calling word is common worship. God is present in such worship, even though they are a pilgrim people—that is, they remain permanently unsettled until Christ returns to power.

If worship celebrates this expectation and is intended to keep this hope alive, then worship is central to any form of expression witness may take. An assembly of people forms a church, but it must be called together by appointment. 'Church' originally referred to the community gathered at Jerusalem by the preaching of the apostles, and as such it was a witness to their work. Gradually, the term came to mean the people of God who inherit and sustain his promise of present and future renewal. The church is the solemn assembly for the liturgy and as such includes all those who take part in it. The Christian community is the messianic community in its local embodiment, and as such it witnesses to the Christ's arrival, potential transforming power, and expected final return.

If the first form of expression of any witness is the formation of a community for worship, as a precondition for that gathering and as a necessity for its maintenance, preaching and teaching and prophecy must continue both within it and as going out from it. This form of witness is the proclamation of God's revelation by those whom the community (and the Holy Spirit within it) has commissioned. This means to preach good tidings, to declare, to announce, or to proclaim as a herald. Teaching must go on within the community to preserve its bonds, but preaching also involves telling the news to all people who have not heard it before. In the New Testament, preaching has nothing to do with the delivery of sermons to the already converted. Teaching can have an internal orientation; however, preaching must extend to those outside the inner group, all of whom (supposedly) believe alike.

The context of the message of preaching is decisive for discerning what forms its expression can take. In New Testament times, the aspects of the gospel are easy to identify: the announcement that (1) the age of fulfillment has dawned; (2) this has taken place through the life and death and resurrection of Jesus; (3) Jesus has been exalted and now shares fully in the power of God as his ministry manifested only partially before; (4) the Holy Spirit has come to be present among the community as the sign of Christ's continued presence and power on earth; (5) the messianic age inaugurated will be consummated in Christ's return; (6) in view of all this, an appeal for repentance and acceptance is in order. All subsequent preaching, if it is to be an authentic form, must be based on these modes of expression, and then its witness can be recognized as such.

The form that witness takes will not always be peaceful, although its message is peace. That is, human life is a struggle between life and death, good and evil. In spite of his message of God's love, Jesus' ministry is, for the most part, marked by conflict, and certainly it ends in a destructive clash. Thus, a witness in any form is bound to engender a conflict with the secular world, since the mark of the secular world is its failure to accept such divine authority. In this sense, Christian life is a constant warfare, and each follower needs to be exhorted to courage in his struggle with the pagan in himself and in the world. The energy needed is not to combat some physical power or realm, but to oppose the invisible and spiritual forces of evil which constantly threaten invasion. One central form of witness, then, is to strengthen the believer against such constant attack.

If this is the case, one recurring form of expression which witnessing must take is 'sacrifice'. Since all sacrifices belong to the class of holy things, traditionally sacrifice was offered at any place where God was discovered to have revealed himself. Since the Christian believes that God revealed himself in Jesus' life and also in God's action to reverse the forces that put Christ to death, he may offer a sacrifice of himself at any place or time where God's command to love and serve demands it. That is where God has and will appear: in need, in the opportunity for service, and wherever unselfish love is present. Sacrifice originally meant, quite literally, a slaughter. In a sense, this meaning remains for the Christian, although it is his self-concern and his pride that now are to be offered up in smoke on a personal altar.

Sacrifice is a gift to God made in return for God's reaching out to restore man. Moreover, sacrifice is a means of entering into communion with God. Thus, *if a man cannot sacrifice himself upon occasion, he has no basis upon which to know*

God, since that quality is what Jesus revealed as fundamental to divinity. In this case, God may appear to die when actually it is man who, in his loss of soul, has become dead to the discovery of God. Thus, rather than being a loss as feared, a sacrifice proves to be a means for releasing life, whether this is for God's benefit or for the worshiper or for the object of his work. A sacrifice is a gift, just as God is believed to have made an unexpected gift of himself. It is a peace offering which, because it fulfills a command, has atoning value and promotes peaceful relations with God. God's anger is kindled by the intrusion of selfish ambitions, but his wrath is rendered peaceful by every selfless sacrifice to aid others.

G. CAN THE PAST BECOME FUTURE NOW?

Can memory have a present effect, particularly if it is the memory of God's action? Can what is promised in full only for the future nevertheless exist and exert some power in the present? These are the twin questions that ultimately define both the form that witness can take and what it claims to be a witness to. When we say that God "remembers," he does so in order to show mercy to that person, to protect or to deliver him. With God, remembering has a certain power, and therefore it can accomplish certain things. God's remembering is at one with his action, whether this is in judgment or for restoration. On the other hand, however well intentioned, our memory is not always effective. In this way, men differ from God.

When we consider Jesus' injunctions to his disciples to "remember," it is clear that he recommends a very concrete form of remembering. He intends so to involve the rememberer as to bring the past back into the present. At times, this is possible for us, but it is not accomplished without a great deal of effort. Whether we can do this involves the question of the efficaciousness of Jesus' sacrifice in the crucifixion. That is, is a sacrifice offered once and for all, so that it becomes unrepeatable, or is it able continually to be renewed in such a way that it can be newly present? If it is the latter, this certainly involves a very special form of remembering. When seen in this light, the relationship between past, present, and future ceases to be so sharply divided. For example, can memory be so powerful as to overcome the natural divisions between the parts of time? If so, it would not seem so unintelligible that what is promised in full only for the future might also exist in the present.

The concept of 'end' and the idea of 'future' are joined together in religious thought. 'Eschatology' simply means thinking of the future as having a limit. It is to consider the future against the idea of an end and a transformation. As such, the limit is the end that contains the whole of existence. That is, *existence can only be understood as a whole as it is held up against this idea of limit.* Certain potentialities are inherent in the cause of the first beginning, but the end refers to the idea of taking full possession of those potentialities at that time— that is, of reclaiming them. As such, the end can be considered the fulfillment of time and not its abrupt termination.

Will there be last things just as there were first things and just as we now have present existence? Do all three add together to make each part more intelligible? For Christians, of course, the end is already given in the events of the life, death, and resurrection of Jesus. In this case, eschatology applies to the present time and not just to some future disruption, insofar as the last days are already thought to have been set in motion by what happened to Jesus. The true and final future has already begun. Yet, in order to understand this, we must return to our twin question of how the past can be powerful in the present via memory, and also how an as yet unreached future can have an effect upon us now. Can an ultimate limit exist and alter the present, without in fact having yet been reached?

Strange as it may seem in speaking of cataclysmic endings, the answer to these questions is bound up with the idea of 'peace'. In a religious sense, peace is thought of as being the gift of God himself, so that, where it comes to exist, God must have visited. (He alone lives in an Age of Aquarius.) As a brief glance at the warlike conditions in which we always live will quickly tell us, peace is an eschatological goal—that is, it is one whose realization in full awaits a radical transformation. Such a future can be brought about as partially present, but, in this age, peace is necessarily in jeopardy and cannot be achieved more than in part. In this situation, 'patience' becomes an important attribute. It has (when properly used under favorable conditions) sacrificial power to transform evil, the disrupter of peace, into good. (Martin Luther King was right.)

To achieve peace is a desire for well-being manifested in every good for man. In addition to patience, 'suffering' is important to peace, since the concept of the 'suffering servant' is "he who brings peace to the nations." Of course, this is eschatological in its full achievement—that is, it represents a final peace as a gift of God in a coming age not yet fully present.

The achievement of peace is, of course, equivalent to the coming of the kingdom of God. Therefore, *to the extent that we find peace now, we experience a future kingdom of God in the present day*. Miracles, the signs of the kingdom's presence, are not unassociated with such peace: they remove disorder and create wholeness. Since peace requires the abrupt end of certain destructive forms of life, its full and permanent presence requires miracles.

Jesus becomes a Christian symbol for the achievement of peace: its lasting presence is dependent on his final victory over its chief enemies—that is, sin and death. Until these forces are contained and reversed, the enduring presence of peace is impossible and its contemporary achievement will always be a precarious affair. In this sense, peace is almost synonymous with eternal life, since death must be overcome to make it possible. Thus, *life in the church and the calling of peace must be coincident*, since the Christian believes that he follows the one through whom peace is possible—just because the ravages of sin and death have been brought under control by God's action on him.

The observance of the 'sabbath' is a memorial to the peace and rest that is God's, and, as such, its restfulness (*vs.* action) is not to be despised. The sabbath becomes primarily a day for the performance of those works that constitute its eventual fulfillment. The sacred day of the week is both a testimony and a preparation for the expected day of peace—to be made possible in the future but often already beginning to be present now.

It may seem strange to conclude a work that proposed to outline how philosophy shapes theology on such a note as this.

However, the theme of "future peace" is philosophically strange only if the reader uncritically accepts certain views about what philosophy is and does. As outlined in Part I, the introduction of eschatology as a primary question alters the character of philosophy and also establishes its relation to theology. The presence of the past and the influence of future peace are both prime themes, if religion is to be understood and if philosophy is to be defined in this relationship.

As a result, it turns out that, in a sense, theology can shape philosophy too. That is, the data selected for consideration alter the form that philosophical analysis can take. Thus, for instance, if selfless 'love' is a theme learned from the religious life or from theological doctrine, insofar as philosophy considers this both seriously and primarily, the concept of philosophy is altered and defined in the process. Of course, religion is not alone in suggesting to philosophy that it should begin with a consideration of love. Plato did this long ago in the *Phaedrus*, the *Symposium*, and other dialogues. And, just because the concept of love is important to Plato, his philosophical thought takes on a different form from anyone who excludes such emotion from the realm of philosophical consideration.

If learning to love (that is, others, not oneself, and the sufferer, not necessarily the good) is the primary form for witness, a philosophy that really stops to consider this transformation must build its account around that hub. Emotion, of course, then becomes a revealer, and philosophy should not try to get by on rational thought alone. Such a path, certainly, is more dangerous for philosophers; Descartes' pure thought is relatively safe, even from doubt.

Philosophy today must accept its obligation to learn from such a precarious world, and, if it does, it cannot control the whole intellectual scene for its own purposes. Philosophy then resigns itself to at best partial rational control, although it does not fail to control with reason when and where it can. It is just that love uncovers forces that are not always subject to our command—but from which we may learn more than if we could always live undisturbed. However, if we remained always calm, we would also be able to teach less of any real assistance to men.

INDEX

71 72 73 74   7 6 5 4 3 2 1